Liberalism and
the Challenge of Fascism

SOCIAL FORCES IN ENGLAND AND FRANCE
(1815–1870)

LIBERALISM AND THE
CHALLENGE OF FASCISM

Social Forces in England and France (1815-1870)

by J. SALWYN SCHAPIRO

1 9 6 4
OCTAGON BOOKS, INC.
NEW YORK

Copyright 1949, by the McGraw-Hill Book Company, Inc.

Reprinted 1964
by special arrangement with McGraw-Hill Book Company, Inc.

OCTAGON BOOKS, INC.
175 FIFTH AVENUE
NEW YORK, N. Y. 10010

LIBRARY OF CONGRESS CATALOG CARD NUMBER: 64-24853

Printed in U.S.A. by
NOBLE OFFSET PRINTERS, INC.
NEW YORK 3, N. Y.

To my wife, Kathrine Kerestesy Schapiro
whose power of organization and gift of penetrating criticism
have shaped the writing of every page in this book

Preface

When the nineteenth century ended historically in 1914, liberalism had become the accepted way of political life in Europe. This does not mean that liberal principles and methods were adopted fully and whole-heartedly by every nation. Far from it. The advance varied in extent, all the way from complete triumph in democratic England to faint beginnings in all but completely autocratic Russia. However, the impact of liberalism was so great that the general belief was that it would inevitably triumph in all Europe. Hardly anyone dreamed of the possibility of a world-wide repudiation of triumphant liberalism. Its future seemed secure.

Yet in less than a decade after 1914 two movements appeared, communism and fascism, that declared war à *outrance* against liberalism. Openly and insistently did these movements proclaim their intention to destroy every vestige of liberalism throughout the world, an intention that they carried out with fanatical zeal and ruthless determination wherever they conquered. Fascism made more rapid headway for a time than did communism. It appeared—so it then seemed—out of the void, as the protagonist of the existing order against social revolution. Before long, however, fascism revealed itself as the deadly and uncompromising enemy of liberalism in all its forms and manifestations.

It might be said almost as an axiom that, wherever liberalism was, fascism was. The strength of the latter was in proportion to the weakness of the former. Fascism was strongest in semiliberal Germany and weakest in completely liberal England, And the prime cause lies deep in the history of nineteenth-century Europe. In describing the great conflicts between liberals and reactionaries during this period, historians have too frequently stressed the triumph of the former over the latter. Convinced of the inevitability of progress, these historians assumed that whatever success the reactionaries won was only temporary, while the successes of liberalism were final and permanent. The truth of the matter, which can now be better seen in retrospect, is that, whereas the reactionaries were beaten, and even discouraged, they were not at all reconciled to the liberal regime. Sullen and menacing, they lurked in the shadows of the liberal structure, watching and waiting for their opportunity to destroy it. Now and then gleams of hope flitted before their eyes. What if liberalism were threatened from the left as well as from the right? In that case the reactionaries would find powerful allies in their erstwhile enemies, the *bourgeoisie*. Had not the threat of universal confiscation been heard in the "June Days" of 1848 and again in the Paris Commune of 1871, when a new genie—proletarian dictatorship—was let loose from the revolutionary bottle. The advent of Soviet Russia as the protagonist of world revolution brought into focus the fears of a century. Promptly did the reactionary elements in every European land consolidate behind fascism as the force that could, at the same time, avert the communist menace and destroy the liberal democratic system.

Liberalism went down to destruction in Germany and Italy and survived in England and France. And the explanation lies not in their national characteristics but in their national history. In Germany liberalism had received a mortal blow as a consequence of the failure of the Revolution of 1848. And the semiautocratic German Empire established by Bismarck prepared the Germans to accept the Nazi dictatorship of Hitler. In Italy the liberal tree had many branches, but weak roots. The government was of the liberal pattern but great masses of Italians, poverty stricken and illiterate, were barely aware of liberal principles, hence indifferent to their appeal.

It was quite otherwise in England and France. If liberalism was secure anywhere, it was secure in England. With the enfranchisement of the lower classes, nineteenth-century liberalism smoothly flowed into twentieth-century democracy, and the fusion of these two powerful forces in England gave the cohesion and strength that come from national unity. In France liberalism scored a great triumph with the establishment of the Third Republic; but it did not flow smoothly into democracy as in England. The French democratic tradition of 1793 was associated with dictatorship and terrorism; and more than once did it arise to combat liberalism, notably in the "June Days" and in the Paris Commune. Dormant during the long life of the Third Republic, the tradition of '93 was revived with the appearance of communism after the First World War, and the consequence was a France deeply divided into left and right. Neither a villain like Pierre Laval nor a hero like Winston Churchill can offer sufficient explanation why France fell and why England stood up in 1940. Only history can explain adequately the united England and the divided France that faced the German onslaught in the Second World War.

This book is devoted to a study of the formation of the pattern of liberalism in England and France, where its ideals and policies became a model, followed more or less by the other nations of Europe. It also treats of the origins of fascist ideology in these countries. The triumph of fascism in Italy and Germany attracted world-wide attention, and many books have appeared dealing with its historic origins in these lands. What still remained to be studied were the historic origins of fascism in England and France, where it did not triumph but where social forces have existed and continue to exist—weak in England and fairly strong in France—that constitute a danger to liberalism.

Chapters 13 to 15, dealing with the Heralds of Fascism, aim to throw a new light on Louis Napoleon, Proudhon, and Carlyle—the light of the present on the past. The system established in France by the strange and enigmatic Emperor cannot be understood without its being seen as a historic preview of the fascist state with its popular, even socialist, appeals cloaking a ruthless personal dictatorship. The author's interpretation of Proudhon is an attempt to explain the violent contradictions in the writings of the "father of anarchy," who denounced property as theft and exalted the middle class. An exhaustive examination of his writings convinced the author, reluctantly to be sure, that Proudhon was a harbinger of fascism in its essential outlook and its sinister implications. The overtones of Carlyle's resounding message were heard but not understood by Victorian England. In retrospect they become clearer than the message itself. The spirit of Carlyle was moral, his language, prophetic; but his political and social outlook is now easily recognizable as being that of fascism, with its exaltation of personal dictatorship in government, its regimentation in society, and its suppression of "inferior" classes and peoples.

The author wishes to thank Professor Henry W. Ehrmann for his assistance in carrying out the research for Chap. 14, Heralds of Fascism:

II. Pierre Joseph Proudhon, Revolutionist. The author also wishes to record his obligation to the *Political Science Quarterly,* the *Journal of the History of Ideas,* the *Journal of Modern History,* and the *American Historical Review* for the permission to publish as chapters in this book articles that originally appeared in these journals. These articles are "Alexis de Tocqueville, Pioneer of Democratic Liberalism in France" (*Political Science Quarterly,* December, 1942); "John Stuart Mill, Pioneer of Democratic Liberalism in England" (*Journal of the History of Ideas,* April, 1943); "Thomas Carlyle, Prophet of Fascism" (*Journal of Modern History,* June, 1945); and "Pierre Joseph Proudhon, Harbinger of Fascism" (*American Historical Review,* July, 1945).

J. SALWYN SCHAPIRO

NEW YORK, N. Y.
December, 1948

Contents

PREFACE vii

CHAPTER

1. What Is Liberalism? 1

2. Liberalism and the Whig Tradition in England 21

3. Liberalism and the Revolutionary Tradition in France . . . 32

4. The Utilitarian View of the Nature of Man and of the Mechanics of Progress 43

5. The Classical Economists and the Apotheosis of the *Bourgeoisie* 60

6. The Malthusians and the New Inequality 81

7. The "Glorious Revolution" of 1832 and the Triumph of Bourgeois Liberalism in England 111

8. Bourgeois Liberalism and the Irreconcilable Conflict of the Two Frances 139

9. The Victorian Compromise in England; the New Liberalism and the New Conservatism 182

10. Rise and Fall of Bourgeois Liberalism in France, 1830 to 1848 . 221

11. John Stuart Mill, Pioneer of Democratic Liberalism in England 256

12. Alexis de Tocqueville, Pioneer of Democratic Liberalism in France 290

13. Heralds of Fascism: I. Louis Napoleon Bonaparte, Statesman . 308

14. Heralds of Fascism: II. Pierre Joseph Proudhon, Revolutionist 332

15. Heralds of Fascism: III. Thomas Carlyle, Prophet 370

16. The Historic Importance of Bourgeois Liberalism 397

BIBLIOGRAPHY 404

INDEX 413

xi

Liberalism and
the Challenge of Fascism

SOCIAL FORCES IN ENGLAND AND FRANCE
(1815–1870)

Chapter 1. What Is Liberalism?

The great issue of the Second World War, openly avowed by both the Axis and the United Nations, was democracy, or liberalism in its most advanced form, versus fascist dictatorship. At the height of Axis success, in 1941, the doom of liberalism, proclaimed by the fascists, seemed to be sealed. Wherever the Axis powers—Germany and Italy—triumphed, liberalism was extinguished swiftly, thoroughly, and mercilessly. England alone remained, defiant and undismayed, to battle for the liberal heritage of mankind.

With the defeat of the Axis powers, the hopes of liberalism rose high. Would the Second World War result in the reestablishment of the democratic system that had prevailed before 1939? Or would a new order come into existence based on liberal principles but with orientation in favor of social security and economic equality? A reevaluation of liberalism in the light of its historic evolution is the only guide to the perplexed liberal seeking for a solution of the problems raised by the greatest war in history. Such a reevaluation will reveal what was permanent and what was transient in the contributions that liberalism made to the progress of mankind.

The expression "liberalism" came into general use only about the middle of the nineteenth century. The word was new, but the attitude of mind that it connoted was old, perhaps as old as humanity itself. In a general way, liberalism comprehended a belief in the power of reason to regulate the conduct of life, in critical views of dogmatic beliefs, and in an experimental attitude toward problems in government and society. Extraordinary individuals—a Socrates, an Abelard, a Milton—had given resounding but fleeting expression to the liberal attitude of mind when confronted with life's great problems. But liberalism as the generating principle of a political system based on representative institutions, of an economic system based on machine industry, and of a social order based on individualism is distinctively modern. Only in the nineteenth century did movements and parties

1

appear that aimed to organize national life in harmony with liberal principles. According to Hobhouse, liberalism was "an all penetrating element of the life-structure of the modern world."[1]

The beginnings of liberalism can be traced to the sixteenth and seventeenth centuries, the period when feudal society was disintegrating and modern society was emerging. Capitalist enterprise during the Commercial Revolution was creating a new economic system. The consolidations of territory and of power into sovereign states was creating a new political system. The revival of the ancient classics, and especially the birth of modern science in the Copernican Revolution, was creating a secular culture far different in outlook from the theological culture of the Middle Ages. All these changes had in them the germinating principle of liberalism.

As a pattern of "the life-structure of the modern world," liberalism was the inspiration of the intellectual revolution that took place in England and in France during the eighteenth century. In that rosy dawn of liberalism, its ideals were proclaimed with a fervor inspired by a new and resplendent vision of man throwing off his evil heritage of brutality, ignorance, and prejudice and becoming his own true self, a rational being living in an enlightened society in which he found security against want, persecution, and war. In France the militant *philosophes* openly attacked the Old Regime on all fronts. They decisively repudiated the religious way of life and thought, and boldly proclaimed the "natural order," revealed by modern science, as the supreme model for the guidance of mankind. They denounced all the institutions of the Old Regime as having their origin in violence and prejudice and their continued existence in the selfishness of the ruling classes and in the ignorance of the masses. The *philosophes,* especially those associated with the French Encyclopedia, were pioneers in what is included today in the term "social sciences." By studying the fundamental principles of human conduct in relation to environment, they sought to establish a harmonious and beneficent social order on the model of the harmonious and beneficent natural order. So influential were the *philosophes* that they succeeded in creating a liberal pattern of ideas that was widely accepted by the cultured classes throughout Western Europe.

[1] L. T. Hobhouse, *Liberalism* (London, 1911), 46.

At the same time, in England, the Industrial Revolution was taking place, which was to prove to be the seed ground of liberalism. By establishing the factory in a strategic position to dominate economic life, modern industrialism swept away the static social order, characteristic of feudalism, and created a society that was constantly in motion, at times feverishly so. The continual changes in the trades and in the professions, the continual shift of population from country to city and from city to city, the passing of old ways and the coming of new ways of making a living—all created conditions hospitable to the dynamic views of liberalism.

Another tremendous impetus to liberalism was given by the French Revolution. Wherever and whenever it penetrated, the French Revolution proclaimed its principles and imposed its policies. One has but to read the speeches delivered in the Constituent Assembly to realize the greatness of the liberal vision and the power behind it. To the peoples on the Continent, liberalism became synonymous with the principles of the French Revolution. Practically every liberal movement on the Continent during the nineteenth century was directly or indirectly inspired by the French Revolution.

With the Reform Bill of 1832 in England and with the Revolution of 1830 in France, liberalism at last scored a definite triumph. This new pattern of life in Western Europe was championed by the new class that came into power—the middle class, or *bourgeoisie*. Its interests, its ideals, and its values superseded those of the landed aristocracy, which for so many centuries had been the ruling class. So rapidly did liberalism spread that, as it might be said, it constituted public opinion in England and France during the nineteenth century. Not to be a liberal meant to be outside the main currents of life and thought.

What are the fundamental views and principles of liberalism? First and foremost, liberalism proclaimed a new view of human nature. "What is man, that Thou art mindful of him?" is the question to which a new answer has been given whenever a new social order appeared. Human nature may never change, but views of human nature have undergone marked changes in the history of mankind. When it found its full voice, during the eighteenth century, liberalism loudly and insistently proclaimed the essential goodness of man. Strangely enough, it was in the sophisticated, cynical France of the Old Regime that belief in man's essential goodness was asserted most uncompromisingly. Fundamental in the views of the French *philosophes* was their belief that man is naturally good and that all evil in the world comes from a bad social order. Despite his disclaimers, Rousseau was the supreme exponent of this view. Even Voltaire, for all his many inconsistencies and his ingrained cynicism, believed in man's essential goodness; otherwise his passionate denunciations of "man's inhumanity to man" would be meaningless. The flaming hostility of all the *philosophes* to the church—the religious Rousseau no less than the irreligious Voltaire —was largely inspired by their repudiation of the Christian view of man's nature. Man, according to Christianity, was conceived in sin and was born to the heritage of Adam's fall; hence he was naturally an evil creature. So evil was man, in his essential nature, that he could not save himself through his own will alone, no matter how determined his efforts. Only when divine grace came to the aid of his will to be saved could man attain salvation. And divine grace would be given only to the faithful.

So all-pervading was the Christian belief in the natural depravity of man that the Protestant Reformation accepted it and even emphasized it. Luther's views on the duty of those in authority to curb man's evil propensities was even more pronounced than those of his Catholic opponents. The horrible tortures and savage punishments meted out to criminals, heretics, and rebels were motivated less by the offenses committed and more by the need felt to uphold authority in its efforts to curb the "old Adam" in man.

Because of its belief in the essential goodness of human nature, liberalism had a profound faith in the good will of the normal human being. Unless moved by fear of insecurity and injustice, the average man tended to be kindly in his personal relations and cooperative for the common good. That being the case, it became the great mission of liberalism to establish a social order that would free man from the fears that constantly beset him by guaranteeing security to his person, to his property, and to his opinions, and by promoting his material and social well-being. To establish this security was the purpose of the English Bill of Rights and of the French Declaration of the Rights of Man. Liberalism shifted the great human struggle: the conflict was no longer between man's evil nature and divine grace but between man, who was good, and society, which was evil. A good society must be established in order to promote the good life of the individuals composing it. What was called "morality," according to liberalism, did not arise from a code imposed on man by God, but from harmonious human relations established by a good social, political, and economic environment. A social order inspired by faith in the essential goodness of human nature would have no need of authoritative repressions to maintain its stability. It would be maintained by the spontaneous loyalty of the average man. Love of mankind and faith in the average man, even more than fear of revolt on the part of the underprivileged, inspired the great reforms accomplished by the liberals during the nineteenth and twentieth centuries.

Closely related to the liberal view of human nature was the belief in the efficacy of the appeal to reason. Liberalism was nothing if not rationalistic. Whether reason was part of man's natural endowment or an acquired characteristic was a much mooted question, but that man was essentially a rational creature was taken for granted. The one faith that liberals had was faith in man's reason. James Mill, in a classic statement on the faith of a liberal, declared that every man "possessed of reason, is accustomed to weigh evidence, and to be guided and determined by its preponderance. When various conclusions are, with their evidence, presented with equal care and with equal skill, there is a moral certainty, though some few may be misguided, that the greater number will judge right, and that the greatest force of evidence, wherever it is, will produce the greatest impression."[2] Some few would persist in holding wrong opinions because of bias and prejudice, which, in time, would dissolve as a consequence of free discussion and better education. In this way the rational standard of a community would continually advance.

Only through reason could man's natural goodness be made effective. Liberals were convinced that "all problems can be solved in a rational manner with the aid of abstract principles that conform to logic and to human aspirations, called the rights of the citizen or of the people,"[3] By directing man's energies, by strengthening his convictions, by broadening his social vision, reason would be the efficient cause of trans-

[2] James Mill, "Liberty of the Press," 22, in *Essays* (London, n.d.).
[3] A. Leroy-Beaulieu, *La Révolution et le libéralisme* (Paris, 1890), 159.

forming man's natural goodness into a dynamic power to create the good society. Without the steel of reason, man's goodness would weaken and disintegrate into aimless sentiment and become the prey of romantic obscurantists. No better illustration can be given of the influence of romantic sentiment than the great vogue of the "Napoleonic legend" in France, which led to such dire consequences. The application of reason to social problems would result in bringing to bear the scientific method of research, experiment, criticism, and verification upon the problems of human relations that had been awaiting solution ever since man became man. The scientific approach to social problems, as seen in the social sciences, was distinctively liberal. It was the very antithesis of the revelation of truth through supernatural intervention. Nothing was so distinctive of the liberal temper as its aversion to dogmatism in any and all forms. The liberal temper was, above all, skeptical, experimental, and disinclined to clutch at finalities. It turned away from the quest for certainty. Truth, according to liberalism, was ever changing, like life itself; hence it was relative and tentative, not absolute and final. It had no bible in which was found the source of all truth, and no prophets to reveal the truth. In short, liberalism was not a religion, inspiring a fanatical devotion to a body of dogmas and a readiness to slay heretics and infidels. "For liberalism," observes Laski, "is the expression less of a creed than a temperament. It implies a passion for liberty, and that the passion may be compelling, it requires a power to be tolerant, even sceptical, about opinions and tendencies you hold to be dangerous, which is one of the rarest of human qualities."[4] The Frenchman, Alexis de Tocqueville, and the Englishman, John Stuart Mill, were almost perfect examples of the liberal temper. Both had a passion for liberty and neither was intolerant of the views even of the greatest opponents of liberty.

Because of this great emphasis on rationalism, liberalism became completely secular in its outlook. Liberals were "freethinkers," definitely nonreligious and militantly anticlerical. Religion in any form was to be tolerated as a variety of individual opinion and of group asso-

[4] Harold J. Laski, "De Tocqueville," in *The Social and Political Ideas of Some Representative Thinkers of the Victorian Age* (F. J. C. Hearnshaw, ed., London, 1933), 100.

ciation, whether the religion was professed by a majority or by a minority of the nation. Religious ideas and influences were to be eliminated from public life; hence liberals favored separation of church and state, secular education, civil marriage, and divorce. Religion being considered a private matter, the powers of government could not be used to coerce men's religious beliefs. The church, being given complete autonomy in its own sphere, could not be used as an instrument of tyranny by the powers of government. A "free church in a free state" became the slogan of the secularist liberals in England, who in the nineteenth and twentieth centuries succeeded in shearing away many privileges of the established Anglican church and in separating church and state in Ireland and in Wales. It was also the slogan of the anti-clerical liberals in France, who succeeded in establishing secular education, civil marriage, and divorce and in separating church and state.

The deep aversion that liberals had for religious dogmas inspired in them an aversion to dogmatic thinking in secular matters as well. They spelled truth with a small "t," not with a capital. Their attitude of mind toward life and life's problems was motivated by "principles" that were indeed universally true, but only relatively so. Liberal principles were to be applied cautiously and moderately, though continuously, to given problems produced by historic conditions in order to keep pace with a constantly changing social order. Liberals believed in *solving* social problems one by one, not in abolishing them altogether all at once, as did dogmatic revolutionists. As a consequence of their objectives being limited, the methods employed by liberals in reaching them were moderate and considerate. Never have liberals believed that ignoble means justify noble ends. Unlike the monolithic Truth of dogmatic faiths, spiritual or secular, the truths of liberalism were many and various. Some could be applied in one place but not in another, in one period but not in another, to one people but not to another. No better illustration of the liberal temper in action could be given than that of Gladstone. Nearly all Gladstone's political activities were devoted to the promotion of reforms of all sorts: Irish land reforms, the extension of the suffrage, disestablishment of the Anglican church in Ireland, and popular education. To Gladstone these reforms were neither final solutions of the problems that he confronted nor parts of a blueprint of a perfect society. Believing in the "inevitablity of gradualness," liberalism beheld no ecstatic vision of a perfect society, either of a past golden age or of a future Utopia. At best, it had a vague ideal of the future that the eighteenth-century libertarians called "perfectibility," when human society would approximate the beneficent harmony of the natural order.[5]

The new social order to be created by liberalism was to be one in which the goodness and rationality of man could function effectively. The pioneers of liberalism in the eighteenth century proclaimed a principle that was as magnificent in its breadth as it was startling in its novelty; namely, the equality of all human beings everywhere and any-where, irrespective of race, sex, nationality, profession, or condition of life. In a sense, this liberal principle was the secularization of the Christian doctrine of the equality of souls. The American Declaration of Independence, asserting that "all men are created equal," and the French Declaration of the Rights of Man, asserting that all men "are born and remain free and equal in rights," gave the weight of legal authority to this principle. Belief in the principle of human equality as against human inequality has, to this day, distinguished liberals of all schools from conservatives and reactionaries of all schools. By pro-claiming equality as the supreme ideal and by establishing a new order inspired by this ideal, the American and French revolutions marked the dramatic entry of the principle of equality into the history of mankind. In the pioneer stage of liberalism, equality meant equality before the law of all human beings. Gunpowder was said to have made all men of one height, so it may be said that equality before the law made all men of one class.

The great vision of human equality has never left liberalism in the many trials and struggles that it has undergone down to this day. Once the principle of equality was accepted, it could not be limited to the legal sphere, because the acceptance of this principle involved a revolutionary change in the attitude of society toward the average man. Inevitably the door was opened to newer and even to greater equalities. During the nineteenth century liberalism became the pro-

[5] There was no better exponent of eighteenth-century liberalism than the French *philosophe*, Condorcet. The last chapter of his *Esquisse d'un tableau historique des progrès de l'esprit humain* gives a picture of the future of mankind. See J. Salwyn Schapiro, *Condorcet and the Rise of Liberalism* (New York, 1934), 254–259.

tagonist of political equality, or democracy. In the movement to establish universal, equal suffrage, it was clear to those who favored it, as well as to those who opposed it, that political democracy would not be the final step in the march toward equality. Once established, political democracy would become a powerful method for applying the principle of equality to economic matters in the interest of the working class. With the establishment of manhood suffrage in England and in France, a movement began in favor of economic equality. Therein lies the significance of the rapid growth of the socialist and labor parties, which fell heir to the egalitarian principle first proclaimed by liberalism. The many social reforms in the interest of the working class, moderate and halting at first, but comprehensive and far-reaching today, have been so many steps in the direction of economic equality.

It was liberalism that proclaimed the worth and dignity of the individual. An egalitarian social order could exist only with the recognition of the importance of the individual in the liberal scheme of life. Liberalism aimed to establish a social order that would free the individual from the many restraints laid upon him by governments and institutions and from the grip of tradition laid upon him by ancient beliefs and customs. Once a free social order was established, the autonomous individual would be free to roam from one occupation to another, from one opinion to another, from one faith to another, from one country to another, from one allegiance to another, in his search to find full scope for his talents and for his ambitions. Liberals were convinced that without fundamental equality of individual rights no freedom was possible; and that the greater the equality, the greater would be the freedom. Not only was freedom essential to the development of the individual's personality; it was also the best means of securing social progress by stimulating individual initiative and enterprise. The welfare of the individual and that of society were inseparable; there could be no prosperity for the individual at the expense of society, except in the case of the unpunished criminal.

It was liberalism that had the first vision of a classless society. During the eighteenth century it launched a truceless war against such caste privileges of the feudal system as still persisted in Western Europe: in an emaciated form, as in England; in a mild form, as in France;

and in full vigor, as in Germany. By a method that was novel in history, it sought to break the fetters of privilege, which were maintained by the guild, the corporation, the manor, the mercantilist system, the official church, and the absolute state. This method was the creation of a great sphere of private life by separating society from the state through the abolition of privileged classes, privileged economic groups, privileged churches, and the coercive power of the state. A free society would appear, composed of individuals most of whose activities would be private—unregulated and uncontrolled by the government. The chief function of the latter was to protect the freedom of the individual by forbidding monopolistic practices and class legislation.

The state, which had previously been the prime source of privileges in society, under liberalism became the guardian of human liberty. The establishment of what are called, in England, "civil liberties" and, in France, "the rights of man" gave official recognition to the dignity of human personality. In the preliberal, aristocratic society dignity of office, of station, or of calling was recognized, not the dignity of the individual man himself. As a consequence the masses of mankind were condemned from birth to "undignified" occupations and were relegated to the "lower orders." Having no dignity, the common man became a "function," an instrument in the hands of "his betters"—to be used or abused as suited their interests or fulfilled their desires. In the liberal writings of the eighteenth century, especially in those of the *philosophes,* passionate pleas were frequently made for the recognition of the dignity and worth of the individual man and woman, irrespective of race, class, faith, or nation. Rousseau, in many an eloquent passage, proclaimed that every individual was an end in himself and should, therefore, not be used as an instrument to serve the needs of others. The establishment of civil liberties was an act of emancipation of the lower classes from the feudal caste system. The common man broke into humanity when the "worker" became a "man," with inalienable rights.

Of all the civil liberties the most basic was intellectual liberty. Without it all the others were in constant danger of being violated. Restrictions on freedom of speech by the reactionary Tory government in England led to the passage of the Six Acts (1819), which all but abolished the traditional "liberty of the subject." Similar restrictions in

France by Louis Philippe led to the September Laws (1835), which flouted the Rights of Man. In the new industrial society freedom of speech, of the press, and of assembly made possible organization and rapid mobilization of the concentrated masses of the population, in case of a conflict between liberty and privilege. Without intellectual liberty the exploited poor would have been compelled to resort to the far less effective methods of secret societies, conspiracies, and sporadic rioting. Those who sought to limit or to destroy this most precious of the civil liberties by means of censorship were themselves convinced that public opinion would always be on the side of their opponents. Publicity was an insinuating threat and a constant danger to the rule of privilege. More than once did public opinion prevail against those who wielded superior power, political or economic. To defy public opinion openly would have been an admission by those in power that they were on the defensive and that they depended on force alone to keep them in power—an admission that no class or government, however powerful, could afford to make. In the struggles that took place in Europe during the nineteenth century between liberals and the reactionary governments, censorship was used by the latter, curiously enough, with the object of creating an impression that public opinion supported those in power, on the theory that silence gave consent.

So great was the emphasis of liberalism on the liberty of the individual that the fact of its being also the champion of the liberty of the group is often forgotten. Liberalism proclaimed the right of association in whatever form—political, religious, social, economic, or cultural. The right of association had a special bearing on the position of minorities that suffered legal discrimination, in one form or another, to a greater or less degree. Minorities, not majorities, needed protection under the law. In the liberal view a minority was a "collective personality," therefore the rights of the individual applied equally to a minority group.

The real test of civil liberties came when a minority group was involved in the prosecution of an individual. For an isolated individual to insist on his rights in violation of laws would have troubled tyrannical governments very little. It involved no threat to their power. But an organized group, a minority, that flouted the government created a quite different situation. No matter how small and how insignificant it might be, an organized minority constituted a threat to those in power. In predemocratic days, the government itself was controlled by a privileged minority; hence it had a wholesome dread of being displaced by a minority, out of power, as a result of a sudden upheaval. In the attacks on civil liberties, involving prosecutions of individuals, the really significant ones were those cases in which the individuals represented organized minorities. The prosecutions of labor leaders in England for violating the Combination Laws were really attacks on an organized minority—the trade-unions. The refusal of Parliament, in 1828, to admit to its membership the Catholic Daniel O'Connell was really an attack on an organized minority—the Catholic Irish. The prosecution of the opponents of the Second French Empire was really an attack on organized minorities—the republicans and the socialists.

Liberalism inspired the struggle for the rights of the "collective personality" that took place during the nineteenth century. It championed national rights, whether those of divided people—like the Germans or the Italians—to form a united nation, or those of minority nationalities—like the Greeks, the Poles, the Hungarians, and the Irish —to gain independence or autonomy. It espoused the cause of persecuted religious minorities. In England this led, directly or indirectly, to the emancipation of the Dissenters, the Catholics, and the Jews; in France, to the emancipation of the Protestants and the Jews. Liberalism also inspired the emancipation of the trade-unions through the repeal, in England, of the Combination Laws of 1799–1800; and, in France, of the Coalition Law of 1791.

The application of liberal principles to the social order predicated a new and distinctively modern concept of social relations, known as "progress."[6] In the ancient and medieval worlds time had been regarded as the universal enemy of man that inevitably brought decay and death. There was always a "decline and fall," the fate of communities as well as that of individuals. As they grew older, empires and peoples disintegrated and they finally passed away, leaving monumental ruins as their tombstones. Change was, therefore, regarded as a portent of evil. This sentiment is so old and so deep that even now it inspires fear in conservatively minded persons.

[6] For an excellent discussion of the history of the idea of progress, see J. B. Bury, *The Idea of Progress* (New York, 1932).

Liberalism came in response to a rapidly changing social and economic order, owing to the progress of the Industrial Revolution in the eighteenth and nineteenth centuries. It, therefore, envisaged a dynamic society constantly changing for the better. To liberalism time was the universal friend, which would inevitably bring greater happiness to ever greater numbers. Faith in progress became a liberal passion that repudiated the Golden Age of a dim past, the Heaven of a future life, and the Utopia of a mythical land and proclaimed the ideal of a better and more abundant life for all mankind here on earth and in every community. Because of its belief in progress, liberalism continually warred against the *status quo*. Either through reforms or through revolution, old nations would be rejuvenated and begin a new and a happy life. Enslaved peoples and depressed classes would be emancipated. Poverty would be mitigated, perhaps even abolished, by the progress of industry and the spread of enlightenment. Hence, in the new vision of the progress of mankind, changes in the social order were to be welcomed, not feared. The all-essential factor was a good environment, to be created through social, economic, and political reforms. Given a good environment, man could rise to the highest moral excellence. Liberalism turned away from the ideal of the medieval saint—supreme goodness aglow in an evil environment, as in the case of Saint Francis of Assisi—and proclaimed the modern ideal of the reformer—a Robert Owen devoting his life and his energies to making the world a fit place for the masses of mankind.

A society constantly in motion had need of a political system that was constantly in motion. The liberal state came into existence in response to this need. Under autocratic rule, the chief function of the state was to freeze the *status quo* in society established by the caste system. It would not be too much to say that liberalism was the creator of the modern state, of its mechanism no less than of its underlying principles. Fundamentally the liberal state is "a government of laws not of men," in that it functions through popularly elected parliaments, which make laws for the people as a whole. A "government of laws" is impersonal in whatever it does; hence it' gives a feeling of security to every law-abiding individual. A "government of men"—namely, autocracy—"even when wisely and humanely wielded, necessarily deprives mankind of many precious and useful possessions, and renders insecure and transitory those they enjoy."[7] The legislation of a liberal state is general, in theory at least; therefore it excludes favoritism as well as discrimination of special groups, on the principle of "equal rights to all and special privileges to none." By creating representative parliaments, liberalism repudiated the age-old view of the relation between government and people as that between rulers and ruled. The law of a liberal state was neither the "command of a sovereign" nor the fiat of a dictator, but the identification of the interests of the people with the power of the state through the medium of representative government. Only that law was valid which enlarged the sphere of individual and collective liberty.

Of equal importance was the liberal idea that with power must go responsibility. Irresponsible power, whether exercised by the divine-right monarch in the past or by the totalitarian dictator in recent times, has been the *summum malum* of all government. Benevolent despotism was a myth invented to make an unjustifiable system acceptable and even glamorous. No one person, no one group could be trusted with a monopoly of power—no leader, no party, no class, no corporation, no church, on the theory that, according to Lord Acton, power always corrupts and absolute power corrupts absolutely. It was the liberal state that invented a political system in which responsibility went with power. This system was parliamentary government. The representatives were responsible to the electors, who chose them and who could retire them to private life at the next election. Those who were in office as ministers were responsible to parliament, which at any time could oust them from office. Even in the England before 1832, when the electors were few and generally corrupt and when Parliament was dominated by aristocratic cliques, officials felt a sense of responsibility to those who held over them the power of political life and death. With the expansion and purification of the suffrage, responsibility of those in office to the electorate became clear and definite. The popular mandate became all important in the political life of the liberal state.

Liberalism has not always been successful in maintaining the identification of the public interest with the power of the state. Often—only

[7] Quoted in Guido de Ruggiero, *The History of European Liberalism*, trans. from the Italian by R. G. Collingwood (London, 1927), 296.

too often—the powerful influences of pressure groups, representing special interests of all sorts, have attained control of legislation. But liberalism did succeed in resolving the various problems confronting the people—social, economic, religious, and cultural—into *political issues* for the voters to decide at elections. By this method the pressure of special interests was weakened and often eliminated through the counterpressure of popular opinion, which became more effective as the suffrage expanded and as the masses became more instructed and more conscious of their power.

Because it favored the solution of problems through political methods, liberalism relied chiefly on legislation to advance its policies. Once a problem was resolved into law, it was solved in society. Even in the early—the laissez-faire—period, when liberalism opposed state intervention in economic matters, it did not at all follow that liberals favored a do-nothing state. Quite the contrary. The liberal state of the laissez-faire period was very active in enacting all sorts of reforms: clearing away the debris of feudalism, abolishing the restrictions of mercantilism, reforming the administration of justice, encouraging industrial enterprise, and promoting economy and efficiency in the government.

By instituting representative government, liberalism created a new power in the state, the power of numbers. Before the advent of liberalism, mankind had always been governed by minorities, which were composed of privileged groups; a change of government had meant a shift of power from one privileged group to another. The "majority" then had no political existence. With liberalism came the new concept of majority rule. Even when the franchise was limited by high property qualifications, as it was in England before the Reform Bill of 1867 and in France before the Revolution of 1848, the power of numbers challenged the power of hereditary privilege for the control of the state. Rule by numbers meant that each individual, whoever he was, counted for one and only for one; whereas, under the rule of privileged groups, individuals of the mass were ciphers and each of the few privileged individuals counted for much more than one. Majority rule made impossible the control of the government by a hereditary class, as the majority was constantly changing in character and in size. The electorate was expected to expand, and it did expand, at first through the acquisition of property and later through the extension of the suffrage to the lower classes. The "liberal method does convert all from subjects into citizens, and gives to all, or to as many as possible, the means of sharing power . . . ."[8]

Government by numbers was a principle that was new, very new, in history. It meant the right of the majority to rule the nation and the right of the minority to oppose the government. These rights rested on liberal faith in the good will, in the good sense, and in the intelligence of the average man. Translated into political terms, it meant that the majority would not abuse its power and that the minority would loyally accept the rule of the majority. Under the paliamentary system majority and minority were interchangeable groups; one might become the other as a consequence of new elections. There could be no permanent majority of one party in a dynamic society in which there was a constant shifting of classes, of economic interests, and of political opinion. What was known as the majority was, in fact, a more or less temporary combination of minorities, formed in order to advance policies favored by all of them. Such combinations produced, in England, the tightly organized two-party system; in France, the loosely organized *bloc* system. In the former there were conflicts within each party of the minorities composing it, the object being to capture the party organization. In the latter, the conflicts took place among the many political groups, to decide the division of the parliament into left and right.

The liberal scheme of rule by number created a new attitude toward the state on the part of the average man. Under the hereditary system of absolute monarchy government was a "mystery" into which only the irresponsible rulers were initiated. Under the parliamentary system government was a political contrivance, open to constant inspection, and those who controlled it were responsible to the people who could oust them by merely scratching a piece of paper. Responsible government meant that the minority, as well as the majority, was responsible; it had to conduct itself in a manner that would inspire confidence in its fitness to become the majority. By recognizing the right of the minority to exist in the nation and to function officially in the government, liberalism gave supreme expression to its faith in man's natural

[8] Benedetto Croce, *History as the Story of Liberty*, trans. from the Italian by Sylvia Sprigge (New York, 1941), 260.

goodness. To quote the eloquent words of the Spanish political philosopher José Ortega y Gasset, liberalism "is that principle of political rights, according to which the public authority, in spite of being all-powerful, limits itself and attempts, even at its own expense, to leave room in the State over which it rules for those to live who neither think nor feel as it does, that is to say as do the stronger, the majority. Liberalism—it is well to recall this to-day—is the supreme form of generosity; it is the right which the majority concedes to minorities and hence it is the noblest cry that has ever resounded in this planet. It announces the determination to share existence with the enemy; more than that, with an enemy which is weak."[9]

It would not be wrong to define political liberalism as the science and art of peacefully choosing an alternative government. The Opposition, officially recognized, constitutes a potential government, which can come into being easily and quickly, provided that the people choose to transform a minority into a majority. This miracle of political transubstantiation can be performed by that utterly mundane act, a general election. In the Opposition lies the fundamental spiritual principle of liberalism.[10] Without it there could be no responsible government, no free elections; there could not be even any civil liberties. Because of the currents of free opinion and of free association in the liberal state, an alternative government, freely chosen, becomes possible. It was not until the appearance of the liberal state that the problem of liberty versus authority arose. Under the autocratic state there could be no civil liberty because no individual had any rights, as over against the authority of the state. Without the right of opposition, functioning fully and freely under the parliamentary system, civil liberties could not exist; and vice versa. History makes this truth only too evident. The English Bill of Rights came only after the supremacy of Parliament had been established by the Revolution of 1688. The French Declaration of the Rights of Man came after Louis XVI recognized the Constituent Assembly. When Charles I sought to rule England without Parliament, he made use of the Star Chamber to destroy the "liberty of the subject." When Charles X planned to undermine the French parliament he

[9] José Ortega y Gasset, *The Revolt of the Masses* (London, 1932), 83.

[10] On the origin and developments of the Opposition in English politics, see *infra*, 24*ff*.

made an onslaught on the rights of man by issuing the July Ordinances of 1830. When totalitarian dictatorships were established in communist Russia, in fascist Italy, and in nazi Germany, both parliament and civil liberties disappeared at the same time.

The core—the hard core—of the liberal state consists of two fundamental principles: (1) government by an assembly freely elected and responsible to the people and (2) constitutional guarantees of civil rights to protect the individual citizen against arbitrary action by the government. As long as a state maintains these principles, it is a liberal state, whether in form it is a monarchy, like Britain; a centralized republic, like France; or a federal republic, like the United States. In the course of its history the liberal state, while upholding its fundamental principles, has pursued different policies in social and economic matters, all the way from *laissez faire,* in the nineteenth century, to social reform and nationalization of public utilities in the twentieth.

Liberalism subordinated the state itself to the "rule of law." This innovation was accomplished by the adoption of a constitution whose authority transcended that of the state by limiting its sphere of action, by checking its powers, and by forbidding the abrogation or limitation of civil liberties. A liberal state is not a Hegelian deity, nor a Hobbesian Leviathan, nor a totalitarian Behemoth. It is an "institution," superior in authority to all other institutions in the nation, in that its supreme object is to promote the good life of all the citizens. Under liberalism the state does not lead a life apart from the people, as it once did under the divine-right monarchs and, in our time, under the totalitarian dictatorships. The liberal conquest of the state and its reduction to the status of an institution were a signal contribution to the cause of human freedom.

It was America that was the pioneer in devising a method of establishing a liberal state through the adoption of a written constitution. The Federal Constitution of 1789, which created a liberal state in America out of hand, was the product of a method new in the annals of government—a constitutional convention. The Philadelphia Constitutional Convention was as near an approach to the "social contract" of Rousseau as history can show. By means of popular approval a new system of government arose, and the "contract" was a written constitution that has survived to this day. Its purposes were (1) to create the machinery of a liberal state based on the principle of popular sovereignty; (2) to guarantee civil liberties by the adoption of a Bill of Rights; and (3) to provide a peaceful mechanism for changing the structure of the government by means of amending the constitution.[11] These objects were meticulously carried out by the Constitution of the United States, and, for that reason, it became the model and inspiration of the liberal movements in Europe during the first half of the nineteenth century.[12]

Itself the product of a revolution, the Constitution of the United States sought to obviate the necessity for future revolutions through the amendment process, the significance of which has not been fully realized. The constitutional amendment was an essential part of the liberal scheme of creating a mechanism of peaceful change in government. It aimed to establish a *dynamic stability* by making possible the gradual adjustment of political institutions to the constantly changing conditions in modern society. The wisdom of the Founding Fathers in adopting the amendment clause, however difficult it may be to apply, was vindicated even more when the United States of America became a highly industrialized nation, in which social conditions changed even more rapidly than during the frontier period. Nearly every amendment to the Constitution that was made after the Civil War was adopted in order to bring government into harmony with changed economic conditions.

A written constitution was a liberal device to produce, in the sphere of government, a balance of the forces of stability and of progress. Only through such a balance could both revolution and reaction be avoided in a dynamic society. Constitutional government, with all that

[11] H. McD. Clokie, *The Origin and Nature of Constitutional Government* (London, 1936), 135*ff*.

[12] The first written constitution in Europe, inspired by the American example, was the French constitution of 1791, adopted during the French Revolution by the Constituent Assembly. Although it did not survive, it created a precedent for constitutional government in France that every subsequent regime followed. Even during the interludes of the dictatorships of the two Napoleons, France had a constitution of a sort, which, in theory at least, recognized popular sovereignty and guaranteed the Rights of Man. The American precedent of a written constitution was followed by Spain in 1812; by Norway-Sweden, Denmark, and the Netherlands in 1815; by some of the states in the German Confederation during 1815 to 1830; by the Latin American nations after they gained their independence; by Portugal in 1822; by Belgium in 1831; by Piedmont and Switzerland in 1848; by Prussia in 1850; and by Austria in 1861.

it implied, was so new that a younger generation had to be educated to maintain it. Liberals, therefore, became ardent champions of popular education in order to create in the rising generation a psychology of consent to the rule of the new authority in the state. The schools were to be training centers for citizenship, where the pupils would be taught loyalty to the Constitution and the rights and duties of citizenship, as well as the three R's. It was liberalism that abolished the old educational system, in which a small part of the nation was highly educated and the great majority illiterate or semiliterate. The pioneers of popular education were outstanding liberals: Jefferson in America, Condorcet in France, and Bentham in England.

Liberalism has written the greatest and most glowing chapters in the story of liberty. Wherever and whenever it was established, liberalism promptly struck off the chains, physical and mental, from those who were enslaved, and it created a social and political order in which liberty became a heritage that broadened down from generation to generation. Because equality was joined to liberty, liberalism never became the exclusive possession of any race, class, or nation. Neither was it limited to any aspect of life; it overflowed from the political and religious to the social and economic spheres. Democracy, the latest form of liberalism, became the way of life and thought of all those who sought new paths of progress, yet held fast to those things in the past which had proved good. Freedom and equality are priceless possessions, which will never be given up willingly by those who enjoy them.

Chapter 2. Liberalism and the Whig Tradition in England

England is the classic land of modern liberalism. There is its original home; there it grew steadily and flourished mightily; there it inspired almost every phase of life and thought; there it has been consistently applied from age to age, from class to class, from problem to problem. It has been said, perhaps by Bertrand Russell, that all Englishmen are liberals: the Conservatives are liberals on the right, and the Laborites are liberals on the left. That is the plain truth. Politics, which divides these parties, is far less important than the ideal of liberalism that unites them. An ardent devotion to individual freedom and an unbounded faith in popular government are the attitude of both parties toward life and toward life's problems.

Liberalism in England was not an acquired characteristic, as it was among the nations on the Continent. It was the mature product of a long historical past, beginning with Magna Charta in the thirteenth century. After centuries of struggle it finally scored a definite triumph in the Revolution of 1688. Since then, in one form or another, liberalism has been an inherited national tradition, accepted by all the people of whatever party and of whatever class. Hence the roots of English liberalism were many and deep, and for that reason it was able, at one time, to withstand the fierce revolutionary storms that blew from France as, in our day, it withstood the fierce fascist storms that blew from Germany.

Prior to the seventeenth century the system of society and of government in England was not unlike that of France. Society was based on the feudal caste system, dominated by a privileged landed aristocracy. The religious system under the established Anglican church, like that in France under the established Catholic church, permitted no deviation from the official faith. The English government was, like the French government, an absolute monarchy on the theory of divine

21

right. It is true that a parliament existed; but it met irregularly and was, in effect, only an advisory body to the crown. Parliament met whenever the king called it, passed whatever laws he desired, and was promptly dissolved when the king so ordered. In reality England, where Parliament met fairly often, was no more of a liberal state than was France, where the parliament was not called for 175 years prior to 1789.

If one wishes a year to mark the birth of the liberal state, that year is 1688. The Revolution of 1688 is known in English history as the "Glorious Revolution" because it was accomplished without bloodshed —at least, without the shedding of English blood. Considerable Irish and Scotch blood was indeed shed before the Revolution was finally over. Every revolution in history has been confronted by the problem of establishing a new, in place of the old and traditional, allegiance. To abolish the existing authority and to set up a new one has been fairly easy for a revolutionary party in power. What has been difficult, very difficult, has been to create a psychology of consent among the people, in order to produce a voluntary obedience to the new authority. Without this consent there could be no stability for the new government; it would not be considered "legitimate." This problem had not been solved by the Puritan rebellion, which never succeeded in winning popular approval either of the Republic, established by the Commonwealth in 1649, or of the Protectorate, established by Cromwell in 1653. For that reason both governments had to resort to dictatorship in order to maintain themselves. The swift and easy restoration of the Stuarts, in 1660, was sufficient proof of the failure of the Puritan rebellion to solve the problem of stability. What made the Revolution of 1688 truly "glorious" was the great political wisdom shown in getting rid of the monarch without getting rid of the monarchy; in giving supreme power to Parliament, without resorting to dictatorship. It is significant to note that in depriving the Stuarts of the throne, Parliament did not specifically repudiate the theory of divine right; and in establishing parliamentary supremacy, it did not specifically assert the doctrine of popular sovereignty. The philosopher of the Revolution of 1688, John Locke, clearly asserted the doctrine of parliamentary supremacy in his great work, *Of Civil Government*. Nowhere, however, did he proclaim the doctrine of popular sovereignty, as did his more famous disciple, Rousseau, in his more famous work, *Contrat social*. The transition that was made by the revolutionists of 1688 from the old authority of the king to the new authority of Parliament was made without ideological conflicts. Actions spoke louder than doctrines and more effectively. The power that James II lost was not recovered by William III, and that power continued to decrease until the monarchy became a national symbol, not a political authority. But the power that Parliament won in 1688 was maintained by its successor and continued to increase until Parliament became the vital source of all political authority in England.

The Revolution of 1688, "the most moderate and most successful of all revolutions," created something new in the history of mankind, the liberal state. It was the first political revolution of modern times that definitely repudiated absolute monarchy and firmly laid the basis of constitutional government. A new era in the history of England and in that of the world now began. By establishing the supremacy of Parliament, the Revolution of 1688 gave a representative body the unexampled position of being the supreme power in the government of the nation. Parliament exercised this supremacy by deposing James II and choosing William and Mary as king and queen of England. Later, in the Act of Settlement of 1701, Parliament again asserted its supremacy by deciding the line of succession to the English throne.

With the fall of absolute monarchy came civil liberty and religious toleration. The "liberty of the subject" was definitely assured by the Bill of Rights of 1689 and by the abolition of the censorship in 1695. Religious opposition to the established Anglican church was officially recognized by the Toleration Act of 1689, which granted toleration to the Protestant Dissenters. Unlike the French Edict of Nantes, which had granted toleration to the Huguenots but which was revoked by Louis XIV, the English Toleration Act was faithfully kept. The equality of civil rights and the toleration of religious dissent made the English people of that period, in the words of Disraeli, a "favored and peculiar people."[1]

Not only did the Revolution of 1688 repudiate absolute monarchy; it likewise repudiated dictatorship, whether that of faction, as under the Commonwealth, or that of the military, as under the Protectorate. The

[1] Benjamin Disraeli, *Whigs and Whiggism* (London, 1913), 229.

meticulous concern for legalistic formulas shown by Parliament in ousting James and in placing William and Mary on the throne betrayed their anxiety lest the new rulers be considered usurpers. No member of Parliament was "purged," and every act of that body was exercised in the traditional form and manner. The Revolution of 1688 was a "legal," as well as a "glorious," revolution.

The vast importance for England of the Revolution of 1688 lay in the fact that it created a national liberal tradition among the people. From that event on, the liberal tradition constituted a counterpoise to the conservative influences that centered around the monarchy, the aristocracy, and the church. An appeal of these elements to maintain their privileges as the inherited traditions of the land could always be countered by an appeal to abolish them to maintain the inherited liberties of the people. And the libertarian appeal was sure to meet a response from many Englishmen, irrespective of their economic interests and of their class prejudices. Two Englands did, indeed, emerge from the Revolution of 1688—aristocratic and liberal England. But, unlike the Two Frances that emerged from the French Revolution, both aristocratic and liberal England have been inspired by common national traditions; as a consequence, they have been loyal to the long-established national institutions of king and Parliament. The conflicts that arose during every generation between the Two Englands have, therefore, been settled peacefully through acts of Parliament, not, as in France, through civil war at the barricades.

Indirectly, the Revolution of 1688 resulted in the creation of a new pattern of political action: the distinctively English two-party system. The original aspect of this system, in which the majority party is officially in control of the government and the minority party is legally in the opposition, lay in the latter. The recognition of the role of the Opposition party in the government of a nation gave the legal stamp of approval to the idea that opposition to the government was not treason, an idea that was startlingly new in the eighteenth century and caused considerable mystification on the Continent.

This distinctively English contribution to the art and science of government was not created out of hand. It appeared as a result of England's political experience during the period of revolution and reaction that began with the struggle between Parliament and James I and lasted for almost a century. Two organized political groups—"parties"—emerged from the struggle and became known as "Tories" and "Whigs." They advocated conflicting principles of government; the Tories favored the supremacy of the king, the Whigs, the supremacy of Parliament, in the government of England. After the Revolution of 1688 these parties became identified with rival dynasties; the Tories championed the exiled Stuarts, and the Whigs championed, at first, the House of Orange and, later, the Hanoverians. After the suppression of the Jacobite uprising in Scotland, led by the Pretender in 1715, the Stuart cause was lost. The Tories in Parliament, led by Lord Bolingbroke—the Disraeli of the period—organized what was called the "Opposition." It aimed to overthrow the Whig ministry of Sir Robert Walpole, and not the Hanoverian dynasty. In this manner the conflict between the two parties was transferred from the hills of Scotland to the floor of Parliament; the party objectives ceased to be the English throne and became the spoils of office. Party strife, in and out of Parliament, was the political equivalent of civil war.

It was the English who first grasped the idea that the great role of a parliamentary Opposition was to stabilize a constitutional system of government. It is commonly supposed that the prime function of an Opposition in Parliament is "to oppose," namely, to criticize the government and its policies. That is only partly true. In a deeper sense, the true function of an Opposition is to be a shadow government, ready at any time to take office should political fortune favor it. An Opposition seeks not only to influence the conduct of the government, but, even more, to become the government by turning its minority into a majority. As a consequence, moderation becomes both a principle and an interest in party conflicts. The party in the government fears that extreme measures might antagonize a sufficient number of its supporters to bring defeat at the polls; and the party in the Opposition shuns extreme policies, lest it fail to win the all-essential majority vote. This concept of the role of the Opposition goes as far back as Bolingbroke, who saw the necessity for the minority to develop its own policy in order to prepare the way to assume power. Those who "engage in opposition," he wrote, "are under as great obligations, to prepare themselves to control, as they who serve the crown are under, to prepare themselves to carry on the administration: and that a party, formed for this purpose, do not act like good citizens nor honest men, unless they *propose true,* as well as *oppose false* measures of government."[2] Without a powerful and militant Opposition—the shadow government—the parliamentary system cannot function effectively. Like the party in power, the Opposition must accept the existing political system, and, along with it, the existing social order; at least it must be willing to adopt a strategy of compromise in order to carry out its ideas and policies. The whole essence of parliamentary government lies in the intention to make the thing work. By voluntarily accepting the rule of the majority in a liberal state, the minority creates a situation approximating the "general will" of Rousseau, which implies that laws, to be legitimate, must be the expression of the unanimous opinion of the community. The "government and the opposition become the two jointly liable instruments of the unique general will and amalgamate their dualism."[3] A progressive Opposition substitutes reform for revolution, and a conservative Opposition, continuity for reaction. An uncompromising revolutionary party, such as the National Socialist party during the Weimar Republic in Germany, or a recalcitrant reactionary party, such as the Royalists during the Third Republic in France, would not be an Opposition, because it could not assume power in a political system that it sought to destroy. The expression, "His Majesty's Loyal Opposition," is no Gilbertian satire on English parliamentary practice, but a perfectly true description of a vital element in the English political system. The Opposition is not only legal, it is also official; the leader of the Opposition in Parliament receives a salary from the government.

That other distinctively English political institution, the cabinet, emerged from the conflicts between Whigs and Tories. Like these parties, the cabinet had its beginnings in the Revolution of 1688, but it took definite form during the long Whig ministry of Walpole, from 1721 to 1743. Corrupt and able, Walpole used both his vices and his virtues to advance party government. As the leader of the Whigs, he had the complete confidence of the Hanoverian kings, George I and

2 Henry Saint-John, Viscount Bolingborke, *Letters on the Spirit of Patriotism and on the Idea of a Patriot King* (Oxford University Press, 1917), 37.

3 Guglielmo Ferrero, *The Principles of Power,* trans. from the Italian by T. R. Jaeckel (New York, 1942), 178.

George II, who appointed officials recommended by him, and who signed bills initiated by his ministry and passed by the Whig majority in Parliament. If Bolingbroke may be called "the first leader of the Opposition," Walpole deserves to be called "the first Prime Minister." In the course of time the two-party system and the cabinet became the efficient secret of the supremacy of Parliament in the government of England.

During the eighteenth century these revolutionary changes in government became accepted national traditions, unchallenged by any organized group and unquestioned by the masses of the English people. During that period England was the unique example in Europe of a great nation that was governed by laws enacted by a parliament, and not by decrees issued by an absolute monarch. Freedom of speech and of the press, though restricted by severe libel laws and by high taxes on printed matter, and religious toleration, though restricted by "disabilities" imposed on non-Anglicans, were sufficiently widespread to excite the admiration and the wonder of liberals on the Continent. During the eighteenth century England was regarded as the promised land of freedom by the great French liberals, Voltaire and Montesquieu, who came to England to study her free institutions. French enthusiasm for the English constitution proved infectious in England itself, where it was normally taken for granted as an old tradition. The English discovered that they had a "constitution," and a constitution worship began, which was spread by the writings of Blackstone, the Tory, and by those of Burke, the Whig. "Of a constitution so wisely contrived, so strongly raised, and so highly finished," wrote Blackstone, "it is hard to speak with that praise, which is justly and severely its due:—the thorough and attentive contemplation of it will furnish its best panegyric . . . . We have taken occasion to admire at every turn the noble monuments of ancient simplicity and the more curious refinements of modern art . . . . To sustain, to repair, to beautify this noble pile, is a charge intrusted principally to the nobility, and such gentlemen of the kingdom as are delegated by their country to parliament. The protection of THE LIBERTY OF BRITAIN is a duty which they owe to themselves, who enjoy it; to their ancestors, who transmitted it down; and to their posterity, who will claim at their hands this the best birthright, and noblest inheritance of mankind." [4] According to Burke, the English constitution was "made by what is ten thousand times better than choice, it is made by the peculiar circumstances, occasions, tempers, dispositions, and moral, civil, and social habitudes of the people, which disclose themselves only in a long space of time. It is a vestment, which accommodates itself to the body. . . . The individual is foolish; . . . but the species is wise, and, when time is given to it, as a species it always acts right." [5]

What really was the English constitution of the eighteenth century that excited so much admiration in Europe and stimulated the rhetorical exaltation of Blackstone and Burke? Unlike the Constitution of the United States, it was not all of one piece, a single document establishing a new system of government in harmony with the advanced ideas of eighteenth-century liberalism. The English constitution was a way of political life, accepted by the nation, that was built upon the traditions and precedents of centuries and on the great milestones of English freedom, such as the Magna Charta, the Bill of Rights, and the Toleration Act. It was the ripe fruit of what may be described in the antithetical terms "aristocratic liberalism," which rested on a class partnership between the landed aristocrats and the wealthy merchant class. The former were the senior partner and controlled the government machinery in all its aspects, legislative, executive, and judicial.

Parliament was supreme, it is true, but Parliament was a pliant tool of the landed aristocrats through the system of rotten boroughs and limited suffrage. The parties of eighteenth-century England fitted almost perfectly into the aristocratic political system. The Whigs and Tories were not political parties in the present popular sense, but two congeries of aristocratic families—the Whig Bedfords, Grenvilles, Rockinghams, and Cavendishes, and the Tory Courtenays, Butes, and Cholmondeleys, united by close family ties and representing the same social class whose economic interests were those of the landed aristocracy. It was not, therefore, conflicts of interest, but a tradition—that of the Revolution of 1688—that separated the Whigs and the Tories. The former accepted this tradition wholeheartedly as an ideal

[4] William Blackstone, *Commentaries on the Laws of England* (Philadelphia, 1893), II, Book IV, 342.

[5] Edmund Burke, "Speech on Reform of Representation," *Works* (Bohn ed.), VI, 147.

of freedom, which made them "liberal"; and the latter accepted it nonchalantly as a fact of long standing, which made them "conservative."

What about the junior partner in this combination, the wealthy merchant class? This class had shown its mettle during the Puritan uprising and had played a not inconsiderable part in the Revolution of 1688. The marked economic progress of England during the eighteenth century had given considerable importance to the rising middle class. Concessions had, therefore, to be made to the "commercial interests" by the aristocrats in power, whether Whig or Tory. These concessions were chiefly economic, as evidenced by England's trade policies during the eighteenth century, which were very favorable to the commercial interests. Outside the class partnership of the aristocrats and the wealthy middle class were the masses of the English people, to whom parliamentary government was as much of a mystery as divine-right monarchy had been to their ancestors in the sixteenth century.

Burke was the great philosopher of the English system of aristocratic liberalism. There lies his true significance in the history of political thought and the real explanation of his bitter antagonism to the French Revolution. With profound insight he diagnosed the English constitution as a system of "guarantees" to maintain an aristocratic social structure. It guaranteed the rights of the individual through civil liberties, the freedom of the nation through the checks on the royal power, and the class divisions in society through the privileged position of property. English liberty, according to Burke, was not a universal human right that had been established according to abstract principles, but a system of privileges created by the constitution, whose purpose was to maintain social, economic, and political inequality. "He [Burke] taught the Tories to regard themselves as the true heirs and protectors of the English Revolution Settlement of 1689 against the false cosmopolitan lights of the French Revolution." [6]

The advent of the Industrial Revolution in the latter part of the eighteenth century was destined to undermine the system of aristo-

[6] G. M. Trevelyan, *The Two-Party System in English Political History* (Oxford University Press, 1926), 23–24. For a contrast between the views of Burke and those of Rousseau, see the excellent work of Annie Marion Osborn, *Rousseau and Burke* (Oxford University Press, 1940).

cratic liberalism. A new, powerful class—the industrial capitalists—arose, seeking to entrench itself as the senior partner and to reduce the aristocrats to the position of junior partner in the government of England. In the struggle that was to take place between the two powerful classes, the advantage lay with the industrial capitalists.

In the first place, the factory system shifted population from the country to the city, thereby depriving the aristocrats of much of their popular support. Without a numerous peasantry, whom they could control, the aristocrats would be at a serious disadvantage in case of open conflict with their new opponents, the powerful industrial capitalists. The advancing industrial order was acquiring a popular base, as a consequence of the rapidly growing urban population. Almost all increases in the population of England were absorbed by the new factory towns in the north. The numerous industrial workers who crowded into these towns were out of reach of the landed aristocrats, but within reach of the industrial capitalists. By appealing to the rising spirit of discontent, the latter would be able to mobilize large masses of laborers against aristocratic rule. In the agitation for political reform that began after the Napoleonic wars, it was the riotous factory workers who constituted the greatest threat to the system of aristocratic liberalism.

In the second place, an economic shift took place from property in land to property in industry. The "broad acres" of the aristocrat could not equal in wealth production the concentrated factory of the capitalist. The rapid accumulation of vast wealth by the new class of industrial capitalists brought money to the fore as the new power in society, before which ancient lineage and exalted rank were compelled unwillingly to bow. The aristocrats, both Whig and Tory, were confronted by the industrial capitalists, who truculently demanded that the direction of public affairs should be placed in their hands.

As the industrialization of England proceeded apace, it became evident that the policies and machinery of the aristocratic Whig state were out of harmony with the ideals of the new generation and with the needs of the new social order, which were insistently making themselves felt. Could a transition be made to a new political and social order without a revolutionary uprising? The French Revolution offered the only modern example in Europe of the fall of aristocratic rule that went down to destruction as a result of a bloody civil war. But in England there was the Whig tradition of 1688, which pointed to a peaceful solution. There was "the age-old spirit of the nation; which had built up its work piece by piece without ever destroying what had once been built, but basing upon it every new departure. Thus it had added institution to institution, privilege to privilege, and insensibly adapted ancient traditions to modern needs. It had instinctively re-coiled from all abstract proclamation of principles and rights; its liber-ties had arisen from keenly felt needs, and had been paid for by sacrifices; . . . ."[7] A parliament existed that had supreme power in the government. Civil liberties existed that protected the "liberty of the subject" in demanding reform. Could the Whigs, as the heirs of the spirit of 1688, be induced to become the champions of parliamentary reform that would deprive the aristocrats of the control of the govern-ment and place it in more progressive hands? The answer to this question would decide whether or not England would make a peaceful transition from aristocratic to bourgeois liberalism.

[7] Guido de Ruggiero, *The History of European Liberalism,* trans. from the Italian by R. G. Collingwood (London, 1927), 81.

Chapter 3. Liberalism and the Revolutionary Tradition in France

France, like England, has a national tradition of individual liberty that makes a powerful appeal to the broad masses of the people. Fundamentally the principles of French liberalism are practically identical with those of English liberalism, yet they have been formulated in a different manner and have been proclaimed in a different spirit. These differences, arising from historical situations and not from innate national characteristics, caused the French and the English to follow different paths toward the same liberal goal.

The Old Regime in France presented, in appearance at least, a complete picture of a feudal caste system in society and of absolute monarchy in government. Unlike the old regime in England, that in France could boast of no parliamentary supremacy, of no Bill of Rights, of no Toleration Act, and of no freedom of speech and of the press. Under the shell of the Old Regime, however, a new social order was beginning to pulsate with life. The economic development of France since the Commercial Revolution of the seventeenth century marked a great advance of commerce and industry; and during the eighteenth century the first stages of the Industrial Revolution made their appearance. As a consequence, a powerful *bourgeoisie* came to the front, which grew in numbers, in wealth, and in influence.[1] As in England, so in France, the *bourgeoisie* constituted the driving force behind the movement to overthrow the Old Regime and to establish a liberal social and political order.

The liberal movement under the Old Regime found intellectual expression in the views of the *philosophes*. So great was their influence that their writings constituted a veritable intellectual revolution. To the *philosophes* belongs the credit of having created the pattern of

[1] See the notable Introduction in Vol. I of Jean Jaurès, *Histoire socialiste de la Révolution française,* 8 vols. (Paris, 1922–1924).

French liberalism. Despite the severe censorship laws and the almost complete suppression of civil liberty, there existed in France a state of affairs resembling that in England. The corruption and cynicism of the Bourbon regime constituted an immoral equivalent to the aristocratic liberalism of England. Widespread skepticism among the *bourgeoisie* and the nobility created a situation favorable to the expression of liberal ideas. The censorship was openly flouted. Deism and even atheism became fashionable. Royal despotism, though absolute in theory, became a spasmodic, rather than a continuous, manifestation.

This illegal liberalism under the Old Regime had an important influence in creating the pattern of French liberalism. Nothing is so conducive to wholesale condemnation and to limitless vistas of reform as an archaic order that can be freely attacked because it is feebly defended. The *philosophes* considered the Old Regime wholly evil, in that its laws and institutions violated their cherished principle of natural rights. Furthermore, they took the logical, though unhistorical, position that this evil system was evil also in origin. Violence and ignorance had given it birth, and tradition and prejudice had maintained it from generation to generation. Therefore the Old Regime could not be reformed either in part or as a whole; it must be totally abolished, in order that man might begin anew his social existence, fortified by rights that nature gave him, which no government could take away. Unlike English liberalism, French liberalism had no deep historic roots, no tradition of "liberty broadening down from precedent to precedent." Although English liberalism owed much to the philosophic speculations of John Locke, it owed much more, very much more, to concrete guarantees, such as the Bill of Rights; to the conciliatory policies of the Whig statesman Sir Robert Walpole; and to practical programs, such as those of Jeremy Bentham.

English liberalism bore the stamp of compromise. French liberalism, on the contrary, was abstract, doctrinaire, and uncompromising. By contrast with the "liberty of the subject" valid only in England, French liberalism proclaimed the rights of man and invoked, not historic precedent, but a mythical natural order that gave man his natural and inalienable rights, valid universally. According to De Ruggiero, French liberalism was "genuinely new, because instead of basing itself upon the privileged liberties of the Middle Ages, it arose from their ashes. It was far more akin to the spirit of absolute monarchy which had already begun to destroy the feudal world and had given to its subjects the feeling of equality. The new Liberalism like the monarchy was egalitarian, but its egalitarianism was inspired and ennobled by a broader rationalistic consciousness attributing to all men one identical spiritual and human value."[2] It was this liberal pattern of the *philosophes* that gave to the moral stature of France those vital elements that have made her so distinctive among modern nations: her respect for the dignity and independence of the individual, her cult of reason, and her genius for the universal.

This pattern was applied by the French Revolution. In making the transition from a "regime of privilege" to a "regime of liberty" it went much further and struck much deeper than had the English and American revolutions. The latter were essentially *political* overturns; their chief objective was to overthrow a despotic and to establish a constitutional government. In one aspect the French Revolution was also political; it overthrew absolute monarchy and established a constitutional system. But it was something more significant, in that it was the first *social* revolution in modern history. During the short decade 1789 to 1799 it destroyed the entire social fabric in France—economic, legal, educational, religious, and even geographical—that had existed for centuries. Not a single institution was left intact. Such drastic changes necessarily involved the fate of the class structure under the Old Regime. The ruling classes were ruined by three great confiscations of landed property: (1) the abolition of feudalism on the "famous night of August 4," (2) the confiscation of the church lands, and (3) the confiscation of the estates of the *émigrés*.

These revolutionary changes caused a shift of property interests unparalleled in history up to that time. New propertied classes appeared as the beneficiaries of the confiscations: peasant proprietors and a landed *bourgeoisie,* who were thereby committed to the cause of the Revolution. The status of landed property itself was changed when it passed from the old to the new proprietors. Under feudalism property was not owned but held under a form of trusteeship, as there existed no

2 Guido de Ruggiero, *The History of European Liberalism,* trans. from the Italian by R. G. Collingwood (London, 1927), 81–82.

absolute right of property in land. The French Revolution made property a natural right, and it was given the legal status of full and complete ownership. The proprietor of an estate after the Revolution was in quite a different—and a far stronger—position than had been the lord of the manor under the Old Regime. Curiously enough, property rights were made more definite, more complete, and more invulnerable by a revolution that had confiscated property on a vast scale.

The constructive work of the French Revolution was as thoroughgoing as was its destructive work. Consciously and deliberately it established a new political and social order, inspired by the principles of the Declaration of the Rights of Man. In building *la nouvelle France* the revolutionists sought no historic justification of precedent and made no appeal to national tradition. According to Renan, the French Revolution was the first attempt of mankind to take into its own hand the direction of its destiny, which marked "the entrance of thought in the government of humanity."[3]

But the new order established by the Revolution posed a serious, even a baffling, problem. This was what has been called "legitimacy," by which is meant the loyal support of the government by the entire nation. Popular acceptance of a political system, whether from a spirit of resignation or from inculcated belief, is essential to its peaceful and continuous functioning. No government can long exist that has to be constantly on guard against enemies that seek to destroy it. Only when it can count on unquestioning obedience by all the people can a government be considered as being legitimate. The strength of legitimacy lies primarily in the long endurance, and only secondarily in the punitive powers, of a government. Until the second half of the eighteenth century, there had been little question in France of the legitimacy either of absolutism in government or of privilege in society.

The first attack on the legitimacy of the Old Regime was made by the *philosophes*. In their bitter denunciation of its institutions, laws, ideals, and traditions they unwittingly loosened the foundations that held the old society together. It was, however, no part of their purpose to overturn the Old Regime in a welter of chaos and bloodshed. Not one of these bold, revolutionary thinkers favored resort to popular

[3] Ernest Renan, *L'Avenir de la science* (Paris, 1890), 25.

uprisings to inaugurate the reforms that they advocated so fervently. They were convinced that the force of public opinion and the spread of enlightened views among the rulers would inevitably bring into existence a new and better system. However, the *philosophes* did succeed in destroying, among the educated at least, the traditional loyalties, thereby opening the way to revolutionary violence. From the very beginning of the French Revolution, popular violence made its appearance; and it increased both in amount and in intensity as the pace of the Revolution quickened. One dramatic act, the taking of the Bastille on July 14, 1789, sounded the doom of the old legitimacy in France. The riot in Paris was a signal to the rest of France. For six weeks uprisings took place all over the country. The aristocratic and monarchic hierarchy "vanished into nothingness, disappeared into an enormous crevasse of history that all at once opened up beneath its age-old foundations . . . . Louis XVI became king without an army, without a police force, without courts, laws, or money; he was despoiled of all his powers, not by right but by deed, without any constitutional conflict and without advantage to a new power. Never in Western history had there been so unexpected and so tremendous an emotional contagion; one of the most grandiose among all historical edifices built by mankind unexpectedly crumbled away within a few weeks in the middle of a peaceful Europe; . . ."[4] The Reign of Terror was but the culmination of the violent overthrow of the old legitimacy begun by "July Fourteenth." Revolutionary violence became a heritage of France from the French Revolution. Its origin lay in the ideals of the Revolution and in the situation created by a social overturn that brought ruin and death to the hitherto ruling classes. The ideal of equality vibrated in almost every paragraph in the Declaration of the Rights of Man. This great promise of mankind was at last to be fulfilled. It aroused desires, hopes, and passions among the French masses, who were determined to sweep aside all obstacles to the march of equality. The constitution of 1791, which established a limited monarchy, was followed by the constitution of 1793, which established a democratic republic. Every step taken in the direction of political equality was followed—sometimes preceded—by steps in the direction of

[4] Guglielmo Ferrero, *The Principles of Power*, trans. from the Italian by T. R. Jaeckel (New York, 1942), 83.

social and economic equality, such as the abolition of aristocratic privileges, the destruction of feudalism, the confiscation of the church lands and of the estates of the *émigrés*. Even a socialist vision of economic equality arose with the Conspiracy of Babeuf. Those who had benefited from the confiscation of the property of the church and that of the *émigrés* became affrighted at the prospect of universal confiscation. They now sought to protect their interests by suppressing the revolutionary elements. In the opinion of a distinguished historian of the French Revolution, Georges Lefebvre, the proclamation of an equality of rights "put in glaring contrast the inequality of existence. Since the latter results, in part, from the unequal distribution of wealth, an unavoidable conflict, at once political and social, arose between property owners and proletarians. This conflict will lead the Revolution straight to democracy; and then, ten years later, it will convince the *bourgeoisie* to resort to military dictatorship in order to restore the domination of the upper classes."[5]

There was another, a practical, cause for popular violence and terrorism during the French Revolution. The treason of the monarchy and the recalcitrant attitude of the aristocracy created a situation that gave the opportunity to the Jacobin terrorists to put through extreme measures, on the plea of saving the country from reaction and invasion. In the opinion of Lefebvre, the Old Regime "would not have yielded to a legal revolution. Having resorted to force it was destroyed by the force that the people, mobilizing in the streets, put at the service of what they considered to be right, without their representatives even having dared to ask them for it."[6]

Owing to the fact that the French Revolution was a social revolution accompanied by civil war and terrorism, it created a division among Frenchmen so deep, so wide, so bitter, and so irreconcilable that nothing could bring the two Frances together. On one side were the upholders of the French Revolution: republicans, democrats, and socialists; on the other side, royalists, imperialists, and clericals. Neither side was ever strong enough to crush the other. Whenever one of the two Frances was out of power, it conspired to overthrow the government by violent methods. Whenever it was in power, it used the machinery

[5] Georges Lefebvre, *Quatre-vingt-neuf* (Paris, 1939), 238–239.
[6] *Ibid.*, 235.

of government to eliminate all influences of the "other" France. A revolutionary *tradition,* something new in history, had been established by the French Revolution, which constituted a threat to whatever regime was in power.[7]

The great schism of 1789 proved to be the effective cause of delaying for a century the establishment of a new legitimacy. All during the nineteenth century there took place in France what might be called the quest for a liberal legitimacy, and it was not until the Third French Republic was firmly established that a government based on the principles of the French Revolution was accepted, if not by all, at least by a majority of the people. By contrast, the English and American revolutions had little difficulty in finding a new, a liberal, legitimacy. After the Revolution of 1688 Parliament was recognized almost universally by the people of England as the supreme authority in the government. The sporadic uprisings in favor of the exiled Stuarts received no popular support outside Scotland. Even the totally un-English king, the Hanoverian Geoge I, had little difficulty in keeping his throne. In America the new government established by the Federal Constitution of the United States had no problem of legitimacy to solve, because it had been freely accepted by all the states. The "spirit of '76" became the traditional bond of union of all political parties in America. The reason in both cases is not far to seek. As has been already stated, the English and American revolutions were primarily political in character. They left the old institutions, the old property system, the old religious beliefs virtually undisturbed. As a consequence, no bitter, uncompromising opposition arose that aimed to overthrow the new order established by a revolution that substituted one political authority for another.

Though it was unstable, the liberal state was established in France, almost in its complete form, by the French Revolution. France took from England the parliamentary system and from America the idea of a written constitution, both of which were incorporated in the constitution of 1791. It has been the general fashion among liberal historians to condemn this constitution as being "bourgeois" because it provided for a propertied suffrage, in violation of the egalitarian spirit of the Declaration of the Rights of Man. But the constitution of 1791

---

[7] For a further discussion of the problem of the two Frances, see *infra,* 146*ff.*

marked a great advance over the British constitution, then the model and hope of the liberals on the Continent. In the first place, it followed the example of the Bill of Rights in the United States Constitution by including the Declaration of the Rights of Man, which guaranteed civil liberties. In the second place, it provided for a unicameral parliament, thereby eliminating the reactionary influence of an aristocratic upper house, as in England. In the third place, the property qualifications for voting were so low that about 60 per cent of the adult males were qualified to vote.[8] At that time only about 5 per cent of the adult males in Great Britain and Ireland were qualified electors. In the fourth place, the constitution gave to the king the powers of an executive only, and even these were sharply limited. For a "bourgeois" document, the constitution of 1791 compares favorably with many "democratic" constitutions of nineteenth-century Europe.

France made an original contribution to political liberalism by anticipating its democratic phase in the twentieth century. The Jacobin constitution of 1793 established, for the first time in the history of Europe, a democratic republic. Supreme power was to be exercised by a unicameral legislature, elected by direct manhood suffrage. The constitution itself was adopted by a nationwide referendum, another democratic innovation. Furthermore, it provided for the establishment of a national system of popular education and guaranteed all citizens the right to a livelihood. Never before in history had such radical innovations been formulated by the government of a nation. French democracy, however, was more of a promise than a performance, as the constitution of 1793 was never applied. For all that, it became the inspiration of the democratic elements in the nation, who, since the French Revolution, have struggled to carry out its promises. In France, far more than in England, was liberalism associated with "the people," whose sovereignty could be made effective only in a republic that was democratic both politically and socially.

Another liberal heritage of the French Revolution was the ideal of a classless society. How was this ideal, then so startling in its novelty, to be attained? The answer was, through a wide distribution of prop-

[8] Of about 7,300,000 adult males in France, about 4,300,000 were "active" citizens, with the vote; and about 3,000,000 were "passive" citizens, without the vote. See Albert Mathiez, *The French Revolution*, trans. from the French by C. A. Phillips (New York, 1929), 86.

erty. Eighteenth-century liberals were convinced that the possession of property was the measure of a man's freedom. Only a nation of property owners constituted a free society. This belief was most strongly held by the most advanced of the liberals of the period: Condorcet in France, Bentham in England, and Jefferson in America. Every man, they asserted, should be given full and free opportunity to acquire property, either in land or in business or through the exercise of a trade or a profession. Because in France no supply of free land existed as there did in America, the only way to give property in land to those who did not have it was by taking it away from those who did have it. The confiscations of landed property by the French Revolution, already referred to, and its sale to peasants and bourgeois constituted a redistribution of property on a vast scale. To preserve the newly established small property system from generation to generation, the French Revolution abolished the aristocratic system of primogeniture and established the system of equal division of inheritance through the *loi de partition,* according to which the estate of the father was to be divided equally among his children.

How was every individual to be given the opportunity to acquire property in business, or through the exercise of a trade or a profession? The answer was, by means of free individual enterprise. The privileged guilds and corporations, relics of mercantilism, constituted a bar to the freedom of enterprise by individuals whose ambition to acquire property was roused by the new economic opportunities offered by the Industrial Revolution. These bodies were abolished forthwith by the French Revolution. The famous *loi Le Chapelier* forbade, under severe penalties, the formation of associations in the same business, trade, or profession. Every such association, it was believed, would tend to establish new privileges for its members through monopolistic practices, and to create new social strata through the acquisition of great wealth by the fortunate few. Those who were poor, the agricultural and industrial laborers, would be stimulated by ambition to acquire property, an ambition that the state would encourage through favorable laws and through popular education. Under such circumstances the poor would not be a "class" but a transitory group on its way to prosperity through the acquisition of property. The few rich, having no privileges, would be an unimportant element in a nation of small property owners. Property, which, through its concentration, had created a society of privileged classes and unprivileged masses, would, through its diffusion, create the classless society of the future.

Property was endowed by the French Revolution with the magic of freedom. That is why it established property rights on a more firm basis than it had enjoyed under the Old Regime. Property, according to the Declaration of the Rights of Man and of the Citizen, was a natural right, which the state itself could not violate. All during the nineteenth century, the *bourgeoisie* insisted on the inviolability of property rights as a heritage from the French Revolution. At the same time, the propertyless proletariat proclaimed the ideal of a classless society as their heritage from the French Revolution. Had not the Revolution popularized the idea that government and society, not fate or personal wickedness, were responsible for the misery of the common man? The socialist movement of the nineteenth century originated in France; the Utopians Saint-Simon and Fourier were its pioneer thinkers. It was in France also that socialism made its first desperate attempts to establish a classless society: in 1797, with the Conspiracy of Babeuf; in 1848, during the June Days; and in 1871, during the Commune of Paris.

Finally there was the liberal heritage from the Revolution of anti-clericalism and the ideal of the "lay state" (*l'état laïque*). The French Revolution declared war *à outrance* against the Catholic church—its powers, its organization, its dogmas, and its authoritative position in the life of the nation. As the Revolution became more violent, its blows against the church increased in intensity. First came the confiscation of church property, then the Civil Constitution of the Clergy, then separation of church and state, and finally the efforts to de-Christianize France. These attacks were inspired by hatred of the church as one of the pillars of the Old Regime and as the primal source of the principle of authority in human thought and in the conduct of life. Inspired by the rationalism of the *philosophes,* the revolutionists sought to isolate and to discredit supernatural authority in all its manifestations in both public and private life. They were convinced that there existed a fundamental incompatibility between the church and the principles of the French Revolution.

Although the church was restored by Napoleon's Concordat of 1801, its moral authority was seriously undermined. All during the nineteenth century anticlericalism was the one bond of union that united the various parties and factions that upheld the principles of the French Revolution: the constitutional monarchists and the republicans during the first half of the nineteenth century, and the radicals and the socialists during the second half. Anticlericalism, as a liberal heritage of the Revolution, appealed both to the *bourgeoisie* and to the working class, despite their conflicting political and economic ideals. Hostility not only to the church but also to Christianity, and even to religion itself, became the distinguishing mark of militant anticlericalism. At best, it sought to divorce the state from all connection with the church, to secularize education, and to allow Catholicism to compete freely in the open market of ideas and beliefs along with other faiths and philosophic schools.

The principles of the French Revolution have constituted, to this day, the liberal tradition in France. Every liberal movement—bourgeois, democratic, socialist—has adhered to the "principles of 1789" as its primal inspiration and rallying cry. Whenever an appeal was made to vindicate these principles, it received an almost spontaneous response, whether at the barricades that overthrew despotic kings, as in the revolutions of 1830 and 1848; or in the underground that conspired against the military dictatorship of Napoleon III; or in the parliament of the Third French Republic, as in the MacMahon, Boulanger, and Dreyfus affairs. Because it had to be constantly on guard, French liberalism was more alert, more militant, and less compromising than was English liberalism. At every showdown it showed up, ready for the fray.

When France fell during the Second World War, the principles of the French Revolution were repudiated by the fascistic Vichy dictatorship established by Marshal Pétain. This repudiation was not the act of the French people, but that of the German conqueror using the French reactionaries as their tools. The "principles of 1789" again became the inspiration of the widespread Resistance movement of all parties that struggled with undaunted heroism to liberate France from the German invaders and their collaborationist tools. After the war a Fourth French Republic arose, grounded more firmly than ever before on the principles of the French Revolution. No other republic is possible in France.

Chapter 4. The Utilitarian View of the Nature of Man and of the Mechanics of Progress

English political and social thought in the first half of the nineteenth century bore a direct and unmistakable relationship to the great social and economic changes ushered in by the Industrial Revolution. As a result of these changes, a struggle for power was arising between the rising middle class and the ruling aristocracy. What the former needed above all else was a popular appeal to win public opinion, as a counterweight to the official influence over the people exercised by the aristocrats through their control of the government. Of the literate element in England, the middle class was by far the most numerous. It was, therefore, essential to consolidate this class into a "public" whose "opinion" would be a powerful weapon in the coming struggle.

The best way to accomplish this would be through the popularization of a philosophy that was universal and liberal in its fundamental principles and, at the same time, in harmony with the rights of property and with the special interests of the middle class. When industrial development has "modified the old class relations," observes Leslie Stephen, "or when the governing classes have ceased to discharge their functions, new principles are demanded and new prophets arise. The philosopher may then become the mouthpiece of the new order and innocently take himself to be the originator. His doctrines were fruitless so long as the soil was not prepared for the seed."[1]

Conditions in England after the Napoleonic Wars were ripe for the appearance of a liberal social philosophy. The pace of industrialism in England had increased, rather than diminished, during the struggle with France. As a consequence of its increase in numbers and in

[1] Leslie Stephen, *The English Utilitarians* (London, 1900), I, 6.

43

wealth, the middle class was in a far stronger position vis-à-vis the landed aristocracy than they had been during the eighteenth century. Furthermore, a large working class had arisen in the factory towns, which were seething with revolutionary discontent during the years of depression that came after 1815. A liberal philosophy with a universal appeal would draw the discontented workers to the side of the middle class in a conflict against aristocratic privilege. To the workers the conflict would be one for the emancipation of the unprivileged and for the establishment of a democratic social order. Utilitarianism was the new social philosophy that appeared in response to the new conditions in England. It proclaimed universal principles, as befitted a social philosophy, even an English one. Nevertheless, its fundamental principles were obviously, plainly, and frankly related to the changed economic conditions and to the changed class relationship in England during the first half of the nineteenth century. Utilitarianism consisted of a blend of new ideas and old traditions that were peculiarly and specifically English. It was not a closed metaphysical system, as was the philosophy of Hegel. Neither was utilitarianism a flaming ideal created by a generous imagination, like that of Rousseau. It comprehended an attitude toward life; a program of social, economic, and political action; and methods of attaining it that were in admirable harmony with the national temper and with the historic traditions of the English people.

Utilitarianism was advocated by a group of intellectuals whose activities constituted an intellectual revolution in nineteenth-century England comparable to that of the *philosophes* in eighteenth-century France. Its fountainhead was Jeremy Bentham, whose ideas influenced the stream of thought and the course of affairs in England as profoundly as did those of Rousseau in France. Bentham was born in 1748, the son of a wealthy London lawyer. Two early experiences made a marked impression on him: one, when he was a student at Oxford; the other, when he was a student of law at Lincoln's Inn. Bentham's experience in England's ancient seat of learning, which he attended from 1761 to 1763, was unhappy and roused in him a hatred of ancient institutions of all kinds. He disliked his rowdy fellow students, despised his clerically minded, conservative teachers, and detested the almost medieval curriculum of Oxford, the home of "lost causes, and forsaken beliefs, and impossible loyalties." After graduating from Oxford at the age of sixteen, Bentham devoted himself to the study of English law. He was admitted to the bar in 1769, but never practiced his profession. His study of law gave Bentham a bad impression of England's legal system. He considered it a hodgepodge of unrelated principles and traditions, irrational in theory and cruel in practice, of which the chief beneficiaries were the lawyers, who waxed fat by ruining their clients. English law had become "a mere jungle of unintelligible distinctions, contradictions, and cumbrous methods through which no man could find his way without the guidance of the initiated, and in which a long purse and unscrupulous trickery gave the advantage over the poor to the rich, and to the knave over the honest man."[2]

Bentham devoted many years to an assiduous study of the common law in order to reform it. During the first years of his career, he was known as a law and prison reformer. His personal situation was ideal for pursuing the career of a reformer: he was rich and a bachelor; and he had the patronage of a powerful aristocrat, Lord Shelbourne. Bentham advocated the establishment of a legal code that would have few rules, easy to learn and easy to apply—a code that would be logical in its reasonings and mild in its penalties. His great work on the reform of English law, *Rationale of Evidence,* became a storehouse of principles and methods, advocated by English law reformers. Bentham, declared John Stuart Mill, "found the philosophy of law a chaos; he left it a science. He found the practice of law an Augean stable: he turned the river into it which is mining and sweeping away mound after mound of its rubbish."[3]

Prison reform likewise engaged Bentham's attention. He devised an ingenious model prison, which he called the "Panopticon," in which the keeper would be able to see from a single point everything that was

[2] *Ibid.,* I, 278.

[3] John Stuart Mill, "Bentham," in *Dissertations and Discussions* (New York, 1874), I, 393. For Bentham's influence on law reform, see William Holdsworth, *A History of English Law* (London, 1923), II, 575; James Fitzjames Stephen, *A History of the Criminal Law of England* (London, 1883), II, 216; A. V. Dicey, *Lectures on the Relation between Law and Public Opinion in England during the Nineteenth Century* (London, 1914), 134*ff.*; and C. Phillipson, *Three Criminal Law Reformers: Beccaria, Bentham, Romilly* (London, 1923).

going on in the prison. The purpose of the Panopticon was, according to Bentham, to reform, not to punish its inmates; it was designed as a "mill for grinding rogues honest, and idle men industrious."[4]

Early in his career as a reformer, Bentham had come to the conviction that the root of England's troubles lay in the famous English constitution. His first book, *Fragment on Government,* which he published anonymously in 1776, was a virulent attack on the constitution and on its great apologist Blackstone. In Bentham's opinion, the "matchless constitution" so much praised by Blackstone was a "cover for rascality," and all that even the "Glorious Revolution" of 1688 accomplished was the substitution of one dynasty for another and the adding of "corruption to force." The main function of the constitution, according to Bentham, was to bolster up a narrow and selfish oligarchy, the sole beneficiary of institutions teeming with abuses and corruption. Blackstone he stigmatized as a man whose "hand was formed to embellish and to corrupt everything it touches. He makes men think they see, in order to prevent them seeing. His is the treasury of vulgar errors. He is the dupe of every prejudice, and the abettor of every abuse."[5] *Fragment on Government* created a sensation; it was generally believed that the anonymous author was a prominent public figure, not the unknown twenty-eight-year-old Jeremy.

Of Bentham's many amazing gifts, not the least was his gift of choosing disciples. Highly talented men were drawn to him, in the belief that he was a storehouse of knowledge and a dynamo of ideas that they could use to advance their own careers. Bentham made good use of his disciples by employing their aid in preparing his writings for publication and in giving publicity to his ideas. There was almost an apostolic succession of Benthamite disciples who became private secretaries to their master. The first was a French-Swiss, Etienne Dumont, who gave Bentham a Continental reputation as a political philosopher by translating into French his book, *Introduction to the Principles of Morals and Legislation.* Of the translator Dumont it may be said that he did not "betray" the original; on the contrary, he

---

[4] *Correspondence,* in *The Works of Jeremy Bentham* (Bowring, ed., Edinburgh, 1843), X, 226. Unless otherwise indicated, the quotations from Bentham's writings are from this edition of his works.

[5] Quoted in C. B. R. Kent, *The English Radicals* (London, 1899), 227.

actually improved it. Owing to Dumont's efforts, Bentham's ideas had a considerable vogue in France during the early days of the French Revolution. Long before Bentham was recognized in his own country, he had achieved an almost world-wide reputation. He was enthusiastically acclaimed as a great legal philosopher in such widely separated places as Russia, Spain, and South America.[6]

Bentham's recognition in England came largely through the efforts of another disciple—the Scotsman James Mill. It was the latter who made Bentham's ideas the philosophic basis of a new political movement, which became known as "Philosophic Radicalism." Mill constantly extolled the greatness of his master in books, articles, and reviews. His son, John Stuart Mill, one of the younger set of Benthamites, greatly helped to spread Bentham's reputation as a law reformer by editing his *Rationale of Evidence*. Prominent among Benthamites, or "utilitarians"—a descriptive expression coined by John Stuart Mill— were Sir James Romilly, the reformer of England's criminal law; Lord Brougham, the Whig statesman and political reformer; Francis Place, the political organizer of radical movements; Sir John Bowring, the editor of Bentham's collected works; George Grote, the historian of ancient Greece; Edwin Chadwick, the famous municipal reformer; and, most famous of all, John Stuart Mill.

There is almost a tradition in England that in order to be a philosopher a man has to be something of a crank. Bentham fully lived up to this tradition. He was, as he himself said, a "comical fellow," an eccentric of genius: egotistic, naïve, cheerful, and benevolent—a type of reformer that flourishes best in the atmosphere of good-humored tolerance characteristic of the intellectual climate of England. "I am a selfish man," remarked Bentham, "as selfish as any man can be. But in me, somehow or other, so it happens, selfishness has taken the shape of benevolence."[7] In his later years, being a bachelor, he lived alone, always working assiduously. His constant companion was a pet cat, and his only relaxations were "trotting" in his garden and playing the organ. From time to time Bentham's disciples would come to sit at the feet of their master, whom they revered as a sort of oracle. And

[6] *Papers on Codification* (Bowring, ed.), IV, 514–530; E. L. Kayser, *The Grand Social Enterprise* (New York, 1932), 82–85.

[7] *Memoirs of Bentham* (Bowring, ed.), X, 95

like an oracle the master would sometimes turn sharply and severely on those who came to seek his wisdom. Bentham worked hard and regularly, but not systematically. He literally shed manuscripts of books, pamphlets, and articles, which were written offhand and often were left unrevised. Like the queen bee, who merely gives birth to many offspring and has "workers" to attend to them, Bentham merely gave birth to many books, which, before they appeared in print, were "edited"—actually, revised—or even rewritten by his secretary-disciples.

Bentham wrote voluminously on many subjects: government, law, politics, religion, education, economics, and prison reform. His earlier works were written in a style that was clear, pungent, and provocative.[8] His criticisms of ancient institutions and hallowed traditions were set forth with a sort of unimaginative vividness that tore through sentimental associations and romantic halos of the kind that surround institutions and beliefs in a state of decay. As Bentham grew older, his eccentricities became more marked and affected his writings. His style became involved, didactic, diffuse, and even obscure; and this made his books difficult—at times, even painful—to read. Bentham's books, declared his disciple Francis Place, are "so written that to comprehend all that is said, each paragraph, nay each sentence, must be studied, and most men think it trouble enough to study the subject itself, be it what it may, even in the plainest language, without being obliged at the same time to make a study of the phraseology of the author."[9] Bentham was so eager to be precise that he actually invented new words, like "codify," "international," "minimize," and "maximize," to express his ideas more clearly. "He became obscure by dint of wishing to be precise."[10] However, as in the case of Thorsten Veblen, with whom he may be compared, lightning flashes of sharp wit and revealing insight now and then pierce through the clouds of Bentham's obscurity.

Unlike Rousseau, who was intoxicated by the exuberance of his prolific imagination, Bentham had a mind that was concrete, cautious,

---

[8] See, especially, *Fragment on Government, Truth against Ashhurst,* and *Book of Fallacies.*

[9] Graham Wallas, *The Life of Francis Place* (London, 1898), 84.

[10] Élie Halévy, *The Growth of Philosophic Radicalism,* trans. from the French by Mary Morris (London, 1928), 305.

practical. His eccentric personality and gnarled style masked a great profundity, which had its sources in the very depths of England's political experience and practical wisdom. Bentham was a philosopher in the true English tradition, being psychological like Locke and practical like Adam Smith. He abhorred abstractions, which were mouth filling but left the stomach empty. In his attitude toward the state, Bentham was as severely critical of the ideology of revolutionary France as he was of the traditions of aristocratic England. He detested the logical application of abstract principles, such as the natural rights of man, to the problems of government. His utilitarian philosophy was indeed rational and logical, but it drew its conclusions from concrete facts, not from abstract ideas. He never reasoned about wholes until he dissolved them into parts, an empirical method that left little to the imagination but much to cool reasoning.

Bentham was a rationalist, if he was anything, but his rationalism was a practical social philosophy, to be applied to given problems in a given situation—not a universal solvent of the ills of mankind. He ridiculed the ideas of a "state of nature" and of a "social contract" arising from it; the "indestructible prerogative of mankind" did not need "to be supported upon the sandy foundation of a fiction."[11] Men living without government, he argued, lived without rights. Therefore the doctrine of natural rights "was simple nonsense: natural and im-prescriptible rights, rhetorical nonsense—nonsense on stilts."[12] The Declaration of the Rights of Man he characterized as a "hodge-podge of confusion and absurdity,"[13] as "bawling on paper," a "perpetual vein of nonsense, flowing from a perpetual abuse of words."[14] These abstract ideas, in Bentham's opinion, hindered rather than helped the solution of political problems by preventing clear thinking on definite issues. Nay, worse, they stimulated revolutionary ardor by putting the mask of high ideals on evil passions. "To add as much force as possible to those passions," he declared, "already but too strong, to burst the cords that hold them in; to say to the selfish passions, there,

[11] Bentham, *A Fragment on Government* (F. C. Montague, ed., Oxford University Press, 1931), 154.

[12] *Anarchical Fallacies* (Bowring, ed.), II, 501.

[13] *Memoirs of Jeremy Bentham* (Bowring, ed.), X, 63.

[14] *A Critical Examination of the Declaration of Rights* (Bowring, ed.), II, 497.

everywhere is your prey; To the angry passions, There, everywhere
is your enemy."[15]

Utilitarianism, as preached by Bentham and his disciples, comprehended a view of human nature, a moral code, and a program of
action that made a great appeal to the rising generation of England
after the Napoleonic Wars. Bentham's view of human nature is strikingly stated in the opening paragraph of his *Introduction to the
Principles of Morals and Legislation.* "Nature has placed mankind
under the governance of two sovereign masters, *pain* and *pleasure.* It
is for them alone to point out what we ought to do, as well as to
determine what we shall do. On the one hand the standard of right
and wrong, on the other, the chain of causes and effects. They govern
us in all we do, in all we say, in all we think: every effort we can
make to throw off our subjection, will serve but to demonstrate and
confirm it. In words a man may pretend to abjure their empire: but
in reality he will remain subject to it all the while. The *principle of
utility* recognizes the subjection, and assumes it for the foundation of
that system, the object of which is the rearing of the fabric of felicity
by the hands of reason and of law. Systems which attempt to question
it deal in sounds instead of sense, in caprice instead of reason, in
darkness instead of light."[16]

According to Bentham's analysis, the ultimate aim and criterion of
conduct is happiness. Man was naturally selfish and pursued his self-
interest—*i.e.,* his "happiness"—incessantly and inevitably toward definite
and concrete goals. And these goals were materialistic in character.[17]
Man, elsewhere observed Bentham, from the very constitution of his
nature "prefers his own happiness to that of all other sensitive beings
put together: but for this self-preference, the species would not have
had existence.[18] And each individual was the best judge of this "self-
preference," because generally "there is no one who knows what is
for your interest, so well as yourself—no one who is disposed with so
much ardor and constancy to pursue it."[19] Furthermore, only the

---

[15] *Ibid.*

[16] Bentham, *Introduction to the Principles of Morals and Legislation* (London, 1879),
1–2.

[17] *Manual of Political Economy* (Bowring, ed.), III, 33.

[18] *Memoirs of Bentham* (Bowring, ed.), X, 30.

[19] *Manual of Political Economy* (Bowring, ed.), III, 33.

expectation of the enjoyment of pleasure or of the avoidance of pain operated as the driving forces of human action. Such abstractions as "justice," "obligations," "rights," "duties" were "fictitious entities," without meaning except in relation to the realities of pleasure and of pain. Most human actions were the result of calculating the pleasures that came from "material consequences associated with them." All men, even madmen, calculated on how their actions would bring them happiness. This view of the nature of man, Bentham was convinced, was so true that it was obvious to anyone. "In this matter," he declared, "we want no refinement, no metaphysics. It is not necessary to consult Plato nor Aristole. *Pain* and *pleasure* are what everybody feels to be such—the peasant and the prince, the unlearned as well as the philosopher."[20]

But there were degrees of pleasure and of pain. How was the extent of each to be measured? Besides, what was pleasure to one might be pain to another. Happiness, in the view of Bentham, was not a state of exaltation ineffably spiritual, but a pervasive feeling of comfort, which was the outcome of "material consequences." Therefore, happiness was a concrete reality that could be subjected to the test of measurement. Bentham evolved a rather intricate scheme of ascertaining the extent of pleasures and of pains, which he called the "felicific calculus." This scheme, Bentham boasted rather naïvely, was so great an innovation that he would be hailed as "the Newton of the moral world," who succeeded in making morals as "clean as mathematics." He tabulated fourteen "simple pleasures" and twelve "simple pains," each unit of which was to be measured according to six criteria: intensity, duration, certainty, propinquity, fecundity, and the number of persons affected.[21] Bentham admitted that different individuals had different ideas on what constituted pleasure and pain. But, he argued, all pleasures, insofar as they were pleasures that produced happiness, were the same, hence "pushpin is as good as poetry if it gives the same pleasure." The "addibility of happiness" was a postulate without which "all political reasoning is at a stand." Promises of pleasure induced action, just as logical argument induced assent, because there

[20] Bentham, *Theory of Legislation* (C. K. Ogden, ed., New York, 1931), 3.

[21] For a good analysis of Bentham's scheme, see W. C. Mitchell, "Bentham's Felicific Calculus," *Political Science Quarterly*, XXXIII (June, 1918), 161–183.

"is, or rather there ought to be, a *logic* of the *will,* as well as of the *understanding.*"[22]

Bentham's "felicific calculus" was designed as a sort of measuring rod, a "moral arithmetic," with which to measure social progress. Though founded on a crude, mechanical psychology it did mark an advance over the eighteenth-century conception of progress as an abstract "law," which operated universally and inevitably. Progress could now be planned and directed according to definite principles, which promised concrete results.

What surprisingly followed from Bentham's materialistic view of human nature was a benevolent social doctrine: the "greatest happiness of the greatest number." Bentham was not the originator of this famous phrase, which was implicit, and even explicit, in the writings of Helvétius, Beccaria, and Priestley. But what had been merely a phrase was made by Bentham into a fundamental principle of morals and of public policy. The "greatest happiness" principle proclaimed a new basis for morality, in that it stressed the importance of social consequences of individual actions almost to the exclusion of individual motives. Love, anger, or patriotism, as expressed by individuals, were not in themselves either good or bad. What made them so were their social consequences. "The creed which accepts as the foundation of morals, Utility, or the Greatest Happiness Principle," declared John Stuart Mill, "holds that actions are right in proportion as they tend to promote happiness, wrong as they tend to produce the reverse of happiness. By happiness is intended pleasure, and the absence of pain; by unhappiness, pain and the privation of pleasure."[23] The innate moral sense, ascribed to man by religious and moral teachers, was, according to Bentham, a "fictitious entity." Bentham convinced himself and his disciples that the "greatest happiness" principle would prove to be the law of gravitation of the social order. When the natural laws that govern human relations would be discovered, he, Bentham, would be hailed as the "Newton of the moral world."

The great problem that confronted the utilitarians was how to transform individual selfishness, which is antisocial, into a social good.

[22] Bentham, *Principles of Morals and Legislation,* Preface, xiii.

[23] John Stuart Mill, "Utilitarianism," in *Utilitarianism, Liberty and Representative Government* (London, Everyman's Library, 1914), 6.

They asserted as a fundamental postulate the view of Adam Smith, that the interest of the public was the sum of the interests of the individuals who composed it. "The interest of the community, then, is what? The sum of the interests of the several members who compose it."[24] Logically it followed that the true interests of the individual must be in harmony with those of the public. Any antisocial action of the individual was a "miscalculation" of his self-interest. How, then, was the individual to develop sufficient capacity for "enlightened" self-interest to make his activities conform to the public welfare? Popular education was the answer. The utilitarians became ardent advocates of "schools for all" as the best means to advance the "greatest happiness" principle and to spread popular enlightenment in regard to public policies. Bentham made the suggestion—very radical for his day—that a ministry of education should be established by the government, to advance the cause of popular education.[25] His disciple, James Mill, became an active advocate of popular education supported by the state, on the ground that the mass of people were too poor to pay for the education of their children.[26] The utilitarians stressed, especially, the study of the social sciences in the colleges and universities.[27]

A more direct method to advance both individual and public welfare, according to the utilitarians, would be the creation of a favorable environment through "radical," or root, reforms of all existing institutions. The old social order, based on privilege, caste, monopoly, and repression, was to give place to the new social order, with institutions that functioned in the interest of the greatest number. In his *Book of Fallacies,* Bentham exposed with trenchant logic and with ruthless ridicule the romanticizing of evil customs and irrational institutions by the conservative upholders of the old regime in England. Those who opposed innovations, he declared, were always alive "to possible imaginable evils, dead to actual ones, eagle-eyed to future contingent evils, blind and insensible to all existing ones."[28]

[24] Bentham, *Principles of Morals and Legislation*, 3.

[25] *Constitutional Code* (Bowring, ed.), IX, 441.

[26] See his article, "Education of the Poor," *Edinburgh Review*, XXI (February–July, 1813), 207–219.

[27] London University was founded, in 1828, by a group of utilitarians, among whom were James Mill and Lord Brougham, with the special object of teaching the social sciences, then neglected by Oxford and Cambridge.

[28] Bentham, *The Book of Fallacies* (London, 1824), 150.

To every law, tradition, custom, and institution, utilitarianism put the simple but devastating question: What is its use? If it promoted the greatest happiness of the greatest number, it should be maintained. If not, it had no right to exist. "I asked myself," declared Bentham, *"how* this or that institution contributed to the greatest happiness.— *Did* it contribute?—If not, what institution *would* contribute to it." [29] Bentham rejected *in toto* the sanctity conferred by history and tradition upon ancient institutions and customs. He had nothing but scorn for Blackstone's apostrophes to the British constitution and for Burke's eloquent defense of traditional values.

It was to legislation that the utilitarians turned as the chief means of promoting the "greatest happiness" principle. "The right and proper end of government in every political community," declared Bentham, "is the greatest happiness of all the individuals of which it is composed, say, in other words, the greatest happiness of the greatest number." [30] To the utilitarians the state was no Hegelian deity, no mystical entity apart and above the people, to be blindly worshiped and obeyed. It was, to all practical purposes, Parliament, a creature of the electors, which was then absurdly misrepresentative, crudely inefficient, and incredibly corrupt. To reform Parliament and make it the instrument of progress by taking it out of the hands of those to whom it was an instrument of privilege became the immediate object of utilitarian activity. Then only would the legislator become the "great dispenser of pleasures and pains in society." [31] Law was the creative force in human activity; therefore, only through legislation could reforms be made permanent by creating a new environment that would mold human behavior. This utilitarian faith in the prime importance of legislation became a heritage of English liberals, who were firmly convinced that no change was real and permanent unless it appeared in the form of an act of Parliament.

However, the action of the state in society should be limited to the negative functions of ensuring that contracts, freely made, be faithfully kept; that compensation be given for damages suffered; and that individuals be not interfered with in their pursuit of happiness. Rarely,

[29] *Memoirs of Bentham* (Bowring, ed.), X, 581.
[30] *The Constitutional Code* (Bowring, ed.), IX, 5.
[31] Halévy, *op. cit.*, 487.

if ever, should the state intervene in economic life to regulate wages, prices, hours of labor, investment, or conditions of production, all of which should be regulated by the natural working of economic laws. The utilitarian policy was to make the nation "master of its own destiny" through "the removal of every definite abuse and the repeal of every unjust law, and especially of any law which pressed unfairly and hardly upon the poor. This being done, law, it was assumed rather than stated, could do no more; for the ultimate cure of social diseases we must trust to general good-will, and above all to individual energy and self-help."[32]

According to Bentham, the objectives of government were "security, subsistence, abundance, and equality."[33] And the greatest of these was security. Without security of life and property, there would be no happiness for anyone. It was the desire for security, not only for the present but also for the future, that impelled men to accumulate wealth. Therefore, the best method of attaining security was by maintaining the rights of property, any menace to which produced pain and any protection, pleasure.[34] Essentially, property was not a natural right; it was something much more real, namely, the legal guarantee of every security in society. Hence the government should be especially concerned about the institution of property. To create economic equality was, in the opinion of Bentham, not an important object of government. All that it could and should do in this direction was to encourage a tendency toward economic equality by bringing about a greater and freer circulation of wealth through the abolition of privileges and sinecures; through the establishment of equal division of inheritance among children; and through the suppression of entail and of primogeniture.[35] If the property system should be destroyed in order to establish a regime of economic equality, security would vanish and society would relapse into its original savage state. "When security and equality are in conflict, it will not do to hesitate a moment. Equality must yield."[36] Revolutionary attempts to establish economic equality would only bring widespread idleness and poverty, with the result that "the miser-

[32] Dicey, *op. cit.*, 213.

[33] *Constitutional Code* (Bowring, ed.), IX, 11–15.

[34] *Principles of the Civil Code* (Bowring, ed.), 1, 308–309.

[35] *Logical Arrangements* (Bowring, ed.), III, 294.

[36] Bentham, *Theory of Legislation*, 120.

able would awaken from their delirium, curse the system and its inventors, and join their endeavors to bring back the former state of things."[37]

In their insistence on maintaining the rights of property, coupled with their demand for wholesale changes in government and society, Bentham and his followers created the pattern of English radicalism. Utilitarianism was a philosophy of reform, not of revolution. It advocated the abolition of specific evils through legislative action, not the freeing of the human race by an upheaval of the downtrodden. All changes, even the most drastic ones, were to be made within the economic framework of the property system, which would assure both progress and security.

As long as the utilitarians were in the front line of battle against England's old regime, their great virtues often obscured their limitations. The fallacies of utilitarianism became evident after they had succeeded in creating the bourgeois liberal order, which, in turn, became the object of attack by a new generation of reformers. Chief among the fallacies of utilitarianism was its exaggeration of the power and the capacity of the individual to be master of his own economic fate. Few individuals had the capacity to know what their best interests were. Fewer still had the freedom of choice and the power to get what they desired. Most individuals had their choice made for them by conditions and situations over which they exercised no control. Even more optimistic was the view of the utilitarians that an "invisible hand" was guiding the individual so that his self-interest would be in harmony with public welfare. In the competitive struggle under laissez-faire capitalism, profit—not public welfare—was the great objective. And profit, provided that it was legally made, was its own justification. The hands that guided the profit seeker were entirely visible; they guided him in the direction of self-interest, not of public welfare.

Utilitarianism cannot be dissociated from the historic conditions out of which it arose. In the opinion of a recent writer, Bentham "was, perhaps unconsciously, the philosopher of the Industrial Revolution, and the Industrial Revolution was rapidly becoming a factor in

37 *Principles of the Civil Code* (Bowring, ed.), I, 364.

politics."[38] The opportunities opened up by machine industry to ambitious men to become rich gave them a view of new vistas of great and unexpected pleasures. Economic success was the new pleasure and economic failure the new pain that were ushered into middle-class consciousness by the Industrial Revolution. For this reason, the bourgeois liberalism formulated by the utilitarians made a powerful appeal to the English middle class, to whom the traditionalism of Burke was the romantic expression of aristocratic privilege, which they hated; and to whom the egalitarian principles of the French Revolution were a new challenge by the propertyless masses, whom they feared. Utilitarian principles and policies taught them how to make drastic changes in the social order without resorting to revolution.

Middle-class England was terrified at the possibility of a social upheaval that might engulf all propertied classes—industrial, as well as landed. It is, therefore, not surprising that utilitarianism became frankly a middle-class philosophy and was universally recognized as such. According to Dicey, Benthamism "was fundamentally a middle-class creed, and the middle classes were more likely to give effect to the aspirations of Utilitarianism than any other part of the community."[39] This view was also that of John Stuart Mill, who declared that utilitarianism voiced "the interests and the instincts of large portions of society recently grown into strength."[40]

Although the number of those professing utilitarianism was very small, their influence was widespread. It went beyond the middle class and became the current intellectual coin of the nation, and all England was speaking the language of utility. Even those who thoroughly disliked Benthamism as a philosophy consisting of cold truisms advocated by calculating materialists, who appealed to the meanest of passions, selfishness, yet were influenced by the stark common sense of the creed. It appealed to practical businessmen, who beheld their self-interest universalized, not as an evil, but as a good. It appealed to social reformers of many kinds, to whom utilitarianism was a working creed with a satisfying intellectual content that spurred

[38] M. Roberts, *The Whig Party, 1807–1812* (London, 1939), 264.
[39] Dicey, *op. cit.*, 187.
[40] Mill, "Bentham," *op. cit.*, I, 357–358.

their efforts to create the "good society." It appealed to idealistic temperaments, like that of John Stuart Mill, who beheld possibilities of broadening the sectarian basis of utilitarianism through a wider application of the "greatest happiness" principle. Though they were far, very far, from accepting utilitarian principles, shrewd Tories, like Sir Robert Peel and William Huskisson, and cautious Whigs, like Macaulay, trod the path blazed by Bentham and his disciples.

The bourgeois stamp, so characteristic of utilitarianism, drew the lightning of devastating criticism from the prophet of fascism, Thomas Carlyle, and from the prophet of socialism, Karl Marx. Carlyle hurled maledictions, as vigorous as they were frequent, against utilitarianism and its prophet, Bentham, who, he declared, sought to make a "swine's trough" of human society and to defile human relations by a "cash-nexus" as the supreme bond between man and man.[41] Marx used the term "bourgeois" as an epithet to describe what he considered the lowest and most vulgar depth to which a social philosopher could descend. The "archphilistine" Bentham, wrote Marx, was "a genius in the way of bourgeois stupidity," the "insipid, pedantic, leather-tongued oracle of the commonplace bourgeois intelligence of the nineteenth century," who in his arid and simple way assumed "the modern petty bourgeois, and above all the modern English petty bourgeois, to be the normal man."[42]

What were the permanent contributions of utilitarianism? Its flat materialism and mathematical hedonism have long since been thrown into the discard. Its rigid equations of happiness of all sorts and conditions of men are now regarded as psychologically naïve. However, the utilitarians did open up vistas of human progress and did devise new methods of creating the "good society," an objective that was always in their minds and in their hearts. By breaking the charm of the English constitution, which had closed English eyes to the great evils of their day, the utilitarians created a state of mind hospitable to new ideas, to new institutions, and to new methods of progress that were struggling for recognition and support.

By its insistence on favorable social and economic conditions as the

---

[41] See *infra.*, 392.

[42] Karl Marx, *Capital*, trans. from the German by E. and C. Paul (New York, Everyman's Library, 1930), II, 671.

prime source of individual happiness, utilitarianism created the acid test of a healthy social order. The great social and economic reforms of nineteenth-century England owed not a little to direct utilitarian inspiration. The reason why the utilitarians were considered common-place was that they sought the plain truth, without any airs of profundity in their analysis of social problems. Profundity and truth are not always the same thing. Finally, the utilitarians created new methods of peaceful progress through legislative action. Reforms had to be continuous, one *after* another; they had to be radical by making substantial changes; and they had to be of benefit to the whole nation by alleviating the conditions of any class or group that suffered hardship and injustice. The utilitarian method of radical reform through parliamentary action became an English national tradition that was followed by the Liberal party in the nineteenth century and by the Labor party in the twentieth. "Inevitability of gradualness" became the recognized English method of achieving social progress.

Chapter 5. The Classical Economists
and the Apotheosis of
the *Bourgeoisie*

Utilitarianism created a new mood in England—the mood of the practical, the definite, the worldly, and the shrewd. Clearly and sharply did it assert the supremacy of material factors in man's happiness and in public welfare. And these material factors became insistently persuasive with the advance of the Industrial Revolution, which rapidly changed the social scene in England. Instead of farms, hamlets, and an occasional town, there appeared immense cities with teeming populations, huddled around gigantic factories. The great manufacturing centers seemed like forests of tall chimneys. Population increased rapidly and the whole increase was absorbed by the cities.[1] Factory production increased even more rapidly and England became "the workshop of the world." New populations appeared, out of which emerged new social classes with new relations to each other. What was most striking was the emergence of a wealthy class of capitalists— "chimney aristocrats"—whose wealth, in many cases, far exceeded that of the old landed aristocrats.

It was the machine, the child of the inventor's brain, that was the primal cause of the remarkable advance of industry. The revolutionary change from the tool to the machine marked a momentous event in the history of mankind. Instead of being an aid to the worker in the production of goods, the machine itself, unlike the tool, became the producer, with the worker serving merely as its aid. Nothing else was more startling than the contrast between living men and "iron men" as producers of goods. The worker was biologically stationary; he could

[1] The population of England and Wales during the period 1801 to 1831 increased almost 57 per cent. G. R. Porter, *Progress of the Nation* (London, 1912), 19.

have only two hands and ten fingers. But the "iron man," the machine, could have as many hands and as many fingers as the ingenuity of the inventor could provide. Moreover, the "iron man" worked tirelessly and endlessly. Production could now advance with giant strides. The skilled artisan was swiftly eliminated. An unskilled laborer, a "hand," took up the task of tending the machine, which, as it developed, became almost human in its automatic intelligence, while the "hand" became almost machinelike in his monotonous labor.

Another artificial creature made its appearance as the efficient aid of nascent capitalism, the joint-stock company. As industry grew, there was an urgent necessity for more and more capital, which, at first, had been supplied in limited quantities by individual entrepreneurs. The joint-stock company was an anonymous, artificial "person," the creature of law. Its function was to accumulate large amounts of capital and to limit the liability of its members to the amount that they had invested. Unlike a single proprietorship or a partnership, the joint-stock company remained intact, regardless of the personality of the owners—namely, the stockholders. It was made possible by the facility afforded by the new method for the rapid transfer of ownership through sales of shares of stock. In England before the middle of the nineteenth century, joint-stock companies could be organized only in special cases. But the need for raising large amounts of capital to finance the rapidly growing railways induced Parliament, in 1856, to enact a law that permitted the organization of joint-stock companies in any business venture.[2] Great funds of capital could now be amassed with which to set in motion the resources of the nation in men and materials.

The chief beneficiaries of the machine and of the joint-stock company were members of the class now designated distinctively as "capitalists." Originally they formed part of what was known as the *bourgeoisie*—the general term used to describe those engaged in commerce and industry. As members of the *bourgeoisie,* the capitalists bore the mark of social inferiority and shared the odium attached to traders from time immemorial. The bourgeois was not a "gentleman," because he was "in trade"—an activity that was associated with dubious relationships, if not with downright dishonesty. Those engaged in trade were regarded as performing semilegitimate, though

[2] K. B. Smellie, *A Hundred Years of English Government* (London, 1937), 24.

necessary and useful, functions. According to feudal tradition, "honor" attached only to the aristocrat, no matter how poor he might be in worldly goods and how outrageous his conduct might be toward his social inferiors.

With the advent of the Industrial Revolution, the bourgeois underwent a transformation. The itinerant merchant, at best a glorified peddler, became a "captain of industry"—a capitalist whose economic power was ludicrously out of proportion to his social position and to his political influence. Often he was far wealthier than the aristocrat who affected to despise him as a vulgar upstart. As the factory system spread, the new class of industrial capitalists grew in numbers and in economic power. Their influence began to be felt even in the government, then under aristocratic control. Before 1832 England presented an economic contradiction to her political setup. Within a comparatively short time, a new class had come into existence, the members of which—aggressive, capable, and energetic—engaged in opening up new avenues of wealth production. But in the seat of government were the landed aristocrats, whose traditions and sentiments were feudal and whose power came from the political privileges conferred on them by law and custom.

In order that the capitalists might be able to assume the place in society and in government to which their economic importance entitled them, there had to take place a reevaluation of social values. The "men of money" must be put in the place of the "men of family," whereby the capitalists became elevated in the social hierarchy. This reevaluation could be accomplished by showing, in the first place, that in the new economic order the capitalists were the sole creative element, on whose energy, enterprise, and foresight depended the prosperity of the entire nation. In the second place, the aristocrats must be shown up as a useless, parasitic class, ornamental at best, who, by means of their privileges, drained the wealth produced in the nation. Finally, the nation was to realize that the capitalists were not merely an isolated group of newly rich but the leaders of a rapidly growing new middle class: businessmen, professionals, scientists, who were now the bone and sinew of the nation. This new situation was clearly seen by the Utopian socialist, Saint-Simon. "Let us suppose," he wrote in 1819, "that France loses fifty of her first-class doctors, fifty first-class chemists, fifty first-class physiologists, fifty first-class bankers, two hundred of her best merchants, six hundred of her foremost agriculturists, five hundred of her most capable ironmasters . . . . As these men are the indispensable makers of her most important products, the minute that France loses them she will degenerate and fall into a state of despicable weakness in the eyes of rival nations. . . . Now let us imagine that France retains all her men of genius, whether in the arts and sciences, or in the crafts and industries, but has the misfortune to lose all at once" the royal family, all the officials in church and state, and the highest nobility. Such an overwhelming catastrophe would surely aggrieve the French, but it "would not cause the nation the least inconvenience."[3] The fact that, for making this statement, Saint-Simon was arrested by a resentful aristocratic government merely confirmed its truth.

In the preindustrial era of privilege and of caste there had existed no such type as the "successful man." One was born successful, with a "golden spoon in his mouth," and a family estate in his name. Those of nonaristocratic origin who had managed to rise from obscure beginnings were called "adventurers," and they were generally unscrupulous men with gifts of personality and talents for intrigue that served them well in getting the backing of influential rulers and courtiers. John Law was a famous example of an adventurer. Early in the eighteenth century he had risen to wealth and power in France by winning, through devious methods, the support of the court for his financial schemes.

When the wealthy factory owners appeared, they were at first regarded with contempt by the aristocrats, who ridiculed them as *nouveaux riches,* parvenus, and upstarts. In reply, the successful man could assert that he, unlike the aristocrat, had created the property that belonged to him. Without his efforts this new wealth would not be at all, and the nation would be the poorer. The larger the number of successful men in a nation, the more prosperous was the nation. The unsuccessful men were those who did not add to the wealth of the nation; being poor in ability, they were poor in worldly goods. Success was the new heaven. Capitalism encouraged hopes of entering it by

[3] Quoted in C. Gide and C. Rist, *Histoire des doctrines économiques* (Paris, 1926), 240–241.

presenting the vision of wealth for anyone who practiced the virtues of economy, sobriety, prudence, and ambition. The promises of wealth and the threats of poverty that capitalism held out to all enterprisers it fulfilled promptly and ruthlessly. There was never any doubt who was a success and who was a failure in business. Those who succeeded —the elect—entered the capitalist class. Those who failed struggled on in the purgatory of ruinous competition or were cast down into the hell of poverty. Who was responsible for their failure? It was then widely believed that if a man was poor he alone was responsible. Either he lacked the capacity to take advantage of the opportunities offered by a free economy or he lacked character, being lazy or a drunkard. If he was not himself responsible, then his parents were, for bringing him into the world without a prospect of "desirable existence."

The capitalists asserted that, unlike the aristocrats, they did not constitute a privileged class; they were really the "public" organized in the most efficient form and led by its most capable members. Anyone could become a capitalist, provided that he had capacity to acquire property. Legal equality and civil liberty would enable him to utilize his acquisitive abilities in a free, unprivileged social order in which individuals, of whatever origin, moved up and down the social order according to their capacity to take advantage of economic opportunities. The successful businessman, just because he had succeeded in acquiring property through his individual efforts, had passed through the severest test of human capacity. In a society of free enterprise, the acquisition of property was prima facie evidence of an individual's natural endowment of superior intelligence and energy; the failure to acquire property, of his incompetence and laziness. He was the "self-made" man, who had created himself as the fit inhabitant of the new economic world.

The outward and visible sign of the successful man was property, which became the badge of the bourgeois, as privilege had been that of the aristocrat. The emphasis placed on property rights by the bourgeois liberals was, in a sense, new—even novel. Property had always played a leading role in human affairs, but its sacred "rights" had never been so insistently proclaimed as during the period of bourgeois liberalism. The possession of a noble estate under feudalism had been, indeed, an important element in the system of aristocratic privilege. But an estate was not property in the sense that the lord had a right to do whatever he willed with his own. His property right had been limited by all sorts of feudal restrictions, which had made the lord more the trustee than the proprietor of his estate.[4]

Now, during the struggle for power that took place between the "men of property" and the "men of family" for the control of the state, property was invested with the character of a sacred institution. For centuries history, tradition, and romance had exalted the aristocrats as the natural rulers of mankind. Government was an art in which only the well born were initiated. But, argued the champions of the capitalists, capacity is even more natural than family descent. The "men of property" had proved their superior natural endowments in competition with others, whereas the "men of family" had compelled others to acknowledge their fitness to rule the nation through special privileges, conferred upon them by law and custom.

Any infringement on property rights or any restrictions on the acquisition of property would constitute, in the view of the capitalists, an attack on the class of successful men. National progress would come to a standstill and all existing wealth would begin to vanish. Governments should do everything in their power to encourage saving by the capitalists, because "according to the idea that considered men only as simple factors in the production of goods it was plainly evident that the capitalists were the most active element in the process of creating wealth."[5] It was capitalist enterprise that was the only source of rent, wages, and profits; and the pivotal of these was profits. By full and free play given to the profit motive the good of the community would be promoted and its wealth would be increased. To the defenders of capitalism the urge for profits was the creative urge that exploited natural resources by building factories and railways and by opening mines. They had no eyes to see the exploitation of human beings that accompanied the advance of industry: the underpaid, overworked laborers and the unsuccessful competitors who fell silently by the wayside. The "capitalist creed was the first and only social creed which valued the profit motive positively as the means by which the ideal

[4] J. Salwyn Schapiro, *Condorcet and the Rise of Liberalism* (New York, 1934), 171–173.

[5] Pierre Quentin-Bauchart, *La Crise sociale de 1848* (Paris, 1920), 14.

free and equal society would be automatically realized."[6] Therefore, let no taxes be laid on industry. Such a policy would result in decreased earnings, the accumulation of capital being thereby discouraged, or in a flight of capital, which would be sent away to be invested abroad. According to John Stuart Mill, a tax on profits in a capitalist country like England would prove to be "extremely detrimental to national wealth."[7] Attacks on the rights of property, asserted Ricardo, should be discountenanced by governments and by public opinion, because the progress of mankind depended "on the conviction of each capitalist that he will be allowed to enjoy unmolested the fruits of his capital, his skill, and his enterprise." Without this conviction, half of productive industry would be at once annihilated, and the result would be more fatal to the laborer than to the capitalist.[8]

Of all the classes in a modern nation, argued the champions of capitalism, the middle class was best fitted for the task of framing its policies and directing its affairs. Its members alone had proved their capacity to rule by increasing the wealth of the nation through their foresight, their ability, their enterprise, and their good judgment. They had property, hence they were independent in their views. They had education, hence they were capable of thinking rationally. They were the "virtuous rank," because they had the moral quality of self-sacrifice; they had forgone the pleasures of today for the good of tomorrow by their frugality and careful saving. In the middle class, asserted James Mill, "are the heads that invent, and the hands that execute; the enterprise that projects, and the capital by which these projects are carried into operation . . . . In this country at least, it is this class which gives to the nation its character."[9] Exaltation of the middle class has persisted to this day. In the novel of Sinclair Lewis, *Prodigal Parents,* published in 1938, the author says the following of Fred Cornplow, a character who symbolizes the bourgeois: "From Fred Cornplow's family, between B.C. 1937 and A.D. 1937, there came, despite an occasional aristocratic Byron or an infrequent proletarian John Bunyan,

[6] Peter Drucker, *The End of Economic Man* (New York, 1939), 37.

[7] John Stuart Mill, *Principles of Political Economy* (with an introduction by W. J. Ashley, ed., New York, 1909), 826.

[8] David Ricardo, "Observations on Parliamentary Reform," in *Works of David Ricardo* (J. R. McCulloch, ed., London, 1888), 555.

[9] James Mill, "Education," *Westminster Review,* I (January, 1824), 68–69.

nearly all the medical researchers, the discoverers of better varieties of wheat, the poets, the builders, the singers, the captains of great ships. Sometimes his name has been pronounced Babbitt; sometimes it has been called Ben Franklin . . . .

"He is the eternal bourgeois, the bourjoyce, the burgher, the Middle Class, whom the Bolsheviks hate and imitate, whom the English love and deprecate, and who is the most of the population worth considering in France and Germany and these United States.

"He is Fred Cornplow; and when he changes his mind, that crisis is weightier than Waterloo or Thermopylae." [10]

By contrast with the middle class, the aristocrats were economically a sterile class, given to luxury and dissipation; the source of their power lay in wealth that they did not produce and in political control conferred on them by special privileges and by an unjust system of parliamentary representation. It would be difficult, declared John Stuart Mill, to point out "what new idea in speculation, what invention or discovery in the practical arts, what useful institution, or what permanently valuable book, Great Britain has owed for the last hundred years, to her hereditary aristocracy, titled or untitled; what great public enterprise, what important national movement in religion or politics, those classes have originated, or have so much as taken in it the principal share." [11]

But a disturbing contradiction soon loomed up. How could bourgeois class rule be maintained in a liberal state that accepted the principle of equal rights to all and special privileges to none? Mankind, according to the apologists of bourgeois class rule, lived at the same time in two worlds: one, legal and moral, in which reigned equality; and the other, social and economic, in which reigned inequality. The modern world of social and economic inequality was created by the new industrial system, which fused the conception of property as a natural right with the tradition of inheritance as a natural privilege. In economics, capital was part of a man's wealth devoted to the creation of more wealth; but in society, capital was part of a man's wealth devoted

[10] From Sinclair Lewis, *The Prodigal Parents* (copyright, 1938, by Sinclair Lewis. Reprinted by permission of Doubleday & Company, Inc.).

[11] J. S. Mill, "M. de Tocqueville on Democracy in America," *Dissertations and Discussions* (New York, 1874), II, 95.

to the acquisition of an income, which became a family inheritance. If wealth that was created argued capacity in its creator, wealth that was inherited argued opportunity to acquire capacity through leisure and education. And who had a better right to rule than the capitalists, the class that had both the capacity to create wealth and the right to transmit it?

The great task of elevating the capitalists to the position of supreme importance in society was accomplished by the classical school of economics. The real father of the school was David Ricardo, who was born in London, in 1772. Ricardo was of Jewish origin, being descended from a family of Portuguese Jews who had migrated from Portugal to Holland, thence to England. As a young man, Ricardo embarked on the career of stockbroker. After making a fortune on the stock exchange, he retired from business to devote himself to the study of economics, in which he was deeply interested. Ricardo was a reserved, even shy, man who was content to study but disinclined to write. He was urged, almost driven, to literary labor by his devoted friend and ardent admirer, James Mill. Ricardo wrote few books, his collected works consisting of only one volume. His chief work, *On the Principles of Political Economy and of Taxation,* which appeared in 1817, was the first great work on economics since the publication, in 1776, of Adam Smith's *Wealth of Nations.* The book made Ricardo's reputation, both as a thinker and as an advocate of free trade. In 1819 he was elected to Parliament, where he became a leader in the movements to reform Parliament and to repeal the Corn Laws. Ricardo voted consistently in favor of parliamentary reform and of lowering the tariff on foodstuffs. He remained in Parliament until his death, in 1823.

Ricardo's *Principles* gave direction to economic thought during the whole nineteenth century. Its influence was as clearly seen in the capitalist theories of the classical school as in the socialist theories of Karl Marx. Yet neither the book nor its author had any of the trappings of greatness. The style of the *Principles* is dry, even turgid, involved, and abstract, having none of the lucidity and elegant simplicity of the *Wealth of Nations.* Neither is the book a work of original research, based on statistical analysis of economic phenomena. In Ricardo's time there existed no great body of statistical material on wages, hours, earnings, output, prices, and costs. Whatever existed of such data was fragmentary and scattering. Therefore, Ricardo had no means of analyzing scientifically the economic behavior of people. His method was that of bold generalization and logical deduction, which made the *Principles* an intellectual tour de force in "imaginary experimentation." Ricardo's mind was his laboratory; logic, his apparatus; and assumption, his materials, in the science of "pure economics." He had a practical knowledge of only one branch of economics, namely, finance; of the practical aspects of industry and of agriculture he knew little. Ricardo's methods were followed, to a considerable extent, by his disciples in England, known as the "classical school." These included Thomas Robert Malthus, John Ramsay McCulloch, Nassau William Senior, James Mill, and John Stuart Mill.

Wherein lay the prime importance of the classical economists? It lay in their development of a system of thought in which the capitalist was placed in the godlike position of being the creator of the modern economic world, the prosperity of which could be maintained only by doing his will. And the capitalist will was in harmony with universal, infallible "economic law," which automatically regulated the economic activities of individuals and of nations. Like divine law of orthodox religion and like natural law of eighteenth-century philosophy, economic law of the economists was beyond human power to control and to regulate. There was "one way, and only one way," remarks a contemporary apologist for capitalism, "that any people, in all history, have ever risen from barbarism and poverty to affluence and culture; and that is by that concentrated and highly organized system of production and exchange which we call Capitalistic: one way, and one alone. Further, that it is solely by the accumulation (and concentration) of this Capital, and directly proportional to the *amount* of this accumulation, that the modern world has risen: perhaps the sole way throughout the whole of eight or ten thousand years of economic history."[12]

How was wealth produced under capitalism? How was it distributed? According to Ricardo, the study of economics was concerned chiefly with discovering the economic laws that determined the *distribution* of the total wealth produced in the nation, namely, the relative amounts received by the three elements engaged in its pro-

[12] Carl Snyder, "By Way of a Preface," in *Capitalism the Creator* (New York, 1940).

duction: landowners, capitalists, and workers.[13] The most important was the amount received by the capitalists in the form of profits. On profits depended not only the prosperity of the capitalists but, what was even more important, the continued prosperity of the nation. Its economic progress vitally depended on the amount of new capital that would be forthcoming to maintain and to extend old enterprises and to start new ones. Without the continual investment of new capital, the human race would not advance a step, because each one would consume his portion; consequently, there would be nothing left for investment.[14]

The extent of industrial development was determined not by the extent of markets but by the amount of capital available for industrial investment. Where did this new capital come from? Not from the workers, who, having just sufficient for their maintenance, had no surplus to invest. Not from the aristocrats, who gave free rein to their self-indulgence by wasting their surplus on all sorts of unproductive luxuries and extravagances. It came from the capitalists, and only from the capitalists. By restricting their consumption they saved their surplus for the purpose of additional investment. More capital meant increased production, which, in turn, meant greater employment. Saving, arising from individual abstinence, was a form of self-sacrifice in order to create capital, which alone made the wheels of industry go round. And saving could arise only from great inequalities of income. Without saving there would be no capital, and without capital, no industrial production. For the inequalities of status characteristic of feudalism, the classical economists substituted the inequalities of income. They preached a "worldly asceticism" with the object of laying up treasures in this world, not in the next. And the reward would be in this world in the form of profits, which constituted, in the view of Senior, the "remuneration of abstinence." The role of the capitalist was recognized as the most vital in the state because his individual profit spelled public gain.[15] Money gains of the individual represented

[13] F. H. Knight, "The Ricardian Theory of Production and Distribution," *The Canadian Journal of Economic and Political Science* (1935), I.

[14] Frédéric Bastiat, *Sophism of Protection,* trans. from the French (New York, 1888), 356.

[15] N. S. B. Gras, "The Business Man and Economic Systems," *Journal of Economics and Business History,* III (February, 1931), 178ff.

a social gain in the amount of goods produced; hence the sum of individual profits in terms of money equaled social gains in terms of goods.

The "universal beneficence of profits" became almost a dogma of classical economy. Profit was endowed with a social purpose; the businessman could not succeed unless the community was prosperous. So pervasive was the tendency to identify the profits of the capitalists with social and national welfare that later classical economists like John Elliot Cairnes experienced a revulsion against this notion. The "whole problem of industry," he declared, "is looked at exclusively from the capitalist's point of view. The advantage *we* derive from our coal-beds and iron-mines are the advantages which capitalists derive from them. 'British trade' means capitalists' profits; and, as the only cost taken account of in production is the capitalists' cost, so naturally the capitalists' remuneration is the only remuneration thought worth attending to. Hence high wages are represented as 'neutralizing' industrial advantage, as if nothing were gain which did not come to the capitalist's maw; and the liberal remuneration of the working-people is deplored as a national calamity because it sets limits to the capitalist's share in the produce of their joint exertions."[16] However, to do justice to the classical economists, they did dispel the notion, held in their day and revived today, that profits represented a loss to everyone except to the capitalists, who were merely shrewd and lucky gamblers. Profits may, and often do, mean the reward of industry and ability and the promotion of the general welfare through increased production.

Never before was man's desire for money so plainly identified with the highest interests of mankind by an influential school of writers. Philosophically, classical economy had its roots in utilitarianism. Virtually every member of the school was directly or indirectly connected with Bentham. Ricardo and the two Mills were the intimates and disciples of the utilitarian sage. Translate "pleasure" into "economic interest" and the "calculating man" of the utilitarian becomes the "economic man" of the economists. Money, according to Bentham, was the greatest of all human desires. The best way to apply the "greatest happiness" principle was to give a money equivalent to the

[16] J. E. Cairnes, *Some Leading Principles of Political Economy* (New York, 1874), 55–56.

different kinds of pleasure. One man's shilling was as good as that of another, therefore it was a perfect equation of pleasure; the more shillings, the more pleasure. Indirectly money served to procure all the pleasures and to avoid all the pains.[17] Even if money were not the cause, it might be the measure of the various kinds of pleasure. As utilitarians, the classical economists held profit to be the primal source of pleasure and the lack of it, the primal source of pain.

The new economic world visualized by the economists needed new inhabitants. They created a new Adam, who never "walked with God" but who was "the walking embodiment of the alleged propensity to barter, truck and exchange one thing for another." This creature was the "economic man," a creature born and cradled in utilitarianism, who directed all his thoughts and all his energies to advancing his selfish interests through the accumulation of wealth. Yet his creators found a way of salvation for the "economic man." His very selfishness, provided that it was illumined by the light of "economic law," would set him on the path leading to the general good. Automatic, impersonal forces harmonized the selfish interest of the individuals with the general interest of the public. Each individual, in the famous words of Adam Smith, "intends only his own gain, and he is in this, as in many other cases, led by an invisible hand to promote an end which was no part of his intention.[18]

Never before in history had there been so complete an identification of class interests with national welfare, with universal justice, with progress, and with the happiness of mankind. The views of the economists typified the attitude of "the English bourgeois class, and bourgeois blinkers are in evidence on almost every page the classical authors wrote."[19] Nothing else is so persuasive, so insinuating as a self-interest infolded in a noble ideal; the drive of the former becomes the high purpose of the latter. The "private interests of a class assumed a vague air of universality. Was not the *bourgeoisie* the general class *par excellence?*"[20] Equally astonishing was the bland concept of "an

[17] Élie Halévy, *The Growth of Philosophic Radicalism,* trans. from the French by Mary Morris (London, 1928), 462.

[18] Adam Smith, *An Inquiry into the Nature and Causes of the Wealth of Nations* (Edwin Cannan, ed., London, 1930), I, 421.

[19] J. A. Schumpeter, *Capitalism, Socialism, and Democracy* (New York, 1947), 75.

[20] Guido de Ruggiero, *The History of European Liberalism,* trans. from the Italian by R. G. Collingwood (Oxford University Press, 1927), 169.

invisible hand" of the general good, guiding the crass selfishness of the "economic man," a being "without bowels, with an interior like a clock, accurately ticking the progress of the human race under the impulse of the magic spring of enlightened self-interest, and never needing to be wound or regulated."

The apotheosis of the *bourgeoisie,* a class long regarded with contempt, becomes plausible when viewed in the light of the historic circumstances out of which it arose. The expansion of capitalism during the period 1815 to 1870 resulted in a rise of industrial production and of foreign trade to unprecedented levels. The capitalists succeeded in amassing huge fortunes and, at the same time, in advancing national prosperity, which gave some justification for the widespread belief in middle-class capacity. By making possible an expanding economy, the Industrial Revolution had opened the door of opportunity to those who were capable of taking advantage of it. The ingenious inventor, the shrewd investor, the enterprising businessman, the ruthless exploiter, all now found scope for their various talents in the "acquisitive society" that was coming into being. One now could become rich by making money—not, as in the traditional way, by inheriting it. In England, especially during the early stages of the Industrial Revolution, obscure men from the lower ranks gathered together great fortunes and became famous as capitalists. James Hargreaves was a weaver; Richard Arkwright, a barber; Thomas Telford, a shepherd; Samuel Crompton, the son of a farmer; James Watt, the son of a carpenter; and the ancestor of Sir Robert Peel, a yeoman. John Galsworthy's novel *Forsyte Saga* gives a remarkable picture of a wealthy capitalist family whose fortune was founded by a yeoman ancestor. "There is probably no period in English history," writes Leslie Stephen, "at which a greater number of poor men have risen to distinction."[21] An entire class was endowed by the intellectual apologists of capitalism with the supreme gift of natural capacity, because some of its members had the ability—and the good fortune—to take advantage of favorable conditions.

These individual successes, striking as they were, did not bring universal conviction of the capacity of the *bourgeoisie* as a class. On the contrary, the apotheosis of the *bourgeoisie* by the classical economists aroused disdain among the aristocrats and hatred among the workers.

[21] Leslie Stephen, *The English Utilitarians* (New York, 1902), I, 111–112.

To ascribe godlike qualities to manufacturers who brought squalor and misery in the wake of their factories seemed satirical. Never before had wealth been so sharply divorced from elegance and urbanity as in the case of the newly rich industrialists. In France, particularly, where the division between the classes was deep and bitter, "bourgeois" became a term of opprobrium.

The emergence of a powerful capitalist class constituted a challenge to the old ruling class—the landed aristocracy. Despite the great advances made by agriculture as a result of the Agricultural Revolution, it was rapidly being displaced by industry as the chief source of wealth production in England. Aristocratic privileges and mercantilist restrictions, however, constituted serious obstacles to capitalist expansion. Before long, a struggle for power began between the lords of the factory and the lords of the land, aiming at control of the state. The former could find no "social space" in the century-old hierarchical order, based on land. Hence they sought to create a new order, in which capitalists could rule the nation without having the privileges of a ruling class. Money would prove to be more powerful than family in the emerging industrial society. Political power was all essential to the former, in order to make England's policies conform to the urgent needs of advancing industry. Here again the classical economists came to the fore with an intellectual justification of the struggle between the two propertied classes. Classical economics was to prove itself to be "the most formidable conceptual instrument ever directed against an outworn social order."[22]

Before Marx was, Ricardo was. The true fathers of the theory of the "class struggle," as that of "economic determinism," were Ricardo and his disciples, though they did not use these expressions. By emphasizing the distribution of wealth as the main problem of economics, they brought to the fore the class conflict implicit in the capitalistic system of production. What was to be the share of the landlords, of the capitalists, and of the workers? Would not the landlords,·who controlled the state, use their political power to their economic advantage by enacting laws that would give them a larger share? According to Ricardo, the class struggle was between the landlords and the capitalists, not between the latter and the workers. It was a dictum

22 K. Polanyi, *The Great Transformation* (New York, 1944), 223.

of the classical economists that the share of the laborers in the national income was fixed by "economic law." According to this law, the purchasing power of wages, or "real wages," was always limited to the amount sufficient to sustain the laborer and his family.[23] As the share of the workers was fixed, the remainder was to be divided between landlords and capitalists. These groups constituted economic classes in the sense that each had economic power, one having land and the other, industry. The workers, being dependent on their daily labor for their livelihood, had no economic power; hence they were not regarded by the classical economists as being truly an economic class. What the workers had to sell was labor, which, like machinery, was part of capital and an element in the cost of production. "A laborer is himself a portion of the national capital and may, without impropriety, be considered . . . in the light of a machine which it has required a certain outlay of labor to construct; . . ."[24]

If an equitable division of the wealth produced was to be made between landlords and capitalists, account had to be taken of the part that each played in the national economy. As the capitalists were, according to the classical economists, the productive element and primarily responsible for the economic progress of the nation, they, not the landlords, should be given first consideration. Ricardo's famous "economic law of rent" proved logically—and conclusively to the capitalists—that landlords were Olympian parasites, above the economic struggle, who contributed nothing to economic progress yet took a heavy toll, in the form of "rent," on all those who did. Ricardo's thesis was as follows. Land was limited in quantity and variable in quality; and fertile land was relatively scarce. As population grew, the most fertile land alone was not capable of supplying the foodstuffs needed by the nation. Less fertile land had, therefore, to be brought under cultivation. The cost of producing the foodstuffs on the land of the second degree of fertility was greater than that on land of the first degree; and this higher cost determined the price of food. The differential between the cost of production on land of the first and second degrees of fertility was "rent," which was pocketed by the landlords. This differential became larger and larger as land of less and less

[23] See *infra, 92ff*.
[24] J. R. McCulloch, *Principles of Political Economy* (Edinburgh, 1843), 356.

fertility was brought into cultivation to produce sufficient food for a constantly increasing population.

It was plain, then, according to Ricardo, that rent was not due primarily to the bounty but to the "niggardliness of nature," of which the landlords took full advantage. The cause of constantly rising cost of living was ascribed by Ricardo to the greed of the landlord, whose interest "is always opposed to the interest of every other class in the community. His situation is never so prosperous as when food is scarce and dear: whereas, all other persons are greatly benefited by procuring food cheap."[25] John Stuart Mill indignantly asserted that the landlords, without exerting any effort, grew richer "as it were in their sleep, without working, risking or economizing."[26] Their income "costs them neither labor nor care, but comes to them, as it were, of its own accord," as a consequence of which the landowners "are indolent, ignorant, and incapable of managing their property in the public interest."[27] The inescapable logic of the "law of rent" was that the great riches of the landowners came from an iniquitous appropriation of wealth produced by the industrial classes. "The dealings between the landlord and the public," observed Ricardo, "are not like dealings in trade, whereby both the seller and the buyer may equally be said to gain, but the loss is wholly on the one side, and the gain wholly on the other."[28] Very plainly did Ricardo's "law of rent" proclaim a class conflict between landlords and capitalists as part of the inevitable working of "economic law." It is now clear why Ricardo emphasized distribution, not production. It was his intention to prove conclusively that, in the distribution of the national income, the capitalist—sole creator of wealth—was the chief sufferer. Ricardo's abstract, impersonal analysis implied plainly, however, that unless this situation were radically altered, all economic progress would cease.

What the capitalists beheld in the increasing rent levied by the landlords was their own gradual ruin. Why? In order to maintain an

[25] Ricardo, "Essay on the Influence of a Low Price of Corn on the Profits of Stock," *Works*, 378.

[26] J. S. Mill, *Principles*, 818.

[27] Smith, *op. cit.*, I, 248.

[28] Ricardo, *Principles of Political Economy and Taxation* (E. C. K. Gonner, ed., London, 1891), 322.

efficient labor force, money wages would have to be increased to meet the cost of living. Wages were determined chiefly by the price of food. The increase in money wages would come only from profits—the just reward of the capitalists for their abstinence, their enterprise, their risks, and their capacity. Profit was the residue after wages had been paid and after used-up capital had been replaced. "There is no other way of keeping profits up but by keeping wages down" was the dictum of Ricardo.[29] That was the law of profits. The worker, even with higher wages, would be receiving only his sustenance; but the increase would come from the pockets of the capitalists and go into the pockets of the landlords in the form of higher prices for foodstuffs. By increasing wages in order to give the workers the same amount of food, the capitalists were "compelled to give a greater value to their laborers without having a greater value for themselves. They are, therefore, obliged to forego a portion of their profits."[30] Constantly increasing wages, owing to constantly increasing rent, would result inevitably in a constantly decreasing rate of profit.

The Ricardian view of industrial change was that, in the long run, rent tended to rise; wages, to remain approximately constant; and profit, to fall. Under these conditions, argued Ricardo and his disciples, new capital would be more and more difficult to obtain, because the tendency of an increase in capital and in population was to increase rent at the expense of profits. Saving, the source of capital, would be discouraged. Finally, a situation would arise when no new capital would be forthcoming, because nearly all profit would have disappeared. In effect, the landlords would, through increasing rent, have confiscated capital, the unique basis of economic progress. Society would then run down like a clock and fall into a stagnant condition, called the "stationary state."[31] Only the situation of the laborers will remain unchanged in the "stationary state"; they received only a sustenance wage in the era of progress and they will receive only a sustenance wage in the era of stagnation. Their standard of living may even be lowered, because the collapse of capitalism would result in the

[29] Ricardo, "On Protection to Agriculture," *Works*, 476.
[30] Ricardo, in *Westminster Review*, III (1825), 398.
[31] J. S. Mill, *Principles*, 746*ff.*; Ricardo, *Principles*, 98*ff.*

impoverishment of the entire nation, which would force the laborers to a lower standard. Unlike the natural law of Adam Smith, which envisaged a beneficent harmony of the interests of individuals, classes, and nations, the economic law of Ricardo envisaged a ruinous conflict of class interests, leading to poverty and stagnation.

England, after the Napoleonic Wars, gave a practical demonstration of the views of the classical economists regarding the conflict of interests between landlords and capitalists. When peace came, in 1815, Parliament, controlled by the former, passed a corn law prohibiting the importation of wheat as long as the price of English wheat did not exceed 10 shillings a bushel. The sharp debate on this measure in Parliament clearly showed the rising conflict between the landed and the industrial interests. The landed interests were insistent on maintaining high duties on foodstuffs in order to keep out the cheap food from the Continent. Opposed to them were the manufacturers, who demanded the lowering, even the abolition, of the duties on foodstuffs—the famous Corn Laws. Cheap food from abroad would result in decreasing the cost of living; its effect would be to lower wages and especially to lower rents, thereby enabling the English manufacturers to meet the competition of the rising industries on the Continent and, at the same time, to weaken the landed interests. Widespread discontent followed the rise in the cost of living that came with the higher duties on foodstuffs. Strikes broke out among the poorly paid factory workers, who demanded an increase in wages to meet the higher cost of living. Their employers contended that it was not they, but the landlords, who, by their greed for more rent, were responsible for the misery of the laborers. The effect of the teachings of the classical economists was to shift the conflict of interest between labor and capital to that between land and labor. By this ingenious strategy the fury of popular discontent was turned against the landed aristocracy, who soon realized that their hitherto impregnable position in the life of England would be assailed by the redoubtable combination of wealthy capitalists and numerous factory laborers.

Uncertain of the outcome of the efforts to reduce rent, sometimes fearful of the consequences of an open conflict between the people and the aristocrats, the classical economists were inclined to see a dismal future for mankind. Their pessimism was so marked that economics became popularly known as the "dismal science." The decreasing rate of profit, owing to increasing rent, would halt economic progress and lead to the "stationary state." The "law of diminishing returns," by giving diminishing returns for increasing investments of capital in land, set definite limits to the production of foodstuffs. The "law of population" presented the Malthusian specter of overpopulation, which, unless checked, would gradually reduce the available food supply and bring mankind to the verge of starvation. The persistent pessimism of the economists is surprising, in view of the plain facts that contradicted their forebodings. Industrial production in England was proceeding at an astounding rate. Agricultural production, owing to improvements in farming, increased the food supply. New methods of transportation, such as the railway and the steamboat, were giving access to the almost unlimited food supply of the New World. In full view of the horn of plenty, the "dismal science" was full of dire forebodings of universal misery.

To understand this contradiction it is necessary to regard the pessimism of the classical economists not as an attitude of hopelessness, but, on the contrary, as an attitude that had revolutionary implications. The "stationary state" was a warning—even a threat—to the aristocrats that, unless landlordism were destroyed and capitalism given free rein, all hopes of a prosperous future for mankind, inaugurated by the Industrial Revolution, would be blasted. Ricardo's pessimism, implied in the "stationary state," was as threatening to landlordism in England as Rousseau's pessimism regarding "civilization" had been to the Old Regime in France. Economic law was used by the classical economists as natural law had been used by the *philosophes,* to furnish a powerful intellectual weapon with which to undermine the old order in England.

It is difficult to regard the classical economists as revolutionists. They certainly did not advocate popular uprisings, terrorism, and revolutionary decrees. Quite the contrary. They regarded with horror, dread, and loathing both the principles and the practices of the French Revolution. Yet they were revolutionary in their ultimate aims, if not in their methods, because they advocated fundamental changes in the economic basis of society, in class relationships, and in political organization. How were these changes to be accomplished peacefully? Unlike France of the Old Regime, England possessed in Parliament a peaceful mechanism of change. But this mechanism was controlled by the aristocratic defenders of the old order, who used that mechanism to defend their vested interests. "Reform of Parliament" became the battle cry of all those who were determined to establish a new order in England by means of a legal revolution.

Chapter 6. The Malthusians and the New Inequality

In the struggle between the two propertied classes, the capitalists and the aristocrats, the classical economists had put the powerful intellectual weapon of "economic law" in the hands of the former. But a new class relationship was arising, that between the capitalists and the numerous nonpropertied working class that had emerged from the Industrial Revolution. What was to be the attitude of the capitalists toward the workers? Unlike the aristocrats, the workers did not, at the beginning of the nineteenth century, constitute a powerful class that could defend itself in a struggle with the capitalists. How were the workers to be prevented from becoming sufficiently powerful to challenge the capitalists as the latter had challenged the aristocrats? That was the question to which the classical economists gave an answer.

The great problem of nascent capitalism in the early days of the Industrial Revolution was how to accumulate a pool of capital. Expanding industry had a constant and pressing need for more capital—to keep existing industry going, to extend its operations, and to start new enterprises at favorable opportunities. Capital, it was then believed, could arise only from savings, and savings came only from ever-increasing profits. The cost of production must, therefore, be kept as low as possible, to ensure profitable returns; and labor was an important element in the cost of production. Labor, under the wage system, was a commodity to be bought and sold in the open market, like any other commodity. What chiefly interested the capitalist in hiring workers was to pay as little as possible in wages and to get as much as possible in hours. Low wages would keep down the cost of production and long hours would increase the productivity of labor; both would spell high profits for the capitalist. According to Ricardo, there was no other way of keeping profits up but by keeping wages down. That was the "law of profits."

Wages were down and profits up during the period of bourgeois liberalism. The evil conditions of the industrial workers in England of the early nineteenth century are too well known to require detailed description. Their places of work were unsanitary, even dangerous; their hours of work, long and arduous; their wages, barely sufficient to keep body and soul together; their homes, in filthy, crowded slums; their family life, a mockery, with wives and children toiling like the workmen themselves in the factory. Unemployment and destitution haunted the laborer all his working life. When hired, he lived in dread of being "fired"; and when "fired," he lived in dread of the poorhouse. "It has been said that in the first forty years of the nineteenth century almost every workman expected to go sometime or other into the workhouse."[1] Politically they were second-class citizens without votes. Without political power, their civil rights were in constant danger of being curtailed. The infamous Six Acts, enacted in 1819, which seriously curtailed freedom of speech, of the press, and of assembly, was directed against the working class. Indeed, the latter could be described as being the helots of the bourgeois liberal order.

The evil condition of the working class was a strange commentary on the extraordinary advance of commerce and industry in England during the first half of the nineteenth century. A new system of inequality appeared, which, in fact though not in law, maintained the age-old division of mankind into rich and poor. On the one side was a small class of immensely rich industrial magnates and on the other, a numerous and desperately poor working class. The economic distance between them was as great as that between rich and poor in the preindustrial era—even greater. Throughout recorded history, human inequality has been the fact, whatever explanations or apologies have been given for it; but inequality took different forms in different periods and in different lands. The form that it took in Western Europe during the medieval period was based on the aristocratic idea of privilege, which predicated a caste system of society. Despite the universal acceptance of the Christian faith, which preached the equality of souls, a caste system prevailed in medieval Europe resembling that in

---

[1] J. L. Hammond, "The Industrial Revolution and Discontent," *Economic History Review,* II (January, 1930), 225. In 1842 one out of every eleven of the total population was officially a pauper. See E. Neff, *Carlyle* (New York, 1932), 197.

India, where it was an article of the Hindu faith. What the European caste system lacked were the iron rigidity that only religion could give and the refinements of subordination, as developed in India, where "caste" and "race" were frequently synonymous terms.

There was no escape from the caste system, as everyone came to his status through heredity. The poor were born poor and the rich were born rich. That the many should live in misery, even starving, and that the few should live in superabundance was determined by fate, over which man had no control. Hence the system could not be questioned as being unjust. By some it was even considered to be part of the divine plan, to alter which was deemed sacrilegious. No solution of the problem of the poor, in this world, was possible; only in the hereafter could the poor obtain salvation on the basis of equality with the rich.

This pessimistic attitude may be explained—in part, at least—by the economic situation during the aristocratic social order. The crude methods of farming and the handicraft system of manufacture did not, in general, produce sufficient supplies of food and of goods to guarantee a comfortable existence to everyone. In that period of "deficit economy," the masses did not "starve amidst plenty"; they suffered because, generally, there was not enough produced to go round. To have taken away the superabundance from the wealthy few for the benefit of the starving many would not have solved the problem of inequality. In all likelihood, it would have resulted in the equality of want.

With the advent of the Agricultural and Industrial revolutions, a new economic system arose, which was based on a "surplus economy." Scientific methods of agriculture increased enormously the yield of the soil. The factory multiplied almost miraculously the production of all sorts of articles, old and new, to satisfy human wants. At last there was a possibility of abolishing poverty by adopting new methods of distributing wealth; but the "creation of riches proved an easier task than their equitable distribution."[2] Those who profited from the new economy did not see in its advance a new society emerging, to be organized, to be assimilated, and to be controlled and guided in the general interest, but merely a quick way to make large fortunes by those who had the means, the ability, the opportunity, and, in some instances, the ruthless-

[2] G. P. Gooch, "The Victorian Age," in *The Social and Political Ideas of Some Representative Thinkers of the Victorian Age* (F. J. C. Hearnshaw, ed., London, 1933), 16.

ness to exploit the new economy. They were blind to the silent economic massacres that came as a consequence of periodic depressions, of the shifting of markets, of the rise of new industries, and of technological improvements.

What the economic changes brought to the poor was not the abolition of poverty but its concentration around the centers of wealth production, the factory towns. The contrast between the underpaid, overworked, miserably housed, ill-clad factory "hands" and their enormously wealthy employers, in the period of "surplus economy," was as great as that between peasants and lords of the manor in the period of "deficit economy." The old inequality, based on the status of caste, was gone; and in its place was a new inequality which, ironically enough, arose from "freedom of contract." The poor were now poor, not as a result of a decree of fate, but of their individual failure to succeed in a free, competitive world. The Industrial Revolution "had delivered society from its primitive dependence on the forces of nature, but in turn had taken society prisoner."[3]

The social order established by capitalism was stoutly defended by the classical economists, who justified the new inequality as being part of the natural order. Furthermore, they turned the powerful weapon of economic law against the new poor as they did against the old rich, in order to protect the interests of the capitalists. The attitude of the classical economists to the problem of poverty constitutes a somber page in the intellectual history of modern Europe. It is a strange and baffling fact that, at the very time when the new agriculture and the new industry were producing food and goods sufficient to eliminate poverty —at least, its extremes—the laborers, as a class, were doomed to inescapable and eternal poverty by the apologists of capitalism. They proclaimed the existence of biologic and economic laws that decreed, at the same time, prosperity for the capitalists and mere subsistence to the workers. And these laws, being natural, were enforced by nature herself; they could not be repealed as could man-made statutes by man-chosen parliaments. It followed logically that the workers were beyond all human help. The Biblical dictum, "For ye have the poor with you always" (Mark 14:7) now received verification at the hands of scientific

[3] J. L. and Barbara Hammond, *The Town Laborer, 1760–1832* (London, 1917), 31.

students of the most advanced economic system that the world had yet known.

In their attitude toward the working class the classical economists exhibited as distinct a class bias as they did in their apotheosis of the *bourgeoisie*. Historically related to Calvinism,[4] capitalism assimilated something of its psychology and of its doctrine of predestination. According to the classical economists, the capitalists were the "elect" of this world, having attained economic salvation. Where there is salvation there must also be damnation. Economic law, universal, impersonal, and implacable, was invoked by the classical economists to justify the economic damnation of the working class. Nature's penalties, in the form of economic law, were greater and surer than penalties imposed by statutes. No police were necessary to catch the offender against economic law; no courts were necessary to try him; and no judge, to sentence him. Inevitably, promptly, and powerfully was the offender hurled to swift punishment in the form of economic ruin. The justice of economic law was never tempered with mercy and was administered with an impersonality as pitiless as was the Calvinist god himself.

Of all the classical economists, the one who most logically, most thoroughly, and most consistently condemned the poor to eternal poverty was Thomas Robert Malthus. Born in 1766, of a middle-class family, Malthus was educated in Cambridge University. In 1797 he was ordained a clergyman of the Anglican church, but he held a curacy for only a short time. In 1798 he wrote, anonymously, a pamphlet, entitled "An Essay on the Principle of Population," which aroused widespread attention because of the novelty of the views expressed in it. In 1803 a second edition appeared, under Malthus's name, considerably revised, enlarged, and modified. The *Essay* was now a book, not a pamphlet, and almost immediately it took rank as a classic in the history of economics because of its careful scholarship and original views. Malthus's work was an inquiry into the nature and causes of poverty, as Adam Smith's *Wealth of Nations* had been an inquiry into the nature and causes of wealth. The *Essay* made an important contribution to the study of economics by stressing the biological factor in the pro-

[4] On the subject of the relation of Protestantism to capitalism, see the excellent study, R. H. Tawney, *Religion and the Rise of Capitalism* (London, 1926).

duction and distribution of wealth. In addition, it was a pioneer work
in a new field of investigation, *i.e.,* demography, dealing with the
statistical study of population. Malthus's book became the point of
departure for all studies of population problems since its appearance.

Malthus, in 1805, was recognized by an appointment as professor in
Haileybury College, an institution established by the East India Company, where he continued to pursue his economic investigations. He
made other contributions to classical economy, notably *The Principles
of Political Economy,* which appeared in 1820. However, it was primarily the *Essay* that gave Malthus his preeminent position as one of
the fathers of classical economy. Though the doctrine associated with
his name was very sensational, there was nothing sensational, nothing
especially interesting in the life and personality of Malthus. He lived
the quiet, retired life of a scholar and died in 1834.

The great success of the *Essay,* apart from its intrinsic merits, resulted
from the historic situation at the time of its appearance. A great wave
of reaction against the principles of the French Revolution was sweeping England as a consequence of the Reign of Terror in France. Dread
of revolutionary violence led many Englishmen to become sharply
critical of the ideas of the French *philosophes* which had gained wide
currency in England during the eighteenth century. Burke's *Reflections
on the French Revolution* convinced them that the revolutionary
violence in France owed its inspiration to the radical teachings of the
philosophes. Definitely and specifically, Malthus's *Essay* was a flat
repudiation of the optimism and generous humanitarianism characteristic of eighteenth-century liberalism. The great error, according to
Malthus, of the exponents of the ideal of human equality and of progress toward perfectibility, such as Condorcet in France and William
Godwin in England, was that they attributed the ills of society to its
institutions, especially those derived from government and from property; whereas the "deeper-seated causes of evil" resulted "from the laws
of nature and the passions of mankind."[5] The establishment of equality
among men, even if possible, would consequently lead, not to universal
happiness, but to universal misery.[6]

[5] Thomas R. Malthus, *An Essay on the Principle of Population* (London, 1890), 308.
This edition is hereinafter referred to as Malthus, *Essay.*
[6] *Ibid.,* 300*ff.*

Conditions in England itself drew attention to the significance of Malthus's views. From 1770 to 1801 the population of England and Wales increased 27½ per cent.[7] A series of bad harvests during the years 1794 to 1800 sent up the price of bread. This situation produced great suffering among the poor, which called attention not so much to their suffering as to the phenomena of increasing population and decreasing food supply. During the first half of the nineteenth century, every census revealed striking—even startling—increases in the population of England and Wales.[8] Despite the increase in the food supply, owing to the progress of agricultural methods, the rate of increase was not so great as that of population. This situation, though it proved to be temporary, brought wide support to the Malthusian doctrine that all efforts to improve the conditions of the poor would encounter an insurmountable barrier in natural law.

The central theme of the *Essay* is boldly and unqualifiedly stated by Malthus. It is that the masses of mankind are doomed to eternal want because it is the "constant tendency in all animated life to increase beyond the nourishment prepared for it." In other words, population tends to increase at a faster rate than the means of subsistence can be made to increase. This idea is strikingly phrased by Malthus in the following manner: "A man who is born into a world already possessed . . . has no claim of *right* to the smallest portion of food, and, in fact, has no business to be, where he is. At nature's mighty feast there is no vacant cover for him. She tells him to be gone, and will quickly execute her own orders, if he do not work upon the compassion of some of her guests. If these guests get up and make room for him, other intruders immediately appear demanding the same favor. . . . The order and harmony of the feast is disturbed, the plenty that before reigned is changed into scarcity; and the happiness of the guests is destroyed by the spectacle of misery and dependence in every part of the hall, and by the clamorous importunity of those, who are justly enraged at not finding the provision which they had been taught to expect. The guests

[7] G. T. Griffith, *Population Problems of the Age of Malthus* (Cambridge University Press, 1926), 13.

[8] The first official census of the population of England and Wales took place in 1801. Before this year, population figures were only estimates. In 1801 the population of England and Wales was, in round numbers, 8,900,000; in 1841 it rose to about 16,000,000, an increase of 80 per cent in 40 years. See Griffith, *op. cit.,* 21*ff.*

learn too late their error, in counteracting those strict orders to all intruders, issued by the great mistress of the feast, who, wishing that all her guests should have plenty, and knowing that she could not provide for unlimited numbers, humanely refused to admit fresh comers when her table was already full."[9]

The great problem of mankind, therefore, was how to maintain a balance between population and food supply. According to Malthus, the "principle of population" was the universal tendency for population to outrun the means of subsistence. The natural instinct of men to procreate caused population to increase very rapidly; if unchecked, it would double every twenty-five years. Far slower in rate was the increase in the food supply, owing to the fact that (1) land was limited in quantity, (2) it varied in productivity from a low to a high fertility, and (3) the "law of diminishing returns" gave a decreasing rate of return for an increasing rate of investment of capital in land.[10] When, because of good harvests, the food supply of a country increased, it was followed by a "devastating torrent of children," and the balance between food supply and population was again restored. If the ratio of food supply was greater to the population, as in a new country like America, emigration would flow to it until population bore the same relation to food supply as in older lands. Malthusianism, therefore, rested on three postulates: (1) the reproduction tendency of man, (2) the limited supply of land, and (3) the tendency of population to increase faster than the means of subsistence can be made to do.

Malthus was a believer in biological determinism. The great, all-mastering, all-determining factor in human life was the passion between the sexes. As the "law of diminishing returns" from agriculture arose from the nature of plant life, so the "law of population" arose from the natural instinct of sex. Owing to this primal force, Malthus was convinced, no permanent improvement could be really effected in the lot of the masses of mankind. Theirs was a dismal future of constant poverty; the rate of population increase would always outstrip the rate

[9] T. R. Malthus, *An Essay on the Principle of Population* (London, 1803), 531–532. This paragraph was not included in the editions of the *Essay* following that of 1803, but Malthus never repudiated the idea expressed in it.

[10] The "law of diminishing returns" was not stated by Malthus. It was, however, implicit in his population theory. Later, that law was developed by John Stuart Mill as an integral part of classical economics.

of food increase. Malthus saw no way by which man could escape from the weight of this law which pervaded all animated nature. No fancied equality, no agrarian regulations, in their utmost extent, could remove the pressure of it even for a single country. Therefore no society could exist in which everyone was happy and prosperous. In order to bring about an equilibrium between population and food supply, both nature and society had developed checks on population growth—nature, through famine and pestilence; society, through war, misery, vice, and hunger.

The system of supplementing wages through the rates, known as the "Speenhamland system,"[11] roused determined opposition on the part of Malthus. He was convinced that poor relief tended to waste capital, to facilitate early marriages, and to encourage large families; therefore, to aggravate the very condition that it aimed to alleviate.[12] For the state to encourage the establishment of old-age pensions and the giving of aid to widows and orphans, as advocated by Condorcet,[13] would merely encourage idleness and laziness among the poor. "It has happened that from the inevitable laws of human nature some human beings will be exposed to want. These are the unhappy persons who in the great lottery of life have drawn a blank."[14] Any plan to improve the condition of the poor met with the opposition of this devout clergyman and earnest scholar. Malthus opposed a suggestion of the agricultural reformer Arthur Young that poor peasants be given small lots of land on which to grow potatoes. This reform would, in his opinion, lead to an increase of population; the peasants, given a secure source of livelihood, would be encouraged to have large families.[15]

In the 1803 edition of the *Essay,* Malthus declared that the only rational method of checking population was by "moral restraint," by which he meant "restraint from marriage from prudential motive with a conduct strictly moral during the period of this restraint."[16] This required continence before marriage and postponement of marriage

[11] See *infra,* p. 189.

[12] Malthus, *Essay,* 470.

[13] Condorcet, *Esquisse d'un tableau historique,* in *Oeuvres* (Paris, 1847–1849), VI, 247, and *Sur les caisses d'accumulation,* XI, 392–393.

[14] Malthus, *Essay,* 316.

[15] *Ibid.,* 510.

[16] Malthus, *Essay* (1803), 9.

until a man had sufficient means to bring up a normal family, which, according to Malthus, should number five or six children. He opposed birth control through "artificial and unnatural modes of checking population," which would "destroy that virtue and purity of manners which the advocates of equality and of the perfectibility of man profess to be the end and object of this view."[17]

Malthus, however, had little confidence in the capacity of the poor for "moral restraint." Lacking property, they lacked prudence; lacking education, they lacked reason. The poor were reckless, irrational slaves to their sex passions; they procreated without a thought of their future or that of their offspring. Their unrestrained tendency to procreate permeated the entire economic organization of society and was the primal cause of all the evils suffered by the poor. Now that they were legally free—hence, in the position of legal equality with the propertied classes—the poor must be convinced that the "principle and permanent cause of poverty has little or no *direct* relation to forms of government, or the unequal division of property." They must be made to realize that their condition was determined by economic law, which could be changed neither by legislation nor by revolution. If the poor man was convinced that the evils from which he suffered were absolutely irremediable, he "would be disposed to bear the distresses in which he might be involved with more patience." He would feel "less discontent and irritation at the government and the higher classes of society, on account of his poverty," and therefore, would be "less disposed to insubordination and turbulence."[18] The clergyman-economist preached resignation to the poor in the new spirit of economic law, as well as in the old spirit of religion.

With this injunction came also a warning. If through ignorance of economic law the poor became discontented, in the belief that their misery came from evil institutions and from "the inequity of the government," the social order would be in danger. Under such circumstances the majority of well-disposed persons "would throw themselves into the arms of a dictator," should the government be unable to suppress the "horrors of anarchy."[19] The poor were now between the

17 Malthus, *Essay* (1890), 301.
18 *Ibid.*, 541–542.
19 *Ibid.*, 472.

Scylla of economic law, which doomed them to eternal poverty, and the Charybdis of despotism, which threatened them with tyranny.

However, because Malthus preferred to enlighten the poor, rather than to repress them, he favored a system of popular education, the general purpose of which was to raise the cultural level of the masses, and the special purpose of which was to teach the lower classes the principles of classical economy.[20] Once they learned these principles, the poor would understand their position in the economic scheme of life as determined by the relation of population to food supply. The poor would then realize that they must depend on themselves to better their conditions through "moral restraint." They would then shun those demagogues who incited them to revolt, because, having the right education, they would be able to detect the sophistries of the agitators.[21] Malthus gave Scotland as the example of a poor country where education had the effect of making the poor "bear with patience the evils which they suffer" by making them "aware of the folly and inefficiency of turbulence."[22] To praise the Scots as a people willing to suffer evils because they had a high standard of popular education was a strange compliment to that militantly democratic people.

The doctrines of Malthus gained wide and ready acceptance and became "almost axiomatic postulates in English political economy."[23] What was obvious seemed true; and what was in the interest of the propertied classes seemed right. The limitations of Malthusianism, however, became clear with the rapid development of the railway and the steamboat, which brought foodstuffs from distant places; with the advance of scientific farming, irrigation, refrigeration; and with the application of machinery to agriculture. Owing to these methods, it has been possible to demostrate the opposite proposition to Malthus's "law of population," *i.e.,* that food supply can be increased faster than population.[24] Besides, the rate of population can be deliberately slowed

[20] The scheme of popularizing the principles of economics was taken up by Harriet Martineau. Her popular books, *The Parish, The Hamlet,* and *Illustrations to Political Economy,* published during 1832–1834, sought to convince her readers that economic law, not society or the employers, was responsible for poverty.

[21] Malthus, *Essay,* 497.

[22] *Ibid.,* 496–497.

[23] See "Population," in *Encyclopedia of the Social Sciences* (New York, 1934), XII, 249.

[24] For an analysis of Malthusianism, see Harold Wright, *Population* (London, 1923), and W. S. Thompson, *Population Problems* (New York, 1935).

up without resorting to "moral restraint." Malthus confused the sexual with the reproductive instinct; the latter is far weaker than the former. Though they are united by nature, the reproductive can be separated from the sexual instinct by use of contraceptive methods. Planned parenthood, with the limitation and spacing of offspring, has now made possible the control of population growth.

Closely related to the Malthusian "law of population" were the "subsistence-wage" and "wage-fund" theories. These doctrines of classical economy constituted a trinity intrinsically united to form a godhead, which sat high in nature, pronouncing eternal doom on the laboring masses of mankind. In order to comprehend fully the meaning and implications of the subsistence wage, it is essential to keep in mind that, in the view of the classical economists, labor was a commodity that was bought and sold in the open market. As a commodity it had a market price, namely wages, the amount of which was regulated by the economic law of supply and demand. But unlike any other commodity, labor was inseparable from the laborer who sold it. Though legally free, the laborer was, perforce, obliged to sell himself along with his labor for a definite part of the day, the workday; hence the expression, "wage slavery." James Mill, who was as trenchant in the expression of his ideas as he was relentlessly logical in formulating them, insisted that, as the capitalist owned the wages, he owned the wage earner. The laborer was, in fact, a slave; the only difference between him and the chattel slave was "in the method of purchasing." Instead of owning the whole time of the worker, as under chattel slavery, Mill argued that the capitalist owned only the week or the month—the part that he paid for in wages.[25]

The position of the laborer, under capitalism, according to the classical economists, was an anomalous one: he was part commodity, part human; part-time free, part-time slave. In order to reconcile these contradictions, the classical economists, especially Ricardo, developed the theory of the "natural price" of labor. "Labor," declared Ricardo, "like all other things which are purchased and sold, and which may be increased or diminished in quantity, has its natural and its market price. The natural price of labor is that price which is necessary to enable the laborers, one with another, to subsist and to perpetuate their

[25] James Mill, *Elements of Political Economy* (London, 1844), 21.

race, without either increase or diminution."[26] More simply, whatever the wage, it was always limited to the subsistence of the laborer and his family.

The "natural price" of labor, or the subsistence wage, was fixed by an economic law that Ferdinand Lassalle later made famous as "the iron law of wages." According to this law, wages could never be more than just sufficient to sustain a laborer and his family under conditions prevalent in the nation at the time. The subsistence wage was not absolutely fixed and constant; it varied in different countries according to climate, soil, morals, and customs. It also varied in the same country, at different periods, as a result of historic changes. It was higher in England than in China; and it was higher in the England of the nineteenth century than in England of the thirteenth century.[27] It followed that the subsistence wage was not necessarily a near-starvation wage but one that could and did rise with economic progress. There were "standards of wretchedness" that even the "iron law of wages" could not lower. How, then, did the standard of living for the worker rise? Sometimes through the introduction of a new food supply, as when the potato was introduced into Ireland. Sometimes through competition for labor in times of great prosperity, owing to increases in capital investments. On the whole, however, the standard of living in a country was fairly constant. When an increase in capital investment took place, the market price of labor, or the "nominal wage," rose; it was higher than the "natural price," or the cost of subsistence. In time of rising prices, the "nominal wage" did not always rise as rapidly as did the cost of living. This discrepancy was counterbalanced, according to Malthus, by a greater demand for labor, owing to increased industrial activity, which gave jobs to more laborers, and by "the opportunity given to women and children to add considerably to the earnings of the family."[28] However, this situation did not last long, owing to the constant pressure of population. It was the invariable rule "that an increase of population follows

[26] David Ricardo, *Principles of Political Economy and Taxation* (E. C. K. Gonner, ed., London, 1891), 70.

[27] *Ibid.*, 74. See the closely reasoned article by F. H. Knight, "The Ricardian Theory of Production and Distribution," *Canadian Journal of Economic and Political Science*, I (1935), 184–196.

[28] Malthus, *Essay*, 427.

the amended condition of the laborer."[29] Prosperity induced the laborers to marry early and to have large families. As a result of increased competition among the laborers, wages again fell to their natural price, because of the tendency of the laborers to "people down their old standard of living" by increasing their numbers. For this reason, the supply of labor would always be greater than the demand; hence the worker could never get more than a subsistence wage. "There is nothing so absolutely unavoidable in the progress of society," wrote Malthus, "as the fall of wages, that is, such a fall as, combined with the habits of the laboring classes, will regulate the progress of civilization according to the means of subsistence."[30] Only in new lands, as in America, was it possible to advance constantly the standard of living, because in America there was a constantly increasing capital investment and an insufficient labor supply. The fall of wages caused by a rise in the number of workers became a fundamental tenet of classical economy.

The pessimistic views of the classical economists concerning wages gained wide currency because of the economic situation in England during the first half of the nineteenth century. There did not exist at that time a sufficient supply of ready capital to finance the rapidly growing enterprises. Industrial expansion outran capital accumulation, which came chiefly from the surplus profits of the wealthy few. Hence every increase in wages and every decrease in hours were at the expense of capital that was badly needed for production. Low wages and long hours were, therefore, condoned by the capitalists and their apologists as necessary to England's industrial progress. "The enforced abstinence of the workers was set side by side with the voluntary abstinence of the capitalist as the twin beacon-light of national prosperity."[31]

It was plainly the belief of the classical economists that the working class did not and could not share permanently in the benefits created by industrial progress. If anything, they were its victims, being constantly "exposed to fluctuations of demand and unsteadiness of wages."[32] In the opinion of Malthus, "the good or bad condition of the

29 Ricardo, *op. cit.*, 400.

30 Malthus, *Inquiry into the Nature and Progress of Rent* (London, 1815), 19.

31 G. D. H. Cole, *A Short History of the British Working Class Movement, 1789–1937* (London, 1937), I, 180.

32 Malthus, *Essay*, 420.

poor is not *necessarily* connected with any particular stage in the progress of society to its full complement of wealth."[33] Invention of machinery brought no lasting benefit to the laborers. "They see invention
after invention in machinery brought forward, which is seemingly
calculated, in the most marked manner, to abate the sum of human
toil, yet with these apparent means of giving plenty, leisure and happiness to all, they still see the labors of the great mass of society, undimin-
ished, and their condition, if not deteriorated, in no striking and pal-
pable manner improved."[34] It was "questionable," declared John Stuart
Mill, "if all the mechanical inventions yet made have lightened the
day's toil of any human being. They have enabled a greater population
to live the same life of drudgery and imprisonment, and an increased
number of manufacturers and others to make large fortunes. They have
increased the comforts of the middle classes. But they have not yet
begun to effect those great changes in human destiny which it is in
their nature and in their futurity to accomplish."[35]

An inescapable conclusion followed: that all permanent advantages
coming from the introduction of machinery went to the capitalists, and
justly so. Because of their abstinence, the capitalists were able to save;
thereby to accumulate capital, without which industrial progress would
be impossible. The wealth of the few, not the welfare of the many, was
the prime consideration of the classical economists, who were convinced
that large profits, rather than high wages, were the acid test of national
prosperity. The laborers, chained to the wheel of labor, ignorant,
animated by a restless desire to propagate, were incapable of getting
more than their subsistence. They did not and could not save; hence
they were not contributors to the new capital, which alone created new
enterprises. In relation to the economic system, the laborer had a double
function: by day he was put in the factory to produce new commodities,
and by night he was put in bed to produce new workers.

The subsistence theory of wages merged with the wage-fund theory
and became inseparable from it, as both theories were inseparable from
Malthusianism. No possible escape from their doom was allowed to the
working class by the classical economists; the wage fund finally and

[33] *Ibid.*, 425.
[34] *Ibid.*, 318.
[35] J. S. Mill, *Principles of Political Economy* (W. J. Ashley, ed., New York, 1909), 751.

completely sealed their fate. This theory was implicit in the views of all the classical economists, even in those of the father of them all, Adam Smith.[36] It was at first accepted, though in a somewhat modified form, even by the most humane member of the school, John Stuart Mill.[37] As might be expected, it received the clearest—and hardest—expression at the hands of James Mill, Senior, and McCulloch, who became the popular exponents of the theory."[38]

According to the classical economists, an economic law definitely determined the portion of labor in the scheme of capitalist economy. At the beginning of each production period the capitalist set aside a definite sum—the "wage fund"—to be devoted exclusively to the payment of labor. Wages did not, and could not, come from any other source. The average wage depended entirely on the ratio between the amount in the fund and the number of laborers employed; it was never more and never less than this amount divided by the number of laborers. It followed logically from this doctrine that wages could not be increased by trade-union action or by government intervention. If wages in one industry were increased—the amount in the fund being predetermined —the increase came not from the pockets of the capitalists but from the pockets of the less fortunate laborers in other industries.

Did then the laborer always receive the same wage? No. The average wage could be made to rise in one of two ways: either by enlarging the fund relative to the number of laborers as a result of larger outlays of capital for investment, which would enlarge the dividend, or by decreasing the number of laborers, which would lessen the divisor. All other schemes for improving the condition of laborers "must be," according to McCulloch, "completely nugatory and ineffectual."

The wage-fund theory would not be complete without visualizing its close relation to the "law of population." An increase in capital did

36 Adam Smith, *An Inquiry into the Nature and Causes of the Wealth of Nations* (Edwin Cannan, ed., London, 1930), I, 69–70.

37 J. S. Mill, *op. cit.*, 349.

38 James Mill, *op. cit.*, Section II; Nassau William Senior, *An Outline of the Science of Political Economy* (London, 1938), 153ff., 173ff., 195ff.; J. R. McCulloch, *Principles of Political Economy* (London, 1870), 173–174. Excellent discussions of the wage-fund theory are to be found in F. W. Taussig, *Wages and Capital* (London, 1896); E. Cannan, *A History of the Theories of Production and Distribution* (London, 1893); and Sidney and Beatrice Webb, *Industrial Democracy* (New York, 1926), 603–635.

enlarge the wage fund, and higher wages for the laborers resulted; but not for long. Nature, the Mephistopheles of the poor man, enticed him to marry early and beget many children, with the result that he soon sank to his former level. The "dividend" had been made larger by the enterprise of the capitalist, but the "divisor" was now also made larger by the reckless improvidence of the laborer. The "quotient," therefore, remained ever the same, namely, the subsistence wage that followed the laborer like a shadow all his life, until he staggered into his grave. As the gloomiest expounder of the "dismal science," Malthus asserted that the "funds for the maintenance of labor do not *necessarily* increase with the increases of wealth, and very *rarely* increase in *proportion* to it."[39] "Abandon hope all ye who enter here!" would have been a fitting inscription for the factory gates.

The wage-fund theory, which doomed the laborers to eternal poverty, acted, according to its advocates, as a stimulus to the increase of profits. Being assured that the share of labor in the product was predetermined by economic law, the capitalists could freely plan to invest where, when, and how the most profit was to be gained. They had little need to concern themselves with the problem of equitably sharing their increasing prosperity with their laborers. The wage-fund theory was the supreme justification of the new *status quo* established by capitalism. It gained wide acceptance during the period of bourgeois liberalism and exercised a powerful influence in thwarting efforts to ameliorate the condition of the working class.[40]

The classical economists were not entirely agreed in their interpretations of the subsistence wage and of the wage fund. They developed refined differences of opinion as to when and how these theories functioned. But they were all united in support of the Malthusian "law of population," which seemed to them the one social truth that could be

[39] Malthus, *Essay*, 419.

[40] John Stuart Mill toward the end of his life repudiated the wage-fund theory; see *infra*, p. 273. It was finally overthrown by the American economist Francis A. Walker, who argued that it was "production, not capital, which furnishes the motive for employment and the measure of wages." If the worker produced more, he would receive more, because his employer could afford to give him more. The general acceptance of the theory, asserted Walker, was favored by the fact that it afforded "a complete justification for the existing order of things respecting wages." Francis A. Walker, *The Wages Question* (New York, 1891), 142.

demonstrated with mathematical precision. The later John Stuart Mill, the "socialist," was at one with the early John Stuart Mill, the "individualist," when it came to Malthusianism. "I ask then," he wrote, "is it true or not, that if their numbers were fewer they would obtain higher wages? This is the question, and no other."[41] One of the reasons why Mill favored popular education was to teach the laborers "the same degree of habitual prudence now commonly practiced by the middle class," who did not assume family responsibilities without due regard for the "customary decencies of their station,"[42] But if the laborers followed the Malthusian injunction, there would have resulted a shortage of labor that might have reduced capitalist economy to dire straits, depending, as it did in the England of that day, on a plentiful supply of cheap labor. "Prudential habits with regard to marriage," declared Malthus, "carried to a considerable extent, among the laboring classes of a country mainly depending upon manufactures and commerce, might injure it."[43] It was Malthus who was now in a dilemma; but he had no confidence in the rationality and prudence of the laboring class. Those of the latter who had a "thought for the morrow" would be few; hence there would be only a slight diminution of population, which would not seriously inconvenience the rich.[44] As a clergyman, Malthus had the moral satisfaction of offering a counsel of perfection; as an economist, he had the practical sense to know that it would not be followed.

The great influence of the classical economists gave a "moral sanction to an exploitation of the working class that shocked the sensibilities of intelligent citizens."[45] With their approval, society was organized into an immense machine, in order to produce the greatest amount of wealth and to give the capitalists the greatest profits, even at the cost of suffering on the part of the workers of any age and of either sex. The laboring masses of England were indeed in what seemed to be a hopeless situation. Intellectually depressed through ignorance,

41 J. S. Mill, *op. cit.*, 358.

42 J. S. Mill, "The Claims of Labor," in *Dissertations and Discussions* (New York, 1874), II, 284.

43 Malthus, *Principles of Political Economy* (London, 1836), 215.

44 Malthus, *Essay,* 458.

45 N. B. S. Gras, "Business Man and Economic Systems," *Journal of Economic and Business History,* III (February, 1931), 179.

physically benumbed through long and arduous labor, and psychologically demoralized by constant worry over their daily bread, the workers were, according to the champions of capitalism, totally unfit to exercise any power in the state. They adhered to the Greek adage that one must never forget to belittle and to decry those to whom he did injustice. The workers were, asserted the classical economists, just creatures of habit whose dominant instinct was sex, in that they had an irrepressible longing to marry and beget children. Their incapacity was proved by the fact that they were unable to earn more than their sustenance, no matter how favorable were the conditions. The new inequality, based on universal, immutable economic laws, constituted a permanent division in society. The poor inherited their poverty as the rich inherited their wealth. Unlike the man-made, complicated caste system of former days, the new inequality had the simplicity and directness that came from universal nature. It was the preserver of civilization because it preserved those who had economic capacity and the power of "moral restraint" to perpetuate this capacity. In his repudiation of the idea of equality, Malthus was the most outspoken, the most consistent, and most logical of the bourgeois liberals of his day. Inequality, asserted Malthus, "offers the natural rewards of good conduct"; hence it was calculated to develop the abilities and rouse the energies of the individual. Were economic equality established by law, it would result not in universal happiness but in universal poverty and in world chaos.[46]

To the poor the new inequality established by capitalism was a galling contradiction of the principle of equality before the law of all men, irrespective of rank or of class. The driving necessity of the worker to accept hard terms or to starve was a baffling aspect of the freedom of the individual proclaimed by the principle of freedom of contract. What was the nature of the new freedom of the individual that brought with it new class divisions in society, whereby onerous tasks were laid on the laborers in the production of wealth and every advantage given to the capitalists in its distribution? Not being a member of a caste, the laborer did not legally inherit his status. He was a member of an economic group, which, in the new industrial order, gave mobility to the individual members of it. Within this group the laborer could freely

[46] Malthus, *Essay*, 297–324.

move from trade to trade, from factory to factory, from place to place. He was free to pass to a higher economic group, provided that he had the means, the opportunity, or the capacity. This freedom of the laborer was not primarily in his interest but in that of the capitalist, who was obviously in a stronger position when it came to applying the principle of freedom of contract. Economic necessity forced the laborer to accept whatever terms were offered to him; but the capitalist was free to dispense with his services whenever it suited the interests of the capitalist.

However, there was one gain for the laborer in the capitalist system: he now had *the right not to work*. This was indeed something new in the annals of the poor. Neither the slave nor the serf nor the journeyman, before him, had had that right. For the individual worker to refuse to work mattered little to his employer. His place would be quickly, almost automatically, filled from the number of unemployed that existed, even in the most prosperous times. But if the workers combined in a trade-union and refused to work collectively, the consequence to their employers might prove disastrous. By organizing trade-unions and asserting the principle of "collective bargaining," the laborers would acquire bargaining power equal to that of their employers, thereby redressing the balance that had been weighted so heavily on the side of the latter. The power to close the factory by means of a strike could be made equal to the power of the employers to dictate terms to the laborers. It was the trade-union, and only the trade-union, that could give economic power to the propertyless workers. The weakness of the individual worker was that he had to sell himself along with his commodity. Now through the union, and only through the union, was it possible to separate the worker—the human being—from labor —the commodity; like the capitalist, the laborer would be able to differentiate himself from the commodity that he sold. It was the union that made a man out of a commodity and gave the worker a sense of dignity and a feeling of power. Paradoxical as it may appear, it was, nevertheless, true that only in combination could the worker obtain individual freedom.

The trade-union asserted the militant refusal of the workingman to accept the position relegated to him by the capitalists and to bow to the economic law of the classical economists. Through their own collective efforts, the workers determined to fight for better conditions. Trade-unionism spread rapidly among the English working class, even in the early days of the Industrial Revolution during the eighteenth century.[47] Strikes were frequent, which greatly alarmed the propertied classes, especially during the period of the French Revolution. The right not to work, when it was exercised in concert, might turn out to be a revolutionary method as efficacious in England as barricade fighting was in France. Closing a factory by means of a strike would ruin a property owner as decisively as would a confiscatory decree by a revolutionary assembly. The factory owners appealed to the government for help, and it was promptly given. In 1799 and 1800 Parliament passed the Combination Laws, which forbade all combinations among laborers for the purpose of increasing wages or of decreasing hours of labor. Strikes were declared conspiracies, and severe penalties were enacted to punish those who participated in them. By means of the Combination Laws, the right not to work was seriously curtailed. To maintain equality before the law, these measures also prohibited combinations of capital. The class character of the Combination Laws soon became evident; they were not enforced against the capitalists, but they were strictly enforced against the laborers.[48]

As might be expected, the classical economists were opposed to trade-unionism. An essential part of the bourgeois liberal creed was free trade in all commodities, and labor was a commodity. Hence, they were opposed to the unions as labor monopolies that fixed prices without reference to the economic law of supply and demand. In the opinion of Richard Cobden, the trade-unions were animated by a desperate spirit of tyranny and monopoly.[49] Moreover, trade-unionism ran counter to the theories of the subsistence wage and of the wage fund. Of what use were trade-unions, argued the economists, if an economic law nullified every "artificial" attempt to raise wages beyond the subsistence level. As usual, Malthusianism came forward to drive home the arguments invoked against bettering the condition of the work-

[47] Sidney and Beatrice Webb, *The History of Trade Unionism* (London, 1920), 69*ff.*
[48] *Ibid.*, 72–73.
[49] John A. Hobson, *Richard Cobden* (London, 1919), 166.

ing class. The unions, asserted John Stuart Mill, "always fail to uphold wages at an artificial rate, unless they also limit the number of competitors."[50] Against the barriers of economic law trade-unions struggled in vain: such was the opinion of Cobden. "They might as well attempt to regulate the tides by force, or change the course of the seasons, or subvert any of the other laws of nature—for the wages of labor depend upon laws as unerring and as much above our coercive power as any other operations of nature."[51] Of what avail were trade-unions if the amount put aside for wages by capital—the wage fund—during a production period was fixed. If a union compelled an employer to increase wages, it would be, not at his expense, but at the expense of the unorganized workers, who would get less because the organized workers got more. The share of the laborers in the product of industry being fixed, there could be no conflict between capital and labor. But there could be a conflict between organized and unorganized labor over the share of each in the wage fund. In this way the rising antagonism between the capitalists and the laborers was to be diverted to an intraclass war within the ranks of the latter.

These views concerning the ineffectiveness of trade-unions for changing economic conditions for the laborers as a class were widely held during the period of bourgeois liberalism. It was then taken "for granted by every educated man, that Trade Unionism, as a means of bettering the condition of the workman, was against Political Economy."[52] It was not belief in the efficacy of trade-unionism that inspired the adherents of classical economy in Parliament, the Philosophic Radicals, to bring about the repeal, in 1824, of the Combination Laws. Quite the contrary! Francis Place, who had engineered the repeal, was convinced that the trade-unions were "but defensive measures resorted to for the purpose of counteracting the offensive ones of their masters." These combinations would go out of existence when the laws against them were repealed, as they "will lose the matter which cements them into masses, and they will fall to pieces."[53]

But the Philosophic Radicals were mistaken. The repeal of the Combination Laws was followed by a great outburst of trade-union

50 J. S. Mill, *Principles*, 402.
51 Quoted in Hobson, *op. cit.*, 166.
52 Sidney and Beatrice Webb, *Industrial Democracy* (New York, 1926), 603.
53 Graham Wallas, *The Life of Francis Place* (London, 1898), 217.

activity. Strikes spread from industry to industry.[54] Once more the capitalists gained the ear of Parliament, which in 1825 virtually restored the Combination Laws. The law of 1825 recognized the right of the laborers to combine, but severely limited the exercise of this right by penal provisions. Strikes and threats of strikes could be and were construed as conspiracies, to which were attached severe penalties. For one worker to persuade another to leave his job unless paid a certain wage was judged to be "in restraint of trade," because such action constituted an obstruction to the employer. Negotiations between a union and an employer could be and were construed by judges as attempts to intimidate the employer. Another law, the Master and Servant Act, "prescribed inequality before the law of workers and employer. If the latter broke a contract with the former it was tried as a civil suit; but if the worker broke his contract he was liable to criminal prosecution. An employer could be a witness in his own defense, a right denied to a worker."[55]

Apart from trade-unionism, the capitalists had another source of anxiety regarding their profits. This was that their class enemies, the aristocrats, would, through their control of Parliament, use government intervention to establish better conditions for the workers. There were good grounds for such anxiety. In the desperate defense of their vested interests against the capitalists, the aristocrats were ready to favor social reform for the workers at the expense of their employers, especially so because such reform would not cost the aristocrats anything, as they were not factory owners.

Again the classical economists came to the rescue of the capitalists, placing in their hands the weapon of *laissez faire,* all bright and burnished, with which to battle against government intervention on behalf of the workers. According to classical economy, wages and hours were matters to be decided in the open market, not in Parliament. Like all other contracts, declared Ricardo, "wages should be left to the fair and free competition of the market, and should never be controlled by the interference of the legislature."[56] Competition among the

[54] Sidney and Beatrice Webb, *History of Trade Unionism,* 104.

[55] James Stephen, *A History of the Criminal Law of England* (London, 1883), III, 209–210.

[56] Ricardo, *op. cit.,* 82.

workers was encouraged, even stimulated. Men competed with other men, with women, and with children; the unemployed, with the employed; the hand worker, with the machine. The low wages that this competition fostered meant high profits for the capitalists. There was no other way of keeping profits up but by keeping wages down.[57] Government intervention, like collective bargaining by trade-unions, asserted the defenders of capitalism, would create a situation in industry wherein the motive for the accumulation of capital would be weakened with every diminution of profit. Cheap labor, as well as improved machinery, was responsible for making England "the workshop of the world" during the first half of the nineteenth century.

Laissez faire became an all-pervading principle in the government policies affecting the working class during the period of bourgeois liberalism. It was ideally suited to keep the laborers in the pitiless grip of economic law that would always force them down to the subsistence level. Any proposal to establish minimum-wage laws roused the ire of the classical economists and sharpened their logic. All such proposals were "founded on mistakes in political economy." It was "as silly and as inefficacious" to pass laws to keep wages up as it had once been to keep wages down.[58] Attempts to circumvent economic law from functioning naturally by the "artificial" method of government intervention were not only futile but also unjust. A situation would arise wherein those "who have produced and accumulated" would be required to support laborers in idleness. "When the pay is not given for the sake of the work," caustically remarked John Stuart Mill, "but the work found for the sake of the pay, inefficiency is a matter of certainty."[59] Invariably the Malthusian overtone was heard in the discussions by the classical economists concerning the future of the working class. It was "a truth which admits not a doubt," declared Ricardo, that the poor could not permanently improve their lot unless they, willingly or unwillingly, consented to limit the number of their off-

[57] Ricardo, "On Protection to Agriculture," *Works of David Ricardo* (J. R. McCulloch, ed., London, 1871), 476.

[58] J. S. Mill, "M. de Tocqueville on Democracy in America," in *Dissertations and Discussions,* II, 115.

[59] J. S. Mill, *Principles,* 363.

spring.[60] If wages were raised by government intervention, population would increase at a constant ratio and production, at a diminishing ratio; in time, the only outcome would be universal poverty. Ignorance of these facts, argued Mill, "on the part of educated persons is no longer pardonable" because they had been so clearly explained by "authors of reputation," meaning Ricardo and Malthus.[61] The policy of *laissez faire* as applied to the workers was a policy of negation, derived from a philosophy of complacency compounded with antipathy to the unsuccessful. It received its harshest justification at the hands of the last of the bourgeois liberals, Herbert Spencer. When seen in connection with the best interests of mankind, he asserted, the privations and harsh fatalities of the poor were "full of the highest beneficence."[62] That the poor were destined to pay the price of progress had become almost an axiom among the bourgeois liberals of all schools.

Was there another way to better the conditions of the working class besides that of trade-unions and that of government intervention? Seriously hampered by legal restrictions, the trade-unions were able to accomplish little in that direction. And the efforts of the social reformers, hampered by the principle of *laissez faire,* had yielded at best only negative results, as in the Factory Acts. Could not substantial and positive improvements be made in the condition of the working class by an appeal to a generous and sympathetic public opinion that would compel employers to share their profits more liberally with their employees? There was the famous example of that enlightened employer, Robert Owen, who had transformed the wretched, squalid factory town of New Lanark into a model community by raising the standard of his employees. And his farsighted generosity had resulted in increased prosperity for his business.

Unfortunately for the workers, their views remained unheard and their interests remained unheeded. Without adequate schooling, without representation in Parliament, without effective organization, they exercised but little influence in the formation of public opinion. What passed as public opinion was largely created by the bourgeois liberals, who popularized the views of the classical economists so successfully

[60] Ricardo, *Princilpes,* 84.
[61] J. S. Mill, *Principles,* 364.
[62] Herbert Spencer, *Social Statics* (New York, 1883), 354.

that they came to be regarded as self-evident, eternal truths. The dismal outlook of the economists concerning the working class gained almost universal acceptance in the England of that day. "The theories of the economists," observe the Webbs, "corresponded with the prejudices of the rising middle class, and seemed to be the outcome of every man's experience."[63] In their penetrating discussion of the "mind of the rich," the Hammonds give a vivid idea of the public attitude toward the new inequality, in which "society accepted the standing misery of the poor as a recognized and indispensable condition of national welfare."[64] Malthus was convinced that a class of permanent poor, dependent solely on daily labor for their existence, was essential to the stability of every state. Had not the fountainhead of bourgeois liberalism, Bentham himself, declared that in "the highest state of social prosperity, the great mass of citizens will have no resource except their daily industry; and consequently will be always near indigence, always ready to be thrown into a state of destitution, by accidents, such as revolutions of commerce, natural calamities and especially sickness."[65] These sentiments concerning the dismal fate of the masses were shared by the liberal statesmen of Victorian England, who were convinced that economic law was responsible for the lot of the mass of men, women, and children who could but just ward off hunger, cold, and nakedness.

To accept "starvation in the midst of plenty" as part of the natural order and to justify it on the ground of national welfare and social progress gives a puzzling view of the mind of the classical economists. To appreciate this contradiction it is important to understand their views regarding nature. Unlike the thinkers of the eighteenth century, who viewed nature as the friend of man and who sought to establish an egalitarian social order in harmony with the beneficent "natural order," the classical economists developed a theory of nature's "niggardliness," to justify their belief in inequality. The normal condition of mankind, they asserted, was that of scarcity; hence nature had decreed inequality as the price of civilization. Because of the law of population and the law of diminishing returns, man's efforts to establish equality

---

[63] Sidney and Beatrice Webb, *Industrial Democracy*, 617.

[64] J. L. and Barbara Hammond, *The Town Laborer*, 196.

[65] Jeremy Bentham, *The Theory of Legislation* (C. K. Ogden, ed., New York, 1931), 127.

would result only in universal misery. According to Malthus, the deep-seated causes of evil in society came "from the laws of nature and the passions of mankind." To the classical economists nature was a cruel and deceitful monster, whose malevolent designs were especially directed against the poor. Through the powerful sex instinct, nature drove the poor to have many progeny; she then refused to satisfy their wants because of her "niggardliness." This view of nature as the enemy of the weak prepared the public to accept the Darwinian theory of natural selection, according to which nature, "red in tooth and claw," ruthlessly eliminated all except the "fit," *i.e.,* those who managed to survive the terrifying ordeal that she placed before them. The eighteenth-century concept of a harmonious and stable natural order, as the inspiration for a beneficent and happy society, gave place to the nineteenth-century concept of a constantly changing natural order in which strife was the law and survival the test. It is, therefore, not surprising that nature became the inspiration of a view of society that condemned the mass of mankind to defeat, to misery, and to inglorious extinction.

As a result of the Industrial Revolution, nature, which had long been an abstraction, took definite form and became a concrete reality in the machine. It was nature operating through the steam engine that made and transported goods with incredible speed and efficiency, impossible to human beings. To the laborers the machine was nature in her most cruel mood. Through the competition of the "iron men," it deprived them of their customary methods of making a living. Then it drove them into the factory, where they experienced a new and strange servitude, tending the machine that remorselessly exacted restless and unremitting toil. Uprisings against the "iron men," the famous Luddite riots, broke out among the laborers—but all in vain, as nothing could stop the march of the "iron men" in industry.

It was not only their view of nature, but also their view of history as it concerned the poor, that confirmed the classical economists in their belief in inequality. In many respects they were progressive thinkers, far in advance of their age. Their attitude toward the laborer, however, betrayed a "cultural lag," in that they subscribed to the traditional views of his inescapable lot. The age-old tradition of servitude of the laborer clung heavily to the free workingman of the machine age.

Let it be recalled that, at the beginning of the nineteenth century, great masses of the lower strata of society in Western Europe were just out of serfdom; in Eastern Europe they were actually in serfdom. Slavery, which had long before disappeared in Europe, had been revived by Europeans in America. Though it applied only to the Negroes and to the American aborigines, slavery had the effect of discrediting labor in general and of degrading the laborer everywhere.

Who were the "new poor" brought into existence by the Industrial Revolution? In the view of the classical economists, they were the failures of the new economic order, which gave free scope to every individual who could make his way in an "acquisitive society." "The industry and the labor of the poor," remarked Bentham, "place them among the candidates of fortune."[66] Those who remained poor, it was assumed, were condemned to their low state by their incapacity, their laziness, their immorality, or their uncontrolled passion to procreate. They were the dregs of society,

> With nothing to look backward to with pride,
> And nothing to look forward to with hope.[67]

The laborers were not considered a class in the sense of being an economic group with interests opposed to those of the capitalists and with sufficient economic power to assert themselves. In the opinion of that day, they were the human residue in a competitive system in which the unfittest survived to be mere cogs in the industrial machine. A new sting was added to poverty, the sting of disappointment in not succeeding in the race for wealth; and the sting became all the sharper because of envy of those who had succeeded.

Along with the attitude of contempt on the part of the propertied classes toward the "lower orders"—a contempt as old as history—there was mingled a new sense of uneasiness bordering on fear. The "factory hands" were a new social stratum, concentrated in the industrial centers, who were numerous, discontented, and influenced by "French ideas." What roused great apprehension among the capitalists was

[66] Bentham, *op. cit.*, 114.

[67] From Robert Frost, "The Death of the Hired Man," in *Collected Poems of Robert Frost* (Copyright, 1930, 1939 by Henry Holt and Company, Inc. Copyright, 1936 by Robert Frost).

that the trade-unions might transform the human "cogs" into a class that would challenge the power of the capitalists, as the latter had challenged that of the landed aristocracy. In this sense the trade-unions were a portent, a new and strange portent of social revolution. Behind every demand for better wages, for better hours, for better conditions in the factories, loomed the lurid and terrifying specter of revolution, with its appeal to the disinherited in all lands to rise against their oppressors. An uprising of the industrial laborers would threaten the existence of all propertied classes, especially of the capitalists, who were hated by them as their special oppressors. Both Malthus and Ricardo had lived during the French Revolution and had retained vivid memories of the Reign of Terror. Should a social revolution start in England, it might prove to be even more widespread than that in France, because the mass of English laborers, long freed from serfdom and from the control of the guilds, were in a position to use their freedom to engage in subversive activities. The overtone of social revolution is heard above the calm pronouncements by the classical economists of economic laws that doomed the workers to eternal poverty. To the ancient contempt felt for the common man was now added the modern fear of him as a social revolutionist.

The importance of the "dismal" views of the economists concerning the working class does not lie in their truth or in their falsehood. It lies, primarily, in their historical significance. The economic trinity—law of population, subsistence wage, and wage fund —which dealt with human beings in an inhumane manner, held a vital place in the ideology of bourgeois liberalism, which consistently and ingenuously identified the interests of the capitalists with the general welfare and with the progress of mankind. The imposing intellectual structure erected by the classical economists reconciled a new contradiction in human society: progress and poverty. Capitalism was progress, and the poverty that dogged its heels was not its creation but the inevitable outcome of biologic and economic laws that determined the portion of the product that went to labor. These laws supplied the supreme justification of class rule, without class responsibility —the new political phenomenon that appeared with the advent of the capitalists to power in the state. The old ruling class, the landed aristocracy, had had responsibilities toward their dependents, because their

position had been due to privileges conferred on them by government and society. But the new ruling class, the capitalists, owed their
position, according to the classical economists, to their abstinence, to
their capacity, to their energy, and to their enterprise. Their wealth
was conferred on them by natural economic laws; hence nature herself
had absolved the capitalists from responsibility for the grave evils
suffered by their dependents: low wages, long hours, unsanitary factories, unemployment, and destitution. The capitalists could say, and
did, in the words of Malthus, that the poor "are themselves the cause
of their own poverty."[68] It took superb moral effrontery and the "dismal
science" of classical economy to condemn the laborers to eternal poverty
and then make them responsible for their fate.

[68] Malthus, *Principles of Political Economy,* 458.

Chapter 7. The "Glorious Revolution" of 1832 and the Triumph of Bourgeois Liberalism in England

The ideas of bourgeois liberalism developed by the utilitarians and the classical economists were not destined to remain philosophic abstractions. They soon became the battle cries of the rising middle class, spearheaded by the industrial capitalists, in its ambition to become the ruling force in England.

No sooner were the Napoleonic Wars over than an intense struggle for mastery began between the aristocrats and the capitalists. The great problem was whether a shift in class power, involving vested interests, historic institutions, and cherished traditions, could be made peacefully. Or would England, like France, have to undergo violent revolutionary upheavals in order to make the great political transformation that new conditions demanded? Unlike the situation in France after the Napoleonic Wars, that in England favored the peaceful triumph of bourgeois liberalism. There did not exist in England, as there did in France, two irreconcilable elements, each bent on the other's destruction. However bitter the feelings between the two Englands, liberal and tory—and they were very bitter—compromise was never precluded from the calculations of either side. The explanation must be sought not in the English national temperament, which is supposedly inclined to compromise, but in the fundamental fact that the English Revolution of the seventeenth century was intrinsically a political, not a social, revolution. As a class, the English aristocracy emerged virtually unscathed from the Puritan uprising and from the Revolution of 1688. Their lands were not confiscated, except in isolated cases. Their social, political, and economic privileges continued without serious modifications. And, most important of all, their heads rested securely

111

on their shoulders. There had been no long processions to the block during the English Revolution, as there had been long processions to the guillotine during the French Revolution. What did take place was a new infusion of wealthy merchants into the ranks of the aristocracy. But the tenants remained tenants, as under their former lords, because the English Revolution "did not materially alter the existing laws in regard to land tenure. . . ."[1] No sweeping abolition of feudal privileges took place, as in France during the French Revolution; neither were estates partitioned among the peasantry.

In 1815 the situation of the landed aristocracy was actually better than it had been in the eighteenth century. Their estates had been enlarged as a result of the enclosures, which, in effect, confiscated the common lands and the holdings of the yeomanry for the benefit of the aristocrats. Furthermore, owing to the application of science and machinery to agriculture, the landlords were able to increase the yield of their lands to supply the need of a growing population. The English aristocracy managed to combine old aristocratic privileges in regard to their estates—such as entail, primogeniture, and the game laws— with larger holdings and with better opportunities to exploit their lands profitably.

However substantial the gains of the aristocrats, those of the capitalists were far greater, owing to the extraordinary progress of industry. The economic future of England lay definitely with the capitalists. A conflict between them and the landed aristocracy, each economically strong and both fearful of revolutionary upheavals from below, was likely to lead to a compromise solution. No deep unbridgeable gulf separated aristocratic from middle-class England.

Another fortunate element in the peaceful development of English liberalism was Parliament. It was then the only representative body in the world that exercised supreme power in the state. Despite the aristocratic character of its organization and membership, Parliament was truly a national institution. It was considered the nation in miniature, no matter how few the electors. Parliament had antiquity and

[1] S. J. Madge, *The Doomsday of Crown Lands* (London, 1938), 267; see also Margaret James, *Social Problems and Policy during the Puritan Revolution* (London, 1930). For the economic aspect of the conflict between the Stuart kings and Parliament, see J. U. Neff, *Industry and Government in France and England, 1540–1640* (Philadelphia, 1940).

continuity, which appealed to the conservative elements of the nation. And because of the revolutionary role that it had played in the struggles against Stuart despotism, Parliament was regarded as the one institution that embodied England's liberal traditions; hence it appealed to the liberal elements of the nation. Both political parties, the Tories and the Whigs, united in upholding the fundamentals of liberalism—parliamentary government and civil rights—which had definitely emerged from the Revolution of 1688. In 1815 England was the only nation in Europe that possessed in Parliament a peaceful mechanism for change that could end the "discord between a changing social condition and unchanging laws."[2]

The aristocracy, however, controlled Parliament. It controlled the House of Lords, directly by the membership of the peers through the principle of heredity; and, indirectly, the House of Commons by proxy, through the rotten-borough system and the restricted suffrage. Aristocratic influences in the government were not limited to Parliament; they extended to the Established Church, to the endowed universities, and to the public services, civil and military. Both the Tories and the Whigs, who worked the parliamentary system and filled the offices, were representatives chiefly of the landed interests. Their power could not be broken without a drastic reform of Parliament that would introduce new elements in the electorate and new constituencies in the representative system. How could such changes be made against the certain opposition of an aristocracy tenacious of its privileges? To lose control of Parliament would mean opening the dikes to floods of radical legislation that would overwhelm the aristocracy as the ruling class. Was England to undergo a revolution against an aristocratic parliament as France had undergone a revolution against an absolute monarch?

It was plain that, in order to realize their aims, the English middle class must gain control of Parliament; and they must do it in a manner to avoid revolution, which might bring disaster to all the propertied elements. The French Revolution had begun as an attack on the property of the aristocrats, but confiscation followed confiscation with something like socialist objectives. This constituted a warning that was

[2] A. V. Dicey, *Lectures on the Relation between Law and Public Opinion in England* (London, 1914), 122.

not lost on the English middle class, who were convinced that, at all costs, Parliament must be kept intact and under the control of the propertied classes, although the control must be shifted from the landed to the industrial interests.

A comprehensive program for the solution of this problem was the extraordinary accomplishment of the bourgeois liberals in England. With their philosophic roots deep in utilitarianism, they created two powerful movements—one, economic, in classical economy; and the other, political, in Philosophic Radicalism—both of which aimed to bring about a transformation of the English systems of society and government. So closely united and so harmonious were the bourgeois liberals that the membership of all three groups, utilitarians, classical economists, and Philosophic Radicals, was almost identical. Whatever was distinctive in each group was largely determined by its leading figure. In the case of utilitarianism, it was Bentham; in classical economy, Ricardo; and in Philosophic Radicalism, James Mill.

James Mill was born in 1773, the son of a shoemaker, in a small town in Scotland. Like so many poor but talented Scotsmen, both before him and since, he early took the road to London. In 1808 he met Bentham and promptly saw in him the all-wise master and in himself the devoted disciple. Mill became Bentham's private secretary, the recognized function of Benthamite discipleship. In order that he might be constantly near his master, he and his family moved to the neighborhood of Bentham's home, where they resided for many years. Mill lived and labored in the shadow of Bentham, whose philosophy he accepted completely and wholeheartedly. It may be said that Mill was a disciple who actually created his master. He found Bentham an eccentric recluse, known in England chiefly as a prison reformer, and left him the leader of a great movement—a prominent national figure. It was Mill who converted Bentham to political action and made him a force to be reckoned with in the politics of England. With his "genius for logical deduction and exposition, which gives a kind of originality to his works even when they are expressing someone else's ideas, Mill rendered Bentham as much service as Bentham rendered Mill. Bentham gave Mill a doctrine, and Mill gave Bentham a school."[3]

[3] Élie Halévy, *The Growth of Philosophic Radicalism*, trans. from the French by Mary Morris (London, 1928), 251.

Though born and reared in the traditions of Scottish Presbyterianism and trained for its ministry, Mill came under the influence of the French *philosophes,* especially that of the materialist atheist Helvétius. He consequently repudiated Christianity as dogmatically and as completely as he had once accepted it. According to John Stuart Mill, his father was convinced that mankind "reached the most perfect conception of wickedness which the human mind can devise, and have called this God, and prostrated themselves before it. This *ne plus ultra* of wickedness he considered to be embodied in what is commonly presented to mankind as the creed of Christianity."[4]

Mill wrote voluminously on all sorts of subjects dealing with social and political problems. Though not a great writer, he wrote sufficiently well to secure for himself a place in the intellectual history of nineteenth-century England. His style is hard, cold, and logical, as was the stern, didactic, humorless author himself. It has a clarity that comes from rigidity rather than from sympathetic observation. The only emotion of which Mill was capable was moral indignation, which was always on tap, flowing in a controlled, though abundant, stream. It was directed chiefly against the political evils of his day, to the abolition of which he dedicated his life.

There is an unforgettable picture of Mill the father by Mill the son in the latter's *Autobiography.* James Mill's early life as a child in a poor family, together with his Calvinist upbringing, must have influenced him to view life as "a poor thing at best, after the freshness of youth and of unsatisfied curiosity had gone by."[5] Handsome and dignified physically, Mill was a logic machine mentally. He exorcised passion and sentiment from human thought and conduct, which were to be guided only by reason and logic. Life to Mill was "a series of arguments, in which people were constrained by logic, not persuaded by sympathy."[6]

In Mill's case, as in that of many other thinkers, it was temperament rather than ideology that determined his ideas and conduct. His temperament was that of a self-denying, fanatical Calvinist, though his standard of morals was hedonistic, based on the "greatest happiness"

[4] J. S. Mill, *Autobiography* (John Jacob Coss, ed., New York, 1924), 29.
[5] *Ibid.,* 34.
[6] Leslie Stephen, *The English Utilitarians* (New York, 1902), II, 39.

principle of utilitarianism. Throughout his life Mill was possessed by "the despairing gloom, the austere fanaticism, the moral power" of Calvinism. He was an ascetic without a monastic rule, a theologian without religion, without "eyes or ears for the beauties of nature and art . . . in short, the Utilitarian whose caricature was soon to become popular."[7] With Mill's death, in 1836, there passed away the early and unattractive type of utilitarian reformer. The later, and more attractive, type was none other than John Stuart Mill, whose personality did so much to eliminate the forbidding aspect that his father had given to utilitarianism.

James Mill was English bourgeois liberalism incarnate. He had all the virtues and all the shortcomings of that school of opinion, and he expressed his views with a frankness and a sharpness that left nothing to be desired. His opposition to aristocracy was as thorough as was his indifference to the working class. It was said of Mill that his radicalism came less from the love of the many than from the hatred of the few. In his vision of a good society, Mill beheld the middle class—and only the middle class—in the seat of power and of influence. The "middle rank" was, in his opinion, the most useful of all classes, because it was free from the necessity of manual labor without being exposed to the vices and excesses of the very rich. The only alternative to a bourgeois social order was either the chaos of anarchy or the still life of caste. It would be hard to imagine a stronger champion of the rights of property than Mill. In his view the possession of property was the best test of ability in the individual and of progress in society. The business of government was properly the business of the rich, and "they will always obtain it either by bad means or by good." The only good means by which the rich could get control of the government was through a free suffrage and a secret ballot. Therefore the rich should always endeavor to gain the good will of the people.[8]

Mill was the organizer and leader of a political movement known as "Philosophic Radicalism." It arose from the very bosom of utilitarianism, all the members being avowed disciples of Bentham. Apart from Mill, the leading figures of the movement were Joseph Hume and Sir Francis Burdett, its most prominent parliamentary representatives;

[7] Halévy, *op cit.,* 309.
[8] James Mill, "The Ballot," *Westminster Review,* XIII (July, 1830), 37*ff.*

Francis Place, the remarkable tailor-politician whose genius for political organization became proverbial; and Sir Samuel Romilly and Sir James Mackintosh, prominent as law reformers. A younger element attracted to the movement included George Grote, the historian of ancient Greece; John Austin, the juristic philosopher; Edwin Chadwick, the administrative reformer; and, most famous of all, John Stuart Mill. Bentham himself was closely identified with the Philosophic Radicals, as were Ricardo and Malthus.

"Philosophic Radicals" was not a felicitous designation of an active English political group, but it fitted the members perfectly. They were all intellectuals, deeply interested in the philosophic aspects of public questions as expounded by their master, Bentham. At the same time, they were active politicians and propagandists engaged in translating utilitarian principles into a political program of radical reform. Like the Fabian socialists of a later day, the Philosophic Radicals were not distinctively a third party, but they were definitely a political group with a comprehensive program of reform far in advance of anything advocated by the two major parties; and, again like the Fabians, they sought to influence public opinion, in order to bring pressure to bear on the two parties to adopt their policies. The great historic importance of English radicalism lies in the fact that it presented alternative methods to those of the French Revolution for the objectives of abolishing an old social order and inaugurating a new one.

Could Parliament be made the instrument of radical reform? Not as it was organized and as it had traditionally functioned. Could the party system be made to serve the interests of the middle class? Hardly, as both Tories and Whigs were dominated by powerful aristocratic families. Very clearly did the Philosophic Radicals realize the necessity for making "radical," *i.e.,* root, changes in the political and social systems. Their program comprehended drastic reforms in every aspect of English life, political, economic, religious, educational, and administrative; in every sphere of activity, local, national, and imperial. However, they concentrated all their energies, all their efforts, all their talents on parliamentary reform. Politically minded, as have been nearly all left groups in England, the Philosophic Radicals were convinced that a reformed Parliament would become the organized expression of an aroused public opinion, which would put into effect the policies that they so enthusiastically advocated. In this constitutional way England would then have a continuous national assembly, without civil strife, without revolutionary dictatorship, without ruthless confiscations. They, more than any other English political group, grasped the idea that the supreme function of a liberal state was to avoid social revolution by dissolving social antagonisms into political issues, which meant transforming class war into party conflicts.

The system of representation, in the opinion of Mill, if made more representative, would abolish separation between the rulers—"those who rob"—and the ruled—"those who are robbed." To be really effective in enacting reforms, Parliament should be all-powerful—"omnicompetent," in Bentham's coined phrase—in the government of England.[9] Publicity should be the only check on legislative power. "Without publicity," asserted Bentham, "all other checks are fruitless: in comparison with publicity, all other checks are of small account."[10] Liberty of the press was the supreme method of giving expression to public opinion, because it threw all men into the public presence. The editor of a journal was, therefore, an unofficial functionary whose importance far outweighed that of many an official one.[11]

How was a Parliament, reformed and "omnicompetent," to come into existence? Certainly not as a result of a revolutionary uprising from below. On that all the Philosophic Radicals were in complete agreement. Could a revolutionary change be made without violence? There existed a historic precedent, the Glorious Revolution of 1688. The Philosophic Radicals set themselves the task of developing a comprehensive plan of parliamentary reform and of devising a political strategy to realize it. Their success resulted in what may be called the "Glorious Revolution of 1832," in the passage of the great Reform Bill of that year.

To understand the remarkable difficulties and obstacles that faced the Philosophic Radicals, it is well to keep in mind that Parliament had virtually ceased to be the national scene of political struggle for the control of the government. With the aristocrats in control of both

9 Jeremy Bentham, *The Constitutional Code,* in *The Works of Jeremy Bentham* (Bowring, ed., Edinburgh, 1843), IX, 120*ff.*

10 *Organization of Judicial Establishments* (Bowring, ed.), IV, 317.

11 *Securities against Misrule* (Bowring, ed.), VIII, 579.

houses, the supremacy of Parliament really meant the supremacy of that class in the government of the country. As both the Whigs and the Tories came from the same class and represented the same economic interest, that of the landed aristocracy, the two-party system had virtually broken down. The two parties played each other's game; and the stakes of the game were public office and the prestige of the aristocratic families. According to Bentham, there existed a tacit cooperation between the two contending parties against the peoples' interests. "His Majesty's Government" and "His Majesty's Opposition" were really smoke screens for a system of family rotation in office, agreeable to both parties, who acted "under the dominion of the same seductive and corruptive influences." What the Tories now have, the "Whigs have before them in prospect and expectancy," sarcastically observed Bentham.[12] What the English people beheld in their parliamentary setup was a "discredited Opposition" facing a "discredited Government." [13]

Elections were sham battles over trumped-up issues. The Tories claimed to be the champions of the glorious tradition of a stable, yet free, England, which had successfully withstood the assaults of Revolutionary and Napoleonic France. As upholders of the traditions of the Revolution of 1688, the Whigs proclaimed themselves to be the champions of English liberty and of the rights of the people. "The Whigs have ever been an exclusive and aristocratic faction," observed the Philosophic Radical, John Arthur Roebuck, "though at times employing democratic principles and phrases as weapons of offense against their opponent. . . . When out of office they were demagogues, in power they became exclusive oligarchs."[14] To maintain the "tacit cooperation" of the two parties, elections were "managed" by wholesale corruption and by an outrageous abuse of government patronage. Voting was farcical, even in those constituencies that were not rotten boroughs. "Freedom of election as against the despotic power of the monarch," declared Bentham, "was established;—freedom of election

[12] *Plan of Parliamentary Reform* (Bowring, ed.), III, 527–528.

[13] Élie Halévy, *A History of the English People in 1815,* trans. from the French by E. J. Watkins and D. A. Barker (New York, 1924), 169.

[14] John Arthur Roebuck, *History of the Whig Ministry of 1830* (London, 1852), II, 405–406.

as against the disguised despotism of the aristocracy, Tories and Whigs together, remained extended."[15]

The Philosophic Radicals realized very clearly that a new balance of classes was arising in England as a result of the Industrial Revolution. A new urban population was growing rapidly, among whom there existed no nostalgia for "merrie England," no ancient loyalties to cherish, no sentiment of devotion to their betters. In the unrepresented industrial towns and in the unenfranchised urban inhabitants they beheld the possibility of a widespread movement to strike the weapon of Parliament from the hands of the aristocrats and to place it in the hands of those who would abolish the system of organized political corruption, with its romantic façade of ancient loyalties.

The plan of parliamentary reform was worked out in great detail by Bentham in his *Constitutional Code*[16] and *Plan of Parliamentary Reform*.[17] What Bentham demanded was a radical reform of the political system that would include the supremacy of the Commons, popular suffrage, and administrative centralization. In 1818 resolutions based on the political views of Bentham and of Mill were introduced in the House of Commons by the Benthamite, Sir Francis Burdett.[18] These resolutions constituted a direct frontal attack on the citadel of aristocratic power, the unreformed Parliament.

In their proposals to broaden the electorate, the Philosophic Radicals came sharply up against the issue of universal suffrage. Logically universal suffrage was the practical application of the supreme principle of utilitarianism, "the greatest happiness of the greatest number," according to which each individual was to count for one and no one for more than one. The equal claim of everyone to happiness involved an equal claim of everyone to the means of attaining happiness, and "everyone" meant poor as well as rich, women as well as men, and ignorant

---

[15] Bentham, *The Book of Fallacies* (London, 1824), 257. For excellent studies of political life in England prior to 1832, see L. B. Namier, *The Structure of Politics at the Accession of George III*, 2 vols. (London, 1929); T. E. Kebbel, *A History of Toryism, 1783–1881* (London, 1886); and A. F. Freemantle, *England in the Nineteenth Century*, 2 vols. (London, 1929).

[16] Bowring ed., IX.

[17] *Ibid.*, III.

[18] T. C. Hansard, *The Parliamentary History of England* (London, 1806 to date), XXXVIII, 1118ff.

as well as learned. In the principle of number, so dear to the utilitarians, lay the logic of political democracy. Therefore Bentham, in theory at least, favored universal suffrage for both men and women.[19]

Prior to 1832, the system of representation and of voting constituted an outrageous violation of the principle of number, so fundamental in utilitarian philosophy. A constituency was a place, not a number of people; and an elector was a privileged person, not a citizen with rights. Yet Parliament legislated in the name of the people of Britain! Extension of the suffrage, abolition of the rotten boroughs, and representation of the new centers of population would vindicate, according to the Philosophic Radicals, the principle of number by making Parliament truly representative of the nation.

Logic, however, was one thing and practical politics, quite another. Being in the political arena, the Philosophic Radicals were willing and ready to compromise on the suffrage issue in the interest of the middle class. "The aim should be to develop the middle class: to this can be reduced the equalitarianism of Bentham and James Mill."[20] Manhood suffrage aroused strenuous opposition because it was then identified with revolutionary democracy, with attacks on property, and with leveling policies. It had been adopted in 1793 by the National Convention in revolutionary France, on the principle of popular sovereignty, which, it was feared, would bring a Reign of Terror in England as it had done in France.

To Englishmen generally the "liberty of the subject," or the protection of civil rights of the individual by law, was a sacred right. But voting was a political *privilege* connected with property. Being strong upholders of the rights of property, the Philosophic Radicals were opposed to manhood suffrage, which aimed to abolish property rights in voting. Once established, it might become a precedent for

[19] *Memoirs of Bentham* (Bowring, ed.), X, 495, 497. However, Bentham did not consider woman's suffrage a practical issue. See *The Constitutional Code* (Bowring, ed.), IX, 107–108. The movement for manhood suffrage had antedated Bentham. In 1780, the Duke of Richmond had presented a resolution in Parliament in favor of manhood suffrage and annual parliaments. See Hansard, XXI, 687. Major John Cartwright had achieved fame as an advocate of manhood suffrage. See his book, *Bill of Rights and Liberties* (London, 1817). For a study of the suffrage movement, see G. S. Veitch, *Genesis of Parliamentary Reform* (London, 1913).

[20] Halévy, *Growth of Philosophic Radicalism,* 366.

attacks on property in general, as well as for attacks on privileges. They feared that, under a system of manhood suffrage, the nonpropertied classes would combine politically to advance their own interest, which might prove dangerous to the middle class as well as to the aristocracy. A vote was not only an expression of opinion; even more was it an exercise of power. Manhood suffrage would give the poor political power, which they would use to redress the balance in the economic sphere. According to the Philosophic Radicals, a lowered property qualification for voting was the solution of the suffrage problem. This would maintain the property basis of voting and, at the same time, make the government "popular" by extending the suffrage. Through the process of expanding the suffrage by contracting the property qualification, the principle of number would be substituted for that of privilege in the electoral system of England. This change would lead to the suppression of aristocratic rule without incurring the dangers of revolutionary democracy. Representation on the basis of number would, according to this scheme, give the controlling power to the middle class, whose numerical superiority was sure to swamp the aristocrats and their political vassals.

In the agitation for the reform of Parliament, the Philosophic Radicals unhesitatingly and definitely favored a lowered property qualification for voting. In their view, property did not constitute a special privilege, because anyone who had capacity could acquire it. Hence control of the government by property owners was not a form of class domination; it was the rule of a natural elite, which constantly maintained a high standard of fitness by eliminating the unfit through competition. That part of the working class, asserted John Stuart Mill, which succeeded in "raising itself becomes a part of the ruling body; and, if the suffrage be necessary to make it so, it will not be long without suffrage."[21] In his essay "Government," James Mill argued that, as the object of government was the increase of happiness, that object could best be attained through the protection of property rights. And of all systems of government the parliamentary system was best fitted to protect property rights, provided that the electorate was large enough to prevent the formation of "sinister interests," *i.e.,* an electorate with a

[21] J. S. Mill, "M. de Tocqueville on Democracy in America," in *Dissertations and Discussions* (New York, 1874), II, 99.

property qualification sufficiently low to include the middle class. "There can be no doubt that the middle rank," he declared, ... "is that portion of the community of which, if the basis of Representation were ever so far extended, the opinion would ultimately decide. Of the people beneath them, a majority would be sure to be guided by their advice and example."[22] Ricardo, whose economic sense sharpened his political views, argued that in order to maintain the sacred rights of property "an extension of the suffrage, far short of making it universal, will substantially secure to the people the good government they wish for, and therefore, I deprecate the demand for the universality of the election franchise."[23]

John Stuart Mill was not one whit behind his elders in upholding the fitness of the middle class to rule the nation. "To most purposes in the constitution of modern society," he declared, "the government of a numerous middle class is Democracy. Nay, it not merely *is* Democracy, but the only Democracy of which there is as yet any example: what is called universal suffrage in America arises from the fact that America is all middle class." It was a "chimerical hope to overbear or outnumber the middle class: whatever modes of voting, whatever redistribution of the constituencies, are really necessary for placing the government in their hands, those, whether we like it or not, they will assuredly obtain."[24] Bentham himself, despite his belief in universal suffrage, was ready to compromise. He declared that he was "not only content, but glad to limit the suffrage to householders who paid direct taxes."[25] Temperamentally an eighteenth-century *philosophe,* he had the saving grace of cynical frankness, a quality lacking in his humorless, rigid disciples. He frankly admitted that he could not find reason for excluding a majority of the people from voting; hence he was willing to leave the defense of such a policy to those who could.[26]

Like all the bourgeois liberals of the time, the Philosophic Radicals identified the interests of the middle class with those of the public. As a

22 James Mill, "Government," in *Essays* (London, n.d.), 32.

23 David Ricardo, "Observations on Parliamentary Reform," in *Works* (J. R. McCulloch, ed., London, 1852), 556.

24 J. S. Mill, "M. de Tocqueville on Democracy in America," *loc. cit.* It is important to note that later Mill changed his mind in favor of universal suffrage. See *infra,* p. 264.

25 *Plan of Parliamentary Reform* (Bowring, ed.), III, 467.

26 *Radicalism Not Dangerous* (Bowring, ed.), III, 599.

consequence, they applied the "greatest happiness" principle in such a manner as to satisfy both interests. They actually advanced a theory of representation of the "lower orders" by the middle class, similar to the theory of "virtual representation" advanced by the supporters of King George III's policy of taxation without representation of the American colonies. Certain elements—namely, children, women, younger men, and the "lower orders"—argued James Mill, need not be directly represented because their interests were indisputably included with those of others." To enfranchise the "lower orders" was entirely unnecessary, because the "great majority of the people never cease to be guided by that rank (middle class); and we may, with some confidence, challenge the adversaries of the people to produce a single instance to the contrary in the history of the world."[27] In other words, the middle class counted as the "greatest number," because they were really the public that included an overwhelming majority of the people. John Stuart Mill, whose liberal views were far in advance of those of his father, yet argued that the interests of the "lower orders" were identical with those of the propertied classes. With a naïveté that is astonishing today, he declared that the rich "willingly make considerable sacrifices, especially of their pecuniary interest, for the benefit of the working classes, and err rather by too lavish and indiscriminating beneficence; nor do I believe that any rulers in history have been actuated by a more sincere desire to do their duty towards the poorer portion of their countrymen."[28] There was one class that was not part of the public, namely, the aristocrcy; therefore, the "sinister interests" of the latter were directly opposed to public interests. It is well to observe that the bourgeois liberals in England were class conscious in relation to the aristocracy but not in relation to the working class. The reason is not far to seek: the former was a redoubtable foe, whereas the latter had not yet seriously challenged the power of the capitalists. Until the appearance of Chartism the revolutionary movement among the working class was negligible. Therefore, the English middle class was not obliged to wage war on two fronts, that on the right and that on the left, as was the French *bourgeoisie* during the same period.

The Philosophic Radicals were determined to destroy every part of

[27] James Mill, "Government," in *op. cit.,* 32.

[28] J. S. Mill, *Representative Government* in *Utilitarianism Liberty and Representative Government* (London, Everyman's Library, 1914), 209.

the political mechanism by means of which the "many-headed incubus," as Bentham called aristocracy, ruled the nation. Apart from such basic parliamentary reforms as the abolition of rotten boroughs, the representation of the industrial centers, and the expansion of the suffrage, they advocated a number of other political reforms designed to weaken the power of the aristocracy. The contraction of the term of Parliament, then seven years, was part of their reform plan. More frequent elections would have the effect of keeping the people keyed up to the political issues that divided them. Bentham favored annual parliaments, but he was willing to accept a term of three years.[29]

The Philosophic Radicals also favored the secret ballot, then considered a very radical reform. The viva voce method of voting was not an unimportant element in the aristocratic control of Parliament, in that it enabled the aristocrats to put pressure on the electors to vote for their candidates. The extension of the suffrage might mean the extension of aristocratic pressure on the new voters if this method of voting were maintained. The immense social prestige of the English upper class might become a subtle form of corrupting the middle class, which was notoriously sensitive to social pressure. James Mill came out boldly and vigorously in favor of the secret ballot, on the ground that it would effectively prevent the wealthy from coercing the poorer electors.[30]

Radical reform to the Philosophic Radicals meant not merely the reform of the representative system, but the abolition of England's ancient and most cherished institutions, the monarchy and the House of Lords. Bentham was an outspoken republican and an enthusiastic admirer of the American constitution.[31] The office of king could not be continued, he declared, "without endeavoring to give perpetuity to, by far the foulest system of immorality, as well as the grossest system of absurdity that the wit of man ever engendered."[32] In place of the king, the "corruptor-general," he favored the election of a chief executive by the Commons for a term of four years.

Bentham's followers, however, maintained a discreet silence on the issue of republicanism versus monarchy. Republicanism had been dis-

[29] H. R. G. Greaves, "Bentham on Legislative Procedure," *Economica,* XI (1931), 324.
[30] James Mill, "The Ballot," in *op. cit.,* 1–39.
[31] *Plan of Parliamentary Reform* (Bowring, ed.), III, 472; *Constitutional Code* (Bowring, ed.), IX, 9, 63, 69, 119.
[32] *Constitutional Code* (Bowring, ed.), IX, 145.

credited by the Reign of Terror in France; like democracy, it was identified with revolution. The weakness of both the English kings of the time, George IV and William IV, convinced the Philosophic Radicals that the monarchy would not constitute a serious obstacle to their plans of reform. An attack on the king might arouse sentiments of ancient loyalties that would increase the already great difficulties that faced them. Hence at the very beginning of the struggle between liberalism and conservatism in England, the monarchy was shelved as an issue.

The House of Lords, however, was a different matter. Here was a legislative chamber that had equal power over legislation with the Commons; and by its constitution, it was the very quintessence of aristocratic privilege. Moreover, it was the citadel of the most powerful economic group, the landed interest, which they were determined to overthrow. No matter how much the representative system was reformed, the will of the Commons could, at any time and for any or no reason, be nullified by the aristocratic House of Lords.

As usual, Bentham was more outspoken and more radical in his views than were his disciples. He advocated very decisively the abolition of the House of Lords and the establishment of a single-chamber parliament with complete power over legislation. In Bentham's view, the House of Lords was the political arm of an entrenched aristocracy; it was such in origin and had continued as such ever since. The upper house gave a small, privileged class the power to veto legislation for the public welfare. Any second chamber was, according to Bentham, "needless, useless, worse than useless—that is to say, purely maleficent:..."[33] It served as a parliamentary screen behind which reactionaries concealed their evil intentions. A bicameral legislature, in the opinion of Bentham, had few, if any advantages, and many disadvantages: conflict of the two houses; unnecessary delay; division of responsibility; minority rule, as the upper house was smaller than the lower; waste of time and money; and complication of government machinery.[34]

[33] Bentham, *On Houses of Peers and Senates* (Bowring, ed.), IV, 420–421.

[34] For Bentham's views on second chambers, see *ibid.*, 419–450; *An Essay on Political Tactics* (Bowring, ed.), II, 307–310; *Constitutional Code* (Bowring, ed.), IX, 114–117. See also L. Rockow, "Bentham on the Theory of Second Chambers," *American Political Science Review*, XXII (1928), 576–590.

In this matter, too, his followers took a more moderate stand. They did not desire to abolish the Lords, any more than they desired to abolish the monarchy. Could not the Lords, like the Commons, be reformed by limiting its power over legislation? Roebuck delivered an attack on the Lords, in which he declared that its existence in its shape at the time was incompatible with the welfare of England.[35] A definite plan for the reform of the upper house was submitted in 1836 by James Mill. It was as follows: "Let it be enacted, that if a bill, which has been passed by the House of Commons, and thrown out by the House of Lords, is renewed in the House of Commons in the next session of parliament, and passed, but again thrown out by the House of Lords, it shall, if passed a third time in the House of Commons, be law, without being sent again to the Lords."[36] Mill's plan for reforming the Lords strikingly anticipated the Parliament Act of 1911, put through by the Liberal ministry of Herbert Henry Asquith, which in effect made Parliament a single-chamber legislature by virtually abolishing the legislative power of the Lords. The long arm of the stern utilitarian reached across the century to deliver a decisive blow to the aristocracy, which he regarded as the most sinister of all England's "sinister interests."

What was the attitude of the Philosophic Radicals toward religion in general and toward the established Anglican church in particular? As might be suspected, they repudiated all revealed religion. Especially did they repudiate Christiantiy, which, because of its otherworldliness, embodied everything that denied the "greatest happiness" principle. In the Benthamite view there could be no spiritual equivalent in the next world. The Anglican church, according to James Mill, was a "sinister interest," closely tied to the aristocracy; together they constituted a serious hindrance to the progress of the English people.[37] All the "sinister interests," he declared, "have a natural tendency to combine together and to cooperate, inasmuch as the object of each is thereby most completely and most easily secured. But between the particular interest of a governing aristocracy and a sacerdotal class, there seems a very peculiar affinity and co-incidence—each wielding the precise

[35] Hansard, *op. cit.*, XXX, 1162ff.
[36] *Westminster Review*, XXX (July, 1935–January, 1936), 297.
[37] James Mill, *Westminster Review*, I (1824), 214.

engine which the other wants." Religion then became a "state-engine," which led to corruption, oppression, and hypocrisy. Bentham advocated the disestablishment and the disendowment of the Anglican church.[38]

Being materialists in philosophy, the Philosophic Radicals were logically led to espouse atheism. But they were soft materialists and mild atheists. They lacked utterly the hard, bitter, uncompromising hostility to the church that was so characteristic of the anticlericals in France. What the Philosophic Radicals favored was the elimination of the church as a "state-engine," not its destruction. The most bitter of all the English anticlericals, James Mill, sought to convert the Anglican church into a secular society that would preach the gospel of the "greatest happiness" to save the greatest number in this world, not in the next. The explanation for the mild anticlericalism of the Philosophic Radicals was that the Anglican church occupied a position in England far different from that of the Catholic church in France. Ever since its establishment by Henry VIII, the Anglican church had been a department of the government, obviously and willingly subordinating itself to the authority of Parliament. Once Parliament was reformed and under radical control, the church would become as amenable to the new authority as it had been to the old. Quite otherwise was the situation of the Catholic church in France. Though officially established, as was the Anglican church, it did not willingly accept its subordinate position. French Catholicism became a powerful ally of the reactionary parties that plotted to restore the Old Regime, under which the church had flourished as a semi-independent corporation, a status virtually that of a state within a state. Fear of the church as a reactionary power was largely responsible for the truculent attitude of the French anticlericals.

There existed another difference in the situation of the two establishments. In France almost the entire population were formal adherents of the Catholic church; Protestantism was almost nonexistent. Hence the influence of the church, however small among some elements, was coextensive with the nation itself. Catholicism could and did make a powerful appeal to national traditions, unbroken for ages past, to reinforce its sacerdotal claims. More than once did the clericals make good use of French nationalism to bolster up their reactionary policies,

[38] *Constitutional Code* (Bowring, ed.), IX, 92–95.

which infuriated the anticlericals and stimulated them to wage war *à outrance* against the church.

Quite otherwise was the situation of the Anglican church. During the thirties of the nineteenth century it could claim the allegiance of only 60 per cent of the British people. It had a powerful rival and competitor in the Nonconformist sects, whose membership was as high as 38 per cent; only about 2 per cent were Catholics. Both the Nonconformists and the Catholics acidly refused to recognize the Anglican church as the "Church of England." Furthermore, Anglicanism could not make a powerful appeal to historic traditions to reinforce its sacerdotal claims. Unlike the Catholic church in France, whose origin went back to Roman times, that of the Anglican church, despite its claims, went back only to the sixteenth century.[39] It was the relative weakness of Anglicanism that was largely responsible for the mildness of English anticlericalism.

Of the many reforms advocated by the Philosophic Radicals few were directly in the interest of the working class. The cause of the industrial laborers, exploited in the factories, and that of the peasants, driven from their holdings by the enclosurers, received scant, if any, attention at their hands. According to Dicey, Benthamism "meant nothing more than the attempt to realize by means of effective legislation the political and social ideals set before himself by every intelligent merchant, tradesman, or artisan."[40] Anyone who favored a democratic suffrage or who favored policies directly in the interest of the lower orders, like the half-Tory demagogue William Cobbett and the Utopian socialist Robert Owen, roused the ire of Bentham and his followers. In the opinion of Bentham, Cobbett was an "odious compound of selfishness, malignity, insincerity, and mendacity."[41] The Owenites were distrusted by the Philosophic Radicals as sentimentalists and feared as potential revolutionists, who, in a crisis, would be found behind the barricades.[42] Owen, in the opinion of Bentham, was a sentimental windbag who "begins in vapor and ends in smoke."[43]

[39] For a good description of religious conditions in England during the early part of the nineteenth century, see Halévy, *A History of the English People in 1815*, 342ff.

[40] Dicey, *op. cit.*, 187.

[41] *Correspondence* (Bowring, ed.), XI, 68.

[42] Graham Wallas, *Life of Francis Place* (New York, 1919), 273.

[43] *Memoirs* (Bowring, ed.), X, 570.

The Philosophic Radicals developed a system of political strategy that was shrewdly calculated to realize their plan of reform without resorting to revolution. This system aimed

1. To create a public opinion severely critical not only of the existing political order but also of the hallowed traditions associated with the English constitution.
2. To "soften" the Tories by continuous attacks upon them and their policies in order to bend them into an attitude of compromise.
3. To create a real opposition in Parliament by converting the Whigs to the cause of reform.
4. To give full and emphatic assurance to the propertied elements in the nation that "radicalism" was not revolutionary; that, on the contrary, it was an uncompromising champion of property rights and of constitutional methods of change.

A propaganda launched by Bentham and his followers poured an unceasing stream of vitriolic criticism of England's historic institutions, methods, and traditions. Nearly all the trenchant political pens of the period were wielded by the Philosophic Radicals and their followers, their "fellow travelers," to use a now current expression. No Burke, no Blackstone appeared, to hail the glories and sing the praises of the English constitution. Bentham's voluminous political writings might be described as an elaboration of his first book, *Fragment on Government,* in which he had violently attacked the constitution. Years later, Bentham, older and more furious, lashed out in his *Constitutional Code* against the constitution, which, he declared, was "composed of the conjunct action of force, intimidation, corruption, and delusion."[44]

James Mill was less furious, but not less critical, than was his master. His essay "Government" was a cogent and trenchant analysis of the English constitutional system, the keystone of which was, according to Mill, the control of the political life of the nation by a landed aristocracy in order to maintain its interests against those of the people. Mill's essay became the political handbook of the Philosophic Radicals, who looked to it for both guidance and inspiration.

Consciously and deliberately the Philosophic Radicals appealed to the well to do and to the educated of the nation. They "abhorred the

[44] *Constitutional Code* (Bowring, ed.), IX, 9.

common herd" and "loved to preach a philosophy at a respectable distance from their hearers," never even dreaming of mingling with the masses.[45] In order to spread their doctrines, the Philosophic Radicals founded the quarterly *Westminster Review* under the editorship of James Mill. They also founded two dailies, the *Morning Chronicle* and the *Scotsman*.[46] In 1828 they founded the University of London, in order to teach the social sciences, which were then sadly neglected by Oxford and Cambridge. The *Westminster Review* became the "official organ" of the Philosophic Radicals, in opposition to the Tory *Edinburgh Review*. Every issue contained trenchant attacks on the "six hundred families" that ruled England, who "inherited the ignorance of their ancestors along with their estates."

A new public opinion arose to confront those in power. It had a jealous regard for freedom of speech, of the press, and of assembly, which then had a special political significance, in that they constituted the power of the unrepresented. Ever since 1695 there had been no established censorship of printed matter in England. But there existed restrictions on the freedom of the press in the blasphemy laws; in the severe libel laws, which forbade attacks not only on private individuals but also on public officials; and in the taxes on knowledge, *i.e.,* stamp duties on journals. But these restrictions were often evaded by the agitators for reform. Before long an aroused public opinion began to exercise great pressure on Parliament. This pressure was reinforced by the wave of discontent among the working class during the period of depression that followed the Napoleonic Wars. The revolutionary threat from below gave point to the agitation for parliamentary reform.

Within the Tory party an element appeared that realized that time was out of joint. Public opinion, or what passed as such in aristocratic England, was not flowing placidly in its old, accustomed channel of Parliament. Something had to be done to conciliate it, lest the revolutionary spirit be wafted from France across the Channel. A reform Tory group appeared, led by the Peels, father and son; William Huskisson; and William Wilberforce, who were inclined to favor moderate social, economic, and religious reform. Largely because of

45 C. B. R. Kent, *The English Radicals* (London, 1899), 364.

46 J. S. Mill, *Autobiography,* Chap. 4, gives an interesting account of the founding of these journals and of their influence in spreading the ideas of the Philosophic Radicals.

their efforts, Tory England, during the Restoration period, was not dominated by a reactionary spirit, as uncompromising as that on the Continent. A number of important reforms were enacted by Parliament: the criminal law reform of 1823; the modification of the navigation and tariff laws, to promote freer trade; the repeal of the Combination Laws against the trade-unions; the repeal of the Test and Corporation Acts against the Nonconformists; and, most important of all, Catholic emancipation. The Tories were undergoing a process of "softening," in preparation for their submission in 1832.

A far more significant result of the tactics employed by the Philosophic Radicals was that the cautious and hesitating Whigs were driven to the side of the reformers. To create a real opposition to the "stern, unbending" Tories meant the restoration of the two-party system to its full vigor. Only in a vigorous opposition, committed to reform, lay the possibility of a peaceful transition to a bourgeois liberal England. The incessant agitation for reform had influenced the Whigs far more than the Tories. In the first place the Whig tradition of 1688 was revived after the danger from Revolutionary and from Napoleonic France had passed away. The Whig party began sprouting a "left wing," led by Lord John Russell and Earl Grey, which looked with favor on plans for moderate parliamentary reform. In the second place, there had long been a sizable capitalist element, the "monied men," in the Whig party, which grew in importance as a consequence of the advance of commerce and industry during the Industrial Revolution. This capitalist element, which had infiltrated aristocratic Whig ranks, lent a willing ear to plans of political reform that would give control of Parliament to their class. Finally, the Whigs were even more sensitive than were the Tories to the rising tide of discontent among the working class. As landlords and as capitalists, they had a double motive for fearing a revolutionary overturn; hence they were more easily convinced by the Philosophic Radicals that the best way to preserve the constitution was to adapt it to changing conditions by reforming Parliament. They took to heart Burke's view that a state without the means of some change was without the means of its own conservation. For these various reasons the Whigs decided to march with the Philosophic Radicals on the reform road, though keeping well to the rear.

On their side the Philosophic Radicals, realizing the necessity of keeping the Whigs in the line of march and the Tories in a "soft" condition, proclaimed their determination to uphold the existing social order. Class diplomacy, not class war, was their line of policy. Like the Fabian socialists of a later day, the Philosophic Radicals were deeply influenced by the English tradition of compromise, and they were willing to collaborate with anyone who was willing to collaborate with them. They were quite ready to accept half a loaf, provided that it was not poisoned by too many aristocratic ingredients. Bitterly hostile to England's aristocratic regime, the Philosophic Radicals were convinced that it could gradually be dissolved by radical reforms. This method would constitute a painless revolution; it could take place, however, only when moderate conservatives joined forces with reformers. To quiet the fears of the former, it was highly essential to assure them that the policies of the Philosophic Radicals were directed toward renovation, not toward innovation.[47] All their proposals would be consistent with constitutional methods, with a restricted suffrage, and with property rights, especially with the last. Bentham insisted that radicalism was not "dangerous" because it was strongly opposed to attacks on property rights. Such attacks, he asserted, resulted in producing more suffering among the poor than among the rich. The latter could save themselves by exporting their capital, thereby causing unemployment and destitution.[48] Moreover, attacks on property rights, by creating a feeling of insecurity among property owners, would cause them to fear losing what was "part of our being and cannot be torn from us without rending us to the quick."[49] Were men discouraged from acquiring property, all progress would be slowed up. If the state was obliged to take over property, such a step "should be attended with complete indemnity." Even sinecures should not be suppressed without compensation. Though strongly in favor of the abolition of slavery, Bentham's tender regard for property rights led him to oppose confiscation of property in slaves. What he favored was gradual emancipation of the slaves with compensation to their masters.[50]

A social revolution, involving wholesale confiscation of property,

[47] Bentham, *Plan of Parliamentary Reform* (Bowring, ed.), III, 446.
[48] Bentham, *Radicalism Not Dangerous* (Bowring, ed.), III, 608.
[49] Bentham, *The Theory of Legislation* (C. K. Ogden, ed., New York, 1931), 115.
[50] *Ibid.*, 207–209.

was, in the view of Bentham, the greatest of all calamities. "No more security, no more industry, no more abundance! Society would return to the savage state whence it emerged." It was easy to arouse among the masses "the savage instinct of plunder" by proclaiming "certain pompous maxims which are a mixture of truth and falsehood." The outcome would be great harm to individuals with but little benefit to the public. By creating general insecurity, revolutionary changes resulted in general unhappiness and retrogression. Economic equality established by confiscation, observed Bentham, could not be maintained "except by renewing the violence by which it was established. It will need an army of inquisitors and executioners as deaf to favor as to pity; insensible to the seductions of pleasure; inaccessible to personal interests; endowed with all the virtues, though in a service which destroys them all." In the end, the system of "political and religious slavery," established by confiscation, "will destroy both itself and security at the same time."[51] These profound observations of Bentham were drawn from the experience of France during the French Revolution, when the great confiscations of church and noble property were maintained by the continuous terrorism of the Jacobins and by the continuous wars of Napoleon.

The readiness of the Philosophic Radicals to agree to a propertied suffrage gave assurance to both Tories and Whigs that a reformed Parliament would not be an instrument with which to effect a revolution in property rights. To those Tories who stubbornly opposed reform, in the belief that an extension of the franchise would lead to equal division of property, Bentham replied that an equal division of property was so absurd that few held such views. "It is not *anarchy* ye are afraid of," he tartly told them, "what ye are afraid of is *good government.*"[52]

The movement launched by the Philosophic Radicals succeeded beyond their fondest hopes. As John Stuart Mill observed in 1832, there was "nothing definite and determinate in politics except Radicalism."[53] Its influence drew many Englishmen away from constitu-

51 *Ibid.,* 119–123.

52 *Plan of Parliamentary Reform* (Bowring, ed.), III, 476.

53 Quoted in K. B. Smellie, *A Hundred Years of English Government* (London, 1937), 54.

tion worship and led them to regard favorably the changes in the governmental system advocated by the Philosophic Radicals. "The class of reasoners, called at this period Radical reformers," declared Roebuck, "had produced a much more serious effect on public opinion than superficial inquirers perceived, or interested ones would acknowledge. The important practical effect was not made evident by converging and bringing over large numbers of political partisans from one banner or class to another, or by making them renounce one appellation and adopt another; but it was shown by affecting the conclusions of all classes, and inducing them, while they retained their old distinctive names, to reason after a new fashion and according to principles wholly different from those to which they had been previously accustomed."[54]

In this newly created public opinion, the industrial capitalists saw a powerful weapon with which to attack the entrenched aristocracy. The power, vigor, and resourcefulness of the wealthy manufacturers were soon enlisted on the side of the reform movement. In the opinion of an authoritative historian of the period, "Capital's desire to break down the Land's monopoly of political power gave the Reform movement after 1820 much of its driving force and most of its respectability."[55]

Conditions after 1815, when the war of classes succeeded the war of nations, were favorable to the growth of a militant opposition to the landed aristocracy. The Corn Law of 1815, enacted by a Tory Parliament, raised duties on foodstuffs to keep up war prices. The cost of living rose, which created widespread popular discontent. Taking advantage of this situation, the manufacturers denounced the landlords as the exploiters of all the other classes, because they alone benefited from high tariffs and high rents. They were silent on their own exploitation of the workers, who then earned starvation wages and labored as many as seventeen hours a day. Popular resentment was, in this way, turned against the class in power by the class that was ambitious to displace it.

Discontent among the workers was spreading rapidly. They were convinced that a reformed Parliament would be an all-powerful means

[54] Roebuck, *op. cit.*, I, 344.
[55] J. R. M. Butler, *The Passing of the Great Reform Bill* (London, 1914), 246.

of bettering their social and economic condition. Hope of emancipation among the underprivileged roused them to revolutionary fervor, which had the effect of terrorizing the aristocrats and of causing apprehension among the capitalists. This situation was clearly seen by Macaulay, who, in a speech delivered in Parliament on March 2, 1831, advocated the Reform Bill on the ground that it would admit to the suffrage only those who were safe and exclude those who were unsafe. "At present," he declared, "we oppose the schemes of the revolutionists with only one half, with only one quarter of our proper force. We say, and we say justly, that it is not by mere numbers, but by property and intelligence that the nation ought to be governed. Yet, saying this, we exclude from all share in the government great masses of property and intelligence, great numbers of those who are most interested in preserving tranquility, and who know best how to preserve it. We do more. We drive over to the side of revolution those whom we shut out from power. Is this a time when the cause of law and order can spare one of its natural allies?"[56]

Macaulay's purpose was unmistakable. It was to unite all propertied elements against the menace of a revolutionary working class, which could not be warded off by the aristocracy alone. Property was the supreme institution, "for the sake of which, chiefly, all other institutions exist."[57] It was now threatened in its entirety; therefore, it should have as its defenders both the aristocracy and the factory owners, who were to unite against their common foe by compromising their differences regarding the reform of Parliament.

The fear of a revolutionary upheaval from below was the prime reason why the Lords yielded to the Commons in the great crisis of 1832. The provisions of the Reform Bill of 1832 were indeed moderate, and for the very reason that the threat of revolution, which had precipitated its passage, led the aristocrats to make concessions to their rivals the capitalists. In regard to the suffrage, the reform was exceedingly modest: the electorate was increased from about 435,000 to about 656,000 by lowering the property qualification for voting sufficiently to include the well to do of the middle class, yet making it

[56] *The Complete Works of Lord Macaulay* (London, 1898–1920), XI, 411–412.
[57] *Ibid.*, 429.

sufficiently high to exclude the working class, the farm laborers, and most of the lower middle class. In one sense, the property qualification for voting was more clearly established by the Bill, which abolished the anomalous franchises in the boroughs that pertained to certain offices and to certain groups and established a uniform property qualification, the £10 franchise, for voting. To balance even this meager extension of the suffrage, the secret ballot was rejected. In the opinion of the reformers, the viva voce method of voting would be necessary, to supervise the new voters, as it was highly undesirable to have a body of electors who were "irresponsible in the exercise of a vast power."

Far more important than the extension of the suffrage was the change in the system of representation. Most of the rotten boroughs were abolished and representation was given to the new industrial centers, like Manchester, Glasgow, Leeds, and Birmingham. Parliament, elected by ever so restricted a franchise, would consist chiefly of members representing manufacturing interests, not, as hitherto, the landed interests. It was the obvious purpose of the Reform Bill to give the control of the Commons to the middle class. However, in the spirit of the compromise of 1832, the reformers showed consideration for aristocratic interests by refusing to accept the principle of basing representation upon population through periodic redistribution of seats. Equality of representation smacked of democracy, which all parties concerned were eager to disown.

"Liberalism of the Benthamite type," declared Dicey, "was the political faith of the time. Its triumph was signalized by the Reform Act."[58] This great measure, which marked the advent of bourgeois liberalism in England, was less a triumph of one party over another, of one class over another, of one principle over another, and more a compromise by all the parties—the Whigs, the Tories, and the Philosophic Radicals— in order to avoid a revolution. The Whigs tempered their demands. The Tories yielded. And the Philosophic Radicals accepted an extension of the suffrage so moderate that it was nothing less than a caricature of their cherished "greatest happiness" principle. It was this compromise that was the chief cause of the peaceful change from aristocratic to bourgeois liberalism. "Riot was softened into peaceable dem-

[58] Dicey, *op. cit.,* 32.

onstration, and civil war became a party strife, waged in accordance with rules, freely admitted on either side."[59]

Despite all compromises, the aristocrats were out and the capitalists were in, as the rulers of the nation. The triumph of the latter was made all the more secure just because the Reform Bill was a compromise measure. The aristocrats were not eliminated from the political scene; hence they were not inclined to resort to reaction in order to restore the old regime in England. In the foreground on the political stage were now the capitalists, who, as leaders of the middle class, were determined to be the architects of the new, industrial England.

[59] Halévy, *A History of the English People in 1815,* 176.

Chapter 8. Bourgeois Liberalism and the Irreconcilable Conflict of the Two Frances

The Reform Bill of 1832 marked the peaceful triumph of bourgeois liberalism in England. This compromise, which issued from the struggle for mastery between the old aristocracy and the rising middle class, augured well for the stability of the new order, controlled by the triumphant middle class. In France, after 1815, the same struggle began between the same classes. Would the outcome be a peaceful triumph for bourgeois liberalism in France, as in England?

The situation in France was not promising for the future of bourgeois liberalism, and the primal cause was the tremendous social upheaval effected by the French Revolution. Memories of confiscation, of exile, of death, and of the Reign of Terror created in postrevolutionary France an atmosphere of bitterness and hatred that made the problem of the transition from an old to a new order far more difficult there than in England. No stable government could be established unless it was based on the principles of the French Revolution, which had now become the great national heritage of the French people. In the words of Guizot, the question after 1815 was whether "from the ideas of 1789 and the social order founded upon them a stable government could arise that would function normally."[1]

Only a stable government could cope with the great problems, national and international, that confronted France in 1815. For a quarter of a century the nation had been in the throes of a continuous upheaval as a consequence of revolutionary changes in the social order, of a rapid succession of governments, and of ruthless wars, both civil

[1] François Guizot, *Histoire parlementaire de France* (Paris, 1863), III, 153.

and foreign. Peace and stability were now the supreme desiderata of the exhausted, disillusioned French people.

As in England, a stable government in France implied that it was accepted by the people—hence safe from both reaction and revolution. Two conditions were all essential to achieve this desideratum. In the first place, a parliament must be established, with supreme power in the state, that would have the loyal support of the propertied classes old and new. In the second place, that parliament must appeal to the masses of the people as a national institution, which, though controlled by the propertied classes, yet held out the promise of becoming the representative of the entire nation through manhood suffrage. These conditions did exist in the England of 1815; hence the peaceful triumph of bourgeois liberalism in that country.

But they did not exist in France. A parliament came into existence in accordance with the famous *Charte,* the constitution granted in 1814 by the restored Louis XVIII. A Chamber, elected by a high-propertied suffrage, was to serve as a counterpoise to the largely hereditary upper house and to the executive powers of the king. To gain popular support, the *Charte* accepted the principles of the French Revolution by establishing equality of all citizens before the law, freedom of speech and of the press, religious toleration, and protection against arbitrary arrest.[2]

The *Charte* organized the political power of the *bourgeoisie* and protected its economic interests. The purpose, frankly avowed, was to create a class balance between the aristocracy and the *bourgeoisie,* which, its framers were convinced, would bring stability to the government of the restored Bourbons. To give security to those who had acquired property as a result of the confiscations of the lands of the church and of the *émigrés*—the *biens nationaux*—the *Charte* contained a provision guaranteeing the inviolability of all property, including that "which is called *national.*" The power of the *bourgeoisie* in the government was recognized by a system of suffrage that gave the vote to those who paid at least 300 francs a year in direct taxes. Only those who paid at least 1,000 francs a year in direct taxes were permitted to be representatives. Age, as well as property, was to ensure conservatism in

[2] F. M. Anderson, *The Constitutions and Other Select Documents Illustrative of the History of France, 1789–1907* (Minneapolis, 1908), 459.

the Chamber. The minimum age required for electors was thirty years; and for candidates, forty. Open voting was prescribed in order to give a "salutary direction" to electors in voting for candidates.[3]

As a consequence of the restricted suffrage, the electorate was limited to about 90,000 out of a population of about 32,000,000. The great mass of the people—peasants, workers, shopkeepers, professionals—were outside the political life of the nation. It was a far smaller electorate in proportion to population than that which chose even the unreformed Commons in England. Yet it was the wealthy bourgeois, *la haute bourgeoisie,* who controlled the lower house, not as in England, where the aristocracy controlled the Commons. The anomalous situation in France was that, in 1815, "few had any voice in the government, but many had a stake in the country."[4] Property was more widely distributed in France than in England; there were a very large number of rural proprietors and a fairly large number of petty bourgeois; but these classes were disqualified from voting by the system of direct taxes, which bore chiefly on land. The ordinary businessman or professional man did not qualify as an elector; but the rich bourgeois who owned an estate on which he paid heavy direct taxes or the manufacturer who paid a tax on his membership in a corporation did qualify, both as an elector and as a candidate for the Chamber. Most of the peasant proprietors did not qualify, because they did not have enough land to pay the tax required for voting.

The class conflict that arose between aristocrats and bourgeois in France had a different slant from the similar class conflict in England during the same period. It came from the great contrast in position and power that existed between them. The French aristocracy of the Restoration was a ghost of its former self. Its ranks had been decimated by the guillotine and by emigration. Many of those who had emigrated had settled permanently in their new homes. Those who had returned found their standing in the nation undermined by the stigma of treason that was attached to them as having been enemies of France

[3] For good descriptions of the government of France under the Restoration, see Sherman Kent, *Electoral Procedure under Louis Philippe* (Yale University Press, 1937), 10*ff.*

[4] Frederick B. Artz, *France under the Bourbon Restoration* (Harvard University Press, 1931), 179.

during the Revolutionary and Napoleonic Wars. Like the Bourbon King Louis XVIII, the *émigrés* returned to France "in the baggage of the Allies." The prestige of the aristocracy was further undermined by the new "nobility of the sword," created by Napoleon from among his faithful generals. Many of the latter were of humble origin, "self-made soldiers become marshals, Jacobin lawyers dubbed barons, unfrocked priests turned into counts." Those thus newly ennobled emerged as "ancestors" of a new aristocracy, alongside the descendants of the aristocrats of the Old Regime.

More important still was it that the old aristocrats, as a class, had been economically ruined by the confiscations of the French Revolution. Few aristocrats in post-Revolutionary France possessed large landed estates—chiefly those who had managed to escape the confiscatory decrees and those who had returned to France after Napoleon came into power. The Restoration did not—could not—restore the confiscated lands to the returned *émigrés*. To enable some of them to acquire estates, the Bourbon government in 1825 granted an indemnity, known as the *milliard des émigrés,* to those whose lands had been confiscated during the Revolution. Many of the indemnified had neither the desire nor sufficient funds to buy an estate; so they invested the funds that they received as indemnity in the new industries that were being established by the Industrial Revolution.[5] One way of "restoring" the *émigrés* could be accomplished without endangering the public order, namely, to give them public office. Revolutionary and Napoleonic officials were ousted wholesale, and *émigrés* were appointed in their places. These changes were greatest in the army and in the diplomatic service, where aristocratic traditions still survived. The aristocracy of the Restoration might, therefore, be described as being even more an office-holding than a landholding class. The class that had formerly sat in the seats of the mighty were now reduced to the position of officeholders,

[5] There have been differences of opinion as to the extent to which the restored nobility recovered its lands. See A. Gains, "La Restauration et les biens des émigrés," *Mémoires de l'Académie Nationale de Metz* (1927), 327–484; (1928), 87–636; (1929), 3–549; I. Loutchisky, *Quelques remarques sur la vente des biens nationaux* (Paris, 1913); Ph. Sagnac, "La Division du sol pendant la Révolution et ses conséquences," *Revue d'histoire moderne et contemporaine,* V (1903–1904), 457–470; and Henri Sée, "Le Progrès de l'agriculture en France de 1815 à 1848," *Revue d'histoire économique et sociale,* IX, (1921).

whose tenure became precarious as hostility to the restored Bourbons rose among the people.

By contrast with the aristocracy the *bourgeoisie* was larger and far stronger under the Restoration than it had been under the Old Regime. It consisted of manufacturers and craftsmen, engaged largely in the luxury industries; small shopkeepers; and professionals. A new bourgeois element, the industrial capitalists, was coming to the fore with the advance of the Industrial Revolution. Machine production had been introduced into France during the eighteenth century; but as France did not have a sufficient supply of coal, modern industry had not made as great progress as it had made in England.[6] The Continental blockade of Napoleon, however, by shutting out many manufactures, gave a spurt to the development of French industry. During the Restoration, industrial progress continued, but at a pace far slower than in England.[7] In that period the tests of industrial progress were the extent of the use of the steam engine and the amount of cotton goods produced. In 1815 the steam engine was used in only fifteen industrial establishments, chiefly in those engaged in mining. The production of cotton goods increased only threefold during the period 1815 to 1840.[8] France continued to be primarily an agricultural country. Out of a population of 31,800,000 in 1826, as many as 22,500,000 were engaged, directly or indirectly, in agriculture; 4,300,000 were industrial workers; and 5,300,000 were bourgeois—businessmen, professionals, and officials.[9] Land was the most important form of property; it accounted for 66 per cent of the national income.[10]

Though not numerous in proportion to the population, the *bourgeoisie* exercised a power in the nation far beyond its numbers or its

[6] On the factory system in France during the eighteenth century, see Ch. Ballot, *L'Introduction au machinisme dans l'industrie française* (Paris, 1923); Henri Sée, "Les Origines de l'industrie capitaliste à la fin de l'Ancien Régime," *Revue historique,* CXLIV (1923), 187–200; and Al. Choulguine, "L'Organization capitaliste de l'industrie existait-elle en France à la veille de la Révolution," *Revue d'histoire économique et sociale,* X (1922), 184–218.

[7] Henri Sée, *La Vie économique de la France sous la monarchie censitaire* (Paris, 1927), 48–67.

[8] E. Levasseur, *Histoire des classes ouvrières et de l'industrie en France après 1789* (Paris, 1903–1904), I, 627.

[9] Artz, *op. cit.,* 281.

[10] Sée, *Vie économique,* 12.

industrial importance. And this power was due to two factors: one, economic; the other, political. The *bourgeoisie* controlled all commerce and industry, old and new. The abolition of the guilds and corporations by the French Revolution gave them the opportunity to develop the resources of the country, of which the *bourgeoisie* took full advantage. *Laissez faire* was now the accepted economic policy. Furthermore, the economic role of the *bourgeoisie* was based upon land, as well as upon industry. The confiscated lands of the nobles and of the church, the *biens nationaux,* had fallen into the hands of bourgeois and peasants, who constituted a new and numerous body of property owners. Many of the large noble estates and most of the small ones passed into bourgeois hands.[11] "All things considered, this fresh influx of bourgeois landowners is the most significant outcome of the revolutionary land settlement."[12]

Political influence constituted another element of bourgeois power. Unlike the situation in England, the French *bourgeoisie* could count on the support of a numerous body of peasant proprietors, in case of a conflict with a reactionary aristocracy or with a revolutionary working class. Backward in his methods of tilling the soil, largely illiterate, deeply religious, the peasant proprietor was the backbone of conservatism in France; but it was a conservatism that became an ever-present threat to those who sought to restore the Old Regime. The farm of the peasant, like the estate of the bourgeois landowner, was secured by a title that was, in origin, Revolutionary. If the title of one was invalidated, so would be the title of the other. Despite the guarantee given by the *Charte* to the purchasers of the *biens nationaux,* they did not feel entirely secure in their possessions. A threat to restore the Old Regime was, therefore, a threat against the economic interest of the liberal bourgeois, as well as against that of the conservative peasant. This common interest of bourgeois and peasant, founded in a common fear of the *émigrés,* was further strengthened by the fact that not a few of the peasant proprietors had acquired sufficiently large farms to be "metamorphosed into bourgeois."[13] These *bourgeois de campagne* con-

---

[11] *Ibid.,* 13.

[12] J. H. Clapham, *The Economic Development of France and Germany, 1815–1914* (London, 1936), 21; *cf.* G. Lefebvre, *Quatre-vingt-neuf* (Paris, 1939), 182.

[13] Loutchisky, *op. cit.,* 149.

stituted a class having political affinities with the bourgeois of the town, who could rely on peasant support when threatened by proletarian uprisings. This unity of the propertied classes in both town and country explains to a considerable degree the persistence of the social structure established in France by the French Revolution. French history during the nineteenth century gives striking illustrations of the solidarity of the two classes when confronted with an attack on their property interests, whether from the right or from the left. When Charles X threatened to restore the Old Regime, he found bourgeois and peasant united to oppose him. Though the Revolution of 1830 took place in Paris, it was accepted nonchalantly, even readily, by the conservative Catholic peasantry.

The mass of peasant proprietors were also a security against threats to the *bourgeoisie* from the socialist workers. The millions of small proprietors had one passionate desire: to keep their farms and, if possible, to add to their holdings. And the millions of landless agricultural workers had one hope: to acquire a little farm, from their savings or from a fortunate inheritance or as a result of a marriage with the daughter of a peasant proprietor. A socialist uprising of the city workers would threaten the security of the peasant proprietor and blast the hope of the agricultural laborer. For these reasons the rural population supported, solidly and efficaciously, the *bourgeoisie* in the towns whenever socialist threats to property rights became menacing. Such threats from the left came in the June Days of 1848 and again in the Paris Commune of 1871, when socialist uprisings were mercilessly crushed by bourgeois governments with the solid support of the rural population.

No sooner was Louis XVIII on the throne than a conflict arose between aristocrats and bourgeois. It was waged on a basis far different from the class conflict in England, where a powerful landed aristocracy, whose estates had been consolidated and even enlarged by the enclosures, confronted the new class of industrial capitalists whose economic power was growing apace with the rapid advance of the Industrial Revolution. In France it was a conflict between an aristocracy, largely shorn of its estates, that was obsessed with reactionary, feudal ideas, and a *bourgeoisie* whose ideas were liberal but whose economic power was based more on commerce, on finance, and on land than on modern industry. It would not be too much of an exaggeration to characterize this conflict as one between aristocrats who had no land and capitalists who had no factories.

Yet this conflict had a tremendous significance for France and for the world. It marked the first battle in the war *à outrance* between the two Frances that had emerged from the undigested French Revolution. One was *la nouvelle France,* the France of the liberals, of the republicans, of the socialists, who, however divided in their policies, were united in their unswerving devotion to the principles of the French Revolution. *La nouvelle France* was libertarian in spirit, egalitarian in social outlook, democratic in politics, and freethinking in religion. It aimed to fulfill the promise of the French Revolution by establishing the reign of equality, when every citizen would have every opportunity to develop his virtues and his talents. The other France was *l'ancienne France,* the France of the reactionaries, of the monarchists, and of the clericals, whose views and policies were inspired by the traditions of the Old Regime. *L'ancienne France* was authoritarian in spirit, aristocratic in social outlook, royalist in politics, and Catholic in religion. The French Revolution, according to *l'ancienne France,* was the source of all evil in the modern world, in that it set loose the spirit of anarchy and disruption, which, unless checked, would destroy everything worth while in civilization. It aimed to restore the Old Regime or, at least, its spirit, by promoting respect for such long-established institutions and traditions as the church, the family, and the monarchy.

As a consequence of the "great divide" created by the French Revolution, a chasm yawned between the two Frances, so deep and so wide that all attempts to bridge it encountered insuperable difficulties. The two never met except at the barricades. The history of France since 1789 might be described as one of continuous civil war, now open, now hidden, now masked. Uprisings, successful or abortive, heralded every generation under different names, with different slogans, and over different issues: reactionaries versus liberals, royalists versus republicans, conservatives versus socialists, and fascists versus communists. The quarrel between the present and the past, which jeopardized the future of France, shook the political structure to its very foundation. It was not least among the causes that led to the fall of France during the Second World War. All the governments from the French Revolution to the Third French Republic were short lived; each came into existence and went out of existence as the result of violence, whether of war, or revolution, or of a *coup d'état*. During the seventy years of the life of the Third French Republic, the war between the two Frances continued; it shifted, however, from the barricade to the floor of parliament, where it was waged in subdued, yet sharp, hostility between the parties on the left and the parties on the right. Now and then, as in the MacMahon, Boulanger, and Dreyfus affairs, the conflicts threatened to shift from parliament to the barricade. In a speech delivered in the Chamber in 1891, Clemenceau, speaking for the left, dramatically and defiantly stated the division in France as follows: "This admirable Revolution from which we have arisen is not finished and still continues. We are still participants in it; always do the same men fight the same enemies. Yea, what our ancestors wanted, we also want. We meet always the same opponents. You have not changed, and neither have we. This struggle must then go on until one side or the other wins a definite and decisive victory."[14]

How to unite the two Frances? That was the problem that confronted the generation after the Napoleonic Wars. Two attempts were made to solve this problem: one by the bourgeois liberals and the other by the clericals. If ever a dynasty needed to create a psychology of obedience to its rule, it was that of the Bourbons. Far from creating stability, the system of compromises established by the *Charte* had the effect of generating a feeling of instability, which pervaded the entire nation. "From 1815 to 1830," remarked that irascible but keen observer, Proudhon, "the country, as legally constituted, was continually at war with authority."[15] The restored Bourbons reasserted the doctrine of divine right, but it received only a mocking response from the people. Parliament was sneered at as a class institution created for the special benefit of the wealthy bourgeois; it was not regarded as a legislative body representing the nation. No regime could long exist under such circumstances. Sooner or later, a misstep that would cause only embarrassment to a stable government was likely to become the prelude to a revolution against the unstable Bourbon regime. The latter, therefore, had to watch its every step. So much energy was consumed by the Bourbons

[14] Quoted in *La République française* (New York, January, 1944).

[15] Pierre Joseph Proudhon, *General Idea of the Revolution in the Nineteenth Century*, trans. from the French by J. B. Robinson (London, 1923), 139.

in merely maintaining themselves that they had little left for the important problems of statesmanship. Bourbon France has little to show in the way of reforms, comparable with Tory England during the same period.[16]

Bourgeois liberalism essayed to overcome these obstacles to a stable order in France. A political group known as the "Doctrinaires" appeared, which played a prominent part in the politics of the Restoration. In numbers the Doctrinaires were so few that, as their opponents derisively said, they "could all find room on a sofa." But their influence on the political thought of the Restoration was considerable. The many liberal groups, both inside and outside of parliament, looked to the Doctrinaires for guidance in the struggle against the forces of reaction and revolution that soon appeared from behind the Bourbon throne. What the Doctrinaires sought to establish was a *modus vivendi* founded on a reconcilation of the Bourbon monarchy with the principles of the French Revolution. They were firmly convinced that the *Charte* was the best means of effecting this reconciliation, in that it created a balance of forces as well as a balance of classes: of legitimacy and constitutionalism, of tradition and progress, of the hereditary principle in the executive and the elective principle in the legislature, of an established church and religious freedom, and of authority in government and civil liberty in society.

In this mood of political compromise, the thoughts of the French bourgeois liberals turned toward England. Once more, as in the days of the Old Regime, the English constitutional system roused the admiration of French liberal thinkers. And their admiration was intensified by the fact that England, alone of the nations in Western Europe, had withstood the shocks of the French Revolution. She had also been the prime factor in liberating the Continent from the domination of Napoleon. The rapid progress of the Industrial Revolution in England had placed her in the very forefront of modern industrial nations. After 1815, England was generally regarded as the strongest, the richest, the freest nation in Europe. "Away from Rousseau and back to Montesquieu!" was now the slogan of French liberalism. Rousseau signified the Reign of Terror, and Montesquieu, ordered liberty under a system of "guaranteeism," with its guarantees of civil liberties, religious toleration, the

16 See *supra*, p. 132.

powers of parliament, the independence of the judiciary, and the rights of property. The English government, declared Royer-Collard, was an "honor to mankind"; it had succeeded in raising the nation "to the highest degree of liberty in domestic affairs and of glory and power in foreign affairs."[17]

Foremost among the Doctrinaires was Pierre Paul Royer-Collard (1763–1845), now just a name, but in his day the most famous parliamentary orator in France. His chief disciple, François Guizot, was destined to become more famous than his master. Others, less known in their day and now almost lost in oblivion, were Camille Jordan and the liberal nobles the Duc de Broglie and the Comte de Serre.[18]

Royer-Collard was the most eloquent and most profound representative of bourgeois liberalism during the Bourbon period. He was elected to the Chamber in 1815 and continued to be a member of that body until his retirement in 1842. His speeches were received with great respect by his associates and were highly influential in bourgeois circles throughout the nation. All during the Restoration, the Chamber resounded with Royer-Collard's eloquent defense of the *Charte,* and he became known as the "philosopher of the *Charte.*" It was his great ambition to give a philosophy to the Restoration, as Rousseau had given a philosophy to the French Revolution. The *Charte,* declared Royer-Collard, was "an indissoluble union between the royal power from which it emanates and the national liberties that it recognizes and consecrates."[19] An uncompromising champion of compromise, he accepted legitimacy wholeheartedly, and tirelessly sought to make it acceptable to the nation by giving it a liberal direction. But whenever the Bourbon government deviated from the *Charte,* either in letter or in spirit, it encountered the strenuous opposition of Royer-Collard.

When read today, Royer-Collard's speeches seem wordy, turgid, abstract, and unrealistic; yet they filled an emotional void in Restoration France. Royer-Collard's eloquent defense of individual freedom and constitutional government gave to the bourgeois the emotional satisfaction of being the champions of freedom, and, at the same time,

[17] A. de Barante, *La Vie politique de M. Royer-Collard* (Paris, 1861), II, 219.

[18] For an excellent description of the Doctrinaires, see C. H. Pouthas, *Guizot pendant la Restauration* (Paris, 1923), 167–172.

[19] Barante, *op cit.*, II, 16.

of being the defenders of the established order against revolution. Altruism joined hands with self-interest to maintain a social order that was, at the same time, a product of a past revolution and a barrier to a future one. A man of high personal rectitude, Royer-Collard was serious-minded, even austere, with a nineteenth-century liberal's manner of presenting his views as if they were eternal truths. Behind his high seriousness and temperamental reserve, there was a genuine and deep humanitarianism, *"un peu hautaine et lointaine."*[20] Royer-Collard, like his more famous contemporaries De Tocqueville and Lamartine, was part of a political tradition that is peculiarly French, in that he was more imposing as an intellectual figure on the political scene than important as a practical statesman.

The Doctrinaires had by no means a monopoly of liberalism in France. On their left in the Chamber appeared a Liberal party, organized in 1817, that advocated a far more progressive regime than that established by the *Charte*. The Liberals accepted the *Charte* not as a finality, as did the Doctrinaires, but only as an installment of a more liberal system of government. They constantly opposed the Bourbon regime as reactionary in its ideals, unscrupulous in its methods, and despotic in its aims. The elections of 1817 showed that the Liberals, not the Doctrinaires, had considerable popular support. Despite active government hostility, they won 180 seats out of about 420.[21]

The spokesman of the Liberal opposition was Benjamin Constant (1767–1830), whose influence on political opinion in France rivaled that of Royer-Collard. Constant was one of the most interesting figures of the Restoration. In his early days, his associations were with the literary lights of Paris, and he became well known as the protégé of Madame de Staël. Constant can be said to have combined three lives in one: a romantic literary life, a dissolute private life, and a liberal political life. As the author and self-created hero of the romantic novel *Adolphe,* he became the glamour boy of the romantic movement in France. In his private life, Constant was as profligate as Royer-Collard was austere. He was so dissolute that he finally passed beyond the boudoir of the mistress to the brothel of the prostitute. Gambling was another of his

20 P. Thureau-Dangin, *Le Parti libéral sous la Restauration* (Paris, 1876), 419.

21 S. Charléty, *La Restauration (1815–1830)*, in *Histoire de France contemporaine* (E. Lavisse, ed., Paris, 1921), IV, 134–137.

consuming passions, which he indulged with nonchalant recklessness. "Constant had insight enough to know his vices but not character enough to overcome them."[22] Yet this romantic profligate had a keen political intelligence and a staunch devotion to liberal principles, which he ardently championed all during the Restoration. As a member of the Chamber, from 1819 to his death in 1830, he consistently opposed the Bourbon government, which he deeply distrusted as being engaged in undermining the liberties of the people. Constant became famous as an orator who had a capacity both "for ironical and disconcerting tricks of argument" and for clear, relentless criticism of Bourbon policies. His "concise and subtle language, his agility in argument, the unexpectedness of his retorts, embarrassed and irritated his adversaries, who were no match for him."[23]

Could the bourgeois liberals who accepted the *Charte* unite the two Frances, thereby bringing stability to the Bourbon regime? From the very outset they were confronted with great difficulties. They were obliged to formulate a philosophy that would reconcile the rule of the wealthy few with the democratic principles of the French Revolution. Unlike the reactionaries, the bourgeois liberals could not appeal to traditional loyalties to uphold the constitutional system established by the *Charte*. They were also in the embarrassing position of supporting a social order that was, itself, the product of the French Revolution. A moderate group defending a revolutionary social order constituted a glaring contradiction, which would arouse distrust among the right and division among the left.

Bourgeois liberalism in France, confronted with more obstacles and with greater difficulties than those in England, developed a political philosophy that was, at the same time, boldly bourgeois and timorously liberal. Intense class consciousness, sharpened by fear of reaction and of revolution, led the French bourgeois liberals to propound theories concerning the position of parliament, the status of the electorate, and the function of political parties in a constitutional state that were strikingly at variance with those of the English bourgeois liberals. In the view of the French bourgeois liberals, the *Charte* established France as a parliamentary state, but without the supremacy of parliament in

[22] Thureau-Dangin, *op. cit.*, 35.

[23] E. W. Schermerhorn, *Benjamin Constant* (Boston, 1924), 33.

the government. That was obviously a contradiction, which the arch theoretician Royer-Collard sought to resolve. The Chamber, he reasoned, was not a representative body; it represented neither the nation nor the electorate nor the constituencies. Only a body elected by manhood suffrage could claim to be a representative institution. Under the *Charte* the electors did not exercise a right, but they did fulfill a function.[24] The French Revolution, in its worst aspects, warned Royer-Collard, "was nothing else than the doctrine of popular representation in action."[25] What, then, was the Chamber? It was a "power," a mandatory of the *Charte* that created the Chamber to be the depository of the *interests* of the nation. Therefore it was not a legislature representing the people; hence the right to vote was given only to those who owned property.[26] In this sense, according to Royer-Collard, the Chamber was a power to be consulted by the king, not a legislature with the right to pass laws. Its chief duties were to act as a guardian of the civil liberties and to call the attention of the government to needful reforms.[27] How could the civil liberties guaranteed by the *Charte* be maintained against encroachments by a despotic monarch? Royer-Collard's answer was (1) by an independent judiciary, appointed for life; (2) by a free press, acting as mediator between government and people; and (3) by a system of local government, which, as in England, would create popular sentiment in favor of liberty.

The refusal of the bourgeois liberals to accept the historic liberal principle of parliamentary supremacy is not hard to explain. In France that principle had a terrifying precedent, the National Convention of 1792 to 1795. It was associated with the revolutionary doctrine of popular sovereignty, which, in the opinion of the bourgeois liberals, had generated the Reign of Terror. As a liberal, Royer-Collard repudiated the sovereignty of one person. As "the living incarnation of the *bourgeoisie* of his age," he vehemently opposed popular sovereignty, which led to the omnipotence of parliament, the "theoretical basis of despotism and of revolution because its implication is that neither fundamental laws

24 Barante, *op. cit.*, I, 228.
25 *Ibid.*, 231.
26 *Ibid.*, 228; II, 36.
27 *Ibid.*, I, 279.

nor national rights have any existence."[28] Popular sovereignty, he asserted, was nothing less than the sovereignty of force, which exercised the most absolute of all absolute power. It had neither limitations nor duties nor conscience and acted without reference to what was good or bad, and without consideration for the past or for the future. The desire of the day alone dominated those who acted according to this evil doctrine, a desire that quickly nullified what had been done "the day before without responsibility for the day after."[29] Where, then, lay sovereignty? According to Royer-Collard, the only sovereignty that merited the name and was superior to that of the people as to that of the king was "the sovereignty of reason, the only true legislator of mankind."[30]

Opposition to popular sovereignty logically led to opposition to its practical application, manhood suffrage. Like the former, the latter was associated with the National Convention, which, in theory at least, had been elected by a democratic suffrage. Democracy, declared Royer-Collard, in its very nature was "violent, militaristic, ruinous."[31] In domestic affairs it had brought anarchy, tyranny, misery, and despotism. Having no property, no stake in the country, the workers were constantly exposed to the temptation of being antisocial. With manhood suffrage "would come the terrible power that engenders revolution." Hence a propertied suffrage was established by the *Charte* to make sure that the elector was above the antisocial passions of the multitude.[32] Only when the state was controlled by the bourgeois was there a certainty of political stability and economic progress. To interest the bourgeois in politics in order to translate his business capacity into political capacity was the real problem in France. That was why the *Charte* created a Chamber, controlled by the bourgeois. "Voilà notre démocratie, telle que je la vois et la conçois."[33]

Even more conservative than his views concerning the suffrage was Royer-Collard's conception of the status of the electorate as a body.

[28] *Archives parlementaires*, XXXIV (Paris, 1876), 132.
[29] Barante, *op. cit.*, II, 463.
[30] *Ibid.*, 459.
[31] *Ibid.*, 469.
[32] *Ibid.*, 36.
[33] *Ibid.*, 134.

In his opinion, the vote was neither a natural right nor a special privilege but a "political function." And the voter was a state *fonctionnaire* with special duties, contingent on special qualifications. The right to vote was "a moral right not a decree of fate, and every one knows that the property qualification is only a sign of this moral right."[34] According to this theory, the electorate was an integral part of the state machine, like the civil service or the army.

Viewing the voter as a state functionary, the Doctrinaires betrayed a fatal incapacity to comprehend that an electorate, even a greatly limited one such as existed in England before 1832, was the primal source of political power in a truly liberal state. And this misunderstanding, as well as the rejection of parliamentary supremacy, arose from the political timidity that was so characteristic of the bourgeois liberals in France during the first half of the nineteenth century. They dared not assert the power of a parliament that they controlled; hence they vitiated the importance of that institution. They dared not appeal to the masses for political cooperation; hence they lowered the suffrage to the condition of a function exercised by a limited group of privileged citizens. It was not until the establishment of the Third Republic that the French bourgeois had sufficient courage and sufficient faith in democracy to entrust their interests to an all-powerful parliament elected by manhood suffrage—"the master of us all," in the words of Gambetta.

More truly a liberal than Royer-Collard was Constant. He had a keener insight into political realities and a profounder understanding of the problem of parliamentary government than that exhibited by Royer-Collard and the Doctrinaires. Like the latter, Constant opposed popular sovereignty, though not so vehemently. In his view, the main problem of liberty was the limitation of sovereignty, whether that of the king or of the people. A bill of rights that protected the liberty of the individual was, according to Constant, a limitation of sovereignty.

Constant was emphatically opposed to manhood suffrage. Leisure, in his opinion, was necessary in order that a man be enlightened and be capable of independent judgment. "Those whom poverty keeps in constant dependence," he declared, "because they are condemned to daily labor are no more enlightened than children.... Property alone, by giving sufficient leisure, renders a man capable of exercising his

[34] *Ibid.,* 283.

political rights."[35] The electoral law in France was, in his view,
"nationale et propriétaire," in that it gave the vote to a large number
of Frenchmen and made the franchise accessible to anyone who
acquired sufficient property. There could be no conflict of interests,
he argued, between voters and nonvoters, because there was no insurmountable barrier to becoming a voter. The best guarantee of social
peace was to have a body of voters who supported the existing order.[36]
The ambition of the poor man should be to acquire property and become
a voter. But, if he were given the vote on the basis of manhood suffrage,
he would use it to acquire property without working, namely, by
invading property rights. Therefore, manhood suffrage would give
the poor unlimited power for mischief, with dire consequences for
the nation, which would become the victim of disorder and corruption.[37]

Possessing a far keener mind than Royer-Collard, Constant realized
that the electoral base, during the Restoration, was not broad enough to
guarantee social peace. The French Revolution, he asserted, had given
the people the habit of rapid change. In critical times little effort was
required to overthrow a government. "The French people do not
attack their government; they merely withdraw from it and the
government quickly collapses."[38] Constant's solution of the problem
of stability was more advanced and more consistent than that proposed
by the Doctrinaires. He had the political perspicacity to realize that an
electoral system, based on property, that excluded the numerous class
of small property owners in France invited disaster. It was the small
property owners between the poor and the rich, he asserted, who were
the strongest supporters of a conservative social order. When a small
owner lost his property, he lost everything; hence he was a passionate
defender of property rights. Constant, therefore advocated the extension
of the suffrage by lowering the property qualification to include every
man who made a living without having to work for wages.[39] An
electorate, *"à la fois nationale et propriétaire,"* that chose deputies

[35] Quoted in Artz, *op. cit.,* 67.
[36] Constant, "De la doctrine politique," *Collection complète des ouvrages* (Paris, 1818),
II, 194–201.
[37] Constant, *Cours de politique constitutionnelle* (Paris, 1872), I, 253.
[38] Quoted in G. de Lauris, *Benjamin Constant et les idées libérales* (Paris, 1904), 50.
[39] Constant, "Histoire de la session de la Chambre des Députés, depuis 1816 jusqu'en
1817," *Collection complètes des ouvrages,* II, 191.

directly would create a true representative system in France, because it would be broadly based, *"large et nationale,"* consisting of the mass of citizens having property, who were interested in maintaining the social order because they had a keen sense of their interests.[40]

Like the Doctrinaires, Constant was a protagonist of a bourgeois social order. But, unlike them, he desired one that would be undefiled by aristocratic influences that came from the ownership of land. Experience had taught him, he declared, "that industrial property in our time was more real and far more powerful than was property in land."[41]

Constant did favor parliamentary supremacy. A parliament elected directly by property owners, small and large, of land and of industry, would be sufficiently powerful to exercise supreme authority in the state. In discussing the parliamentary system in England, he had the mistaken notion that the king was a "neutral power," whose chief function was to bring about the cooperation of parliament, ministry, and judiciary in order to have unity in the government. In appointing and dismissing a ministry the king should, therefore, consult the wishes of parliament.[42]

Neither the moderate liberalism of Royer-Collard nor the advanced liberalism of Constant made a sufficiently powerful appeal to the French nation. To succeed, bourgeois liberalism had to have at least the passive support of the aristocracy or, failing that, the active support of the masses. It got neither. On the contrary, it encountered the bitter hostility of both. The *Charte,* on which rested the hopes of the bourgeois liberals, was a political compromise that could not for long be maintained, because of the deep social divisions created by the French Revolution. In the opinion of Louis Blanc, the struggle between reactionaries and liberals during the Restoration was a class struggle between artistocrats and bourgeois.[43] That was also the view of De Tocqueville, who declared that the period between 1789 and 1830 was "a long and violent struggle between the old feudal aristocracy and

40 *Ibid.*, 183*ff.*; 200–201.

41 Constant, *Cours de politique constitutionnelle,* I, 251*n.*

42 *Ibid.*, 19–21; see also J. Heistand, *Benjamin Constant et la doctrine parlementaire* (Geneva, 1928), 71–77.

43 Louis Blanc, *The History of Ten Years, 1830–1840,* trans. from the French by W. K. Kelly (Philadelphia, 1848), I, 100*ff.*

the *bourgeoisie*." [44] A political system based deliberately on compromise was novel in France, which, since 1789, had lived dangerously, going from one political extreme to another. It was "an ensemble admirably perfect in its logic and in its fragility."[45] The reactionary policies of the Bourbons were due less to the tyrannical impulses of a dynasty that "had never learned anything and had never forgotten anything" and more to the desperate desires of a dying aristocracy to regain its former privileges, estates, and prestige. What the bourgeois liberals failed to understand was that the system of compromise in England, which they so much admired, was the outcome of a long historic process. Like their forebears, during the French Revolution, who believed that liberty could be established by a Declaration of the Rights of Man, the Doctrinaires believed that compromise could be established by a *Charte*.

Without the cooperation of the aristocrats, there was always the possibility of reaction, as fatal to stability as was revolution. Realizing this situation, the Doctrinaires made earnest appeals to the aristocrats to accept *la nouvelle France*. Two propertied classes exist, argued Guizot, who must unite to rule the nation. They were, on the one hand, those belonging to the traditional aristocracy, who possessed social influence and desired to maintain their importance; on the other hand, those who were ambitious to acquire property and to rise in the social scale.[46] The latter, the "new interests," had once been aggressive, in order to conquer a place for themselves in society, but now, having succeeded in becoming property owners, they were on the defensive. The *Charte,* "having found them strong, recognized them as legitimate."[47] These "men of the Revolution" were, therefore, no longer intractable and would gladly cooperate with the aristocrats to establish stability in France. By accepting the changes made by the French Revolution, Guizot argued, the aristocrats would follow the wise example set by the Jacobites in England, who had accepted the changes made by the Revolution of 1688. In this way they would create a powerful, conservative party in the Chamber, representing the landed

[44] Alexis de Tocqueville, "Note sur la classe moyenne et le peuple," *Oeuvres complètes* (Paris, 1864–1867), IX, 515.

[45] E. Spuller, *Royer-Collard* (Paris, 1895), 139.

[46] F. Guizot, *Des moyens de gouvernement et d'opposition* (Paris, 1821), 252.

[47] *Ibid.*, 187.

interests as did the Tory party in England.[48] By a "happy combination of luck and wisdom" the two propertied classes in England were reconciled to the sharing of political power. This "political entente" between the contending classes resulted in establishing stability with liberty. Guizot was convinced that the *Charte* would bring about a similar happy situation in France, provided that the aristocracy loyally adhered to its provisions.[49]

With the appeal came also a warning. None were so strong and, at the same time, so quick to take alarm as property owners, admonished Guizot. The aristocrats who dreamed of recovering their confiscated estates should keep in mind that both Napoleon and Louis XVIII had guaranteed the property rights of those who had acquired the *biens nationaux*.[50] The bourgeois liberals were adamant in their opposition to a restoration of the Old Regime. "Control by privilege," declared Royer-Collard, "can no longer be imposed on this nation.... The existing social order, confirmed by our misfortunes, by our glory, by our sacrifices, must not be put in jeopardy. However serious the situation that might confront the monarchy it should not under any circumstances appeal to the privileged class for help."[51]

The bourgeois liberals were not slow to admonish the government that the wealthy *bourgeois accredités* would resent attacks on the holders of the *biens nationaux* as attacks on property rights in general.[52] Only by guaranteeing these beneficiaries of the Revolution could France be saved from a complete overturn, which would ruin the holders of the *biens nationaux* without benefiting the original aristocratic owners.[53] By insisting on the maintenance of the *status quo* in post-Revolutionary France, the *bourgeoisie* sought to cover with the mantle of conservatism a social and political order that had come into existence as a consequence of a social revolution. And the beneficiaries of the revolution, "gorged with the *biens nationaux*," now appealed to its victims for cooperation to maintain their gains!

Neither the appeals nor the threats of the bourgeois were heeded by the aristocrats. Dispossessed of their estates, deprived of their privileges,

[48] *Ibid.*, Chap. XIII.
[49] Guizot, *Mémoires pour servir à l'histoire de mon temps* (Paris, 1858), I, 111.
[50] Guizot, *Des moyens*, 191.
[51] Barante, *op. cit.*, II, 8.
[52] Guizot, *Des moyens*, 344-345.
[53] Constant, *Discours à la Chambres des Députés* (Paris, 1827-1828), I, 8.

shorn of their prestige, the aristocrats were in an anomalous position during the Restoration. They were in office but not in power. And they fluttered among the ruins of their ancient seats of power, furious at the work of the Revolution and burning with hatred against those responsible for it. To the bitter conflict of class interest was added the blind fury of revenge. Many aristocrats gave themselves over "to caste egotism or to bitter memories. Their pretentions were arrogant, and their pride, puerile, which resulted in widespread distrust and irritation."[54] The French aristocrats became hopelessly reactionary and lent a willing ear to every plot, to every scheme, to every suggestion to overthrow the constitutional system established by the *Charte,* in order to restore the Old Regime.

An irreconcilable aristocracy was not the only problem that confronted the bourgeois liberals in France. Equally serious was the appearance of a revolutionary working class that had inherited the Jacobin traditions of the Reign of Terror. Hence the bourgeois liberals had to wage war on two fronts—on the left as well as on the right. The new social order that was emerging as a result of the progress of the Industrial Revolution exhibited economic inequalities almost as glaring as those under the Old Regime. And these inequalities were all the more galling to the workers, in that the French Revolution had proclaimed the principle of equality, a principle that the *Charte* had, in some measure, recognized by decreeing equality before the law of all citizens.

The brunt of the new economic inequality fell upon the working class. Freed from the restrictions imposed by the guilds of the Old Regime, they became the victims of nascent capitalism, which was as eager to exploit human labor as it was to develop natural resources. Hours of labor were inhumanly long; wages were indecently low; and conditions in the factories were dangerously unhealthy. In the textile mills of Alsace, in 1828, the normal working day was from fourteen to fifteen hours. In the Lille factories, the average wage was twenty cents a day for an adult male. Women and children were employed under outrageous conditions.[55]

In desperation, the workers turned to trade-unionism as a means of

[54] Guizot, *Du gouvernement de la France* (Paris, 1820), 184.

[55] Ch. Rist., "Durée du travail dans l'industrie française de 1820 à 1870," *Revue d'économie politique,* XI (1897), and P. Quentin-Bauchart, *La Crise sociale de 1848* (Paris, 1920), 52ff.

raising their standard of living. But they encountered a great obstacle in the *loi Le Chapelier,* enacted in 1791, which, like the English Combination Laws, forbade unions of employees or of employers. Wages were to be determined by freedom of contract *d'individu à individu.* Under the Empire, a system of industrial passports—the *livret*—had been instituted, which became a convenient method of controlling the movements of the workers by the authorities.[56] Heavy penalties were imposed by the *Code pénal* of 1810 on violations of the *loi Le Chapelier;* but these penalties were applied on combinations of workers, not on those of employers.[57] The word of the employer, not that of the employee, was to be taken as to the amount of wages paid to the latter.[58] Because of the antiunion laws, the workers either organized secret unions or masked their unions as mutual benevolent societies. Despite the law, strikes were frequent and violent, more like revolutionary uprisings than peaceful stoppages of work.

Disfranchised by the *Charte,* forbidden to form trade-unions, their movements recorded and controlled by the *livret,* the French workers were convinced that the only road to freedom lay in revolution, the open sesame to universal happiness. Of the working class in France can it be said more truly than of the working class in any other country that it was revolutionary almost from its appearance on the scene of modern industry. Discontent with conditions and hostility to the government might, at some critical moment, sound the call to the barricades; and the call was certain to be answered.

Both bourgeois and aristocrat recoiled with dread at the specter of revolution, which was ever before their eyes. They had a wholesome fear of the element in the nation other than that "which reads the papers and follows the debates in the Chamber, which invests capital, commands industry, and owns the soil."[59] The propertied classes agreed on one policy, at least, *i.e.,* the suppression of all working-class aspirations. According to the property qualifications required by the *Charte* the workers were completely eliminated from the political life

[56] Sée, *Vie économique,* 116–118.

[57] A. V. Dicey, *Lectures on the Relation between Law and Public Opinion in England during the Nineteenth Century* (London, 1914), 468*ff.*

[58] O. Festy, *Le Mouvement ouvrier* (Paris, 1908), 20.

[59] Quoted in Thureau-Dangin, *op. cit.,* 498.

of the nation. Just because they upheld the parliamentary system, the bourgeois liberals were all the more eager to disfranchise the workers, who, if given the vote, would control parliament because of their great numbers. A high property qualification for voting gave the bourgeois numerical superiority over the aristocrats and, at the same time, reduced to political nullity the most numerous class in the nation. Bourgeois class interests could ask for nothing better in the sphere of government.

The bourgeois liberals in France were in the curious and trying position of defending the French Revolution against the reactionaries on the right and of defending the established order against the revolutionaries on the left. *La nouvelle France,* observed Guizot, "had at the same time a revolution to preserve and a revolution to combat. It is, therefore, necessary that she hasten the consolidation of the new order, and, at the same time, resist attempts to restore the old order."[60] To accomplish this twofold task, the bourgeois liberals were compelled to make two different appeals for support. To the aristocrats they turned the defiant face of liberty and appealed to the nation to uphold the liberties established by the French Revolution. To the workers they turned the cold face of property and appealed to the numerous bourgeois and peasant proprietors to uphold the rights of property against socialistic threats of confiscation. Even more than those in England did the bourgeois liberals in France ring the changes on the importance of property in the social order and of the *bourgeoisie* in the conduct of the government. A veritable cult of property arose among the French bourgeois liberals, and it became more and more ardent as their interests were more and more challenged by both left and right. That section of the *bourgeoisie* the origin of whose wealth was the *biens nationaux* owed their riches less to their capacity as capitalists than to the Revolutionary legislation of which they had been the beneficiaries.

In the light of this historic fact, the bourgeois liberals could not maintain—at least, logically—that property was a natural right. The more advanced of the group, notably Constant, propounded the theory that property was a "social convention," the essential institution on which rested the security of society. Nevertheless it was sacred and inviolable.

[60] Guizot, *Des moyens,* 342.

Without property, humanity would have remained in a savage state, because there would have been no division of labor, the basis of all the arts and the sciences.[61] The two forms of property, land and industry, had need of each other and should, therefore, cooperate to preserve the constitutional system that protects them both. What industry especially needed was peace, in order to get every benefit from its enterprise. For this reason the influence of industry was to be exerted against reaction and revolution.[62]

As a "social convention," property, according to Constant, was subject to control by society, which had the power over property that it did not have over life and over opinion.[63] Of property owners, capitalists were the most important; without their consent "no loan could be floated, no treaty signed, not a shot fired.[64] Though not a natural right itself, observed Constant, property was the bulwark of the whole system of natural rights. Attacks on property provoked resistance, which, in turn, led to violations of liberty and human rights.[65]

The sensitiveness of the French bourgeois liberals regarding property rights led them to emphasize the importance of the *bourgeoisie,* whom they considered the special custodians of property rights. It was in France, even more than in England, that the idea of the predominant role of the *bourgeoisie* in society and in government was assiduously and fervently advocated. Like Royer-Collard and even more truculently than he, Guizot believed that the interest of the whole of society was best represented in the *bourgeoisie,* which he considered the most vital element in the modern social order. "In the class above," he declared, "there exists a tendency to dominate against which we must be on guard. In the class below there is ignorance and the lack of independence as a result of which there is a complete lack of political capacity."[66] The power of the *bourgeoisie* did not come from legal privileges, he argued, but "it is a powerful and formidable fact, a theory in action, capable of defending itself against opponents. Past centuries had prepared the way for it; the French Revolution proclaimed it. All new

[61] Constant, *Cours de politique constitutionelle,* I, 113–114.
[62] Constant, *Discours,* II, 446–447.
[63] L. Dumont-Wilden, *Vie de Benjamin Constant* (Paris, 1930), 178.
[64] Constant, *Discours,* II, 446.
[65] Constant, *Cours de politique constitutionelle,* I, 114.
[66] Barante, *op. cit.,* I, 290.

interests promptly attached themselves to the *bourgeoisie,* whose security could not be disturbed without danger to the established order."[67] There was a profound difference between a system of inequality arising from aristocratic privilege and one arising from bourgeois capacity to acquire wealth. The former was established by law and custom, but the latter, *inégalité de fait,* conformed to natural law. It was idle to dream of restoring the aristocracy to power. All that now remained for the former ruling class were *les souvenirs de l'histoire.* The *bourgeoisie,* and only the *bourgeoisie,* could serve as a medium of reconciliation of the two Frances, by drawing both within the orbit of its interests and by establishing ordered freedom and security of all property.

Far from bolstering up the regime established by the *Charte,* the bourgeois liberals infuriated all the elements opposed to it. The complete identification of the social and political order with bourgeois class interests left no alternative to the aristocrats except reaction, and no alternative to the workers except revolution. The bourgeois liberals had failed to solve the problem of uniting the two Frances.

Was there another solution possible of the problem of stability? Could a method be devised to unite the two Frances other than that proposed by the bourgeois liberals? To answer these questions, a new school of thought arose in France, which became known as "clericalism." Its supporters were deeply convinced that only a revival of Catholicism could unite the two Frances by re-creating the psychology of obedience to the rule of the Bourbons among the French people. Deeply impregnated with the spirit of the Old Regime, the clericals proposed to reconstitute the ancient unity of throne and altar that the French Revolution first had sundered and then had separately destroyed. To be effective, clericalism needed to be advocated by intellectuals who could express their ideas persuasively and attractively. Logic and style were all important in the creation of public opinion in France. The clerical philosophers had both, and their influence in France and in other Catholic lands was deep and wide throughout the nineteenth century.

Chief of the clerical philosophers was the Savoyard Joseph de Maistre (1753–1821). For many years De Maistre was the diplomatic representative of Savoy in Russia. His chief interest, however, was philosophy,

[67] *Ibid.,* 456.

not diplomacy. He became famous as the philosopher of reaction during the Restoration; and his writings were the authoritative sources of reactionary ideas that inspired the policies of the despots of that period. In some respects, this "prophet of the past" resembled the rationalist *philosophes* of the eighteenth century, whom he greatly detested. Like them he had logic, he had style, and he had wit.

According to De Maistre, the supreme importance of the church in history was political and social, not theological or even religious. More than any other institution did the church prove itself necessary for the preservation of the social and political order in human society. Rarely, if ever, did De Maistre discuss Catholic doctrines in their purely religious meaning and in their theological setting. Really interested not in the salvation of man's soul but in the safety of the existing social order, De Maistre was as devoid of religious feeling as the century (the eighteenth) that he attacked in the name of revealed religion. For Christ he had neither love nor worship, nor even an idea of his mission.[68]

De Maistre's ideas had their origin in his pessimistic view that man was by nature evil, and that injustice was the law of the universe. Man was a creature devoid of reason and dominated by emotions, fears, and prejudices. Punishment, consequently, governed all mankind and preserved civilization everywhere. In a graphic passage De Maistre described the executioner as both "the terror and the bond of union of human society, hence the indispensable basis of the body politic."[69] These pessimistic views of human nature logically led De Maistre to repudiate the principles of the French Revolution and to denounce the political and social institutions founded on them. No individual rights could exist and no individual welfare was possible, because the individual, according to De Maistre, was inconceivable apart from the social and political order. Injustice to one man or to many was of no importance and might even serve a useful purpose in preserving the existing order, which alone was all important. He poured ridicule on the cosmopolitan ideals of the *philsophes* of the eighteenth century—*"ce vilain siècle"*—who constantly exalted the love of mankind. "In my life," he declared, "I have seen Frenchmen, Italians, Russians. Thanks to Mon-

[68] Émile Faguet, *Politiques et moralistes du dix-neuvième siècle* (Paris, 1890), I, 59.
[69] De Maistre, *Les Soirées de Saint-Petersbourg* (Paris, 1854), I, 38–41.

tesquieu, I even know that one can be a Persian. But man I have never met in all my life. If he exists I do not know him."[70]

God, not the social contract, according to De Maistre, created the state. A constitution was, therefore, an infringement upon God and a usurpation of the divine plan. Disobedience to God's will was revolution, which testified to the essentially sinful nature of man. Order, not liberty, was the primal need of civilization; hence, a stable society was not possible without Christianity, the most efficient form of which was the Catholic church. Stability in France, asserted De Maistre, could be established only through the acceptance by the nation of the two fundamental human sentiments: supernaturalism and traditionalism, which were, in their very nature, flat contradictions of the "principles of 1789." The divine plan of government could be realized only through absolute monarchy, because that was a natural method of ruling. Popular government was artificial, because it was based on the abstract theory of the social contract. Absolute monarchy alone was able to combine sovereign authority with national unity, thereby ensuring continuity in the life of a people. For a parliament to make laws was inherently absurd, because law was the expression of the traditions and customs, not of the general will of a people.

De Maistre had a most unflattering opinion of the common man. "We see daily in the law courts," he observed, "children, lunatics, and absentees represented by men who are given this power by the law. The mass of people is exactly in the same situation being a perpetual child, a perpetual lunatic, a perpetual absentee."[71] How then could the common man, that irrational creature, be a lawgiver? Laws and institutions should be inspired by "healthy" prejudices, which are all important in human conduct.

The perfect model of government, according to De Maistre, was that of the Catholic church. His famous work on the papacy, *Du Pape,* which appeared in 1819, became the bible of Utramontanism. It was an uncompromising defense of the rule of the church by the pope against the advocates of church councils, of Jansenism, and of "Gallican liberties." Papal rule should be both the model for, and the check on, civil government. The pope "is the natural head," declared De Maistre, "the

[70] Quoted in Faguet, *op. cit.,* I, 9.
[71] *Ibid.*

most powerful protagonist, the great god of universal civilization. His powers have no limits except those set by the blindness and evil will-fulness of princes."[72] Without unswerving loyalty to the pope, there could be no sovereignty, no unity, no government, and no faith. The greatest of all evils was revolution, which began with the Protestant attack on the authority of the pope. And Protestantism prepared the way for the French Revolution, which plunged the entire world into chaos and anarchy. The existing order could be maintained only by giving the church supreme influence in the conduct of the state, in the education of the people, and in the shaping of social policies. All revolu-tionary ideals of liberty and equality should be rooted out as being false, iniquitous, and dangerous to civilization. Once that is done, a cerebral Catholicism would bring an automatic acceptance of an authoritarian government based on divine right and a hierarchic social order based on natural inequality. In the opinion of Faguet, the Christianity preached by De Maistre was a doctrine of "terror, passive obedience, and religion of the state."[73]

Another famous clerical philosopher was Vicomte de Bonald (1754–1840). An *émigré,* De Bonald returned to France with Louis XVIII, full of hatred for the French Revolution. He entered politics and was elected to the Chamber as an ultraroyalist; but his chief interest was political speculation, not practical politics. Unlike De Maistre, De Bonald lacked style and wit; his books were dull, dogmatic, and abstract. His views were similar to those of De Maistre and even more dogmatic. De Bonald was a strong and uncompromising upholder of absolutism in government and of the supremacy of the church. His ever-recurring theme was that unless the world accepted political unity in absolute monarchy and religious unity in the Catholic church, man could never discover truth nor could society hope for salvation. Author-ity and power always came from God; hence popular sovereignty was false and evil. De Bonald attacked the French Revolution because it established individualism in society and centralization in government. The only solution of all France's problems lay in the restoration of the medieval guilds, which, according to De Bonald, was a truly liberal system because it guaranteed the rights of all classes. "With the

[72] De Maistre, *Du Pape* (Paris, 1860), 257.
[73] Faguet, *op. cit.,* I, 59.

clairvoyance of hatred and the cold fanaticism of a scholastic theologian gone astray in the modern world he [De Bonald] has delved to the very bottom of the split" between the French Revolution and the Old Regime.[74]

De Bonald's influence was not so widespread as was that of De Maistre. His humorless identification of Providence with reactionary ideals and policies and of constitutional freedom with feudalism created cynical doubt instead of profound belief. Moreover, his turgid method of argument in the form of triads—cause, means, result—which began with a dogmatic premise and ended with a dogmatic conclusion, gave the effect of petrified logic, which repelled his readers. De Bonald influenced only those reactionaries who were already convinced of his reactionary views.

Far more influential in promoting clericalism than was the *esprit* of the Voltaire of reaction, De Maistre, or the logic of the "last of the scholastics," De Bonald, was the romantic, literary appeal of Chateaubriand. Like De Bonald, René, Vicomte de Chateaubriand (1768–1848) was an *émigré,* who returned to France after 1815 and devoted himself to the Bourbon cause. His famous book *Génie du Christianisme* created a sensation in Europe. Written in a style that was reminiscent of the poetic eloquence of Rousseau, it pictured Catholicism as a romantic faith that had an eternal appeal to the heart and to the imagination. Chateaubriand was a Rousseau in Catholic dress. As the "natural religion" of the Savoyard vicar had been floated by Rousseau on a tide of sentiment, "stained-glass" Christianity was floated by Chateaubriand on a tide of aesthetic mysticism. But the mysticism of Chateaubriand and his many disciples was an artificial product, contrived to turn men's minds away from the social problems that the French Revolution had so dramatically posed before mankind. "To make the antiquated principle of authority look young and attractive, they painted it with the rouge of sentimental enthusiasm; but they only succeeded in making the principle that had once been so awe-inspiring, ridiculous."

Though he was a clerical and a royalist, Chateaubriand was not so extreme in his political views as were De Maistre and De Bonald. Unlike them, he accepted those changes made by the French Revolu-

[74] A. Koyré, "Louis de Bonald," *Journal of the History of Ideas.* VIII (January, 1946), 56–73.

tion that were recognized by the *Charte*, but not the revolutionary principles that had produced those changes. The *Charte,* according to Chateaubriand, would unite the two Frances by mingling the institutions of new France with the memories, the ideals, and the traditions of old France.[75] What was all essential in realizing this purpose was to envelop the Restoration in a Catholic atmosphere. The Revolutionary principles would then disappear from view, overwhelmed by emotional waves of Catholic devotion. Only in this way could the Bourbon regime acquire stability in the new France, won to Catholicism by a popular belief that the salvation of the established order was part of the divine plan.

Clericalism, as a movement, was essentially political in character. None of the clerical philosophers was a deeply religious man, and their efforts resulted in creating in France an anomalous type of opinion, one that was strenuously Catholic without being fervently Christian. They were more interested in cherishing the traditions of royalist France and in maintaining a conservative social order than in advancing the teachings of Christianity. The appeal of clericalism was really to unbelievers, especially to the Voltairian bourgeois, who were fearful of revolution in this world, not of hell in the next. As the revolutionary elements became more and more threatening, their eyes were opened to the utility of an authoritarian church as a stabilizing force in an unstable social order. Especially did clericalism appeal to the bourgeois after the socialist uprising in the June Days, 1848. Many terrified bourgeois, notably Adolphe Thiers, were ready to throw themselves at the feet of the bishops.[76] As John Stuart Mill observed, "the utility of religion did not need to be asserted until arguments for its truth had in a great measure ceased to convince."[77]

The influence of the clerical philosophers was clearly seen in the royalist movement during the Third French Republic, known as the *Action Française*. Its philosophic mentor and intellectual leader, Charles Maurras, was openly an agnostic, even an anti-Christian. According to Maurras, Catholicism, like royalism, was part of France's historic past, not a set of dogmas imposed by priests on the people. On such subjects

[75] Chateaubriand, *De la monarchie selon la Charte* (Paris, 1816), 147.
[76] See *infra,* p. 314.
[77] John Stuart Mill, *Nature, the Utility of Religion and Theism* (London, 1885), 70.

as the immortality of the soul or papal infallibility a member of the *Action* might think what he pleased without injury to the traditions and interests that united France and the Catholic church.[78] Maurras freely acknowledged his debt to the clerical philosophers, especially to De Maistre, whom he greatly admired.[79] So far did political Catholicism separate itself from religion that the *Action Française* was clerical without being Christian.[80] "Je suis Catholique mais je suis athéistique," was the comment of a member of this group.

War *à outrance* was declared by the clerical philosophers against the French Revolution. In their view, it was the movement that was responsible for the appearance in history of an "irreligious social order" with emphasis on happiness in this world, not on salvation in the next. When the common man turned away from religion, the joys of future life would become dimmer as the miseries of this earthly life became sharper. Only the establishment of a religious social order, reasoned the clericals, would quiet popular discontent by turning men's minds away from the problems of this world to visions of the next. "In the measure as instruction descends into the lower classes," observed Chateaubriand, "they will discover the secret plague which infects the irreligious social order. The too great disproportion of conditions and fortunes could maintain itself as long as it was concealed; but as soon as this disproportion was generally perceived, the mortal blow was struck. Reconstruct, if you can the aristocratic fictions; try to persuade the poor man,—when he knows how to read and has no beliefs, when he possesses the same education as you;—try to persuade him that he must submit to all privations, while his neighbor possesses a thousand-fold superfluity; as a last resort, you will have to kill him."[81] Only a revival of Catholicism could save the social order from revolutionary upheavals. The Christian rulers, Catholic and non-Catholic, were exhorted to proclaim Christianity as their ideal and guide in public affairs. And the Catholic rulers were admonished to take the papacy

[78] Charles Maurras, *Dictionnaire politique et critique* (Paris, 1932), I, 242.

[79] *Ibid.*, III, 13–15.

[80] In 1926 the Pope condemned the *Action Française* and forbade Catholics to be members of that organization and to read its publications. See D. Gwynn, *The "Action Française" Condemnation* (London, 1928).

[81] Quoted in P. T. Moon, *The Labor Problem and the Social Catholic Movement in France* (New York, 1921), 15.

as their model of government and to look to the pope for guidance in political as well as in religious matters.

The church in France adopted clericalism with alacrity. It was not at all satisfied with the Concordat, which established state supremacy over the church by making it a department in the civil service, whose officials were appointed and paid by the state. It soon discovered that, no matter how friendly the government, it was "held in a grip which relaxed only as a reward for complete subservience."[82] Moreover, the Concordat had provided for religious toleration; both Protestants and Jews were officially recognized. Under this system, Catholicism, despite its favored position, was merely a variety of religious "opinion," in competition with other faiths in the market place of ideas. This was contrary to the deep and unshakable attitude of the church that it, and it alone, was the sole repository of the faith of Christ. It professed the Truth, not an "opinion." At best, the Concordat had established Gallicanism by making the church subordinate to the state. At worst, it had accepted the liberal view of religion as a form of opinion, to be tolerated along with other opinions. Ever since the days of Louis XIV, the church had stubbornly fought against Gallicanism, and for it to be tolerated along with other faiths in a Catholic land was unthinkable! The church could be restored to "her own" only when there was a restoration of the Old Regime, when it was the only recognized faith and when it enjoyed the status of being virtually a state within a state. An agitation was launched by the church to abolish the Concordat.[83]

The church became the ardent and unfailing supporter of the Bourbons in their efforts to undo the work of the French Revolution. Clericalism pointed the way to restore the Old Regime. In return, the Bourbons did all in their power to extend the influence of the church. Divorce was abolished. All grades of education—elementary, secondary, and higher—gradually fell under church influences. Bishop de Frayssenous in 1824 was made head of the Université de France, which dominated all education in France through its control of appointments, curriculums, and examinations. He promptly embarked on a

[82] R. Soltau, *French Political Thought in the Nineteenth Century* (Yale University Press, 1931), 64.

[83] A. Debidour, *Histoire des rapports de l'église et de l'état en France de 1798 à 1906* (Paris, 1898), 325–326.

policy of clericalizing French education through the appointment of clerical teachers. "Those who have the misfortune to live without religion, or without devotion to the royal family," he declared, "lack the essential qualities that qualify instructors of youth."[84] A royal ordinance decreed that the teacher should base his instructions on religion, on monarchy, and on the *Charte*. Clerical influences were all powerful in the determination of public policies and in the appointment to public office.[85]

Priestly influence in government was certainly not new. What was new was the formation of a *parti prêtre*, which consciously and deliberately used Christianity to preach loyalty not merely to established government but also to a particular regime and to a particular dynasty. King and priest together had mounted the Revolutionary scaffold;, together they were to be in the seats of power, each supporting the other. "It seems that Christ died on the cross eighteen hundred years ago for the Bourbon dynasty," was the comment of cynical Paris. Louis XVIII himself asserted that the bishop should "persuade his subjects of the intimate connection between the altar and the throne, and show them that, as they can not count on any happiness in the life to come without religion, they can not hope for any in this life without the monarchy."[86] As might be expected the aristocrats, whatever their private opinions, became vociferous advocates of clericalism. A restoration of the absolute power of the king and of the influence of the clergy could not fail to restore also the third pillar of the Old Regime, namely, the privileges of the nobility. How far all three reactionary forces were willing to go to uphold the church was seen in the Sacrilege Law of 1825, which prescribed the death penalty for the profanation of sacred vessels under certain circumstances. In France, as in the other clerical countries, everywhere "might be perceived a mingled odor of sacristy and police station."[87]

The clericals, like the bourgeois liberals, failed to solve the problem of reconciling the two Frances. The church was generally regarded more

[84] Quoted in J. B. Wolf, *France, 1815 to the Present* (New York, 1940), 61.

[85] Artz, *op. cit.*, 136*ff*.

[86] Quoted in J. Lucas-Dubreton, *Louis XVIII*, trans. from the French by F. H. Lyon (New York, 1927), 108.

[87] Benedetto Croce, *History of Europe in the Nineteenth Century*, trans. from the Italian by H. Furst (New York, 1933), 93.

as a part of the bureaucracy than as the repository of the faith of Christ. Its activities on behalf of the Bourbon regime intensified old hatreds and bred a new division among Frenchmen, that between clericalism and anticlericalism. As a movement, anticlericalism took definite form in France during the Restoration, when hatred of the church as the pillar of reaction became the political passion of all parties on the left: constitutional monarchists, republicans, and socialists. To be a liberal in politics was equivalent to being a Voltairian in religion.[88] *Le cléricalisme, voilà l'ennemi!* was a powerful sentiment on the left in France long before it became the battle cry of Gambetta.

As France was almost entirely a Catholic nation, opposition to the church tended to become anti-Christian, even antireligious, in character. To French anticlericals, Protestantism was not an alternative religion but a variant of Catholicism, denuded of its grandeur and bereft of its universality. So widespread was anticlericalism that even Catholic liberals were infected with it; what they favored was "perfect obedience in the spiritual and entire independence in temporal matters." Comte de Montlosier , a devout Catholic, assailed clericalism, which, he declared, was undermining religion and conspiring against government and society.[89] Royer-Collard, likewise a devout Catholic, denounced the political activity of the church. "The theocracy of our time," he declared, "is religious rather than political. . . . It is part and parcel of the universal reaction that is now with us. What recommends it to some is its counterrevolutionary appeal."[90] The growth of anticlericalism brought a revival of the writings of the eighteenth-century *philosophes*. Between 1817 and 1829 no fewer than twelve new editions of the works of Voltaire and thirteen of those of Rousseau were published.[91] The widely circulated pamphlets of Paul-Louis Courier and the popular verses and songs of Béranger were bitterly anticlerical. Some of the liberal journals, like the *Constitutionnel,* had regular anticlerical features. A school of anticlerical historians appeared, chief of whom were Jules Michelet and Edgar Quinet. They attacked the

[88] P. Thureau-Dangin, *Le Parti libéral sous la Restauration* (Paris, 1876), 322.

[89] Comte de Montlosier, *Mémoire à consulter sur un système religieux et politique* (Paris, 1826).

[90] Barante, *op. cit.,* II, 258.

[91] Artz, *op. cit.,* 164*ff.*

church as the most redoubtable enemy of the principles of the French Revolution and the greatest obstacle to the progress of liberalism in France and in Europe generally.[92]

As long as an intransigent spirit dominated the two Frances revolution or reaction was always in the offing. Whichever side was in control had to devote its energies to maintaining itself in power, rather than to advancing the progress of the nation. All through the Restoration the country seethed with reactionary intrigues and with revolutionary conspiracies to overthrow the government. It became evident to the Bourbons that they were sitting on a throne perched on a volcano, within which the fires of revolt were constantly smoldering. The one popular element in the regime set up by the *Charte,* the Chamber, excited the greatest opposition. Though similar in organization and in power to the English Parliament, the Chamber had nothing like the prestige that the mother of parliaments had in England. It was not generally regarded as a national institution and, therefore, evoked neither enthusiasm nor popular support. By the king, parliament was regarded as a concession to the wealthy bourgeois, in order to reconcile them to the rule of the restored Bourbons. By the aristocracy, it was regarded as a hateful obstacle to the restoration of their privileges and their estates. By the lower classes, it was regarded as a political organ of the wealthy bourgeois to protect their class interests. Parliament aroused little political interest among the people generally. It was something connected with "privilege," yet without social distinction— the peculiar appanage of the *nouveaux riches,* who were despised by the aristocrats and hated by the masses. "The people were completely indifferent to the elections, which they regarded as matters concerning only the rich."[93]

The political complexion of the Chamber during the Restoration clearly indicated the state of public opinion in France. A large number of political groups appeared whose ideas and interests were in such sharp conflict that they could neither unite into two powerful parties, as in England, nor combine into blocks, as was so frequently the case during the Third French Republic. On the right were the Constitutional Royalists, who accepted the *Charte* and supported the Bour-

[92] Soltau, *op. cit.,* 76*ff,* 115*ff.*
[93] A. Pilenco, *Les Moeurs électorales en France* (Paris, 1928), 26–27.

bons at all times. On the extreme right were the Ultras, an "unreconstructed" group of reactionaries who were "more royalist than the king and more Catholic than the pope." They demanded nothing less than the restoration of the Old Regime. In the center were the Doctrinaires and their allies, who were loyal to the Bourbons as long as the Bourbons were loyal to the *Charte*. When Charles X, leader of the Ultras, came to the throne, the Doctrinaires shifted definitely to the left. On the left were a number of liberal and revolutionary groups—the "tricolor" party—all of whom were anti-Bourbon, some being even antimonarchical. These aimed to establish a thoroughgoing parliamentary regime. At one extreme "was a party that was ultradynastic but anticonstitutional, and at the other extreme, a party that was ultraconstitutional but antidynastic."[94]

As there were no organized political parties in the English sense, political leadership was personal rather than party. The most prominent member of the Chamber was Constant, who was a "leader" because he was an able opponent of the Bourbon regime, not because he had an organized group of followers. Political prominence was generally an attribute of opponents rather than of upholders of the government. Other popular members of the left were General Foy, an eloquent orator of romantic temperament; the banker, Laffite; and the manufacturer, Casimir-Périer—all of whom hated aristocrats and favored the establishment of an undiluted bourgeois monarchy. A veritable symbol of opposition to the Bourbons was Lafayette, republican by tradition. Disinterested, ingenuous, "incapable of resisting flattery or suspecting anyone of disloyalty, and always ready to stand forth in times of crisis," Lafayette became a rallying cry of the republican opposition.[95]

The Chamber exhibited another curious phenomenon: it contained a permanent majority on the right and a permanent minority on the left. In order to be sure of continuous support in parliament, the government instituted a system of "official candidates," which became notorious in France and continued long after the demise of the Bourbons. During elections one of the candidates was openly designated as a friend and supporter of the government. He was favored by the officials, who used bribery, coercion, patronage, and even terrorism to

[94] J. Barthélemy, *L'Introduction du régime parlementaire en France* (Paris, 1904), 151.
[95] Georges Weill, *La France sous la monarchie constitutionnelle* (Paris, 1902), 4.

induce the electors to vote for him.[96] As voting was public and voters were few, the "official candidate" generally won the seat. In this manner the government managed to elect a sufficient number of its supporters to control the Chamber and to uphold the ministry, which was appointed by the king. By using corrupt methods to win a majority in parliament which supported the ministry, the political regime of the Bourbons in France, like that of George III in England, gave the appearance of having ministerial responsibility.[97]

The reason why no real ministerial responsibility existed lay in the fact that no real parliamentary opposition existed. Opponents of the government did succeed in being elected to the Chamber, where they formed a permanent minority, with no prospect of coming into power through regular parliamentary channels. By contrast with the English Commons, the French Chamber contained opponents of the government but not an opposition that aimed to turn a minority into a majority in order to assume power. Deprived of the prospect of becoming the government, the opposing political groups developed a sense of irresponsibility in relation to their own demands, as well as in relation to the government itself. As a consequence, they indulged in bitter factional strife, each faction more intent on discrediting its rivals than on formulating a constructive program. The opponents of the Bourbons sought to prevent the government machinery from working by resorting to obstructive tactics inside parliament and by threatening demonstrations in the streets.

Influenced by the traditions of the French Revolution, the opponents of the Bourbon regime could not comprehend the English idea of an opposition's being a stabilizing force in government through the mechanism of ministerial responsibility. Royer-Collard was opposed to ministerial responsibility, the fulcrum of parliamentary supremacy, because in his opinion the king, not parliament, had the right to control and to direct the government. If ever the Chamber succeeded in imposing a ministry on the king, he asserted, France would no longer

96 G. D. Weil, *Les Élections législatives depuis 1789* (Paris, 1895), 110–130.

97 There was no definite provision in the *Charte* for ministerial responsibility, but it became the practice for the king to appoint ministers agreeable to the Chamber. Only twice during the Restoration were ministers appointed without having the support of the Chamber: one was the Richelieu ministry of 1815 to 1816, and the other, the Polignac ministry of 1829 to 1830.

be a kingdom but a republic.[98] The more radical Constant was like-wise opposed to ministerial responsibility. A vote of "no confidence" by the Chamber, argued Constant, which would overthrow a ministry appointed by the king, was a direct attack on the royal prerogative established by the *Charte*. Parliamentary conflicts, Constant insisted, should not be between government and opposition but between the upper house, which represented conservatism, and the lower house, which favored change.[99] Guizot, who had a better understanding of the English political system than did his fellow bourgeois liberals, realized fully the importance of a parliamentary opposition. But he doubted the possibility of its functioning in France. To be truly effec-tive, he argued, an opposition must be devoted to the general interests of the nation. But in France the moderate parties, alone capable of being an opposition, had received a *triste héritage* from the Reign of Terror. Attacks on property rights frightened the moderates, spokesmen of the *bourgeois accrédités,* into the belief that all rank and station were in peril; hence they rallied to the side of the government. This situation seriously hindered the formation of an opposition, which was thereby deprived of many of its natural supporters.[100]

What both the government and its opponents failed to realize was that a powerful parliamentary opposition would have brought stability to France, as it had to England. In transplanting the English parlia-mentary system, France could not bring with it the soil in which it had grown. The result was that the French parliament did not develop strong roots in the life of the people, part of whom looked to the king as the source of all authority and part, to the barricade as the only way to freedom.

Though a parliamentary opposition was lacking, there was opposi-tion everywhere in France. Curious and contradictory as it may seem, the strength of the opponents of the government lay in their very powerlessness, because, as Guizot expressed it, "l'opposition, c'est la France."[101] Not the government but its opponents could count on the

[98] Barante, *op. cit.,* I, 217.

[99] Constant, "Observations sur le discours prononcé par le ministre de l'intérieur," *Collection complète des ouvrages,* II, 93; *Cours de politique constitutionelle,* I, 383–444.

[100] Guizot, *Des moyens de gouvernment,* 344–349.

[101] *Ibid.,* 352.

national tradition of revolution. The opponents resorted to open criticism of the government in the press and in the Chamber and to secret revolutionary societies, which conspired to overthrow the regime by violent methods. During the Bourbon period, the nation was in a state of permanent conspiracy against the government. What was called "public opinion" was outside the government and in opposition to it. It found expression in the influential Paris press, which made its appearance during the Restoration. Journals were established that exercised great influence, such as the *National,* the *Figaro,* the *Consitutionnel,* the *Temps,* and the *Globe,* all of them liberal and opposed to the government. The Paris press soon gained an importance far greater than that of the press in any other country. Because of the influential role of the press, a tradition arose in France that the government and public opinion were necessarily on opposite sides.

Though the circulation of the journals was limited, their readers were numerous. A passion for reading became widespread in France among all classes. Those who could not afford to buy reading matter would form reading circles, which would purchase journals and books for the members. The French passion for reading was well described by a visitor to Paris in 1830. "Everybody reads," he wrote, "the cab driver while he waits for a customer; the fruit dealer in the market; the porter in the hallway. A thousand persons are to be found every morning in the Palais Royal reading newspapers."[102] The cafés became newspaper-reading centers, and many patronized them less for food and drink than for the purpose of reading the antigovernment journals they provided for their patrons. In their files were also liberal English journals and liberal French journals published in Switzerland, Holland, and Belgium.[103] The Paris cafés were imitated in the provincial towns, where the Paris press had a far larger reading public than did the local journals.

The government was greatly concerned over the hostile attitude of the people; the distance in France between "opinion" and "barricade" was both short and inviting. Despite the guarantees of the freedom of the press contained in the *Charte,* the government was assiduous in its efforts to nullify them by all sorts of methods, ranging from harassing

[102] Quoted in S. Charléty, *op. cit.,* 125.
[103] Artz, *op. cit.,* 82–90.

regulations to downright suppression. Newspapers had to deposit funds with the government as a guarantee of good behavior. The issues of a journal had to be passed upon by a censor before publication. Severe penalties were imposed for attacks on monarchy and on religion.[104]

Opposition to the censorship was universal among the bourgeois liberals. There was no more stout and unflinching upholder of the freedom of the press than Royer-Collard. "If that is lost," he declared, "the nation would sink into political slavery of the most absolute type."[105] Freedom of the press, he insisted, was not merely a private right, it was even more a political institution and a social necessity. It gave stability to the government by calling attention to necessary reforms; it gave liberty to the people by exposing violations of civil rights; and it was the basis for freedom of debate in parliament itself. Moreover, it was futile to suppress a journal because it promptly reappeared under another name, with the same writers and the same readers.[106] The sensitive property nerve in the bourgeois liberal was irritated by the suppression of a journal. Royer-Collard insisted that a newspaper was property; to suppress it was equivalent to confiscation, hence a plain violation of property right.[107]

Constant was even more uncompromising than was Royer-Collard in his championship of freedom of the press, which he regarded as the very basis of all popular liberties.[108] A free press, he argued, protected the liberty of the average citizen by giving him a powerful means to make known his complaints and his desires. Without a free press, no public opinion was possible, and without public opinion, no constitution could long last.[109]

Opposition to the Bourbon regime had revolutionary implications, because it was more powerful outside than inside of parliament. Instead of a parliamentary opposition planning to become the government, as in England, there existed in France conspiratorial groups plotting to overthrow the government by a popular uprising or by a *coup d'état*.

[104] *Ibid.*, 82*ff.*
[105] Barante, *op. cit.*, II, 136.
[106] *Ibid.*, 129–148, 500.
[107] *Ibid.*, 302–303.
[108] Constant, *Cours de politique constitutionelle*, I, 383–560.
[109] *Ibid.*, 494.

"The Liberal party," wrote Guizot, "numbered in its ranks men who favored revolution more than liberty, and stoutly defended the French Revolution and all its works.... Many refused to believe that political liberty had returned to France with the old enemies of the Revolution and in the very midst of our defeat."[110]

Secret societies were organized that plotted to overthrow the hated Bourbons. The most famous of these societies was the *Charbonnerie,* which was modeled on the Italian *Carbonari.* Its aim was to establish a republic; its membership consisted largely of young people who were ardent champions of *la nation nouvelle.* "Nearly all the young people who, at that time, dedicated themselves to intellectual life were more or less in the ranks of the opposition."[111] They were stirred by the pamphlets of Paul-Louis Courier and by the songs of Béranger that ridiculed and denounced the dynasty, the aristocracy, and the clergy. The *Charbonnerie* became the active fomenter of conspiracies and uprisings that culminated in a widespread outburst in 1826. The uprising was, however, suppressed.

Nothing "is more customary in man," remarked De Tocqueville, "than to recognize superior wisdom in the person of his oppressor."[112] The French Revolution had, however, destroyed this "customary" attitude among large masses of the French people. Hence they saw in the reactionary government of the Restoration not "superior wisdom," but the insensate stupidity of a dynasty that "never learned anything and never forgot anything." As the Bourbon regime passed from the constitutional royalism of Louis XVIII to the ultraroyalism of Charles X, the situation became critical. The reactionary measures of Charles pointed straight to a restoration of the Old Regime: the payment of a billion francs indemnity to the expropriated nobles; the attempts to restore primogeniture and entail; the Sacrilege Law, which presaged clerical dominance; and the appointment of the Prince de Polignac as premier, despite an adverse vote of the Chamber. Finally in July, 1830, Charles decreed the July Ordinances, which suspended the liberty of

[110] Guizot, *Histoire parlementaire de France,* I, Introduction, lxxx–lxxxi.

[111] Thureau-Dangin, *op. cit.,* 199.

[112] Alexis de Tocqueville, *Democracy in America,* Henry Reeves text, as revised by Francis Bowen, now further corrected and edited by Phillips Bradley (New York, 1945), II, 11.

the press, dissolved a newly elected Chamber, and raised the property qualifications for voting. Despite their earnest efforts, the bourgeois liberals were unable to prevent the Bourbons from "jumping out of the *Charte.*" Would the reactionary measures of Charles lead to a restoration of the Old Regime? "The memories, the passions, and the interests of 1789," remarked Proudhon, "were the soul of the July Revolution."[113] Fearful of losing the political and economic gains that had come to them from the French Revolution, the *bourgeoisie,* in a panic, appealed to the despised *canaille* to mount the barricades against the government. In the July Revolution of 1830 the two Frances met in mortal combat.

The uprising was a success, in that it eliminated the reactionary Bourbons from the throne and made impossible a restoration of the Old Regime. In the deeper sense, however, the Revolution of 1830 marked a great failure, the failure of the bourgeois liberals to establish stability in France through the constitutional regime of the *Charte.* Because of its class character, parliamentary government during the Restoration had neither the popularity of a democratic regime nor the prestige of an autocratic one; hence it became the seat of strife, not of authority. "The principle of authority," observed Louis Blanc, "was attacked with excessive ardor and it succumbed. The power of the state, divided into two forces perpetually bent on mutual destruction, lost by its instability its title to general respect. Incapable of directing society, since it was itself the seat of strife and anarchy and could hardly maintain its own existence, it accustomed men's mind to the dominion of license."[114] The bourgeois liberals could neither maintain the order established by the *Charte* nor make a peaceful transition to a more liberal order. Confronted by reactionaries on the right and by revolutionists on the left, themselves torn by fears and doubts, the bourgeois liberals were dragged into an uprising that they really did not wish to enter. Their state of mind was well exemplified by Royer-Collard. On the morrow of the July Revolution, he declared, "Moi aussi, je suis des victorieux, triste parmi les victorieux."[115]

113 P. J. Proudhon, *La Guerre et la paix* (Paris, 1927), 356.
114 Louis Blanc, *op. cit.,* I, 82.
115 Guizot, *Histoire parlementaire,* I, Introduction, cv.

To the barricade, not to the floor of parliament, the French people now looked for the overthrow of an unpopular government. Political progress became associated with the idea of permanent revolution, in which one class was constantly arrayed against the other. The bourgeois victors of 1830 were soon to realize that, in order to maintain their victory, they would have to pass to the other side of barricade.

Chapter 9. The Victorian Compromise in England; the New Liberalism and the New Conservatism

The early thirties of the nineteenth century witnessed bourgeois liberalism triumphant in both England and France. The new political setup was carefully adjusted to the needs, the interests, and the ideals of the *bourgeoisie*. The suffrage was sufficiently extended to overwhelm their old opponents, the landed aristocracy, and sufficiently restricted to exclude from the government their new opponents, the working class. In France the aristocrats were all but eliminated from the political scene; and in England they were subordinated to the middle class and destined to play an ever-decreasing part in the government. However, there was a striking difference in the methods by which the bourgeois liberals in each country had achieved their triumph. In France they had triumphed through revolution and, try as they would, they could not rid themselves of the stigma of the barricade. In England they had triumphed through reform, which created a precedent for radical change that, later, was to influence profoundly those in power, as well as those who were seeking to establish new political and social systems.

The Reform Bill of 1832 was another "Glorious Revolution." Like the Revolution of 1688 it marked a great shift of political power without recourse to a violent uprising. In 1832 a revolutionary change took place when the middle class superseded the aristocracy in the control of Parliament, as had happened in 1688, when supreme power in the government of England passed from king to Parliament. In still another significant manner did 1832 resemble 1688: it was a compromise, not a complete overturn. In 1832 the compromise resulted in the subordination, not in the elimination, of the aristocracy in the new parliamentary pattern, just as in 1688 the compromise resulted in the subordination, not in the elimination, of the monarchy in the new governmental pattern. The spirit of compromise in the Reform Bill of 1832 became the inspiration of the many reform measures that were enacted by the bourgeois liberals during the Victorian era.

A new balance of classes appeared as a consequence of the Reform Bill. Under the rule of bourgeois liberalism, the middle class became the senior partner and the aristocracy, the junior partner in the combination that ruled England. This was the reverse of that which had existed prior to 1832. The aristocracy continued to control the public services, civil, military, and diplomatic; to monopolize the House of Lords; and to exercise a paramount influence in the hierarchy of the Established Church. Indirectly they wielded great power through their widespread social influence, which radiated from the throne and from the peerage. Especially was this true of the throne during the long reign of Queen Victoria. "Good form" exercised an invisible, but potent, social pressure, which had a double effect: it stimulated the ambitions of the rising capitalists to enter the ranks of the aristocracy and, at the same time, dampened the ardor and chilled the hopes of the discontented lower classes. The depressive effect of caste influences and ideals was felt most by those at the very bottom of the social hierarchy, who were enjoined to accept "the station in life" into which they had been born.

What the middle class won was the House of Commons. After 1832 the Commons dominated and fashioned English political life to a far greater degree than ever before in English history. What had been the supremacy of Parliament now was, in fact, the supremacy of the Commons, which popularly became known as "Parliament." As a legislature, the Lords were definitely subordinated to the Commons. The threat to pack the Upper House, which induced them to pass the Reform Bill, constituted, in effect, an "unwritten" amendment to the "unwritten" English constitution. It was now established as a precedent that, in case of a conflict between the two houses, the Lords must yield when popular sentiment was clearly on the side of the Commons. After 1832 "the Lords were still a power in the land, but they were a minor power."[1] Thereafter they were regarded more as an obstacle to radical innovation than as a second chamber exercising normal legislative functions.

[1] W. J. Jennings, "Cabinet Government at the Accession of Queen Victoria," *Economica*, X (November, 1931), 146.

Even more important was it that the Commons gained full control of the executive power. Before 1832 the king had appointed the prime minister and his associates in the cabinet, who then had to get a majority in the Commons. Party lines had not been very rigid in England during the eighteenth century. After 1832 came a clearer application of the principle of ministerial responsibility, as a consequence of a more definite demarcation of party lines and of a tighter organization of the two political parties. Party government, long rooted in English politics, did not assume its present-day definiteness until after 1832, when the king appointed the prime minister and his associates *because* they had a majority in the Commons. Whatever remnants of political power had remained to the crown were now lost to the Commons. The king as the symbol of national and imperial unity really dates from 1832.

These great changes in England's political setup took place within its traditional framework of King, Lords, and Commons. There was a shift of power, not of place, from the first two to the third. The king continued to "rule" the country "by the grace of God." The Lords continued to be the "Upper House." But the real governing center, both legislative and executive, was the Commons, which had become the sole heir of the prerogatives of the crown and of the legislative power of the Lords. This significant transformation was an outstanding illustration of the political genius of the English, who developed reform into a subtle art of making vast changes in the depths of the political order while maintaining a calm, unruffled surface of traditional forms and customs. Unlike revolution in France, reform in England had the advantage of maintaining continuity in the life of the nation by satisfying the demands of new powerful elements without creating an irreconcilable opposition among the defenders of the old order. Continuity was maintained by the preservation of England's oldest institutions, the monarchy and the Lords; the more they ceased to function as vital parts of the government machinery, the more hallowed did they become as the bearers of national traditions.

The passage of the Reform Bill had been attended with so much bitterness that the question uppermost was this: would the Tories, representing the aristocracy, accept the supremacy of the Commons, destined henceforth to be dominated by the Whigs, representing the middle class? The answer came in a highly significant declaration by the Tory leader, Sir Robert Peel. In his famous Tamworth Manifesto, Peel declared that he considered "the Reform Bill a final and irrevocable settlement of a great Constitutional question—a settlement which no friend to the peace and welfare of this country would attempt to disturb, either by direct or by insidious means." In his view the spirit of the Reform "implies merely a careful review of institutions, civil and ecclesiastical, undertaken in a friendly temper, combining, with firm maintenance of established rights, the correction of proved abuses and the redress of real grievances. . . ." He promised that the Tory party would give "just and impartial consideration of what is due to all interests—agricultural, manufacturing, and commercial." [2]

The Tamworth Manifesto gave an indelible impression to the new Tory party that emerged from the Reform Bill of 1832. Plainly it was to be a conservative—even a reforming—but not a reactionary party. In other words, the Tories, as after the Revolution of 1688, agreed to accept the role of an opposition party, which gave assurance to the reformers, both Whig and Radical, that their gains were safe from attack.

The struggle between aristocrats and middle class, which before 1832 had threatened to result in revolution, now assumed the peaceful, though acrimonious, form of parliamentary contests. Political stability was now more assured than it had been at any time since the outbreak of the French Revolution, because the government now had the support of both propertied classes. "The battle in the House of Commons," wrote Roebuck, "has been, since the Reform Act, not between those having property and those having none, but between the possessors of different kinds of property—between the landed proprietors, on the one hand, and possessors of manufacturing capital, on the other."[3] But the battle, it is important to note, was that between a government and an opposition, in a political system that both fully accepted, and over issues in a social order based on property and on class divisions that both parties strenuously upheld. In the political struggles for mastery that took place between the two propertied classes during the period of bourgeois liberalism, it was taken for granted that, whichever party was the government or the opposition, the rights of property were to be

[2] *Memoirs* by the Right Honorable Sir Robert Peel (London, 1857), II, 58–67.

[3] J. A. Roebuck, *History of the Whig Ministry of 1830* (London, 1852), II, 417–418.

respected and the class divisions in society were to be upheld. This understanding became famous as the "Victorian Compromise," an arrangement between the aristocrats and the capitalists that guaranteed the property of both and the rule of the latter. But let it be noted, the famous compromise was at the expense of the workers. Politically they continued to be outside constitutional life in liberal England. Economically they continued to be at the mercy of economic laws that worked well for their masters and badly for them. For a generation after 1832, the two leading parties agreed to accept the Reform Bill as—to use the expression of its father, Lord John Russell—the "final" solution of the problem of parliamentary reform.

A great change took place in the historic Whig party after the Reform Bill of 1832. It gradually ceased to be the party of aristocratic families, which had dominated it since the Revolution of 1688. By the middle of the nineteenth century, the Whigs came to be almost exclusively the party of the middle class, whose interests it represented by advocating policies that were directly opposed to those of the landed aristocracy. When the Whigs left their ancient moorings, they began to drift more and more in the direction of Philosophic Radicalism, which greatly appealed to their middle-class supporters. Traditional Whiggism could not encompass the larger vision of the future of England, produced by rapid industrialization and by the appearance of the industrial capitalists whose influence was now nationwide. When the Whigs became the "Liberals," leadership passed from the aristocratic Russells and Greys to the bourgeois Gladstones and Brights. However, Whiggism, with its cautious, historic, traditionalism, and Benthamism, with its cold, logical materialism, never blended sufficiently to form a coherent political pattern. What took place was the typical English method of keeping the form and changing the substance. The Liberals continued to speak the Whig language of Burke, but their policies were those of Bentham.

No one else so completely typified English bourgeois liberalism, as exemplified in the Liberal party, as did William E. Gladstone (1809–1898), the unchallenged leader of the party for almost half a century. A devout churchman, saturated with political traditionalism as a result of his Oxford education, Gladstone was indeed far from being a Benthamite. Nevertheless, he became the outstanding champion of policies that were, in origin and even in formulation, the unquestioned product of materialistic, traditionless utilitarianism. Magniloquent, in deadly earnest as an orator, but cautious and moderate as a statesman, Gladstone appealed greatly to many sections of English opinion. To both propertied classes he was the very incarnation of the Victorian Compromise; hence he won the enthusiastic support of the middle class and roused only halfhearted opposition among the aristocrats, who cynically pretended to fear his bark, at the same time discounting his bite. Throughout his long political career Gladstone constantly and steadily broadened his vision. Beginning as the "brightest hope of the stern, unbending Tories," he ended as an advanced Liberal with a renewed faith in the future of democracy.

What became of the Philosophic Radicals, the fermentative political group that had galvanized the Whigs into a real Opposition and had given ideas and policies to their successors, the Liberals? As a separate political group, they elected about twenty members to the first reformed Parliament, of whom the most prominent were John Arthur Roebuck and Sir William Molesworth. Their influence was far greater than their numbers, as their ideas and their political strategy had been the vital elements in the triumph of 1832. "In 1832," writes Halévy, "Benthamite radicalism was the term, possibly unattainable, to which every deliberate reformer in his measure approached."[4] In the forties, however, the Philosophic Radicals were a vanishing sect, which caused Macaulay to remark sarcastically that they consisted only of George Grote and his wife. The pattern of liberalism that the Philosophic Radicals had created from the various strands of utilitarianism was taken over by the Liberal party. Their work now over, the Philosophic Radicals passed into history.

The period from the Reform Bill of 1832 to the Reform Bill of 1867 was the high noon of bourgeois liberalism in England. Once in power, the bourgeois liberals beheld in Parliament a highly efficient instrument with which to make great changes in the social and economic order —changes that would have behind them the power, the authority, and the prestige of the most popular institution in the land. Parliament seemed to be endowed with a new life, once the spell of custom and

[4] Élie Halévy. *A History of the English People 1830–1841*, trans. from the French by E. I. Watkin (New York, 1924), 70.

tradition was broken by the Reform Bill. A series of radical measures was enacted that resulted in a profound transformation of English society; in other words, in a social revolution on the installment plan. At the end of the bourgeois liberal period, England was essentially a bourgeois state in political structure, in economic policy, and—despite the persistence of aristocratic forms—even in social organization. The great changes were brought about by the painless methods of reform and compromise, without bloody uprisings, without reigns of terror, and without irreconcilable class conflicts, such as had taken place in France during the transition from aristocratic to a bourgeois regime. Again unlike France, every gain that England made during this period was a gain that England kept.

From the beginning of the Reform period until about 1870, the spirit of Bentham was the dominant spirit in English legislation and in English liberal thought. From Bentham's writings "burst forth an impetuous drive to legislate that soon dominated Liberalism."[5] In his quizzical way, Bentham had declared, "Twenty years after I am dead I shall be a despot."[6] That his prophecy was fulfilled to an amazing degree is the testimony of two eminent historians Dicey and Clapham.[7]

In no field of reform was the influence of Benthamism more direct and more potent that in that of local self-government. There its practical genius found ready scope to transform the life of the local communities without disturbing the nation as a whole. There, after the passage of the Municipal Corporations Act of 1835, the middle class had predominant power and could, therefore, freely refashion urban life in accordance with the demands of the new day. "It is to Jeremy Bentham, the prophet of the Philosophical Radicals," wrote Sidney and Beatrice Webb in their authoritative work on English local government, "that we owe the insidiously potent conception of a series of specialized departments supervising and controlling from Whitehall, through salaried officials, the whole public administration of the community,

[5] B. Guttmann, *England im Zeitalter der bürgerlichen Reform* (Berlin, 1923), 554.

[6] Bentham, *Correspondence,* in *The Works of Jeremy Bentham* (Bowring, ed., Edinburgh, 1843), X, 450.

[7] A. V. Dicey, *Lectures on the Relation between Law and Public Opinion in England during the Nineteenth Century* (London, 1914), 126–210; J. H. Clapham, *An Economic History of Modern Britain* (Cambridge University Press, 1932), II, 386–387. See also Graham Wallas, *Men and Ideas* (London, 1940), 29.

whether police or prisons, schools or hospitals, highways or the relief of destitution."[8]

Of the many notable reforms affecting the localities that were put through by the bourgeois liberals, the most important was the Poor Law of 1834. Since 1795, there had grown up in England a practice of supplementing low wages from the rates, or local taxes. This practice, known as the "Speenhamland system" of "outdoor relief," gave subsidies from parish rates, in the form of supplementary wages, to those workers who did not earn enough to support themselves and their families. In effect, the Speenhamland system guaranteed a minimum income to laborers, without establishing a minimum wage. The "squire's law" operated chiefly in the rural districts, but the practice became so widespread that, at one time, the number of "assisted poor" was estimated at about a quarter of the population. The evils of supplementary wages from taxes became notorious. It induced employers to pay low wages and encouraged the worker to depend on public charity for part of his livelihood.[9] The burden of the system was borne chiefly by the small, self-employed farmers, who paid heavy rates in order to supplement the low wages paid by the large farmers who employed many laborers.[10]

Upon the Speenhamland system was vented the full fury of all the classical economists, who "emphasized the allegedly injurious effects on the productive capacity and the will to work and to save of the poor which would result from generous, long-sustained, and assured poor-relief to the able-bodied. They stressed even more the growth of population and the consequent impairment of the basic earning power of labor which they believed would ultimately result from any substantial liberation of the poor from dependence solely on their own efforts for the means of subsistence of themselves and their children."[11] Malthus, as might be expected, led in the attack on the Speenhamland system. He argued that the poor really did not benefit from it, because higher wages were followed by higher prices, which kept real wages at the

[8] Sidney and Beatrice Webb, *English Local Government* (London, 1929), VIII, 27.

[9] For an excellent description of the Poor Laws of England, see G. T. Griffith, *Population Problems of the Age of Malthus* (Cambridge University Press, 1926), 129–169.

[10] G. M. Trevelyan, *English Social History* (New York, 1942), 470.

[11] Jacob Viner, "The Short View and the Long View in Economic Policy," *The American Economic Review*, XXX (1940), 3–4.

subsistence level. By regulating wages without regulating population, the Speenhamland system encouraged the poor to continue in their improvident habits of marrying early and begetting more children, thereby increasing competition in the labor market. Reduced wages were inevitable, the funds reserved for labor being limited. Moreover, the Speenhamland system greatly increased the rates, which burdened the entire community.[12] In his hostility to the Speenhamland system, Malthus rang true to his fundamental principle of population: that man does not have the "right of subsistence when his labor will not fairly purchase it"; to get such a right, he would have "to reverse the laws of nature."[13]

The strong opposition of the classical economists to the Speenhamland system was inspired by their uncompromising belief in an economic system based upon free enterprise and free labor. The growing factory system needed a large and constant supply of cheap labor, which, in the England of that time, would come chiefly from the peasantry driven from the land by the enclosures. But the Speenhamland system, by making many laborers "parish serfs," seriously interfered with the supply of labor for the factories. It prevented the growth of a wage-earning class, whose labor would become a commodity in a free labor market subject to the law of supply and demand.[14]

The Poor Law of 1834 was a direct outcome of the views of the classical economists. It constituted an important application of the principle of *laissez faire* to labor in the system of economic liberalism that held sway in England during the Victorian period. For the most part, the new poor law was the work of the Philosophic Radical Sir Edwin Chadwick, whose famous *Report on the Poor Law* was inspired by utilitarian principles.[15] In the drafting of the law, many details "were taken from Bentham's unfinished but amazing Constitutional Code."[16]

[12] T. R. Malthus, *An Investigation of the Cause of the Present High Price of Provisions* (London, 1800). Bentham, too, was strongly opposed to outdoor relief. See his *Observations on the Poor Bill* (Bowring, ed.), VIII, 440–461.

[13] T. R. Malthus, *An Essay on the Principle of Population* (London, 1890), 476.

[14] For a new interpretation of the Speenhamland system and the Poor Law of 1834, see K. Polanyi, *The Great Transformation* (New York, 1944), 77–103.

[15] Sidney and Beatrice Webb, *op. cit.*, VIII, 79. The most radical of all the Philosophic Radicals, Francis Place, was likewise a supporter of the Poor Law. See Graham Wallas, *The Life of Francis Place* (New York, 1919), 332–334.

[16] M. Marston, *Sir Edwin Chadwick* (London, 1925), 22; see also Graham Wallas, *Men and Ideas* (London, 1940), 29.

The law abolished "outdoor relief" and established a new system, which gave relief only to the sick and aged among the poor and work to the able bodied among the unemployed. Another Benthamite innovation was the system of the administration of the Poor Law; it was made national, not local as previously. Workhouses were established, to which were committed those laborers who were not able to find employment; they were given work that paid less than the least paid jobs. Furthermore, the law was "as Malthusian as it dared to be."[17] The influence of Malthus is seen in the rigid segregation of the sexes in these "poor man's Bastilles," so as to discourage marriage. Nothing was more condemned by the Malthusians than the bringing of children into the world by the very poor.

By establishing workhouses, the reformers gave a satiric answer to the socialist demand for the "right to work." To be sent to the workhouse was a stigma, and it soured the hearts of the workingmen, who were convinced that the Poor Law of 1834 recognized poverty as a crime and the helpless workers as criminals.[18] Workhouses were stigmatized as "jails without guilt." If a laborer was willing to work he must be imprisoned in a factory, and "if he found himself out of work, he could only obtain relief by entering another prison." That, in the judgment of Halévy, was "the achievement of the new liberalism which had conquered in 1832."[19] The basic assumption of the Poor Law was that destitution was due either to the moral fault of the individual or to his lack of capacity in the competitive struggle. Neither in Chadwick's *Report* nor in the law itself was any idea expressed of social responsibility for mass poverty. "Never perhaps in all modern history has a more ruthless act of social reform been perpetrated; it crushed multitudes of lives while merely pretending to provide a criterion of genuine destitution in the workhouse test. Psychological torture was coolly advocated and smoothly put into practice by mild philanthropists as a means of oiling the wheels of the labor mill."[20]

Taking the "long view," the Poor Law of 1834 did result in the abolition of the evil practice of supplementing wages through public charity. As long as the cushion of charity was ever present, the workers were

[17] Clapham, *op. cit.*, I, 578.
[18] *Ibid.*
[19] Halévy, *op. cit.*, 291.
[20] Polanyi, *op. cit.*, 82.

disinclined to stand up and battle for an equitable wage system. Trade-unionism did not and could not thrive under the Speenhamland system, which, by its very nature, prevented the organization of the working class. The great advance of English trade-unionism took place after the passage of the Poor Law.[21]

The Poor Law of 1834 removed the last obstacle to the commercialization of labor. Now labor was recognized as a commodity with a market price, wages; and the workers were free to compete in the labor market. At last there appeared a plentiful supply of labor that factory owners could "hire and fire" as suited business conditions. In abolishing the last security for labor, the Poor Law established, at the same time, greater security for capital, which could now plan new enterprises, assured in advance of a supply of labor, cheap, plentiful, dependent, and docile.

Flushed with triumph, bourgeois liberalism determined to free the land from feudal privileges, as it had freed the workers from "parish serfdom." Deprived of the feudal restrictions on the buying and selling of land, such as primogeniture and entail, and placed on an equal footing with other property, land would cease to be an "estate" and become "property" in the modern sense—free to be divided, to be inherited, to be bought, and to be sold. The bourgeois liberals were convinced that the repeal of the Corn Laws would accomplish this purpose by delivering a body blow to the landed interests. Free trade would be a silent "night of August 4," which, in effect, would ruin the landed aristocracy as a class without peasant uprisings, without the burning of title deeds, without the decrees of a revolutionary assembly —by contrast with occurrences in France during the French Revolution. Once the Corn Laws were repealed, the economic forces of competition, set in motion by the free importation of foodstuffs, would deprive the landowners of the domestic market, which was their only outlet. The value of their estates would sink; land would be forced on the market; and the landowners, as a privileged class, would cease to exist.

According to the teachings of the classical economists, the parasitic

[21] Sidney and Beatrice Webb, *The History of Trade Unionism* (London, 1920), Chap. IV.

position of a landed aristocracy in a capitalist economy justified their elimination from the economic scene. As they produced nothing, they should get nothing. But as property rights in general might be jeopardized by such drastic actions, the free traders advocated a policy that would have the effect of ruining the landed aristocracy, as a class, without attacking the property rights of any individual in that class. The repeal of the Corn Laws would be a "Glorious Revolution" in the economic sphere; an act of Parliament, put through by those who rigidly upheld the "sacred right" of property, would result in expropriating the landed aristocracy. Had not the latter, when they controlled Parliament, set a precedent for such action by putting through the enclosure acts, which, in effect, expropriated the yeomanry? Now that the middle class controlled Parliament, they determined to use that political mechanism to ruin the aristocrats.

Behind the fiscal issue of protection versus free trade there raged in England the most bitter—and the last—conflict between the aristocrats and the capitalists. The latter found themselves seriously hampered by the restrictions of the Corn Laws, which maintained high prices of food and, consequently, of wages, thereby raising the cost of manufactures.[22] A great surplus of goods began to pile up in England, which needed an outlet. Such an outlet could be found in foreign countries, provided that the latter were permitted to send their foodstuffs freely into England. Free trade would have a twofold effect: it would reduce "rent" to a minimum and raise profit to a maximum. It would avoid the necessity of cultivating poor land in England, which raised the cost of living, thereby increasing wages and decreasing profits. The cheap food from the more fertile lands on the near-by Continent would be sent to England at a low cost of transportation. Free competition of cheap food would drive the English landowners to the wall. "Rent" would fall and with it would fall the cost of living and, consequently, the "natural price" of labor, namely, the subsistence wage. Wages being an important element in the cost of production, the English manufacturer would be in the enviable position of always being able to produce at a minimum cost. Had not Ricardo taught

---

[22] In 1835 the price of wheat averaged 39*s.* 4*d.* a quarter, which rose, in 1841, to 64*s.* 4*d.* a quarter. See G. D. H. Cole and R. Postgate, *The Common People* (London, 1938), 306.

the manufacturers that profits depended on "high or low wages, wages on the price of necessaries, and the price of necessaries chiefly on the price of food"?[23] In return for food imports, the English factory owners would export manufactured goods, which, during the first half of the nineteenth century, encountered little competition in the markets of the world. Buying food in the cheapest market and selling manufactures in the dearest market constituted the economic paradise envisioned by the free traders.

All the bourgeois liberals—utilitarians, classical economists, Philosophic Radicals, and the Manchester school—united to demand the repeal of the Corn Laws and the establishment of free trade with the whole world.[24] Free trade, they argued, would be the reform of reforms, in that the markets of the world would be opened to the vast quantities of manufactured goods that poured from English factories; and the rising demand for food in England, grown richer and more populous, would be met by free imports from agricultural lands near and far. As the factory system introduced division of labor in the ways of manufacturing goods, free trade would introduce division of labor in the process of distributing the world's goods. Both as a political and as a social philosophy, liberalism was "the line of policy which seeks to reform the social order to meet the needs and fulfill the promise of a mode of production based on the division of labor."[25] A geographical division of labor would then arise in the world economy: each nation would specialize in those products for which it was best fitted, depending on its natural resources, on its geographical location at a trade center, and on the special abilities of its people. In this way the special advantages of every part of the world would be shared by every nation. Labor and capital would freely migrate to those parts of the world where they could be most advantageously employed; waste and idleness would then be reduced to a minimum. A prosperous and peaceful world was the goal envisaged by the free traders, which could be reached merely by abolishing the tariff duties.

[23] David Ricardo, *Principles of Political Economy and Taxation* (E. C. K. Gonner, ed., London, 1891), 97.

[24] Bentham, *Manual of Political Economy* (Bowring, ed.,) III; *The Works of David Ricardo* (J. R. McCulloch, ed., London, 1871), 203*ff.* On the activity of the Philosophic Radicals in the free-trade movement, see the article by Sir John Bowring in *Howitts Journal*, II (1847), 123*ff.*

[25] Walter Lippmann, *The Good Society* (Boston, 1937), 180.

To its champions free trade took on the character of a world crusade for liberty of enterprise, for equality of opportunity to exploit the world's riches, and for the fraternity of nations united in lasting peace as a consequence of a removal of the tariff barriers that divided them into hostile economic camps. The free traders were ardent in their belief that, once universal free trade was established, universal peace would be sure to follow. "Free trade! What is it?" asked its great apostle, Richard Cobden, "Why, breaking down the barriers that separate nations; those barriers, behind which nestle the feelings of pride, revenge, hatred, and jealousy, which every now and then burst their bounds and deluge whole countries with blood; those feelings which nourish the poison of war and conquest;..."[26] England, by establishing free trade, would become the center of a new world revolution, which would be spread among the nations, not by revolutionary armies, but by the peaceful exchange of products between nations in a world market free to all.

The free-trade movement began early in the nineteenth century, but it did not gain much momentum until after the passage of the Reform Bill of 1832. Associated with this movement was the famous Anti-Corn-Law League, founded in 1836, which was financed by the manufacturers and led by the bourgeois liberals Richard Cobden and John Bright. As in the movement for the reform of Parliament, the bourgeois liberals saw the necessity of gaining popular support, which could be used, as in 1832, as a threat to the landowners. They won the adherence of many workers by blaming the rising cost of living on the landowners. Great masses of the poor rallied to the cause of free trade, which held out to them the promise of immediate relief from hunger and from want.[27] The numerous mass meetings organized by the Anti-Corn-Law League were threats of revolt against aristocratic economic privileges, just as had been the great popular demonstrations before 1832 against aristocratic political privileges. So great was the popular pressure that a section of the Tory party, led by the Prime Minister, Sir Robert Peel, joined the free traders. In 1846 the Peel ministry carried through Parliament the repeal of the Corn Laws. One of the great economic objectives of the bourgeois liberals was at

[26] Richard Cobden, *Speeches on Questions of Public Policy* (London, 1870), I, 79.

[27] Élie Halévy, *The Growth of Philosophic Radicalism,* trans. from the French by Mary Morris (London, 1928), 337.

last realized when free trade supplanted protectionism as the commercial policy of England.

Free trade was a body blow to the English aristocracy from which it never recovered. The landed interest was shattered and, with it, the historic Tory party.[28] The cheap food that poured in from the Continent and from overseas had a disastrous effect upon English agriculture, which gradually declined. In the middle of the nineteenth century, agriculture was still the greatest economic activity of the English people.[29] By the seventies, England became predominantly an industrial state, and agriculture sank into relative insignificance.

However, the landed interests made no attempt to restore the Corn Laws. When Disraeli succeeded Peel as the leader of the Tories he cynically repudiated his former protectionist views and frankly accepted free trade as the best policy for an industrialized England. As in the case of the Reform Bill of 1832, the aristocrats accepted the repeal of the Corn Laws in the interest of social peace. Once more the Victorian Compromise was vindicated.

Industry, in contrast with agriculture, advanced by leaps and bounds. The three decades following the establishment of free trade was the period of England's economic golden age, when the economic life of the world pivoted on her industry, on her commerce, and on her finance. England became the workshop of the world, the forge of the world, the commission merchant of the world, the shipper of the world, the banker of the world, and the broker of the world. From all lands flowed a golden stream of profits toward England. Immense fortunes were piled up by her capitalists, whose influence became all powerful in the conduct of the government.

Closely associated with free trade was a movement that can best be described as "antiimperialism." The old colonial system, which continued into the nineteenth century, was based on mercantilism. One aspect of mercantilism—that in relation to colonies—was the restriction of colonial trade and manufactures for the benefit of the mother country. Another aspect was the special protection given to colonial interests at the expense of the mother country. A good illus-

[28] M. Ostrogorski, *Democracy and the Organization of Political Parties,* trans. from the French by F. Clarke (London, 1902), I, 56*ff*.

[29] Clapham, *op. cit.,* II, 22.

tration was the protection of the sugar interests in the British West Indies. The production of sugar in these islands was stimulated by bounties, by monopolies, and, especially, by a prohibitive tariff on foreign sugar. The West India planters, using slave labor, had almost a monopoly of the market in England. Competition of cheaper sugar from Brazil, Cuba, and the French West Indies was shut out; as a consequence, the British consumers had to pay high prices for sugar. This was a serious hardship to many English poor, who consumed large quantities of sugar when tea drinking became a national habit.

An even more glaring abuse of the old colonial system was the trade of India, which continued as a monopoly of the British East India Company. The members of the company amassed vast fortunes through their control of the Indian trade. However, the cost of protecting their factories and plantations against uprisings and invasions fell upon the British taxpayer, who bore the expense of the British armies in India. To the reformers the old colonial system appeared as the very negation of a free economy.

An attitude of aloofness, not to say of hostility, to the Empire characterized the bourgeois liberals, one and all. Their prophet, Bentham, had asserted that colonies were more of a burden than an advantage to England and that their real use was to provide highly paid positions for the aristocracy. English trade would benefit as a result of emancipating the colonies; and Bentham gave as an illustration the trade of England with the United States, which was greater than the trade of England had been with the Thirteen Colonies. "Hear a paradox—it is a true one. Give up your colonies, they are yours: keep them, they are ours." In case of war, the colonies were a source not of strength but of weakness. "Are you attacked at home? not a man can you ever get from them; not a sixpence. Are they attacked? they draw upon you for fleets and armies."[30]

James Mill asserted that colonies were not held in the interest of the nation but in that of the "ruling few" for whom they were a source of political patronage, such as "governorships and judgeships,

[30] Bentham, *Emancipate Your Colonies* (Bowring, ed.), IV, 414–415. Toward the end of his life Bentham modified his drastic views on imperialism. He supported the plans of the colonial reformers who sought to retain the colonies as places of settlement for British emigrants. See R. C. Mills, *The Colonization of Australia* (London, 1915)

and a long train of *et ceteras."* Moreover, colonies were "a grand source of wars"; they were both a cause of war between ambitious nations and an additional burden in time of war.[31] The leader of the Philosophic Radicals in Parliament, Joseph Hume, declared that the colonies, "instead of being an addition to the strength of the country, increased its weakness; and he believed it would be better able to cope with any contingency which might arise, if those colonies were freed from their allegiance, and became their own masters. The commercial advantages to England would be still the same; for we should continue to be the principal suppliers."[32]

John Stuart Mill lent his powerful support to the attack on imperialism. Colonies, he argued, held out few advantages and many disadvantages to the mother country, which could get along perfectly well without them. Especially did their defense constitute a heavy burden on the mother country. But unlike his fellow Benthamites, Mill was opposed to the abolition of the British Empire, so long as the colonies did not desire separation. What he favored was a loose connection between England and her colonies—one that would protect the latter from being conquered by aggressive, despotic nations.[33]

Antiimperialism was convincing after the American Revolution had proved that colonies could revolt successfully and after the Industrial Revolution had shown the economic fallacies of mercantilism. Cobden and Bright regarded with equanimity the eventual separation of the colonies from England. Cobden was an outspoken Little Englander. He was convinced that England would benefit from the dissolution of the Empire, as the colonies would continue to be good customers, and the mother country would not have the expense of maintaining and protecting them.[34] In a modified form, antiimperialism was the policy of Gladstonian liberalism, which concentrated all its energies on domestic problems to the exclusion of imperial ones. After

[31] James Mill, "Colonies," in *Essays* (London, n.d.), 31–33; A. Bain, *James Mill* (London, 1882), 242.

[32] Hansard, *Parliamentary Debates,* New Series (1823), VIII, 250.

[33] J. S. Mill, *Representative Government,* in *Utilitarianism, Liberty and Representative Government* (London, Everyman's Library, 1914), 379–380; J. S. Mill, *Letters* (H. S. R. Elliott, ed., London, 1910), II, 268. For a good description of the antiimperialist views of Bentham, Ricardo, and the Mills, see K. E. Knorr, *British Colonial Theories, 1570–1850* (Toronto, 1944).

[34] Cobden, *Political Writings* (London, 1867), 25–31.

the repeal of the Corn Laws, the English manufacturers regarded the whole world, not the British Empire, as the proper field for their economic activity. Were the colonies to become independent, they, like the rest of the world, would send foodstuffs and raw materials to England in return for manufactured articles. With what other nations could they do business as well as with England, then the only highly industralized nation in the world, engaged primarily in foreign trade?[35]

It was during the period of bourgeois liberalism that the British Empire experienced a second birth. The charter of liberties of what has been called the "second" British Empire was the famous *Report on the Affairs of British North America*. Its author was Lord Durham, who was assisted by Charles Buller and Edward Gibbon Wakefield, all utilitarians. The *Report* was issued in 1839, as a result of an investigation by Lord Durham of the situation in Canada that had led to the rebellion of 1837. In Parliament, the Canadian rebels had the support of the Philosophic Radicals Joseph Hume and Sir William Molesworth, who criticized the conduct of the British government in the colony.[36] Lord Durham's recommendations created a profound impression in England and led to the establishment, in 1847, of responsible government in Canada. The *Report* was also the inspiration of the British North America Act of 1867, which established in Canada, for the first time, the Dominion system of self-government within the British Empire. For the most part, the bourgeois liberals did not advocate the dissolution of the British Empire; they were content to accept colonial self-government as a policy of *laissez faire* applied to imperial affairs.[37]

Antiimperialism was an important element in the movement to abolish slavery in the Empire. The abolitionists, led by the humanitarians William Wilberforce and Henry Brougham, were bitterly

[35] The definitive work on Victorian antiimperialism, in relation to free trade, is Robert Livingston Schuyler, *The Fall of the Old Colonial System: A Study in British Free Trade, 1770–1870* (Oxford University Press, 1945).

[36] Hansard, *op. cit.*, XXXIX, 1446, 1456.

[37] In the latter part of his life, Bentham advocated a system of self-government within the Empire. See Graham Wallas, *Men and Ideas* (London, 1940), 31. That strenuous Benthamite J. A. Roebuck proposed a scheme of self-government for the colonies as a solution of the imperial problem in his *The Colonies of England* (London, 1849). For an excellent study of English opinion regarding the Empire, see R. C. Bodelsen, *Mid-Victorian Imperialism* (Copenhagen, 1924).

opposed by the small but powerful group of English slaveowners in the West Indies, whose sugar interests were props of the old colonial system. Boer slaveowners on the farms and pasture lands of South Africa did not figure much in the struggle. To the side of the abolitionists came the rival sugar interests in the East Indies, who were not favored by the English tariff as were the sugar interests in the West Indies. "God and Mammon joined hands."[38] Moreover, freedom for the Negro in America meant cheap sugar for the Englishman in Europe. Emancipation would be followed by the destruction of the sugar monopoly, which would open the English market to the sugar raisers elsewhere. On the morrow of the Reform Bill, in 1833, Parliament passed a law abolishing slavery in the Empire. Emancipation was to be gradual and the slaveowners were to be compensated by an indemnity of about one million dollars. Some years later, the discriminatory tariff in favor of British colonial sugar was removed.

The fate of India also was affected by Victorian antiimperialism. The uprising of the Indians against the British in 1857, known as the "Indian Mutiny," turned hostile eyes in the direction of the British East India Company. The uprising was suppressed, but it resulted in ending the career of this famous corporation. In 1858 Parliament passed a law abolishing the East India Company. The rule of British India now passed directly to the crown. In the new system of government there was no provision for Indian self-government, though there was a vague promise of it. Yet the new order was an expression of the antiimperialist trend in England, in that one of the great pillars of the old colonial system collapsed with the abolition of the East India Company.

The triumph of bourgeois liberalism in England was greater and more complete than its pioneers, the utilitarians, had expected or had even hoped. The struggle over free trade in 1846, like that over parliamentary reform in 1832, revealed the great strength of the middle class in their conflict with the entrenched aristocracy. Their comparatively easy triumph in both instances gave them a feeling of assurance, which led to an attitude of complacency. The middle class began to see its triumph in the light of a universal scheme of life and work for all

[38] For a description of the antislavery movement in England, see Paul Knaplund, *The British Empire, 1815–1939* (New York, 1941), 100*ff.*

mankind that made for progress, for peace, and for prosperity. The "universal beneficence of profits," arising from adherence to economic laws, seemed to justify this heightened conception of their role in human progress. The history of England during the period of bourgeois liberalism, from 1832 to 1870, was a period of great progress, of undisturbed peace, of mounting prosperity, and of political stability.

To what extent did the mass of people share in the prosperity that came from England's expanding economy? Did the "universal beneficence of profits" include the workers as it did their employers? These questions become pertinent in our day, when high wages, rather than large profits, are considered the supreme test of national prosperity. To a limited extent the workers did share in England's economic golden age. Real wages rose during the three decades that followed the repeal of the Corn Laws. And it was the very fact that their condition had improved that caused the workers to be dissatisfied. The rising discontent of the workers was fed by the conviction that they shared unequally in national prosperity. Profits rose far higher and much faster than did wages. Immense fortunes were piled up by the capitalists, whereas the workers continued to get a bare minimum for existence. In the deficit economy before the Industrial Revolution the masses had been poor in a poor country; now in the surplus economy created by high production they found themselves poor in a rich country. This situation aroused bitter and active resentment among the industrial workers. How could a more just distribution of wealth be brought about? Could it be done by trade-union action? Hardly. After the repeal of the Combination Laws in 1824, there no longer existed any statutory prohibitions of trade-unions; but the severe limitations placed on collective bargaining and on the right to strike by judicial decisions so hampered the trade-unions that, to all intents and purposes, the Combination Laws continued in full force.

In the view of the English workers, there was only one way to better their situation and that was through political action. The vote was not only a symbol of full citizenship; it was also a powerful weapon that the workers could use to obtain reforms in their interest. Disappointment with the Reform Bill of 1832, which had left them voteless, did not lead the workers to repudiate Parliament, now securely in the hands of their employers. Their active participation in the agitation for parliamentary reform had made them politically conscious. They were now convinced that constant and active pressure from without, which, in 1832, had forced the aristocrats to yield to the middle class, would now force the latter to yield to the working class.

It was this trend that led to the launching of a new political movement, known as "Chartism." In one sense, Chartism was a continuation of the movement for parliamentary reform that had culminated in the Reform Bill of 1832. In another and more significant sense, it was the first nationally organized class-conscious movement of the English workers with something like socialist objectives. Though rather hazy in its social outlook, Chartism managed to combine all the forces that came to life in the early days of the labor movement: democratic government, trade-unionism, workers' education, the cooperative movement, social reform, and socialism. Though he was not directly identified with the Chartists, the man who most nearly represented their ideals was Robert Owen, the father of English socialism. The program of the People's Charter, adopted in 1838 by a workingmen's association in London, was, however, distinctively and exclusively political. It demanded the famous Six Points: (1) manhood suffrage, (2) vote by secret ballot, (3) abolition of property qualifications for members of parliament, (4) salaries for members of parliament, (5) annual elections, and (6) equal electoral districts. This program, formulated in political terms, involved the acceptance of the liberal state by the most radical element of the nation. There was no suggestion of dictatorship in Chartist ideology.

As the Chartist agitation proceeded, socialist overtones were heard in revolutionary threats to the capitalist order. The workers were convinced that the combined property interests in Parliament—land in the Lords and industry in the Commons—constituted a more serious obstacle to democracy than had been the unreformed Parliament under aristocratic control. And they became infuriated when they reflected that the Reform Bill had been put through largely because of their demonstrations, their petitions, their rioting. The workers now vented all their fury upon the middle class, the former ally who had betrayed them by denying them the suffrage. What added bitterness to their disappointment was the Poor Law of 1834, which gave "prison sentences" to unemployed workers.

The Chartists concentrated their agitation on manhood suffrage, which became the symbol of democratic liberalism, as propertied suffrage was that of bourgeois liberalism. Hostility of the Chartists to the property-owning classes created great alarm in middle-class England. It was feared that manhood suffrage, once granted, would be followed by universal confiscation. This fear was voiced by Macaulay, who, in a speech on the People's Charter, declared that universal suffrage was "incompatible, not with this or that form of government, but with all forms of government, and with everything for the sake of which forms of government exist; that it is incompatible with property, and that it is consequently incompatible with civilization."[39]

As the revolutionary year 1848 approached, the Chartists became more and more threatening in their demands. The movement fell under the control of the "physical-force" element, led by Feargus O'Connor, which openly preached social revolution. Not even in 1832 did England experience so great a fear of a revolutionary uprising as it did in 1848. Thousands of citizens were appointed special constables to fight the revolutionists. However, the Chartist threat fizzled out in isolated riots that were easily suppressed. There were no June Days in London, as there were in Paris. England was the one country in Western Europe that managed to maintain political stability during the revolutionary year 1848, when government after government was overturned by the revolutionary tide that rolled on from Paris to Vienna.

Chartism did finally triumph, but in the English manner of the "inevitability of gradualness." Nearly all Six Points became law in time.[40] Bourgeois liberalism proved itself amenable to extensions of democracy, once it was convinced that democracy would respect property rights and civil liberties. Chartism, not Marxism, has been the inspiration of English working-class movements, such as trade-unionism, the cooperative movement, and that distinctively English brand of socialism, the British Labor party.

Chartism was not the only challenge to triumphant bourgeois liberalism. About the middle of the nineteenth century, a new challenge

[39] *The Complete Works of Lord Macaulay* (London 1898–1920), XII, 8.

[40] The property qualification for membership in Parliament was abolished in 1858; universal suffrage was established by the Reform Bills of 1867, 1884, 1918, and 1928; the secret ballot, in 1872; payment of members, in 1911; and in 1944 a law provided for the periodic redistribution of seats.

came from an unexpected quarter—a revived Conservative party under the leadership of Benjamin Disraeli (1804–1881). It was Disraeli
who first grasped the idea that a Conservative party could not exist
in England as the defender of the *status quo*. There was no *status quo*
to defend, so constantly did political and economic institutions and
policies change under the impact of rapid industrialization. He vividly
brought home to his aristocratic associates that the "age of ruins" was
past and that they must face the issues of the day if they wished ever
again to rule England. It was Disraeli, too, who saw the gaping void
in the schemes of the bourgeois liberals to reorganize the national life
of England—namely, the elimination of the working class from any
significant part in shaping their country's future. Far more clearly
than any of his contemporaries did Disraeli realize the shift in class
control of the government that had followed the Reform Bill of 1832.
The capitalists, unlike the aristocrats of former days, enjoyed power
without responsibility by adhering to the philosophy of *laissez faire,*
the very essence of which was, according to Disraeli, a "union of oli-
garchical wealth and mob poverty."[41] Disraeli repudiated *laissez faire*
and excoriated its upholders. The architects of a new and better
England should not be the Benthamites, "philosophers who practice
on the sectarian prejudices of a portion of the people," but a revivified
throne, an apostolic church, and, especially, a regenerated aristocracy,
who were—in his view—the natural leaders of the English people.

In his grand scheme of political reorganization Disraeli proclaimed
an ideal of conservatism. Previously conservatism had meant obstinate
clinging to the *status quo* and rigid adherence to inherited traditions.
Disraeli developed a concept of conservatism that was dynamic, not
static. English conservatives were to be in the vanguard of progress
by becoming the champions of reforms far more radical than those
advocated by the liberals. And these reforms were to be primarily in
the interest of the workers, who were to be enfranchised and raised
from their low economic level through social legislation. But the
inspiration of these reforms was not to be found in the doctrines of
democratic equality, but in the "national past of England"; and they
were to be in harmony with "the manners, the customs, the laws, and
the traditions" of the English people.

Disraeli was far from being a democrat. He was convinced that the

41 Benjamin Disraeli, *Whigs and Whiggism* (London, 1913), 350.

common man was incapable of ruling the nation; all that he could do was to choose his rulers from either of the two propertied classes, aristocrats or capitalists. If the former were willing to extend a friendly hand to him, the common man would gladly prefer the old ruling class, rooted in the nation's history, to the newly rich capitalists, whose chief concern was to keep profits up by keeping wages down. Disraeli developed his ideas, attractively and forcefully, in a trilogy of novels— *Coningsby, Sybil,* and *Tancred*—which aimed to popularize his views. *Coningsby* exposed the failure of the two old parties, the Tories and the Whigs, to deal with the new problems because their ideas were based on social and economic conditions that were passing away. "The crown has become a cipher; the church a sect; the nobility drones; and the people drudges." *Sybil* contained realistic descriptions of what Disraeli called "the two nations" in England, "between whom there is no intercourse and no sympathy; who are as ignorant of each other's habits, thoughts and feelings as if they were dwellers in different zones, or inhabitants of different planets; who are formed by a different breeding, are fed by a different food, are ordered by different manners, and are governed by the same laws. . . . The Rich and the Poor." *Tancred* called for a religious revival to regenerate the English people, in order to make them receptive to the new conservatism. Disraeli made an appeal for the support of the Anglican church on national, rather than on religious, grounds. In his view the church was distinctively an English institution, which, even in worship, expressed the spirit of moderation so characteristically English. "Happy the land where there is an institution which prevents enthusiasm from degenerating into extravagance, and ceremony from being degraded into superstition." [42]

Disraeli spent the major part of his political life "educating" his party, which became known as the "Conservatives." Its reorganization and reorientation proceeded slowly and painfully under his leadership. Finally, he succeeded in persuading the Conservatives to abandon their Tory past and to embark on a career of reform. The Conservatives began outbidding their Liberal opponents in advocating reform measures. This was strikingly illustrated by the Reform Bill of 1867, a Conservative measure that went beyond the proposals of the Liberals to extend the suffrage to the working class.

Secure in the control of the government, fearing neither aristocratic

[42] Earl of Beaconsfield, *Selected Speeches* (London, 1882), II, 558.

reaction nor proletarian revolution, the bourgeois liberals yet sat uneasily in the seat of power. Disraeli's Tory democracy constituted an even greater challenge to them than did Chartism. What if the impossible happened, and the aristocrats and workers united to oust the bourgeois liberals? For different reasons and with different objectives, Tory democracy and Chartism repudiated *laissez faire,* the life principle of bourgeois liberalism. In the struggle against the entrenched aristocracy before 1832, *laissez faire* had proved to be a powerful weapon of offense in the hands of the bourgeois liberals. Could it now function as a powerful weapon in defense of the new order that had issued from the Reform Bill of 1832?

Laissez faire constituted the intellectual bond that united the various types of bourgeois liberals: the tart and acid Bentham and the florid, imaginative Macaulay; the conservative James Mill, and the radical Francis Place; the abstract Ricardo and the concrete Cobden. To understand the great significance of *laissez faire,* it is necessary to keep in mind that, to its upholders, economics and government were two separate and different systems of human activity, having two separate and different tasks, each performed by an organization especially adapted for its special purpose. Like the "world machine" of Sir Isaac Newton, the new economic world ushered in by the Industrial Revolution was an automatic, self-regulating mechanism. It was "a Newtonian economic order wherein matter is replaced by wealth; attraction and repulsion give way to utility and disutility; the phenomena of the market, like those of the heavens, are given an equilibrium; a system of checks and balances keeps the machine in order; and the theory of the conservation of energy finds a parallel in the law of the economic maximum."[43]

There was now an economic world machine, governed by universal economic laws that were harmonious, uniform, and beneficent. As an engineer planned a bridge so that its stresses and strains were in accordance with the laws of physics, so did a businessman plan his enterprise in accordance with economic laws, discovered by the classical economists. Failure to observe these laws would lead to economic disaster in the latter, as it would lead to physical disaster in the former case. Above all, the enterpriser must have full freedom of contract, that

[43] Walton H. Hamilton, *The Pattern of Competition* (New York, 1940), 11.

he might buy in the cheapest market and sell in the dearest; that he might hire labor on terms most favorable to himself; and that he might transport his goods by the cheapest and shortest route. Only by having freedom of contract could he bring persons, machinery, and natural resources into units of profitable production. Unlike feudal society, which was one of "status," industrial society was one of "contract," which allowed only temporary and limited agreements between buyer and seller, and between employer and employed, owing to the dynamic economic changes that were constantly taking place. The moving index of prices was the enterpriser's mariner's compass, pointing to safe investments in a free market in which "demand and supply found their adjustments without anyone estimating the one or planning the other. The individual producer pushed and groped his way to a new and expanding market, intent only on the share of the market which he could capture.... His guide was no estimate of world demand and production, but the moving index of changing prices." If the amount of goods on the market was more than the consumers could buy, prices would fall and the less efficient and the less fortunate producers would be squeezed out. In time, supply would fall below demand, prices would rise, and "the prospect of higher profits would attract more capital and enterprise to production. So supply and demand would circle round a central, though moving, point of equilibrium."[44] This was "economic liberalism" based upon a self-regulating economic system, in which there was an exchange of goods for profit; in which the market price of a commodity meant that its supply equaled its demand; and in which existed a plentiful supply of stable currency, based on the gold standard.

The other sphere of human activity, the government, was subordinate to the market. Unlike the latter, which was the vital connecting link preventing monopoly through combinations, whether of capital or of landowners, the former was a secondary, though a necessary, institution, which functioned best when it functioned least. In the eyes of the bourgeois liberals, the state occupied no such exalted position as it had in the days of divine-right, absolute monarchy. It was a convenient mechanism, designed to do only those things which the individual could not do, such as protecting the free activities of the market by

[44] Sir Arthur Salter, *Recovery* (London, 1932), 10–11.

preventing monopoly through combinations, whether of capital or of labor; enforcing contracts; protecting life, liberty, and property of the citizens; and defending the nation against foreign aggression. In addition the government was to do things that had not been done before, such as protecting the health of the community, building harbors and post offices, and aiding in the development of railways. Macaulay put the case for *laissez faire* in his characteristically emphatic manner. "Our rulers will best promote the improvement of the nation," he declared, "by strictly confining themselves to their own legitimate duties, by leaving capital to find its own most lucrative course, commodities their fair price, industry and intelligence their natural reward, idleness and folly their natural punishment, by maintaining peace, by defending property, by diminishing the price of law, and by observing strict economy in every department of the state. Let the Government do this: the People will assuredly do the rest."[45]

In the view of the bourgeois liberals, *laissez faire* ideally suited England's expanding industry by giving free rein to the exploitation of natural resources and to the utilization of a cheap labor supply. Capital was free to move to those places which possessed natural resources; and labor was free to move to those places where capital found profitable investment. The relics of feudalism and the restrictions of mercantilism were so many hindrances to the "freedom of the individual" to acquire property, the supreme test of economic capacity under capitalism.

Curiously enough, it was the negative aspect of the state that received the greatest emphasis at the hands of the bourgeois liberals. Government was not to interfere with the operations of the market by controlling or regulating its activities. The battle of competitive forces would be real and fruitful only in a market that was free to act automatically in accordance with economic laws. Government intervention in the operation of the self-regulating economic world machine would be useless, mischievous, and even disastrous. It would bedevil and bewilder all economic relationships, the result of which would inevitably be universal ruin.[46] *Laissez faire* had as its fundamental concept

45 Lord Macaulay, *Essays and Biographies,* in *Works,* VII, 502.

46 F. C. Mills, "Economics in Time of Change," *The American Economic Review* (March, 1941).

the natural harmony of economic forces. What is now regarded as anarchy of production was then regarded as the perfection of the orderly operation of economic laws, which brought deserved success to those who worked in harmony with them and equally deserved failure to those who flouted them. When all governmental restraints are abolished, declared Adam Smith in a notable passage "the obvious and simple system of natural liberty establishes itself of its own accord. Every man, as long as he does not violate the laws of justice, is left perfectly free to pursue his own interests in his own way, and to bring both his industry and capital into competition with those of any other man, or order of men."[47] In this "obvious and simple system" capital and labor must be free to come and to go in search of profit or of wages, from industry to industry, from region to region, from country to country.

Obviously there was no place in this "mechanically conceived economics" for a "planned economy" centrally organized and directed by the government. Nature's "simple plan" was a far safer guide than planning by the nation according to rules promulgated by bureaucratic officials. Only when the government followed a laissez-faire policy would the economic law operate to increase the wealth of a nation. "With the view of causing an increase to take place in the mass of national wealth," declared Bentham, "or with a view to increase of the means either of subsistence or enjoyment, without some special reason, the general rule is, that nothing ought to be done or attempted by government. The motto, or watchword of government, on these occasions, ought to be—*Be Quiet*." Any interference on the part of government with business was needless. "Generally speaking, there is no one who knows what is for your interest, so well as yourself." Government interference was "universally and constantly pernicious in another way, by the restraint or constraint imposed on the free agency of the individual." What agriculture, industry, and commerce asked of government was as "modest and reasonable as that which Diogenes asked of Alexander: *'Stand out of my sunshine.'* "[48]

However, it would be incorrect to state that Bentham and his disciples advocated a weak, do-nothing state. Quite the contrary. The

---

[47] Adam Smith, *The Wealth of Nations* (Edwin Cannan, ed., London, 1930), II, 184.
[48] Bentham, *Manual of Political Economy* (Bowring, ed.), III, 33–35.

Benthamites favored a strong, efficient, economical government to carry on the common affairs of the nation and to promote social and economic progress by removing the hampering restrictions imposed by mercantilism on commerce, industry, and labor. Legislation was their supreme method of effecting these far-reaching reforms. Hence they advocated the establishment of administrative centralization, functioning under a hierarchy of civil servants appointed through competitive examinations.[49] The chief functions of the Benthamite state were those of "inspectability": to administer the civil and criminal laws; to register births, marriages, and deaths; to care for the safety of communications by highway, railway and waterway; to maintain the health of the nation through sanitary regulations; to protect contracts; and to provide information on social and economic matters in the form of statistics. Nor did the Benthamite state shy from intervening in economic matters under certain conditions. The Benthamites favored state intervention to protect those who, like children, were not free agents in making contracts.[50] A good illustration was their support of the Factory Act of 1833, the first important law in the history of English factory reform. Among other provisions, the law prohibited the employment in the textile mills of children under nine; provided for an eight-hour workday for children between nine and thirteen; and for a ten-hour workday for those between thirteen and eighteen. [51] However, the Benthamites were opposed to the legal protection of adult laborers, who, they believed, were free agents in making contracts. That a child was not, but that an adult was, a free agent when confronted with the grueling fact of economic pressure was a distinction that permitted a humanitarian escape from the impersonal rule of economic law. In reality, the economic pressure to gain a livelihood was not on the child, but on the father of the child, who was an adult.

From *laissez faire,* as a central doctrine, were derived a new principle of social action, namely, "individualism"; a new view of property that justified capitalist rule; and an attitude of irresponsibility for

[49] The Factory Act of 1833 initiated the Benthamite state by establishing a national system of factory inspection. It was followed by a provision in the Poor Law of 1834, which established a national board of final control.

[50] Halévy, *A History of the English People, 1830–1841,* 114–115.

[51] *Ibid.,* 115.

the evils of industrialism suffered by the workers. Bourgeois liberalism conceived an "atomic" society, composed of individuals each striving to advance his personal interest. Every individual was to be free to contract for anything that he had to sell or wished to buy: the merchant, his wares; the professional man, his services; the worker, his labor; the capitalist, his investment; the landowner, his land. As an "economic man," the individual was the best judge of his own interest; in his efforts to advance it, he was guided by an "invisible hand" to advance also that of the public. The more property individuals accumulated through industry, the richer was the community; its wealth was the sum total of the wealth of the individuals composing it. Harmony of individual and general welfare was, therefore, a fundamental idea of the bourgeois liberals. Social problems were to be solved not by class conflicts but by bringing the interests of class, like those of the individual, into harmony with general welfare. Competition among capitalists was not at first regarded as a struggle of "each man for himself and the devil take the hindmost." It was not strife but a fruitful rivalry that resulted in advancing the prosperity of the nation, in which all would share, though not equally. There was only one alternative to competition, according to the bourgeois liberals, and that was monopoly bolstered up by privilege. Wherever "competition is not, monopoly is," declared John Stuart Mill, and monopoly was "the taxation of the industrious for the support of indolence, if not of plunder."[52]

Laissez faire had a distinct bearing on the ambitions of the capitalists to succeed the aristocrats as the rulers of England. The privileges of the aristocrats were conferred by laws and by customs that Parliament could abolish without attacking the "sacred right" of property. But the power of the capitalist came from the possession of property, which, though it conferred no special legal privileges to its possessors, gave them immense power in the nation whose economic life they controlled. The most obvious example of privilege was income without personal labor; and the most obvious example of despotism was the control of the life and labor of human beings by men who were responsible for their actions only to themselves. Freedom to acquire, freedom to sell, and freedom to transmit, coupled with the protection

[52] J. S. Mill, *Principles of Political Economy* (W. J. Ashley, ed., London, 1909), 792.

of property rights, resulted in placing the capitalists in the position
of a ruling class without the onus of legal and customary privileges.

Property, in its new status of "sacred right," was the sum of all
privileges. Those who possessed it could break down the barriers to
social recognition, to political power, and to economic affluence.
The property of the capitalists was immune to state intervention on
behalf of labor, through *laissez faire,* which prohibited the regulation
of wages and hours. A successful capitalist, whose property was safe
from legislative attack and who had the right to transmit it to his
descendants, was in a far more secure position as a member of a ruling
class than was the landed aristocrat, whose privileges were being rapidly
shorn away by the reforms that followed the Reform Bill of 1832.
Laissez faire resulted in creating something unique in history—a ruling
class without legal privileges and without social responsibilities.

Especially did *laissez faire* absolve the capitalists from responsibility
for their dependents, the factory workers. The "cash nexus" that bound
the capitalist and the worker was an impersonal relationship, which
could be snapped at any time and for any reason. This relationship
was in striking contrast with that between the landed aristocrat and
his dependents, in which many personal ties, reminiscent of feudalism,
bound the lord and his "tenantry" from generation to generation.
The bourgeois liberal doctrines of the "liberty of the subject" and
"freedom of contract" constituted the most powerful influence against
factory reforms.[53] That complete classical economist Nassau William
Senior opposed the Factory Act of 1833, on the ground that the reduction of hours in the factory would bring ruin to England's textile
industry, because the net profit of a cotton factory, operating on a
twelve-hour workday, was "derived from the last hour."[54] All too
frequently did *laissez faire* come to mean the "freedom of consumers
to pay what the traffic would bear, the freedom of farmers to bankrupt
each other, the freedom of women to work in factories at night, and
the freedom of little children to use their own judgment in deciding
whether they shall go to college or go to work in the mill."[55]

[53] William Smart, *Economic Annals of the Nineteenth Century* (London, 1910), I, 669.
[54] S. Leon Levy, *Nassau W. Senior* (Boston, 1943), 241.
[55] C. S. Ayres, "Basis of Economic Statesmanship," *The American Economic Review*
XXIII (1933), 210.

What passed as public opinion in Victorian England had the indelible imprint of *laissez faire*. It was generally accepted as a self-evident truth in the abstract, and as an infallible guide to good government in the concrete. The famous principle blended the English heritage of individual freedom with the selfish interests of the capitalist class. The most vociferous advocates of *laissez faire* were the "Manchester school," so called because the great cotton-manufacturing center, Manchester, became the symbol of industrial England. Its famous spokesmen Richard Cobden and John Bright were the strident voices of triumphant capitalism that boldly and frankly defended its interests against those of the working class. "Manchesterism" became notorious as a body of capitalist doctrines that identified the prosperity of the manufacturers with economic laws that made for universal progress.[56] Greed for money, long regarded as the root of all evil, was translated by the Manchester school into a cosmic urge to benefit mankind.

Of the many reforms put through by the bourgeois liberals, few were directly in the interest of the working class. The social reforms of the period, notably the Factory Acts of 1833 and 1847, were the work of socially minded Tories, like Lord Shaftesbury, Michael Thomas Sadler, and Richard Oastler. These humanitarian reformers did realize the existence of another England, which was unseen and unheeded by the bourgeois liberals: the England that toiled long and arduously in factories, in mines, and in shipyards, for wages barely sufficient to keep body and soul together. The high-souled Lord Shaftesbury became the leading advocate of legislation to protect the workers against the worst evils of the factory system: unhygienic conditions, long hours, and the employment of women and children. Largely through his efforts, Parliament in 1847 passed the famous Ten Hours Law, a landmark in the history of factory reform.

The Ten Hours Law raised less the issue of hours than that of the regulation of the labor of adults. By reducing the workday, in the textile factories, of women and young persons to ten hours, the law, in effect, established a ten-hour law for men as well. The factories could not have been kept open with only the men at the machines.

[56] For a good description of the ideas of the Manchester school, see C. B. R. Kent, *The English Radicals* (London, 1899), 381*ff*.

All schools of bourgeois liberals—Benthamites, such as Roebuck, Bowring, Hume, and Brougham; classical economists, such as Senior; and leaders of the Manchester school, such as John Bright—united in bitter opposition to the Ten Hours Law. They feared, and with good reason, that it would be the first breach in their sacred edifice of *laissez faire*. Anticipating the law, Roebuck had introduced in Parliament a resolution opposing government interference with the power of adult laborers in factories to make contracts respecting hours of employment.[57] Lord Shaftesbury in defending the law flouted *laissez faire* and stoutly maintained that the state had "an interest and a right to watch over, and provide for the moral and physical well-being of her people."[58]

The efforts of the factory reformers in Parliament were seconded by the Tories. Their unexpected support made certain the passage of the Ten Hours Law through the Lords, as well as through the Commons. This great humanitarian measure was the only important reform in the interest of the workers during the period of bourgeois liberalism. Karl Marx was astonished that a law directly in favor of labor should be enacted by a bourgeois parliament, and he hailed the Ten Hours Law as the first victory of the socialist movement. Sympathy with the wretched factory workers, so deeply felt by Shaftesbury, was not, however, the underlying motive that animated the Tories. To them the law was a blow aimed at their class enemies, the capitalists, and part of "the wider struggle between the agricultural landlords and the manufacturers over the repeal of the Corn Laws."[59] To the cynical the passage of the Ten Hours Law presented curiously inverted attitudes on the part of both its supporters and its opponents. The former, the Tories, were animated by a spirit of class revenge that drove them to favor a great reform; and the latter, the bourgeois liberals, were motivated by the ideal of individual freedom that led them to uphold selfish class interests. Seldom has a reform been enacted under circumstances in which the overtones of the debate were more real than the speeches.

The struggle over factory reform revealed the antagonism, not so

[57] B. L. Hutchins and A. Harrison, *A History of Factory Legislation* (London, 1926), 92.
[58] Hansard, *Parliamentary Debates,* 3d Series (March 15, 1844), LXXIII, 1075.
[59] Hutchins and Harrison, *op. cit.,* 62.

much between capitalist and worker as between capitalist and aristocrat. But it was the last battle between the two propertied classes.
Deeper tendencies in the new social and economic order were making
for a *rapprochement*—even for an amalgamation—of capitalists and
aristocrats in order to preserve the interests of both as against the
rising discontent of the workers. An essential part of the Victorian
Compromise was the role of each in maintaining the stability of the
new social order. The aristocrats continued to be the "upper" class
and to set the social tone of the nation, though reduced to a subordinate
position in the political and economic life of England. There were good
reasons why the triumphant middle class desired to maintain the aristocracy in a position of power and influence.

In the first place, a conservative propertied class would be a powerful
ally in the new class struggle that was arising—that between capitalists
and workers. Chartism gave warning of a revolutionary movement,
and this frightened both propertied classes, who saw their common
danger in case of a socialist upheaval. In the second place, the middle
class desired to maintain the aristocracy, because its wealthy members
were ambitious to enter aristocratic ranks in order to become assimilated to the traditional ruling class. By this method the rule of the
"moneyed men" would be legitimized in the popular mind and made
part of the national heritage. Finally, it became evident that a counterweight was needed to the elastic political system in which the supremacy of Parliament and ministerial responsibility might open the door
to dangerous innovations. A rigid social order, pervaded by class feeling, would prove to be a powerful counterweight to the flexible parliamentary system. Conservative sentiments and ideals among all classes
would moderate the political efforts of radical parties to upset the established order.

That an aristocracy firmly established and widely respected could
transform class sentiments into political conservatism was well understood by the middle class when they came into power. It led to the
cultivation of what has been called "snobbishness," which became an
all-persuasive sentiment. In England snobbishness was not an individual
failing, as in other lands, but almost a political necessity in the social
order that emerged from the Victorian Compromise. It implied the
acceptance of that "station in life" in which a person was born; there-

fore it precluded resentment on the part of those in the lower ranks and encouraged them to look up to their "betters." Of all the ranks, those in the most precarious position were the middle class, whose station in life depended on money, not on family. Business failure was always in the offing, owing to the uncertainties and insecurities of laissez-faire capitalism. It compelled a man of the middle class to be constantly on the alert to improve his position, lest he be plunged into ruin and become *déclassé*. The Queen in *Alice in Wonderland* must have had the situation of the middle class in mind when she remarked: "Now, *here,* you see, it takes all the running you can do, to keep in the same place."

After 1832 the great problem of England was to reconcile the triumphant middle class "to the settled institutions of the country," and the aristocracy to the ideas and policies of bourgeois liberalism. A process of class assimilation began, which, in the course of the nineteenth century, consolidated into one powerful class the men of family and the men of money. Many of the aristocrats were reconciled to the rule of the capitalist as a consequence of engaging in business, either as investors or as highly paid, decorative members of boards of directors of corporations. "The [English] aristocracy is a sleeping partner in all the industries," was the observation of that acute social analyst, Louis Blanc.[60] Laws permitting joint-stock companies to be organized with limited liability gave a great spurt to large-scale investment, in which the aristocrats took full part. In this way they salved their aristocratic consciences by not engaging "in trade," retail or wholesale. Aristocratic names profusely decorated boards of directors of great industries, especially coal, iron, steel, and shipping. After the repeal of the Corn Laws, agriculture no longer offered inducements for profitable investment. The aristocrat now looked to his estate as the source of his social prestige and to his corporate investments as the source of his wealth.

Another aspect of the consolidation of the propertied classes was the ennoblement of the wealthy capitalists. The elevation of rich businessmen into the ranks of the aristocracy had become a fairly familiar phenomenon in the eighteenth century. Wealthy members of the East India Company, the "nabobs," had bought seats in Parliament, "the

[60] Louis Blanc, *Organization of Work,* trans. from the French by M. P. Dickore (Cincinnati, 1911), 41.

most exclusive club in England." Rich manufacturers had bought estates and had set themselves up as aristocrats, the "Squires of 'Change Alley," as the newly rich aspirants to high society were derisively called. After 1832 this process was accelerated. Distinction in the acquisition of wealth often counted as much as distinction in politics, in war, in the arts, or in the sciences in gaining a title of nobility.

A new aristocracy gradually made its appearance in England, in origin middle class, that became indistinguishable from the old members of the "ruling families."[61] The process of merging the two propertied classes was accelerated by intermarriage. As the sociologist Hobhouse remarked, the old aristocracy took "its toll of the new wealth by marrying its daughters;" the "Lady Annes and Lady Claras were deliberately married by their families to bankers or brewers."[62] If a wealthy capitalist himself failed to become a lord, he might succeed in becoming an ancestor of one.

Culture, like intermarriage, became a process of assimilating the wealthy bourgeois to the aristocracy. As a movement, "culture" was a novel social phenomenon, in that it made education a means of social climbing by smoothing the path of the bourgeois in his progress toward aristocratic exclusiveness. The famous "public" schools—Eton, Harrow, and Winchester—and the ancient seats of learning—Oxford and Cambridge—welcomed the children of the rich capitalists, where they mingled with the children of the aristocracy, to be educated as "gentlemen." The parents met at fox hunts and at directors' meetings, and their children met in the halls of the exclusive schools and colleges. "The old landed gentry, the professional men and the new industrialists were educated together, forming an enlarged and modernized aristocracy, sufficiently numerous to meet the various needs of government and of leadership in Victoria's England and Victoria's Empire."[63] Class divisions were accentuated by class education: the rich had all the opportunities for higher education, and the poor received only elementary instruction or none at all. What has been called the "old

[61] Of the 681 hereditary peers in 1936, only 47 sat by virtue of titles prior to 1689. Over 700 peerages, including life peerages, were created between 1830 and 1936. See W. I. Jennings, *Parliament* (Cambridge University Press, 1939), 369.

[62] See "Aristocracy," *Encyclopedia of the Social Sciences*, II.

[63] Trevelyan, *op. cit.*, 520; Edward C. Mack, *Public Schools and British Opinion, 1780–1860* (London, 1938).

school tie" had a significance far more important than the sentimental appeal to old associations; it was the tie that bound generations of wealthy families, aristocratic and middle class, into a new ruling class. The social significance of the great critic and essayist Matthew Arnold was that he became the "apostle of culture" to the middle class. Despite the fact that Arnold was aristocratic in temperament, his essays appealed chiefly to this new "social stratum," whom he severely castigated as "Philistines," but to whom he offered social salvation through culture.

An outstanding example of this process of class assimilation was none other than the famous Liberal statesman Gladstone. The son of a wealthy capitalist, Gladstone was sent to Eton and to Oxford. His rise to be one of the rulers of Victorian England was due to his wealth and to his culture, as well as to his great ability. He refused the crowning achievement of bourgeois aspiration, a title of nobility, preferring to be known to posterity by the name by which he was known to his contemporaries. But his son Herbert, lacking his father's claim to distinction, had no such scruples. He succumbed to being assimilated into the aristocracy by accepting a title of nobility.

The Anglican church, too, played a part in this process of class assimilation. As the official religion, Anglicanism was identified with the aristocracy; its clergy, especially those high in the hierarchy, generally came from aristocratic families. To a considerable degree did English class divisions correspond to religious divisions. The aristocracy and those dependent upon them, the agricultural population, belonged to the Anglican church; and the middle class and those dependent upon them, the industrial workers and the "white-collar" clerks, were generally Nonconformists—Protestants belonging to the various denominations. It became almost a fashion for a wealthy manufacturer, as he rose socially and received a title of nobility, to leave the "chapel" and enter the "church." Conversion to Anglicanism gave the seal of spiritual salvation to Nonconformists who were seeking to be among the mundane elect. Moreover, Anglicanism, even more than Nonconformity, preached acceptance of the existing social order in a spirit of resignation. A member of the church was. taught by the Anglican catechism, "To honor and obey the King, and all that are put in authority under him: To submit myself to all my governors, teachers, spiritual pastors and masters: To order myself lowly and reverently to all my betters: . . . and to do my duty in that state of life, unto which it shall please God to call me."

Owing to the consolidation of the propertied classes, Victorian England gave an impression of massive social stability. This impression can be recaptured in the novels of Thackeray, in the histories of Macaulay, and in the poems of Tennyson. Deeply significant was the fact that the social stability of Victorian England rested, not upon a despotic, but on a free, political system, in which the civil liberties of the citizens were guaranteed and in which an elected legislature—Parliament—exercised supreme power in the government. England as the land of stability and of freedom was celebrated by Tennyson in memorable lines:

> It is the land that freemen till,
>   That sober-suited Freedom chose;
>   The land, where, girt with friends or foes,
> A man may speak the thing he will;
>
> A land of settled government,
>   A land of just and old renown,
>   Where Freedom slowly broadens down
> From precedent to precedent.

The real contribution of bourgeois liberalism in England can be measured not merely by its great and lasting reforms but even more by its success in maintaining a stable government in a revolutionary age. It stabilized as it reformed. The laws put through by the bourgeois liberals, though fundamentally in the interest of the middle class, were applied in a manner and at a time that easily adjusted the nation to the changes. Bourgeois liberals never forgot that they came peacefully into power in 1832 as a result of a compromise. And the lesson of the Reform Bill convinced them that they could stay in power only by ruling in a spirit of compromise. At no time did they attack vested interests by confiscatory legislation. And at no time did they present an uncompromising opposition, as did the bourgeois liberals in France, to the enfranchisement of the working class. The English ruling class, having the great advantage of long experience in parliamentary gov-

ernment, learned to recognize new social forces when they appeared
on the historical scene. After the failure of Chartism, Conservatives and
Liberals began outbidding each other in the movement to extend the
suffrage.

Neither was the lesson of 1832 lost on the working class striving for
political recognition. Even in the trying days of Chartism the workers
realized that the door to power in the state, though closed, was not
locked. There was no need in England, as in France, for the workers
to mount the barricade in order to obtain the vote. All that they needed
to do was to demand it loudly, insistently—sometimes, threateningly—
and both parties would begin to outbid each other in their efforts to
extend the franchise. The easy transition from bourgeois to democratic
liberalism made by the reform bills of 1867 and 1884 sufficiently attested the political wisdom of the English working class. And the easy
transition from democratic to socialistic liberalism made by the Labor
party after the Second World War sufficiently attests the political wisdom of the English propertied classes.

Compromise brought stability and stability brought a sense of solidarity of those in power with those out of power, of those in the manor
with those in the factory, of those in the church with those in the
chapel. This solidarity became evident whenever the nation was in
danger. There was one England in the greatest crisis of her history—the
Second World War. From that struggle England emerged as the only
nation in Europe that could boast of a system of government unbroken
for centuries past.

Chapter 10. Rise and Fall of Bourgeois Liberalism in France 1830 to 1848

Bourgeois liberalism in France was to run a different course from that in England. Conditions in England, as already explained, were favorable not only to the peaceful triumph but also to the continued rule of the bourgeois liberals. It was quite otherwise in France. Unlike the Reform Bill of 1832 in England, it was the barricade that ushered in the new regime, established by the July Revolution of 1830. The barricade might be glorious to the revolutionists, but it was rather disconcerting to the bourgeois liberals, both of the old and of the new vintage. That old Doctrinaire Royer-Collard, who remembered '93, viewed with uneasiness and trepidation the vindication of constitutional principles by violent uprisings. As the "philosopher of the *Charte*," he "accepted" the July Revolution because Charles X had attempted to restore absolute rule. However, Royer-Collard evinced little desire to be an active leader in the regime that emerged from the barricade. He remained in the Chamber until his retirement in 1842, but participated little in its activities. "We shall all perish; that will be the solution," he is said to have remarked. The Doctrinaire philosopher, together with the philosophy of the *Charte*, virtually disappeared from the political scene.

As a result of its complete triumph in 1830, bourgeois liberalism was in a position to organize a stable government, freed from the opposition of an irreconcilable aristocracy and of a reactionary dynasty. Louis Philippe, "King of the French," accepted the parliamentary regime and readily agreed to be a constitutional monarch. He consented to cooperate wholeheartedly with the new class in power, the *bourgeoisie*, and, as a consequence, the French monarchy became what had never before existed in Europe—the representative of purely bourgeois in-

221

terests in the nation. The change in fashions was symbolic of the profound change in government. Louis Philippe, who boasted of being the "Citizen King," ostentatiously dressed like a prosperous, respectable bourgeois. His frock coat, trousers, top hat, and cane were as symbolic of the bourgeois monarchy as knee breeches, wig, and sword had been of the aristocratic Restoration.

In 1830, as in 1815, the great unsolved problem was how to unite *les deux Frances* by the establishment of a stable government, safe from overturn either by reactionaries or by revolutionaries. How did the July regime, itself the product of revolution, propose to solve this problem? The answer given by the triumphant bourgeois liberals was twofold. In the first place, they appealed to old sentiments and historic traditions by maintaining the monarchical principle in placing the Orleans dynasty on the throne of France. In the second place, they paid homage to the "spirit of 1789" by expanding the suffrage, by restoring the Revolutionary tricolor, and by making parliament supreme in the government of the nation. They believed that in France, as in England, parliamentary supremacy would result in shifting the conflicts of classes and of parties from the barricade to the floor of parliament. The bitter hostility of the two Frances, which so often had led to civil strife, would be mollified in the peaceful atmosphere of debate; and the outcome would be the great desideratum, a stable France.

The system established by the July Monarchy was ingeniously contrived to give exclusive control of the government to the wealthy bourgeois and, at the same time, ensure this control against all constitutional efforts to overthrow it. The suffrage was expanded by a contraction of the property qualifications for voting from 300 to 200 francs a year in direct taxes. This "liberal" provision excluded from voting all the wage earners, both industrial and agricultural, and many shopkeepers and peasant proprietors. The electorate increased from about 99,000 in 1830 to about 241,000 in 1846; yet this increase gave the vote to only 3 per cent of the adult males in France. Almost 90 per cent of the electorate derived their right to vote from the ownership of land; the rest, from commerce, industry, and the professions. As a result of the rapid development of industry during the July Monarchy, prosperous bourgeois bought estates, in order to be in the fashionable ranks of the landed gentry. More definitely than before was there now a landed *bourgeoisie* in France. The curious situation that resulted from the electoral system of the July Monarchy was the contradiction between the economic status and the political privileges of the voters. As a consequence of the system of taxation, the electoral power of property in land was infinitely greater than that of industrial property.[1] Those in control of the government were a *bourgeoisie* whose political power came from land, but whose economic power came from business; hence they were hostile alike to aristocratic pretensions and to democratic demands.

More important than the expansion of the electorate was the increase in the power of the Chamber. It now definitely exercised supreme power in the government. Ministerial responsibility was not clearly defined, yet in practice it was established; executive, as well as legislative, power rested finally with parliament. Constitutionally, at least, France was now a parliamentary monarchy like England. There took place, however, a far greater shift of class power in France as a consequence of the July Revolution than that which took place in England as a consequence of the Reform Bill of 1832. What the July Revolution accomplished was the overthrow of an aristocratic regime in which the bourgeois had considerable influence and the establishment of a completely bourgeois regime purged of all aristocratic influences. Unlike the Doctrinaires of the Restoration, the liberals of the era of Louis Philippe were determined to bring the conflict of the two Frances to an end by eliminating one of them—the embittered, recalcitrant, uncompromising protagonists of the Old Regime. Louis Philippe was convinced that the only upper class that could direct the destinies of the new France was an upper class whose wealth came from commerce and industry, and not from land. Every change made by the July Monarchy was a blow aimed at the old aristocracy. The increase in the electorate was at their expense; nearly all the new voters were bourgeois, which proportionately decreased the electoral strength of the aristocrats. The largely hereditary Chamber of Peers was abolished and a senate was created, consisting of members appointed for life by the king. "All

[1] For a description of the electoral system under the July Monarchy, see Sherman Kent, *Electoral Procedure under Louis Philippe* (New Haven, 1937), Chap. II; P. Meuriot, *La Population et les lois électorales en France* (Paris, 1916), 44; and A. Pilenco, *Les Moeurs électorales en France* (Paris, 1928), 29.

relations with the legitimism of the Restoration were broken off; at last the *bourgeoisie* had a government all its own."[2] During the reign of Louis Philippe the reactionaries, together with the Bourbons, virtually disappeared from the political scene.

Not only was the aristocracy reduced to almost political nullity, but its social prestige was seriously undermined. During the July Monarchy there took place wholesale ennoblement of newly rich bankers, stockbrokers, industrialists, and merchants. These "July nobles" were despised by the aristocrats, who regarded them as upstart bourgeois disguised as nobles. But they were welcomed by their creator, Louis Philippe, who virtually banished the old aristocrats from his court. Excluded from public life, their social prestige lowered, the old families lived more or less in seclusion amidst "lavender and old lace" in the exclusive Quartier Saint-Germain in Paris. Aristocratic traditions and sentiments were kept alive, but their influence was felt chiefly as a form of nostalgia among the romantically inclined and as a mood of resentful exasperation among the reactionaries against "bourgeois France." The one permanent accomplishment of the July Revolution was the destruction of the power of the aristocracy, which now passed from the historic stage to the pages of history.

It has been the peculiar attribute of French political life that every regime since the French Revolution has been the subject of intellectual controversy, as well as of political strife. So intimate have been the relations between public life and philosophic speculation concerning social problems that even an established regime sought intellectual approval. In France the *status quo* was seldom its own defense. An almost perfect intellectual representative of the July Monarchy was the historian-statesman, François Guizot (1787-1874). His political life, which began in 1815 and ended in 1848, spanned the period of bourgeois liberalism in France. As statesman, political philosopher, and historian Guizot was French bourgeois liberalism incarnate. To his contemporaries, Guizot seemed almost to have been "invented," especially created, for the purpose of interpreting and defending bourgeois France, so perfectly did Guizot's mind reflect the lights and shadows of the July Monarchy that he served most faithfully and defended most convincingly.

[2] G. de Ruggiero, *The History of European Liberalism,* trans. from the Italian by R. G. Collingwood (London, 1927), 177.

As a bourgeois liberal, Guizot had served his apprenticeship during the Restoration under Royer-Collard. Though one of the "younger set" of the Doctrinaires, he deserved the appellation "doctrinaire" better than did his older associates. His mind was of the sharp and rigid type, and its impact on liberal principles resulted in hardening them into set doctrines that, to Guizot, were eternally true under any and all circumstances. Guizot, says his biographer Pouthas, sought "to establish a political system according to rational ideals and to arrange facts into a philosophic system." [3] As a consequence, he became that rare phenomenon, a fanatical liberal, narrow and dogmatic in his opinions and uncompromising and tyrannical in his actions.

Guizot's rapid rise in political life was due in part to his great ability and to his undaunted ambition and, even more, to the great upsurge of bourgeois power that rose like a flood in 1830, to sweep away the flimsy structure of the Restoration. Like Royer-Collard, he viewed with trepidation and uneasiness the July uprising as a manifestation of violence on the part of the lower orders. "À la lumière de la révolution, le libéral Guizot se révèle conservateur." [4] But he also "accepted" the July Monarchy—not, however, in a spirit of resignation, as did his master, but in the spirit of opportunity. Instinctively he felt that a regime was coming into power in which his talents, his temperament, his ideals, his policies, his very personality would find free and ample scope. More bourgeois than the Citizen King, Guizot rose rapidly in his political ascent. He was elected to the Chamber in 1830 and became a member of several ministries. From 1832 to 1837 he was Minister of Public Instruction. In 1842 he rose to be premier and completely dominated the government of Louis Philippe until its overthrow by the February Revolution of 1848.

As premier, Guizot was the bourgeois liberal triumphant. Now the historic moment had arrived when the age-old conflict between despotism and freedom would at last be ended by policies that Guizot determined to inaugurate. Modern history, sarcastically comments Faguet, "was a preparation for the ministry of Guizot." [5] Unlike his predecessors Constant and Royer-Collard, who had battled in vain

[3] Charles H. Pouthas, *Guizot pendant la Restauration, 1814–30* (Paris, 1923), 399.
[4] *Ibid.*, 474.
[5] E. Faguet, *Politiques et moralistes du dix-neuvième siècle* (Paris, 1890), I, 328.

against the intransigent Bourbons, Guizot sat at the right hand of
Louis Philippe and directed the policies of the regime, both in the
Chamber and in the ministry. His domination, however, was not so
much personal as ideological. Cold, narrow, with a rigid adherence
to political formulas, always ready to defend the class interests of the
bourgeoisie, Guizot was a maddening spectacle to the French. He
had neither the sonorous eloquence of a Royer-Collard nor the imagination of Constant, qualities which had made liberal principles seem
almost like a romantic quest. In the liberalism of Guizot his opponents
saw only the crass materialism and the mean selfishness of a class devoid
of public spirit and avid of power. Guizot's religion added to his
unpopularity. He was a Protestant, a strict Calvinist, hence a religious
alien among his people, who were either Catholics or freethinkers.
Guizot's Calvinism accentuated his shortcomings rather than his virtues. It gave him a sense of self-righteousness that caused him to regard
with complacency his limitations as a statesman. To Guizot they were
not *his* limitations but those of his opponents, who stubbornly and
blindly refused to see the truth, which he saw so clearly and presented
so logically. A "stiff, lonely, tragic creature," Guizot was a political
leader without a following, whose power lay in his ability to serve
the rising *bourgeoisie* in France.

Behind Guizot's cold exterior, however, there was a vehemence,
an intellectual pride, an iron determination to persist in his course that
made him disliked by his associates almost as much as he was by his
opponents. Guizot, writes Pouthas, was distinguished by his "close
reasoning, by a mixture of vehemence and cold logic, by the ardent
faith which lay behind his attempts to be impartial, by a capacity at
times to enunciate formulas that remained in one's memory, and by a
strange power of disdain that hurt more than invective."[6] An example
of Guizot's disdain was seen in his biting reply to attacks on him in
the Chamber. "As for the insults, calumnies, and angry attacks," he
declared, "one can multiply them, heap them up as much as one wishes
and, no matter how high, they will never reach the height of my
disdain."[7]

Guizot's writings and speeches well repay close study. Though not

[6] Pouthas, *op. cit.,* 272.

[7] Guizot, *Histoire parlementaire de France* (Paris, 1863–1864), IV, 238.

a profound and original thinker, he had the peculiar quality of being remarkably second rate, in that he fashioned the ideas of bourgeois liberalism into a militant creed that dominated the France of his day. Guizot's political vision was limited, but what he saw, he saw so clearly and stated so frankly and so trenchantly that his political views constitute the classic expression of bourgeois liberalism in France. It was Guizot's fate to defend his ideas against a socialist working class, inspired by revolutionary principles; therefore, they were sharper, clearer, and more challenging than those of the Doctrinaires of the Restoration, whose foes had been a decaying aristocracy and an ineffectual dynasty.

It was Guizot's firm conviction that under the July Monarchy France at last found the political and social stability that she had for so long sought. Thenceforth neither revolution nor reaction would trouble the nation, because the July Revolution by bringing into existence the July Monarchy had, at the same time, abolished the right of revolution. "When it was a question of overthrowing absolutism and privilege," Guizot declared, "it was indeed necessary to appeal to anyone and to everyone in the land, dangerous or useful, legitimate or illegitimate, good and bad. They all appeared on the field of battle, and after the victory each demanded his share of the booty. But now the battle is over, peace has come, and the treaty is signed. And the treaty is the present constitution and government."[8] But the "principle that presided over our Revolution must not preside over our government,"[9] he warned. Under the July Monarchy, argued Guizot, the fundamental principles of the French Revolution were reaffirmed, but purged of violence and terrorism. Whatever was sound, whatever was progressive in the French Revolution, came from the Constituent Assembly, whose great reforms during 1789 to 1791 laid the foundation of *la nouvelle France*. These reforms, based on the principle of equality before the law, constituted a social revolution that was both necessary and just. Unfortunately, however, the French Revolution, argued Guizot, led to democratic experiments that were no part of the original plan of the Constituent Assembly. The "national desire" in 1789, he asserted, was not democracy but a combination of free insti-

[8] *Ibid.*, III, 108–109.
[9] *Ibid.*, I, 147.

tutions with hereditary monarchy.[10] But this national desire was frustrated by democracy, whose very origin and very nature were inimical to the establishment of a stable order. The French Revolution, Guizot believed, had popularized two great errors among the French people. One was that man was naturally good and that all evil in the world arose from bad institutions. The other was that no one was morally bound to obey laws that he did not help to make. Therefore, it was highly essential to purge the principles of 1789 of the "anarchist alloys" that had debased them in the eyes of the nation.[11]

The July Monarchy, asserted Guizot, was a restoration not of the feudal and autocratic Old Regime but of *la nouvelle France* of the Constituent Assembly. It established a political system, which was, at the same time, liberal and antirevolutionary: liberal, in that parliamentary government was fully reorganized; antirevolutionary, in that the new regime was a constitutional monarchy. Having studied English history, he believed that the best way to maintain stability was to follow in England's political footsteps (1) by establishing parliamentary supremacy and ministerial responsibility; and (2) by following a middle-of-the-road policy, the *juste milieu,* analogous to the Victorian Compromise. "Guizot invented the party, the government, and the doctrine of the *juste milieu.*"[12] This policy, he asserted, would close forever "the era of revolutions," because the new social order that had been created by the French Revolution now had a political guarantee in the liberal government of the July Monarchy.[13]

The stability of the July Monarchy had also an economic guarantee. The development of modern industry that was taking place in France and in Western Europe generally was bound to result in domestic tranquility and in peace between nations. Capitalism spelled peaceful progress; hence it made for the stability of governments. Thenceforth the people would be awakened by the sound of the factory whistle, instead of by the ringing of the revolutionary tocsin or the beating of the regimental drum. To maintain stability, the government should follow a pacifist policy in foreign affairs at almost any price. War

[10] Guizot, Preface to *Histoire des origines du gouvernement représentatif,* 2 vols. (Paris, 1874).

[11] Guizot, *Histoire parlementaire,* I, Introduction; III, 153.

[12] Faguet, *op. cit.,* I, 307.

[13] Guizot, *Mémoires* (Paris, 1863–1864), VIII, 521.

and even preparations for war would revive Napoleonic memories that would be sure to upset the much-desired peace. The July Monarchy "had need of excessive tranquility at home and abroad to enable it to seat itself firmly."[14] In domestic affairs the government should pursue the policy of *juste milieu,* the true mean between what Guizot regarded as the rival absurdities of divine right and popular sovereignty. The Bourbons had failed to bring stability to France, argued the upholders of the July Monarchy, because they were closely affiliated with the reactionary aristocrats, who were seeking to upset the *Charte* and to restore absolutism. The outcome was the July Revolution. But now that constitutional government was firmly established, with parliament recognized as the supreme authority and with a responsible ministry in the seat of government, the dread of both reaction and revolution would be forever banished from France.

With stability were inextricably tied up the interests of the *bourgeoisie.* No other advocate of bourgeois liberalism in all Western Europe was so profoundly convinced as was Guizot that the *bourgeoisie* and only the *bourgeoisie* could be the guardian class of the liberal order. He was even more narrowly class conscious, more plain spoken in defense of this class than was James Mill. Reading Guizot today gives one a vivid sense of the militant class spirit of bourgeois liberalism when it was fighting enemies on two fronts: reactionaries on the right and socialists on the left.

The problem of bourgeois liberalism everywhere in Europe was how to fit the class rule of the *bourgeoisie* into the framework of liberal principles. This problem was especially insistent in France, where the July Monarchy claimed as its primal inspiration the "principles of 1789." By a specious appeal to history and by an ingenious use of logic, Guizot proved—to his own satisfaction—that the all-too-obvious class government of the July Monarchy was in harmony with the liberal heritage of the French Revolution. In his historic studies he sounded the keynote that the fundamental fact of modern history was the rise of the *bourgeoisie.* Since ancient times the history of Europe had been the story of the slow and arduous development of this class. It came to maturity with the French Revolution,

[14] Louis Blanc, *The History of Ten Years, 1830–1840,* trans. from the French by W. K. Kelly (Philadelphia, 1848), II, 628.

when it overthrew a social order based on privilege and a political system based on irresponsible autocracy. Since then, the *bourgeoisie* has been "the best organ and the most faithful guardian of the principles of 1789"; of liberty, as of order; of civil rights, as of political freedom; of progress, as of stability.[15] Like all other bourgeois liberals, both in England and in France, Guizot was convinced that the *bourgeoisie,* because it had no legal privileges, was not a class at all but the public itself, consisting of all the able and intelligent men in the nation. They alone were enlightened as to the needs of the nation; they alone were capable of conducting the government in the general interest. Having no privileges to defend, their views constituted public opinion.

Guizot squeezed the entire nation into the narrow confines of the *bourgeoisie.* He was firmly convinced that public opinion was the expression not of the *volonté générale* of democracy but of this enlightened minority, "*épurée, spiritualisée, corrigée,*" in which were concentrated all the living forces of the nation. Its ranks were constantly being filled with the ablest individuals from every social group: the workingman who had inventive ingenuity, the aristocrat who took advantage of opportunities in business to enlarge the family fortune, the peasant with a little capital to invest, the ambitious clerk who rose in the enterprise in which he was employed. There could then be no legitimate conflict between *la bourgeoisie et le peuple.* "In the large space that the former fills in the very heart of society," declared Guizot, "there is room for anyone who is capable and willing to enter it."[16] The way to unite the two Frances seemed clear to Guizot —all power to the *bourgeoisie.*

Guizot's prescription for bourgeois rule was to give the vote only to those who had property. Now that the July Monarchy had established parliamentary supremacy and ministerial responsibility, it was vitally important to limit the suffrage to the propertied classes, of which the bourgeois constituted a large majority. Guizot stressed his argument for a propertied suffrage on the ground that only those who had capacity had the moral right to wield political power. All

[15] Guizot, *Mémoires,* I, 294–298; VIII, 522–523.
[16] *Ibid.,* VI, 348–349.

means of acquiring power, such as wealth, ability, and knowledge, he argued, had their origin in natural capacity. Where was capacity to be found? Promptly Guizot eliminated women, who, he asserted, were naturally incapable of conducting affairs rationally; hence they were placed by God in the home. What men had the capacity to act freely and rationally in the public interest? Owing to differences in individuals, reasoned Guizot, only a few were capable of having true ideas of justice in society; hence only these few had the right to rule the nation. The great problem was to gather from all corners of society the capable few and to organize them into an electoral body. Only such a body could form a government that would function properly, easily, and peacefully. "The principle of political capacity introduced into our government as the source of political rights," declared Guizot, "is perhaps the finest and most useful conquest that we have made in fifteen years."[17] Representative assemblies, according to Guizot, were devices to transform the capable few into electors, not machines for recording the individual preferences of the voters.[18]

Guizot's very mental processes had congealed in bourgeois grooves. He sought to prove conclusively that the capable few were and could be only those who had property. In society, he argued, there were to be found three economic categories: (1) the class that lived from income, and, therefore, had leisure to acquire education in order to develop capacity; (2) the businessmen, who were actively engaged in exploiting capital or land, the nature of whose occupation itself obliged them to have knowledge and to develop their abilities; and (3) the laborers, "who worked in order to live and lived in order to work." Unlike the leisure class, the laborers had no time for education; and, unlike the businessmen, they had an occupation the nature of which—long, hard, and tedious manual labor—unfitted them to act intelligently on public questions.[19] It was self-evident to Guizot that political capacity came as a result of the ownership of property, inherited or acquired. Of all the propertied elements, according to Guizot, the *bourgeoisie* was best fitted to rule the nation.

[17] Guizot, *Histoire parlementaire,* I, 214.
[18] Guizot, *Histoire des origines du gouvernement représentatif,* II, 150.
[19] Guizot, *Discours académiques* (Paris, 1861), 390.

It alone had all the essential qualifications for governing: (1) being rich, it had economic power; (2) being fairly numerous, it had a popular basis; and (3) being successful, it had capacity.

A propertied suffrage, insisted Guizot, was not a class privilege. On the contrary, it served as an inducement to energetic, capable men among the poor to acquire property in order to become voters. The saying, "Get rich and you will get a vote," ascribed to Guizot, truly described the attitude of that most bourgeois of all bourgeois liberals. Such was the virtue of the July Monarchy, he declared, that political rights could be "extended in proportion to the growth of capacity within the nation." While the electoral law set a limit to voting, at the same time it "assiduously encourages the growth of capacity"; as a consequence, the limit was constantly modified, thereby raising the standard of the entire nation. In this way the benefits of a government controlled by the *bourgeoisie* were shared by everyone to the degree that a man rose in the social scale and met the conditions required for participation in political life.[20]

As Premier, Guizot was obliged to defend bourgeois rule against the rising tide of discontent with the July Monarchy. Especially did the resentment of the workers show itself in menacing demonstrations and in riotous strikes. The Premier's attitude toward the unenfranchised workers was coldly and brutally frank. In reply to their demand for the vote, he told them, in effect, that they constituted a class that had failed in life because of the limitations placed upon them by nature, not by society. Therefore the workers were not, and could not be, entrusted with the power to direct the state. Guizot insisted that the rights of the workers as citizens were protected by the constitution, which guaranteed civil equality to everyone. For them to demand political equality was "to confuse two matters that are essentially distinct and different," namely, civil with political rights; the liberty of the individual with the government of the nation.[21] Inequality was the principle of political rights, as equality was that of civil rights; political rights were based on property, the foundation stone of the social order, and civil rights on the equality of all citizens, rich and poor, before the law. The workers, having no

[20] Guizot, *Histoire parlementaire*, III, 105; V, 213.
[21] *Ibid.*, I, 309.

property, concluded Guizot, had no right to the franchise. Then why the demand for manhood suffrage? Guizot asserted that the demand did not arise spontaneously from the workers themselves, who were contented with the protection afforded them by the civil liberties and had no real desire for the vote. The movement for manhood suffrage, in his opinion, was "artificial, superficial, and dishonest," organized by cliques of evil journalists and revolutionists, *"la petite société maladive,"* who were plotting to overthrow the sound bourgeois order, *"la grande société saine et tranquille."* The workers had no need of the vote, said Guizot, to protect their interests as against those of the propertied classes. Quite sincerely and with complete naïveté did the bourgeois historian and statesman assert that the great contribution of capitalism was the solution of the age-old conflict between rich and poor. This it did by creating a bond of common interest between them. "The upper classes are now closely bound to the lower, whom they represent, protect, and do not oppress." Now at last, argued Guizot, harmony exists among people of different occupations living under conditions of economic inequality.[22]

Guizot's political and social views voiced accurately public opinion in bourgeois France. It was during the reign of Louis Philippe that the rising power of the *bourgeoisie* became sharply evident, owing to the progress of the Industrial Revolution. Previously halting and intermittent, it now took even and fairly long strides. Good indexes of the extent of industrialization in France during the reign of Louis Philippe were (1) the amount of horsepower and the number of steam engines in use, (2) the extent of railway mileage, and (3) the consumption of cotton. In 1832 there were in France 525 steam engines, with a capacity of 900 horsepower; in 1847, 4,853 steam engines, with 62,000 horsepower. In 1831 there were 38 kilometers of railways; in 1848, 1,921 kilometers. In 1831 France consumed 28,000,000 kilograms of cotton, in 1846, 65,000,000 kilograms.[23]

Even further advanced than industry was finance. Banking and stock-exchange operations assumed an importance even greater than

[22] *Ibid.,* III, 554–567.

[23] S. B. Clough, *France, A History of National Economics, 1789–1939* (New York, 1939), 148, 153; P. Quentin-Bauchart, *La Crise sociale de 1848* (Paris, 1920), 36; E. Levasseur, *Histoire des classes ouvrières et de l'industrie en France de 1789 à 1870* (Paris, 1903–1904), I, 627; and A. Viallate, *L'Activité économique en France* (Paris, 1937), 90.

that of factory production or railway construction. The savings of the many thrifty small farmers and shopkeepers flowed into the great banks that financed the government and the new enterprises. Yet so great was the need of capital that France imported large amounts from England.

Though France's economic path was now definitely in the direction of industrialization, the majority of the population remained rural. By the middle of the nineteenth century, only one-quarter of the people lived in towns of 2,000 or more. A capitalist class—*aristocratie d'argent et d'industrie*—appeared, which, though small, was exceedingly powerful; its influence penetrated all sections of the new industrial life. This new wealthy class was bitterly resented, both by the aristocrats and by the workers—by the former as a rival for the control of the state, and by the latter as a new oppressor.

The worker's share in the advancing prosperity during the July Monarchy was negligible. "Little if any of the increase in national wealth ever reached the workers because it was absorbed by the *bourgeoisie*."[24] But they suffered from all the evils of early industrialism. Conditions were especially bad in the cotton factories, where, it was said, wages were the lowest, hours the longest, and unemployment the greatest.[25]

The position of the French workers was far worse than was that of the English workers. The former did not benefit indirectly, as did the latter, from the class conflict between aristocrats and capitalists. There was no French Lord Shaftesbury to plead the cause of the exploited in factory and mine. There was no Tory party to put through factory legislation. The French aristocrats had neither the intelligence nor the willingness to champion the demands of the workers as a method of fighting their class enemies, the bourgeois. To the French aristocrats the socialist workers were the violent, bloodthirsty successors of the Jacobin sans-culottes who had dragged their forebears to the guillotine. Hatred and fear of the workers by the

[24] A. L. Dunham, "Industrial Life and Labor in France, 1815-1848," *Journal of Economic History*, III (November, 1943), 139.

[25] *Ibid.*, Henri Sée, "Quelques aperçus sur la condition de la classe ouvrière et sur le mouvement ouvrier en France de 1815 à 1848," *Revue d'histoire économique et sociale*, XII (1924), 493–521; Charles Rist, "Durée du travail dans l'industrie francaise de 1820 à 1870," *Revue d'économie politique*, XI (1897).

aristocrats made impossible in France anything like Disraeli's Tory democracy. Moreover, the aristocrats, as has already been explained, had little part in the all-bourgeois regime of Louis Philippe.

Needless to say, *laissez faire* was a policy strictly followed in France. French bourgeois liberalism was more bourgeois and less liberal than its English counterpart; hence even more averse to social reform. *Laissez faire* was the chief doctrine of a school of economists, known as the "liberal economists," who derived their ideas from Adam Smith. Chief among the liberal economists were Jean Baptiste Say (1767-1832) and his disciple Frédéric Bastiat (1801-1850).[26] They advocated doctrines substantially the same as those of the classical economists in England, whom they greatly admired. Frequently they carried these doctrines, especially *laissez faire,* to extreme—even absurd—lengths, in a manner sharper and more challenging than that of the English economists. The explanation is that the French economists waged war on two fronts: against protection on the right and against socialism on the left. In England protection was regarded as the selfish policy of a landed aristocracy in conflict with the interests of the nation. But that was not the case in France, where the free-trade doctrines of the liberal economists encountered a powerful popular opposition from the numerous peasant proprietors, a class that did not exist in England. On the left, the socialist challenge to bourgeois liberalism was far more powerful in France than in England. The influence of Saint-Simon and his followers was much greater in France than was that of Robert Owen and his followers in England.

There was one well-known economist, Jean Charles de Sismondi (1773-1842), who was not a socialist and who did not belong to the liberal school. His best known work *Nouveaux principes d'économie politique,* published in 1819, was a devastating criticism of classical economics and of laissez-faire capitalism. Sismondi analyzed the hardships of the workers under industrialism and advocated state intervention in their behalf. Government, in his view, was to be the protector of the economically weak against the economically strong. "The more a nation progresses in the arts and in industry," he declared,

[26] The chief work of Say is *Traité d'économie politique,* published in 1803; that of Bastiat is *Les Harmonies économiques,* published in 1850. In 1841 the liberal economists founded the *Journal des économistes,* to advocate their ideas.

"the greater becomes the disproportion in the condition between those who work and those who enjoy. The more the former toils the more the latter has of superabundance." Therefore the state should intervene in order to correct the maldistribution of wealth so that a larger share would go to those who work.[27] But Sismondi's views had little influence on the policies of the July Monarchy.

The liberal statesmen Constant and Guizot championed the doctrines of the liberal economists. Constant was a strong and enthusiastic advocate of *laissez faire,* which, he asserted, would work for the best interest of mankind by allowing economic laws to regulate labor and industry.[28] As might be expected, Guizot was especially insistent on following a laissez-faire policy in the relations between capital and labor. "In the ordinary course of events," he declared, "these relations settle themselves. I am convinced that any attempt by the government to intervene would be chimerical and disastrous." According to Guizot, all state efforts to aid the poor were useless, as men were born in an unequal world. He cited the Speenhamland system of outdoor relief in England as an especially bad example of state intervention, because it created a system in which the poor lived at the expense of the rich all the time.[29] To accept the principle that all poverty comes from an evil system of society and that therefore it is the bounden duty of the government to protect the unfortunate by redistributing wealth would destroy the sense of responsibility in men and rouse evil passions by raising false hopes of economic equality.[30]

The liberal economists in France had no such vogue as did the classical economists in England. Like the regime of the July Monarchy, the doctrines advocated by the economists and the policies pursued by Guizot were generally regarded as part of the bourgeois system of controlling national life. As such, they were bitterly resented by the "other France," the socialist workers. Their resentment of liberal economy was well stated by Louis Blanc. "To augment the mass of wealth without any regard to its distribution," he wrote,

27 Sismondi, *Nouveaux principes d'économie politique* (Paris, 1827), I, 80.
28 Constant, *Collection complète des ouvrages* (Paris, 1818), I, 358*ff.*
29 Guizot, *Histoire parlementaire,* I, 327.
30 Guizot, *Mémoires,* VI, 347.

"this was the sum and substance of the economic doctrines adopted by liberalism. They were heartless doctrines; they forbade the intervention of any tutelary power in matters of trade and manufacture, they protected the strong and left the weak to the mercy of chance."[31]

Bourgeois liberalism in France developed a philosophy of bourgeois rule with a logic and a passion that betrayed a feeling of insecurity. As beneficiaries of revolutionary confiscations, the bourgeois strongly opposed a return of the Old Regime. As property owners, they constituted a powerful conservative force, and they opposed all working-class movements, fearing that a new overturn would result in their being themselves expropriated. The idea of revolution in France was indissolubly connected with confiscation of property. As a consequence, the July Monarchy was more completely bourgeois than was the regime established in England by the Reform Bill of 1832. As has already been described,[32] the English aristocracy continued to wield a powerful influence in public life. Not so the economically weak and politically discredited French aristocracy. The government was frankly bourgeois, frankly avowed; the other elements were made to feel that they did not belong. Their interests, their views, their desires were disregarded as either unimportant or dangerous to the welfare of the nation. In the opinion of that profound observer and keen analyst Alexis de Tocqueville, the triumph in 1830 of the *bourgeoisie* "had been definite and so thorough that all political power, every franchise, every prerogative and the whole government was confined and, as it were, heaped up within the narrow limits of this one class, to the statutory exclusion of all beneath them and the actual exclusion of all above. Not only did it thus alone rule society, but it may be said to have formed it."[33]

Ministers now came from the ranks of the bourgeois. The aristocratic Richelieus, Villèles, Martignacs, and Polignacs of Bourbon days were succeeded by the bourgeois Lafittes, Périers, Guizots, and Thiers. It was the bourgeois monopoly of the government under the July Monarchy that led Karl Marx to characterize it as "a stock company

[31] Blanc, *op. cit.*, I, 82.

[32] See *supra*, p. 183.

[33] *The Recollections of Alexis de Tocqueville*, trans. from the French by A. T. de Mattos (New York, 1896), 5.

for the exploitation of France's wealth" and convinced him that the
liberal state was merely an "executive committee" for the manage-
ment of common bourgeois affairs. Not only was the machinery of
government in bourgeois hands, but it was directed to advance business
interests to a degree unknown in France. Again to quote De Tocqueville, "Master of everything in a manner that no aristocracy had ever
been or may ever hope to be, the middle class, when called upon to
assume the government, took it up as a trade; it entrenched itself
behind its power, and before long, in their egoism, each of its members
thought much more of his private business than of public affairs, and
of his personal enjoyment than of the greatness of the nation."[34] By
appealing to the acquisitive instinct of the people, the July Monarchy
sought to identify itself with those who were successful in conducting
business enterprise. A prosperous *bourgeoisie* would—and could—be
depended upon to give powerful support to the government against
the new antagonist that had appeared from below, the working class.
This situation was noted in 1837 by an American visitor George
Ticknor. "The middling class, on the other hand," he wrote, "is growing rich and intelligent, and, the lower class, with very imperfect and
impractical knowledge, is growing discontented and jealous. The governments are everywhere trying to associate to their interests the wealth
of the middling class and to base themselves on property."[35]

Literature as well as history bears witness to the dominance of the
"middling class" during the July Monarchy. Balzac's famous *Comédie
humaine* consisting of a hundred novels gives a wonderful picture of
the life of the period. It is a bourgeois epic in which money is the theme,
the moral, and the tale. Plots in Balzac's novels concern themselves
less with the rivalries and intrigues of love and war and more with
the *stratégie des intérêts* of bourgeois ambitions for materialistic
success. The passion for money has always been portrayed in literature, but generally as the degenerate passion of the miser or the
ignoble passion of men of low character. In the pages of Balzac,
despite the author's own predilections, money is considered a social
and political power and the fulcrum of the new order in France.

The complete control of the state by the wealthy bourgeois was

[34] *Ibid.,* 6.
[35] George Ticknor, *Life, Letters and Journals* (Boston, 1876), II, 75.

something new in France. Having no roots in the French past, these newly rich capitalists did not have the prestige appertaining to a ruling class, as did the old aristocracy. Neither could they appeal to a great emotion, as the military rulers of the Napoleonic era had appealed to *la gloire*. Therefore the rule of the capitalists in the July Monarchy roused not only hostility but scorn among the people. Having neither tradition nor *la gloire,* the July Monarchy decided to appeal to the acquisitive instinct of the nation to enlist support for its rule. The "magic of property" was to dazzle the French into the belief that a new *carrière ouverte aux talents* was before each and every one of them as a consequence of the progress of industry. An ambitious Frenchman now dreamed of some day becoming a financier or an industrialist. *Enrichissez vous!* was the injunction pronounced by the government to the citizens. The social order established by the French Revolution was firmly joined to the political order established by the Revolution of 1830. Stability, it seemed, had at last come to the nation by the elimination of the reactionary aristocracy and of the dynasty that "never learned anything and never forgot anything." There was now only one France, the France immersed in business and intent on achieving material prosperity, as indifferent to the romantic sentiments associated with the Old Regime as to the democratic ideals associated with the French Revolution. The *juste milieu* seemed to be the final solution of the problem of the two Frances that had defied all efforts to solve it until the advent of the July Monarchy.

It became evident, before long, that the "great divide" continued. The class conflict merely shifted from that between aristocrats and bourgeois to that between bourgeois and proletariat. It was the proletariat who became the new antagonist in a new division of the two Frances that appeared during the July Monarchy. And the new division was even deeper and sharper than the old one had been, because it was a division between two groups, both of which were inspired by the French Revolution. Nothing is so bitter as a conflict between a moderate and an extreme left, as witness the conflict between Girondins and Jacobins in the French Revolution and that between Menshevists and Bolshevists in the Russian Revolution. The workers who had fought behind the July barricades were infuriated when they saw all their hopes turn to ashes with the establishment of the July Monarchy.

Opposition to the July Monarchy, deep and bitter, arose almost on the morrow of its appearance. And it came from the "other France" —the working class, now acutely conscious of a new issue, capitalism, which they denounced as *la féodalité nouvelle,* and under which they were the new serfs and the capitalists were the new lords. In the latter the workers beheld their uncompromising enemies, who were determined to prevent them from sharing in the new wealth that was being produced and from participating in the new political order that had been established. Forbidden by law to organize trade-unions or to engage in strikes, the workers formed secret unions or masked their unions as mutual benefit societies *(associations des mutuellistes).* Strikes took place frequently during the July Monarchy, and they were more like revolutionary uprisings than peaceful stoppages of work. A famous strike of this kind was that of the silk weavers of Lyons in 1831. Driven to desperation by a reduction of their already low wages, the weavers rose in revolt, declaring that they would either "live by working or die fighting." Many died fighting, as the uprising was mercilessly suppressed. In 1834 another strike insurrection took place in Lyons. The demands of the workers for higher wages and shorter hours were couched in revolutionary terms. This uprising, like the one in 1831, was suppressed.[36] More stringent laws were enacted against trade-unions, but repression only served to increase the revolutionary ardor of the workers. These strike revolts marked the gathering storm of a proletarian uprising that was to break out in the "June Days" of 1848.

What the workers really desired was the abolition of the capitalist system and the establishment of a socialist order. The liberal bourgeois appeared to them as even greater tyrants than did the reactionary aristocrats. The latter were far away, having little connection with the urban laborers, and social distance had the effect of mitigating their tyranny. But that was not the case of the bourgeois, who, as employers, were near; hence their tyranny could be felt quickly and surely. As the capitalist system and the bourgeois political order were in close relationship, the new revolutionary movement had a

[36] Dunham, *op. cit.,* 146*ff.*; O. Festy, *Le Mouvement ouvrier* (Paris, 1908), 325*ff.*

different emphasis and a different direction from that which had led to the July Revolution. The political passions of 1830 were now transformed into social passions, which sought to overthrow not merely the government, but even more, the social order.[37] No longer did the revolutionists seek "to upset this or that law, ministry, or even form of government, but society itself," because they were convinced that "the present distribution of goods throughout the world is unjust; that property rests on a foundation which is not an equitable foundation."[38] Political revolution was merely a means; social revolution was the goal.

This new revolutionary movement, generally known as "socialism," looked to the French Revolution as the inspiration of its ideal of economic equality. In France precedent was a revolutionary, not a conservative, force. Had not the French Revolution taken strides toward economic equality by means of confiscating property? The liberal monarchists of 1789 had confiscated feudal and church property. The democratic republicans of 1793 had confiscated the estates of the condemned nobles. And the egalitarians of 1797, in the Conspiracy of Babeuf, had actually advocated confiscation of all property. As a consequence of these precedents, confiscation of property and revolution had become almost synonymous terms in France. In no other country of Europe were the propertied elements, large and small, so greatly haunted by fear of confiscation as they were in post-Revolutionary France. "We have not forgotten," declared Royer-Collard, "that confiscation is the very soul and nerve of revolution. After confiscating as a consequence of condemning one passes to condemning in order to confiscate. Ferocity becomes sated but greed never."[39]

It is an astonishing fact that socialism became the chief issue in France during a period when the overwhelming majority of the inhabitants were rural. The explanation lies in the tradition of revolution as a method of progress, established by the French Revolution. Tradition proved more powerful than economic conditions in determining political action. The tradition of revolution had been upheld in a rather unexpected way by the uprising of July, which had been organ-

[37] De Tocqueville, *op. cit.*, 14.

[38] *Ibid.*

[39] Quoted in M. E. Spuller, *Royer-Collard* (Paris, 1895), 121.

ized and led by the *bourgeoisie,* the very class that, after 1815, had conceived a wholesome dread of popular uprisings. What gave encouragement to the new revolutionary movement of the socialist workers was the ease with which the Bourbons had been overturned. All that was necessary was a feverish night of barricade building in the streets of Paris. The morning would see the swift collapse of a hated government.

With a revolutionary situation in the background it is not surprising that the period 1830 to 1848 in France saw an efflorescence of social theorizing that subjected the capitalist system to far greater criticism than in England during the same period. An intellectual left appeared, which trained its guns on capitalism with as much determination as the *philosophes* of the eighteenth century had trained their guns on feudalism. Capitalism was attacked by the democratic liberal Lamartine; the social liberal Louis Blanc; the Christian socialist Lamennais; the Utopian socialists Cabet, Leroux, and the Saint-Simonians; and the prefascist Proudhon. Their attacks differed in intensity but not in aim, which was to substitute a cooperative social order for that of competitive capitalism. A most uncompromising enemy of capitalism was Louis August Blanqui, an extraordinary character, whose importance lay not in his socialist theories but in the nature of his revolutionary activity. Blanqui might be described as the precursor of a new social type, the professional revolutionary, whose sole occupation was that of an organizer of conspiracies and revolts of disciplined revolutionary groups, dedicated to the violent overthrow of the capitalist system.[40] When arrested in 1836 for complicity in an uprising, Blanqui was asked by the judge what was his occupation. His reply was "Proletarian." "That is no occupation," said the judge. "No occupation!" replied Blanqui, "it is the occupation of thirty-million Frenchmen, who live from their labor and who are robbed of their rights."[41]

This period also saw the appearance of Karl Marx, who came to Paris in 1843 to study firsthand the new social theories that were causing such a stir in France. For Marx the attack on capitalism and on its supporters, the *bourgeoisie,* took the form of an all-embracing

[40] The best sketches of Blanqui in English are in Max Nomad, *Apostles of Revolution* (Boston, 1939), and R. W. Postgate, *Out of the Past* (New York, 1926).

[41] Quoted in Postgate, *op. cit.,* 7.

universal philosophy. It was Marx who sharply proclaimed the workers a *class*, through his insistence on their "class consciousness" and on the "class struggle" between them and the capitalists. The great importance of Marx in the revolutionary history of the nineteenth century was that he shifted the emphasis of class struggle from that between the aristocrats and bourgeois to that between the bourgeois and the proletariat.

The threat of the barricade was not the only danger to stability in France. Another opposition to the July Monarchy appeared in the new and even more ominous threat, that from the barrack. The "Napoleonic legend" had been in the process of formation, as the great exploits of Napoleon were sufficiently recent to be remembered and sufficiently in the past to be romanticized. Bonapartism made a powerful appeal to national pride, because the pacifist policy of the July Monarchy had resulted in reducing France to a humiliating position in international affairs. There began a movement to revise the treaty of 1815, inspired by *"le poignant souvenir de Waterloo."* "Blinded by mean considerations of thrift and prosperity," wrote Louis Blanc, "the bourgeoisie saw nothing but pecuniary loss in the possible agitations of Europe, hence the system of implored peace."[42] The reaction against pacifism was seen in the extraordinary outburst of enthusiasm for Napoleon when, in 1840, the remains of the dead Emperor were brought back from Saint Helena and deposited in a magnificent tomb in Paris. The heir of the Napoleonic legend, Louis Napoleon, was conducting a provocative agitation to revive the great emotion associated with the power and splendor of the First Empire. In the general dissatisfaction with the July Monarchy, Bonapartism had a powerful appeal, in that it promised revolution without terrorism. It seemed impossible that the barricade and the barrack would join forces against the July Monarchy. But, as they say in France, "it is the impossible that always happens."

The great conflict between the new two Frances—bourgeois and proletariat—came to a head during the premiership of Guizot, from 1840 to 1848. It arose over the issue of manhood suffrage, which was advocated by all left groups, who bitterly resented the rule of the capitalist oligarchy. Especially bitter were the workers, who opposed the propertied suffrage even more than did their fellow workers in

[42] Blanc, *op. cit.*, II, 628.

England. A propertied suffrage was traditional in England; even the Philosophic Radicals, in theory democrats, accepted the limited reform of 1832 as an installment of a more extensive electoral program. But in France manhood suffrage was associated with the great tradition of the Rights of Man proclaimed by the French Revolution. It had actually been incorporated in the constitution of 1793, which itself was adopted by a popular referendum. Even Napoleon had bowed before the tradition, though he bastardized it in the form of plebiscites. To go to the barricades under the tricolor, to overthrow the Bourbon dynasty, and then to be presented with Louis Philippe and his bourgeois parliament produced a mood of exasperation and bitterness among the French workers. Almost solidly socialist, the workers of Paris, where political issues were decided for France, hated the July Monarchy with an intensity that came both from disappointment with the outcome of the Revolution of 1830 and from hope of the coming of a socialist commonwealth.

The government of Louis Philippe turned a face of flint toward any suggestion to expand the suffrage beyond the settlement of 1830. In the opinion of Proudhon, the "reformers of 1830 halted only before capital. It was capital that they worshipped by maintaining a property qualification of 200 francs for voting. It was capital that they made both god and government."[43] Opposition by the French bourgeois to manhood suffrage was far more uncompromising than was that of the English bourgeois to the same demand after 1832. To the middle and upper classes in England the workers were the "lower classes," upon whom they looked down with snobbish condescension as upon their inferiors. With this condescension was often mingled a kind of Christian feeling of remorse, not unlike that of the "penitent noblemen" of czarist Russia. Chartist rioting did not entirely change this attitude. If anything, it sharpened the feeling of remorse and prepared the way for the enfranchisement of the workers in 1867.

Quite different was the attitude of the French bourgeois toward the workers. To the former the latter were the rabble, *la canaille,* ever ready for a bloody uprising. The Reign of Terror had left an

[43] P. J. Proudhon, *Les Confessions d'un révolutionnaire* (C. Bouglé and H. Moysset, eds., Paris, 1929), 96.

indelible impression of fear on the imagination of the French bourgeois, who dreaded nothing so much as a parliament, elected by manhood suffrage, having supreme power in the state. It brought reminders of the National Convention and its confiscatory decrees. Manhood suffrage pointed the way straight to a class war between the propertyless many and the propertied few, the only outcome of which would be barbarism and anarchy. According to Guizot, both God and nature had established an eternal hierarchy of labor, ranging from the lowest unskilled manual worker to the highest creative intellectual. Democracy would be the gateway to socialism, the red specter that aimed to reduce all labor to the same level, and that level, the lowest.[44] Dread of *le peuple* caused the terrified *bourgeoisie* to cling more tightly to the monarchical system as a protection against revolution. Even its antipathy to the aristocracy "was tempered by an excessive dread of the people, and by appalling recollections. At bottom it liked monarchy in so far as it presented an obstacle to democratic aspirations: it would have wished to subjugate royalty without destroying it."[45]

In another and different way manhood suffrage roused fear among the bourgeois. The rule of Napoleon, with its military dictatorship, unbridled imperialism, and almost continuous war, in their view, had been the outcome of the manipulation of manhood suffrage by means of plebiscites. Manhood suffrage in France, in the opinion of Guizot, had never been anything but a means of destruction or of deceit: destruction when the masses themselves possessed political power; deceit when manhood suffrage was used by Napoleon, through his plebiscites, to abolish all political rights.[46] The French bourgeois were now completely surfeited with revolution that led to terrorism and with dictatorship that led to war; and they desired nothing so much as peace, both internal and external. Moreover, they were convinced that democracy and dictatorship were temporary aberrations of normal government. Had they not beheld the collapse of the democratic First Republic after a strenuous rule of seven years? And of the auto-

[44] Guizot, *Des moyens de gouvernement* (Paris, 1821), 145–150, and *Democracy in France* (Paris, 1869), Chap. V.

[45] Blanc, *op. cit.*, I, 101.

[46] Guizot, *Mémoires*, I, 166.

cratic First Empire after a victorious career of eleven years? "Popular tyranny or military dictatorship," declared Guizot, "may be the expedient of a day, but can never be a form of government."[47]

Almost from the day of its accession to power, the July Monarchy had to struggle for its very existence. Like the restored Bourbons before 1830, it confronted opponents both inside and outside parliament, who grew more numerous and more menacing with advancing years. Neither the system of government, "a monarchy limited by a limited number of citizens," nor its political philosophy nor its social policy appealed to any section of the people except the wealthy bourgeois. An electorate of 241,000 in a population of 33,000,000 was a mockery of representative government. The *pays légal,* as the electorate was called, represented neither privilege in the aristocratic sense nor numbers in the democratic sense. It was plainly and openly a plutocracy, whose control was resented by the aristocrats and hated by the masses. In practice, parliamentary supremacy meant bourgeois supremacy.

The various opponents of the government could be classified into three main divisions. A moderate group, known as the "Dynastic Opposition," opposed the interference of Louis Philippe in the government and subscribed to the formula pronounced by Adolphe Thiers, their leader, that "the king reigns but does not rule." Under the Bourbons, argued Thiers, the problem had been to prevent the king "from jumping out of the *Charte"* in which he had been confined. The same problem now existed under Louis Philippe, and with less reason, because the king had acknowledged his constitutional limitations by accepting the crown from parliament. A more advanced group was the *Tiers Parti.* Not only did they oppose the king, but they also sought to widen the *pays légal* by expanding the suffrage. The *Tiers Parti* favored the enfranchisement of the professional classes who had "capacity," but not the necessary property qualification. Radical leaders were the scientist François Arago, the banker Jacques Lafitte, and the journalist Garnier-Pagès.

On the extreme left were the Republicans, a small but highly influential group. They had come to the conclusion that a French king, whether Bourbon or Orleanist, could not be anything else but a despot.

[47] Guizot, *Democracy in France,* 65.

Absolutism, and only absolutism, was the historic tradition of monarchy in France; and they pointed to the tyrannical acts of the constitutional king, Louis Philippe, as being in harmony with this tradition. Some of the Republicans favored the overthrow of the July Monarchy and the establishment of a democratic republic on the model of the First French Republic. Others, fearful of the violence and terrorism associated with the French Revolution, desired to establish a republic on the model of America.[48]

These groups never consolidated into a *bloc* to form a parliamentary opposition. An effort was made in 1837 to form such a *bloc,* but without success. No opposition parties were in power throughout the period of the July Monarchy.[49] From this situation arose a curious political phenomenon: the government had many opponents, but no opposition existed as in England, ready to assume office on the overthrow of a ministry. These opponents were not "a consciously well-knit political organization, and to use the word 'opposition' in any but a generally negative sense is to give an entirely incorrect impression of its political nature."[50] Because no well-organized, disciplined opposition existed in parliament, the various factions opposed one another as strongly as they opposed the government—even more strongly. As a consequence, the debates in parliament were popularly regarded as "exercises of the intellect rather than as serious discussions," and the differences between the various political factions were derided "as domestic quarrels between children of one family trying to trick one another."[51] In the view of the opposition groups, parliament was not part of the government at all, but a free forum where they could openly express their hatred of the July Monarchy and incite the nation to overthrow it by speaking "through the windows" to the unfranchised masses outside.

There was more political activity outside than inside of parliament. Secret political societies appeared, some of them being liberal monarchist, like the *Aide-toi, le ciel t'aidera;* others, republican, like *Les Amis du peuple;* and still others, socialist, like Blanqui's *Les Saisons,*

[48] Guizot, *Mémoires,* VIII, 527.
[49] Kent, *op. cit.,* 132*ff.*
[50] *Ibid.,* 132.
[51] De Tocqueville, *op. cit.,* 10.

all of which organized conspiracies against the government. Their efforts were seconded by two powerful journals—the moderate *La National,* edited first by Thiers and then by Armand Carrel, and the radical *La Réforme,* edited by Ledru-Rollin and Louis Blanc. So widespread was the hatred of the July Monarchy that opposition went beyond political bounds. "Out of sheer disgust some looked towards a utopia; others, inspired by romantic novelists, turned passionately toward feudal reaction or toward universal, direct suffrage; others dreamed of a Committee of Public Safety, or of the Empire, or of Plato, or of Panurge."[52]

Unquestionably the July Monarchy had not brought stability to France. The antagonism between the new two Frances—bourgeois and proletariat—was daily becoming more bitter. Where would the new conflict lead? "Socialism" was the only answer, and this, to the bourgeois liberals in power, was the end of all things. How then could the order established by the July Monarchy be maintained in the face of the growing menace of a socialist revolution? An answer was given by Guizot when, in 1842, he became Premier, determined to cope with the situation. The highly moral Calvinist Guizot decided that corruption was better than revolution. He would keep the parliamentary system of the July Monarchy intact, but make it function only in the interest of those in control by having a permanent government majority in the Chamber. Opposition parties would be permitted, but they would be rendered futile by being made to function as a permanent minority. Guizot knew English history very well, especially the period of the eighteenth century when the parliamentary system functioned smoothly and peacefully through the corruption of both the electorate and the ministers. These methods, erected into a national system by the knavish genius of Sir Robert Walpole, had proved highly successful in maintaining the Hanoverian dynasty. Could not the Orleans settlement in France maintain itself by the same methods as had the Hanoverian settlement in England? Again like Walpole, Guizot would also follow a peace-at-any-price policy, in order to prevent the country from being distracted by foreign problems. Business enterprise would be encouraged, in the belief that material prosperity would distract the attention

[52] Proudhon, *La Révolution sociale démontrée par le coup d'état du Deux Décembre* (C. Bouglé and H. Moysset, eds., Paris, 1936), 217.

of the people from political problems at home and from militarist adventures abroad.

These views of Guizot resulted in the establishment of the *Système Guizot,* which flourished in France during his premiership. Its aim was to organize political life in such a manner that, while the forms of parliamentary government would be strictly observed, political power would be exclusively controlled and manipulated by a group of politicians devoted to the Orleans settlement. The *pays légal* was organized into a political machine, with the object of grinding out majorities in favor of the government. A local official expressed the government's opinion when he declared that "prudence insists that the electors should not be left to their own convictions."[53] The voters, being few, were generally known by the officials; and each was labeled *bon, douteux,* or *mauvais.* The machine, directed from Paris by the Minister of the Interior, was operated in the departments by the prefects and their subordinates to produce "good elections," on which the government counted. During elections, "official candidates" appeared, openly designated as such, who were aided in every way possible by the local officials. They received government money with which to finance their electoral campaigns; and they were supported by newspapers that were subsidized by the government and distributed free to the voters. The latter were plainly told that only the "official candidate," if elected, would have access to the "pork barrel" for local improvements.[54] Frequently voters were bribed with government jobs to support the "official candidate" or were threatened with reprisals if they refused to do so. The opposing candidate, faced with these serious handicaps, seldom succeeded in winning an election. "From the elections can emerge an excellent citizen, a man of genius, who is willing to accept the system," declared an official. . . . "But I do not believe that it is possible for a successful candidate to be an enemy of the throne and of the prefect."[55] To have any chance of election the opposing candidate had to be a famous man whose reputation

[53] Quoted in Kent, *op. cit.,* 109.

[54] *Ibid.,* 119*ff.*

[55] Quoted in L. Deries, "Une Élection dans l'arrondissement de Valognes sous la Monarchie de Juillet," *La Révolution de 1848* (May–June, 1914), 139. An interesting and lively picture of political life under Louis Philippe is to be found in Balzac's novel *Le Député d'Arcis.*

would overcome the fear of the voters. Great names were in demand, and such opponents of the government as Arago, Lamartine, De Tocqueville, and Lafitte managed to be elected to the Chamber, where they constituted an eminent but futile opposition. Such methods of controlling the Chamber had existed in France before Guizot; but under the latter, parliamentary corruption was developed into a well-organized, well-directed political machine, which became notorious. The narrow, humorless Guizot "faisait la corruption par grande politique, de l'intrigue par naïveté, de la violence par vertu."[56]

As might be expected, the system produced a compact, permanent majority in the Chamber. It became known as *La Résistance,* which used parliament as a government machine to register decisions already made by the King and his ministers. To make doubly sure of the loyal and continued support of *La Résistance,* deputies were bribed with government jobs and contracts. Were it not for the fact that Guizot was devoid of a sense of humor, what he said to the Chamber in 1842 would have been an example of irony in the best French manner. "Like us ministers," he declared, "you have duties to fulfill; you are part of the government; you have your share of responsibility in public matters before the country. Never forget that."[57] To all appearances, France had the full apparatus of parliamentary government: popular elections, parliamentary supremacy, and ministerial responsibility. What made the entire system a farce was the absence of a genuine opposition that could be freely elected and that could freely become the government. Under the *Système Guizot* the King "had so thoroughly corrupted the Chamber," commented De Tocqueville, "that he had no parliamentary opposition to fear. He had so thoroughly corrupted the 200,000 electors that he had nothing to fear from an electoral opposition."[58] Without a parliamentary opposition, politics, in the English sense, did not exist in France under the July Monarchy. Political life, observed De Tocqueville, "could neither come into being nor be maintained within the legal circle which the constitution had traced for it: the old aristocracy was vanquished, the

[56] Proudhon, *La Révolution sociale,* 198.

[57] Guizot, *Histoire parlementaire,* III, 566–567.

[58] *Correspondence and Conversations of Alexis de Tocqueville with William Nassau Senior* (M. C. M. Simpson, ed., London, 1872), I, 78.

people, excluded. As all business was discussed among members of one class, in the interest and in the spirit of that class, there was no battlefield for contending parties to meet upon."[59]

It was plain that bourgeois liberalism in France had failed to establish a stable government based on the parliamentary system. The parliamentary experiment of the July Monarchy, very hopeful at its advent in 1830, turned into a sorry and evil caricature at its demise in 1848. Because of fear of social revolution, Guizot was convinced that opposition to the government was bound to lead to its overturn. "Beware of weakening, for insufficient reasons, the power that you desire to uphold. Beware of diminishing the strength when you do not diminish the burden of those who rule," he cautioned his opponents.[60] Guizot forgot what he himself had once written about an opposition's being a stabilizing, not a disruptive, force in a liberal system of government.[61] His intense bourgeois prejudices, his fear of disturbing the *status quo,* his narrow outlook, his unsympathetic personality prevented him from applying generous principles to a disturbed situation. Believing in moderation but lacking a sympathetic imagination, Guizot became a fanatical moderate; a dogmatic, opinionated, narrow, and tyrannical upholder of the *juste milieu.*

As hostility to the government grew, so did Guizot's determination to uphold it. Driven by fear, the liberal Guizot veered toward authoritarian power. He began to see in the monarchy an ancient hereditary element that could serve the cause of stability in France. The throne, he asserted, was "not an empty armchair, which is locked up so that no one would sit in it." As he was continuously in authority, the king represented stability in the government of the nation. As chief executive, he ruled in cooperation with parliament; hence the chief function of the ministry was to act as the mediator between king and parliament.[62]

Before long the government of Louis Philippe became as despotic as that of the Bourbons. The civil liberties, so expressly guaranteed in the constitution, were undermined by all sorts of special measures.

[59] De Tocqueville, *Recollections,* 9.
[60] Guizot, *Histoire parlementaire,* III, 566.
[61] Guizot, *Des moyens de gouvernement,* 299–301, 320.
[62] Guizot, *Mémoires,* II, 184–185; *Histoire parlementaire,* III, 683.

Already in 1835 the September laws had put severe restrictions on the freedom of the press. Under Guizot the restrictions were increased, and the nation was reminded of the reign of Charles X. As usual, Guizot had a historicophilosophical reason for every reactionary measure that he supported. The French, as a people, he argued, were peculiarly sensitive to journalistic influence as a consequence of the dramatic events of the French Revolution. As the social order that had emerged from the Revolution had not yet become stabilized, the people were afflicted with a *susceptibilité sociale,* which made them respond quickly to suggestions of revolt that were constantly given by an irresponsible press. At the same time, the government, highly centralized by the French Revolution, became vulnerable at every point. Hence it needed special protection against the attacks of the press.[63]

Naturally a regime that was so anxiously engaged in merely preserving its existence had neither time nor energy left for the creative work of government. As in the case of the Bourbons, and for the same reason, the rule of the July Monarchy was largely a sterile period in French history. In marked contrast with the many reforms of the bourgeois liberals in England were the few and meager reforms of the bourgeois liberals in France. The educational reform of 1833, known as the *loi Guizot,* was fathered by Guizot when he was Minister of Public Instruction. It provided for the establishment of a primary school in every commune, to be supported by local taxes, aided by government subsidies. Education, however, was neither free nor compulsory. Fees were charged, except to the very poor. Religious instruction was officially sanctioned because, as Guizot said, the sentiment of religion "was put by God in the heart of the poor as in that of the rich to maintain the dignity of human life and to protect the social order."[64] Local control of the popular school, under the *loi Guizot,* was put into the hands of a committee, consisting of the mayor, the curé, and a "notable." The government frankly proclaimed its purpose of using the schools to create conservative sentiment among the masses. "Certainly if safety is any concern of ours we must praise the Government for having tried to secure it through public education."[65]

[63] Guizot, *Histoire parlementaire,* I, 1–13.

[64] Guizot, *Histoire parlementaire,* II, 6.

[65] From a report of an educational commission, quoted in E. H. Reisner, *Nationalism and Education since 1789* (New York, 1922), 52.

About all that the July Monarchy contributed to social reform was a weak and inadequate factory law, enacted in 1841. The law was so innocuous that even Guizot favored it.[66] Children under eight years of age were forbidden to work in factories; those from eight to twelve were forbidden to work more than eight hours a day; and those from twelve to sixteen, more than twelve hours a day. The law applied to only a few factories—those which used steam power and which employed twenty or more workers. However, even this law became a dead letter, as no appropriations were made to enforce it. Except for the factory law and the railway law of 1842 giving government aid to railway companies, not a single piece of important legislation was passed by parliament. The deputy was not wrong who exclaimed, "What have we done in the past seven years? Nothing! Nothing! Nothing!"[67]

Opposition to the July Monarchy grew greater and more menacing as its acts became more tyrannical. Conspiracies, uprisings, and strikes became more frequent and more violent. Popular opinion, whenever audible, resounded with hatred of the regime. Even the constitutional opponents of the government "saw more and more clearly that the pacific methods of their choice were of dubious value."[68] Like the regime of the Bourbons, that of Louis Philippe exercised power but not authority over the people. The weak parliamentary traditions of France were not strengthened by parliamentary supremacy, as worked by the *Système Guizot*. A parliament arising from the *pays légal* and a ministry from *La Résistance* could have no prestige in the nation. The monarchical traditions were not strengthened by constitutionalism, as they had been in England. On the contrary, they were weakened by the glaring contradiction between the promise and the performance of the July Monarchy. The other France, the unenfranchised, discontented *pays réel*, sought to express itself in other than parliamentary ways, which it did through the secret revolutionary societies.

The bourgeois liberal regime roused not only hatred but contempt, a contempt so general and so profound that it affected even the supporters of the regime.[69] The very word "bourgeois" became a term of opprobrium, denoting an individual who lacked all the finer

[66] Guizot, *Mémoires*, VI, 362.
[67] J. B. Wolf, *France, 1815 to the Present* (New York, 1940), 156–157.
[68] Kent, *op. cit.*, 215.
[69] De Tocqueville, *Recollections*, 81.

qualities of human personality and a class that was hard, grasping, selfish, and cowardly. "Liberalism" became associated with an economic system that exploited the laboring masses with impersonal ruthlessness by identifying the class interests of the capitalists with universal economic laws. To the opponents of bourgeois liberalism Guizot was the very incarnation of these evil qualities, "the unyielding champion of a monarchy limited by a limited number of bourgeois." He became the personification of the issue between the two Frances, which were making ready to settle it at the barricade.

Secure in his control of the government machinery, Louis Philippe remained oblivious to the true situation in France. "His only occupation was to keep it in order, and to make it work according to his own views, forgetful of society, upon which this ingenious piece of mechanism rested; he resembled the man who refused to believe that his house was on fire, because he had the key in his pocket."[70] Equally obtuse was Guizot, who saw only that the Revolution of 1830 had overthrown the reactionary Bourbons, but who failed to see that it had, at the same time, roused the hopes and liberated the energies of those who dreamed of a far greater revolution. He mistook the "end of the act for the end of the play."

As the year 1848 approached, it became evident on all sides that the July Monarchy, like the Restoration, had failed to solve the great problem of uniting the two Frances. If anything, Louis Philippe and Guizot made that problem more difficult of solution by placing the government in a more precarious position through policies that greatly increased the number of its enemies. The July Monarchy was confronted by a united revolutionary front of workers and petty bourgeois; and this combination received the unexpected support of the Bonapartists, who saw a chance of fishing in troubled waters, and of the Legitimists, who were smarting to avenge the July Revolution. What made the failure of the bourgeois liberals all the more significant was that they were in power during the July Monarchy, not in opposition as they had been during the Restoration. Not the least of the reasons for the tragic failure was that Guizot had neither the social generosity nor the political imagination to win the working class to the side of the government. That aspect of the situation was

[70] *Ibid.*, 11–12.

evident to the luminous De Tocqueville. "Universal suffrage," he declared, "is now the only source that I know from which governmental power can be drawn. This is its great and, so to say, its only merit in my opinion."[71]

It was chiefly the disappointed workers, with their revolutionary heritage, that made dangerous the opposition to the government, in and out of parliament. They were convinced that the July Monarchy was the dead end of all hopes of fulfilling the promise of the French Revolution. This conviction was shared by idealistic bourgeois to whom a democratic republic was the only sure guarantee of political freedom. Once more the two Frances prepared for combat. What followed was the Revolution of 1848.

[71] De Tocqueville, "Nouvelle correspondance," *Oeuvres complètes* (Paris, 1864–1867), VII, 239.

Chapter 11. John Stuart Mill

Pioneer of Democratic
Liberalism in England

Did bourgeois liberalism in England, like that in France, bear within itself the seeds of its own destruction? Or did it possess a capacity for generating new ideals and new forces that would deepen its social outlook and widen its political base? In England the situation was especially favorable for a new "liberal settlement" that would aim to solve the problems of the great masses who politically were thrust outside the constitution and economically were put at the mercy of laissez-faire capitalism. Bourgeois liberalism in England, unlike that in France, was not seriously challenged either by a reactionary right or by a revolutionary left. A new liberal settlement could, therefore, be made without incurring the dangers of civil conflict.

The herald of the new liberalism was John Stuart Mill. Though steeped in Benthamism, he yet came to realize its limitations and he emerged as the champion of a social order far more enlightened, far more generous, and far more humane than that envisioned by Bentham and his disciples. Rarely have the characteristics of an age and of a nation been found integrated in the life and work of a single individual. Mill is the unique example of a man who incarnated the liberal movement in nineteenth-century England: utilitarianism, classical economy, and Philosophic Radicalism in its early phase; and universal suffrage, including women, and social reform in its later phase. In Mill, one "sees an age, and one sees a man";[1] and it might be added, one sees a nation—liberal England.

Mill's *Autobiography* is an extraordinary human document. In it

[1] John Jacob Coss, Preface to *Autobiography of John Stuart Mill* (New York, 1924), hereafter cited as Mill, *Autobiography*.

we get a brief, yet intimate, picture of the author's life as he developed from childhood to the year 1873, when the book was published. Mill was born in London on May 20, 1806, "the eldest son of James Mill, the author of the *History of British India.*"[2] His appearance in the world might almost be said to have been due to "spontaneous generation" from the atmosphere of utilitarianism, rather than to the union of his parents. Throughout the *Autobiography* there is no mention of his mother. The wife of a famous man and the mother of a great one, Mrs. Mill was relegated to oblivion by both. She was not beloved by her husband, James Mill,[3] and probably because of that, she aroused only indifference in her son. The only figure that stood out, clear and sharp, in Mill's early life was his father, who, to his son, was not a father, but the "author of the *History of British India*" and his one and only teacher. Mill had no emotional family ties, not even to his father, whom he greatly admired and respected—and feared—but never really loved. In the *Autobiography,* there are only casual references to his brothers and sisters, who seemed to have played no part at all in his life. Mill was neither a son nor a brother but a product of an educational experiment conducted by his father.

James Mill, with the aid and the encouragement of his "master" and neighbor, Jeremy Bentham, determined on a rigid plan for bringing up young Mill, with the object of making him a missionary of their utilitarian faith. Both were deeply influenced by the idea of the French materialist philosopher Helvétius, that education and environment, not original endowments, were the most important factors in the development of an individual. In early childhood young Mill was given hard intellectual tasks by his father, who acted as his private teacher. At the age of three he read Greek; at eight, Latin; and at twelve, he had read nearly all the classics in the original. History, logic, and philosophy were the other subjects taught him by his father-teacher. James Mill, being an atheist, naturally did not give religious instruction to his son. Young Mill was never truly a child; he read few children's books and he had no playmates other than his brothers and sisters, whose teacher he himself became. Practically the only persons with whom young Mill associated intimately were

[2] *Ibid.*, 2.

[3] Leslie Stephen, *The English Utilitarians* (New York, 1902), II, 39.

his stern, rigid father and that eccentric bachelor, Bentham. It was chiefly his father who fashioned John Stuart Mill's early life and profoundly influenced his ideas and conduct. So deep was the influence of the father on the son that, even after the death of the former, the latter felt his father's ghostly hand on his shoulder to the end of his days.

Mill never went to a college or to a university. For all that he was intellectually as mature at the age of fifteen as an intelligent man who had had all the advantages of a higher education. The first intellectual task assigned to young Mill was the editing of Bentham's great legal work, *Rationale of Evidence,* a task which he performed with striking ability. Utilitarianism was the creed in which Mill was suckled, cradled, and nurtured by his father and Bentham. Naturally, when he came to make a systematic study of the doctrines of Bentham, he came with a will to believe in their everlasting truth. As he stated in his *Autobiography,* the "feeling rushed upon me that all previous moralists were superseded and that here, indeed, was the commencement of a new era in thought. . . . I now had opinions; a creed, a doctrine, a philosophy; in one among the best senses of the word, a religion."[4] At the age of seventeen, Mill began writing for Benthamite journals, especially for the *Westminster Review,* the organ of utilitarianism. At the same time he was appointed to a clerkship in the office of the East India Company, where his father held a high position. Young Mill now had not only a philosophy, but also economic security and prospects of a career as a writer.

All seemed bright for the precocious young man whose life and career had been so carefully planned and arranged. But Mill had arrived at maturity emotionally starved; the development of the human emotions had been given no part in his early education. Music, poetry, games, novels, all had been anathema to his teacher-father; and women and sex were outside the utilitarian concept of happiness. As a consequence, Mill at the age of twenty suffered a nervous breakdown. His recovery was a slow process, and he emerged from his illness a healthier man mentally. Wordsworth was his "doctor." By reading the poetry of Wordsworth, Mill caught glimpses of emotional and imaginative aspects of life previously denied him. He began to

[4] Mill, *Autobiography,* 46–47.

consider happiness in terms of concrete, emotional experiences of individuals, very different from the abstract happiness of utilitarianism. He now sought, consciously and deliberately, to cultivate his emotions by devoting himself to poetry, music, and art.

The peak of Mill's emotional development, however, came when, at the age of twenty-four, he met Mrs. Taylor—a sensitive, intellectual woman married to a plain businessman. Mill found her a stimulating companion and sought her out on all occasions. He became a frequent visitor to the Taylor home and often found himself alone with Mrs. Taylor. The intellectual friendship ripened into love, a relationship that was regarded as scandalous by Mill's family and friends. Nevertheless, it is highly doubtful whether, in this English version of a *ménage à trois,* there was anything more than a platonic relationship on the part of all three. The intimacy of Mill and Mrs. Taylor lasted for twenty years. When her husband died, in 1851, she and Mill were soon married.

Mrs. Taylor exercised a profound influence on Mill's life and thought. She was his one emotional outlet; without her he would, in all likelihood, have withered and dried up in early manhood. It was his profound belief that Mrs. Taylor had opened his eyes to newer vistas of human progress through her great sympathy with the working class. So highly did Mill think of her originality that he regarded his writings as inadequate attempts on his part to express her ideas. Mill's opinion of the extraordinary ability of Mrs. Taylor was not shared by his associates, who believed that she merely echoed his own opinions. In this case, the echo sounded more colorful and more vivacious than did the voice.

The period of Mill's relationship with Mrs. Taylor was the fruitful period of his life. His first book, *A System of Logic,* which appeared in 1843, had a great success. When the *Principles of Political Economy* appeared in 1848, it quickly became the most widely read book on economics since the publication, in 1776, of Adam Smith's *Wealth of Nations.* Mill widened the scope of classical economy by applying its doctrines far more fully than had its founders, Ricardo and Malthus, to concrete human experiences and problems. For half a century, Mill's *Principles* was the standard textbook in economics throughout the English-speaking world. When, in 1859, *On Liberty* appeared,

Mill was universally acclaimed as the great liberal philosopher of his age and of his nation.

Mill's prominence as a writer on politics and his pronounced views on the questions of the day brought him into the political arena. In 1865 he was elected to Parliament as an independent Liberal; but the philosopher in politics did not play much of a parliamentary role. As an orator he was as "cold as a statue" and made but a poor impression on a body that knew Gladstone and Bright. "His figure was spare and slight, his voice weak; a constant twitching of the eyebrow betrayed his nervous irritability."[5] Mill's activity in Parliament was not very great; but he attracted considerable attention, partly because of his advocacy of proportional representation and woman suffrage. When he again ran for Parliament in 1868, he was defeated. Mill thereupon retired from politics. Five years later, in 1873, he died in Avignon, France, at the age of sixty-seven.

Mill has an assured place in the intellectual history of nineteenth-century England. However, it cannot be fairly said that he was an original and creative thinker, as were his fellow utilitarians, Bentham, Ricardo, and Malthus. What especially distinguished Mill was his intellectual honesty and receptive open-mindedness, which gave to his views the unique quality of moral originality. A popularizer of genius, he was "unsurpassable as an interpreter between the abstract philosopher and the man of common-sense."[6] Mill's complete tolerance of opposing views and his candor in regard to his own views enabled him to make utilitarianism more palatable to those who accepted its doctrines and more attractive to those who at first had been repelled by them. The rigid angles of Benthamism were trimmed away and rounded into the curves of a new liberalism, which appeared all embracing in its humaneness and sweet reasonableness. Mill's liberalism became a classless, national ideal—one that appealed to all sorts and conditions of men and women. Strangely enough, it was from the hard soil of Benthamism that grew the fairest flower of English liberalism, which was Mill. In consideration of his early influences and peculiar upbringing, he might have become a logic machine like his

[5] Stephen, *op. cit.*, III, 64.
[6] *Ibid.*, 17.

father or a benevolent crank like Bentham, had it not been for his naturally sweet disposition and—Mrs. Taylor.

If ever the style was the man, it was that of Mill. His was a "white" style, clear, distinct, and precise, an excellent example of the noble simplicity of the best English prose. The appeal of Mill's argument becomes more convincing because the language used is as clear as the logic is impeccable. But Mill's style lacks color; it is without warmth. Occasionally, as in *On Liberty* and in "The Subjection of Women," the intensity of his convictions on matters very dear to him is so deep that the style becomes tinged with emotion and rises to a restrained kind of eloquence. There is hardly a trace of humor or of satire in any of Mill's writings. What is present—and constantly present—is an intensified moral earnestness, which filled the void in his life resulting from the absence of religious convictions. In a writer less gifted than Mill, this moral earnestness would probably have resulted in making his writings sound commonplace to succeeding generations. What saves Mill for posterity is that his moral earnestness is refined by a cool intellectuality, as a consequence of which the writings of this "saint of rationalism" have a luminous integrity that gives them, or the best of them, a place among the classics of political philosophy.

Mill was no unexplainable phenomenon. He was quite definitely the product of his environment, of his age, and of his nation. Apart from these fundamental factors, there were influences that helped to mold him as the leading spokesman of nineteenth-century liberalism. One influence came from France. In his youth he had spent a year in France and had breathed "the free and genial atmosphere of Continental life."[7] "Continental," to Mill, meant French. He knew French very well and was an assiduous student of the writings of Comte, Michelet, De Tocqueville, Guizot, and the Utopian socialists, especially those of Saint-Simon. For a time he was an intellectual intimate of Comte, with whom he frequently corresponded. Mill's sympathies in France were decidedly with the elements on the left. He was in France during the Revolution of 1830, which inspired in him a feeling that he had entered on "a new existence." The Revolution

[7] Mill, *Autobiography*, 40–41.

of 1848 found in Mill an ardent supporter, even of its more radical phase. He expressed sympathy for Louis Blanc's scheme of national workshops.[8] German political ideas had little or no influence on Mill. Two great German political philosophers, Hegel and Karl Marx, were his contemporaries. He knew the work of Hegel, the reading of which gave him "a sort of sickening feeling." As a result of his attempts to "unwind" Hegel, Mill came to the conclusion that to read that German philosopher tended to deprave one's intellect.[9] Although Marx was a fellow Londoner of his for many years, Mill seems never to have known even of his existence. There is no mention whatever of Marx in his writings.

Another influence in the shaping of Mill's thought came from America. It was an indirect influence, as Mill first became interested in America by reading De Tocqueville's *Democracy in America*.[10] This book convinced him that the American experiment in democracy was a success and that democracy was both inevitable and desirable for all mankind. From America he also learned that a greater social equality was possible through a wider distribution of property. During the Civil War, he became a strong supporter of the North as the side that, in his opinion, was fighting to maintain political democracy and social equality.

In "his single person he [Mill] spans the interval between the old and the new Liberalism."[11] From the liberalism identified with propertied suffrage and laissez-faire policies Mill passed to the new liberalism of universal suffrage and social reform without entirely abandoning his fundamental utilitarian principles. It is the opinion of Dicey that the labor of Mill's life "was the reconciliation of inherited beliefs, from which he never departed, with moral and intellectual ideals and sympathies, which, belonging to himself and to his time, were foreign, if not opposed to the doctrine of his school."[12]

[8] Mill, "Vindication of the French Revolution of February, 1848," *Dissertations and Discussions* (New York, 1874), III, 5–81.

[9] Mill, *Letters* (H. S. R. Elliott, ed., London, 1910), II, 93.

[10] Mill, *Autobiography*, 134–135.

[11] L. T. Hobhouse, *Liberalism* (London, 1911), 107.

[12] A. V. Dicey, *Lectures on the Relation between Law and Public Opinion in England during the Nineteenth Century* (London, 1914), 424.

What elements of utilitarianism did Mill retain? What elements did he transform? What elements did he abandon? And what new principles did he advocate? The answers to these questions will give an appraisal of Mill's place as a pioneer of democratic liberalism and of his influence on his own and on succeeding generations. Mill accepted the basic principle of utilitarianism, namely, "the Greatest Happiness for the Greatest Number." But he rejected Bentham's method of applying this principle by calculating, weighing, and measuring pleasures and pains according to the scheme of "felicific calculus." Mill revolted against this method of balancing accounts of man's emotions; he stressed the quality rather than the quantity of pleasure. To Bentham "push pin was as good as poetry." Not so to Mill, who believed that it was better "to be Socrates dissatisfied than a fool satisfied." Furthermore, he concluded that happiness came as a by-product; therefore it could not be, as Bentham had taught, a direct result of political and social policies. By stressing quality instead of quantity, Mill transformed the "greatest happiness" principle from a system of psychological bookkeeping into a moral ideal that appealed to many who recoiled from the all-too-practical rationalism of the utilitarians.

What Mill retained of bourgeois liberalism, as formulated by the Benthamites, was parliamentary government, which he prized above all other English institutions. Like all English liberals, of whatever school, Mill did not separate civil liberties from self-government; one supplemented and protected the other. Parliamentary government was better than any other system, if for no better reason than that it made necessary the political education of the people, thereby making them acutely conscious of the necessity of maintaining their liberties. Of all the systems of representative government, he regarded the British system as the best, and precisely because it was not a symmetrical political system with the powers of government neatly arranged according to universal principles of political science, as they were in the United States and French constitutions. In the British system the powers of government, vested in the King, Lords, and Commons, did balance, he reasoned; but the scales never hung exactly even.[13] Despite

---

[13] Mill, *Representative Government*, in *Utilitarianism, Liberty and Representative Government* (London, Everyman's Library, 1914), 228.

the hereditary monarchy and the bicameral legislature, it was the Commons that exercised preponderance in the British system, because it had the great moral advantage of being the popular element.

In Mill's day, the political problem in England turned on the suffrage. After 1832, the issue between the old and the new liberals was whether Parliament should be chosen by the propertied classes or by the masses of the people through manhood suffrage. The old liberals feared the masses even more than they did the privileged aristocracy. In their opinion the masses, once enfranchised, would use their political power to confiscate property, to oppress minorities, and to suppress civil liberties; hence they were strongly opposed to the extension of the suffrage.

Mill had the foresight and the generosity—and the good sense— to favor a democratic suffrage. He did so not because he regarded the suffrage as an abstract natural right to be given to everyone just because he was born. As a Benthamite, Mill repudiated the doctrine of natural rights; he favored the extension of the franchise because he was convinced that democracy was the most essential security for good government.[14] When every class could protect its interest by means of the ballot, the supremacy of Parliament, with its power to make or to break ministries, would be used to advance "the Greatest Happiness for the Greatest Number."[15] There could be no greater security for good government than that given by democracy. Therefore, the poor should be given the vote in order to protect their interests; otherwise Parliament, representing the propertied classes, would judge questions affecting labor from the employers' viewpoint.[16] Manhood suffrage would prevent the wealthy middle class from becoming an oligarchy that would rule the country in its own interests like any other oligarchy. Mill lent his great influence in favor of the movement to extend the franchise, which resulted in the reform bills of 1867 and 1884.

In no aspect of his political philosophy was Mill more in advance of the Victorian liberals than in his attitude toward woman. To him, women were "people"—hence, part of the general public. In his famous essay "The Subjection of Women," Mill took an advanced feminist position

14 Mill, *Autobiography*, 75.
15 Mill, *Representative Government*, 239.
16 *Ibid.*, 209; *Letters*, II, 268.

by advocating the equality of women with men, the most practical and, at the same time, the most symbolic expression of which would be woman suffrage. He was convinced that whatever differences existed between the sexes arose from environment, from education, and from legal discrimination, "due to the accident of sex."

Mill's essay brought the question of woman suffrage prominently to the fore for the first time since it had been raised in the eighteenth century.[17] He presented his reasons for extending the franchise to women with his characteristic lucidity, candid sincerity, and "sweet reasonableness." The granting of the franchise to women, he held, would be the supreme symbol of equality with men that would arouse in women a new sense of dignity. As a Member of Parliament, he showed considerable courage in offering a woman-suffrage amendment to the Reform Bill of 1867. It received only 73 votes, but Mill's amendment may be said to have launched the woman-suffrage movement, which achieved a resounding triumph in the twentieth century.

Though he was converted to the principle of a democratic suffrage, Mill never entirely freed himself from a feeling of distrust of the "rule of the numerical majority." Property, leisure, and education were, in England, so completely identified with the governing elements that he looked with misgiving at the prospect of the government's falling into the hands of the illiterate, work-benumbed poor. In the class-ridden England of his day the mass of poor were the "lower classes," doomed to remain in that station of life into which they were born. And yet Mill was convinced that the "ascendancy of the numerical majority is less unjust, and on the whole less mischievous, than many others, but it is attended with the very same kind of dangers, and even more certainly."[18] Majority rule was the only feasible plan in a democracy; the problem was how to have universal suffrage and, at the same time, avoid the possible tyranny of majority rule. Regarding the vote, not as a natural right, but as a power over others, Mill favored checks on this power, lest democracy prove as tyrannical as absolute monarchy. So

[17] The pioneer of woman suffrage in France was Condorcet. See J. Salwyn Schapiro, *Condorcet and the Rise of Liberalism* (New York, 1934), 187–195. Mary Wollstonecraft's pamphlet, *A Vindication of the Rights of Woman*, published in 1792, raised the question of woman's rights in England.

[18] Mill, *Representative Government*, 268.

fearful was he of the tyranny of the majority that he became more fertile and more insistent in devising checks on universal suffrage than in advocating its establishment. He favored a literacy test for voting, which, he believed, was "a political principle at once liberal and conservative." It was liberal, he reasoned, in that a literate electorate would favor liberty; it was conservative in that universal suffrage would not be established all at once. In order to prepare the masses for the franchise, Mill urged the establishment of a system of popular education. Convinced that the rich "had more to fear from the poor when uneducated, than when educated," he appealed to the propertied classes to favor popular education "in order to ward off really mischievous errors, which would lead to unjust violations of property."[19]

Education, to Mill, was almost a universal solvent of the problems of democracy. Even a wholly literate electorate, he argued, was liable to commit acts of tyranny, as the majority would be dominated by special interests—class, religious, or sectional, particularly the first. The "sinister interests" of the privileged classes in an aristocracy might yield to the evil of "class legislation" in a democracy. Was it reasonable, he asked, to expect that the poor would resist the temptation "to follow their own selfish inclinations and short-sighted notions of their own good, in opposition to justice, at the expense of all other classes and of posterity?"[20]

The political situation in England during the first half of the nineteenth century helps to explain Mill's fear of class legislation. Infuriated at having been left out in the cold by the Reform Bill of 1832, many workers turned a willing ear to revolutionary appeals. The new class conflict that followed—that between the workers and the middle class—became even more bitter than had been the conflict between the aristocrats and the middle class. Though its famous Six Points were definitely political, Chartism had a menacing socialist overtone that greatly alarmed the Liberals, as well as the Conservatives. With all his generous sympathy for the unenfranchised masses, Mill dreaded a social upheaval of the lower orders. These fears were confirmed by the riotous demonstrations of the Chartists, which gave a vivid idea of social revolution that brought terror to the propertied classes.

[19] Mill, *Autobiography*, 121.
[20] Mill, *Representative Government*, 254.

To avoid the danger of class legislation, Mill proposed schemes of plural voting and of proportional representation as checks on the "rule of the numerical majority." Plural votes, according to Mill, should not be given to those who owned property in different constituencies, as was then the practice; they should be given to the highly educated element—to the graduates of higher institutions of learning and to the members of the liberal professions. In a democracy, the authority of the educated, few in number, would be augmented by "superiority of weight justly due to opinions grounded on superiority of knowledge."[21] Votes were to be both counted and weighed: counted in accordance with the "greatest happiness" principle and weighed in the scale of intellectual achievement. Democratic government was, in essence, according to Mill, government by public opinion. The public in a modern nation, he argued, consisted roughly of two groups—employers and employees—each of which was dominated by selfish class interests that dictated their opinions. Apart from both was a group of educated persons, who, because of their intelligence and learning, were primarily concerned with general, not with class, interests.[22] In a democracy the highly educated would, Mill believed, make an irresistible appeal to the masses. It was not "in the nature of uninstructed minds to resist the united authority of the instructed."[23] If the highly educated were convinced of the necessity of change, they would create sufficient public opinion in favor of new laws. Great steps of progress, according to Mill, came as a result not of a "change in the distribution of material interests," but of a change in opinion, a "social power" far greater than any other. It was the educated element that was primarily responsible for the changes of opinion that made possible social progress. "One person with a belief is a social power equal to ninety-nine who have only interests."[24] In the political conflicts between the two interested groups—employers and employees—the educated elite, strengthened by plural votes, would join forces with that minority in each group who were sufficiently enlightened to subordinate their class interests "to

---

[21] Mill, *Autobiography*, 180. See also "Thoughts on Parliamentary Reform," *Dissertations and Discussions* (New York, 1874), IV, 28*ff.*

[22] Mill, *Representative Government*, 255.

[23] Mill, "Bentham," *Dissertations and Discussions*, I, 358.

[24] Mill, *Representative Government*, 183

reason, justice, and the good of the whole." In this way the enlightened section of the electorate would be sufficiently powerful to direct legislation in the public interest.[25]

Mill's plea to give special influence in the government to the "scholar in politics" was typical of the Benthamite radical. It was really an alternative to the aristocratic control of the government by the "gentleman in politics." Seen across Mill's temperament, democracy meant the substitution of one ruling group for another: an elected, educated elite for a hereditary aristocracy. An independent, educated group, chosen by universal suffrage to govern the nation, would accomplish the political objectives that Mill had most at heart: the elimination of aristocratic government and the limitation of the power of the "numerical majority."

To Mill faith in the disinterestedness of the educated element seemed plausible. Being few in number and in a highly privileged position, the highly educated could, according to Mill, take a position "above the battle" of interests. Today, after a century of democratic experience, it would be somewhat naïve to believe that the highly educated are sufficiently free from personal interests and from class bias to be given greater political power than their numbers warrant. Plural votes for the highly educated is, therefore, not on the agenda of progressive movements.

Proportional representation was advocated by Mill as another check on the power of the majority. He was convinced that the method of electing representatives by a majority vote was bad, in that it resulted in giving all the power to the party that won by ever so narrow a majority. According to Mill, this method greatly exaggerated the already dangerous power of the majority. Elections once over, the minority, be it ever so large, found itself the helpless prisoner of the majority, be it ever so small. In the scheme of proportional representation through the method of preferential voting, as devised by Thomas Hare, Mill saw one of "the very greatest improvements yet made in the theory and practice of government."[26] By giving both to the majority and to the minority representation in proportion to their numbers, it would tend to decrease the power of the former and increase that of the latter.

25 *Ibid.*, 255.
26 *Ibid.*, 263.

Mill's special tenderness for the rights and opinions of minorities caused him to see in proportional representation a means of obviating the danger of majority tyranny.

Mill's advocacy of universal suffrage and his fear of the "rule of the numerical majority," seemingly contradictory, were yet consistent with his fundamental individualism. "The worth of a State in the long run," he declared in the notable ending of *On Liberty,* "is the worth of the individuals composing it; . . . a State which dwarfs its men, in order that they may be more docile instruments in its hands even for beneficial purposes—will find that with small men no great thing can really be accomplished." Democracy to him was the political recognition of the moral worth of every individual, every woman as well as every man. Mill did not greatly fear persecution of isolated individuals who expressed heterodox opinions, because such individuals were seldom considered dangerous to the community. What he did fear was persecution of minority groups, because organized minorities roused fears for the safety of the established order. Protection of minorities was, therefore, the true test of freedom of individual opinion. Proportional representation, in Mill's view, constituted the most effective method of protecting the freedom of the individual, because it gave every minority the power to assert itself politically.

As a liberal, Mill was opposed to a hereditary upper house. However, he favored a bicameral system as another method of preventing the "tyranny of the majority." In place of the hereditary Lords he advocated the establishment of a "Chamber of Statesmen" so constituted that it would be a check on a democratically elected lower house. This body was to consist, in general, of high government officials, of university professors, and peers elected by the entire peerage.[27] Such an upper house would prove an effective bar, Mill thought, to tyrannical measures that might come from a democratically elected lower house.

Curiously enough, Mill opposed the secret ballot and favored open voting. The secret ballot, he thought, was an inducement to the voter to hide his selfish motives and to give vent to his prejudices. Therefore, the elector should vote "under the eye and criticism of the public";

[27] *Ibid.,* 328–329. It is interesting to note that a similar scheme for an upper house was advocated by the opponents of the Parliament Act of 1911, which abolished the veto power of the House of Lords.

it was his moral obligation to consider the public welfare first and fore-most. The "mere obligation of preserving decency," through public vot-ing, would be a check on the abuse of the power of the vote. As pro-portional representation involved the use of the ballot, Mill recom-mended that each voter should affix his signature to his ballot. He was well aware that open voting encouraged coercion, but he minimized it on the ground that the power to coerce was declining, whereas class consciousness and class antagonism were growing among the electorate.[28]

Mill's opposition to the secret ballot can be explained only by his extreme caution in regard to the very thing that he generally favored—a democratic suffrage. In this case, his caution landed him on the side that he detested—the conservative. Like the Puritan that he was, he condemned those who yielded to coercion even more than those who did the coercing. Mill expected the poor voter, at the mercy of his landlord or of his employer, to hold out against threats of economic ruin, thereby proving himself a moral hero. He failed to see that the secret ballot was a device that enabled every citizen to vote according to his opinions without fear of consequences.

Another curious and contradictory view of Mill was his opposition to the payment of Members of Parliament. He opposed the payment of Members on the ground that it would tend to create a class of pro-fessional politicians and demagogues who would be attracted to the calling of parliamentary representative by the inducement of salary. "It amounts to offering 658 prizes for the most successful flatterer, the most adroit misleader of a body of his fellow-countrymen."[29] He failed to see that the payment of salaries to Members of Parliament would be an inducement to honest, not to dishonest, legislators. There were far greater monetary temptations than salary to dishonest legislators.

As Mill lived during the great upsurge of nationalism in Europe, it is surprising to note that he had comparatively little to say on the subject. His *Representative Government* contains a short and rather indifferent chapter dealing with nationality. In general, he believed that "the boundaries of governments should coincide in the main with those of

[28] *Ibid.*, 300–307.
[29] *Ibid.*, 311–312.

nationalities," as an essential "condition of free institutions." A "united public opinion, necessary to the working of representative government," could not exist in a state containing different nationalities. Mill was thinking of Austria during the Revolution of 1848, when the government effectively used one nationality against another to suppress the liberal movement.[30]

Mill's political views marked the extent of his departure from the bourgeois liberalism of his day. Not only was he more democratic in his definite proposals, but his general outlook on the political problems of his day was far broader than that of his liberal contemporaries. He realized what they did not or would not realize, that under modern conditions the affairs of state concerned directly everyone in the community. Hence the organization of the state, as well as its policies, should be controlled by everyone in the community. This was the democratic idea which Mill grasped fully and firmly, despite many saving clauses, and which makes him a pioneer of democratic liberalism.

Was Mill's liberalism as advanced in its economic as it was in its political aspects? In the first edition of his *Principles of Political Economy* Mill accepted the principles of classical economy and gave them wide currency not only in England but throughout the world. Nevertheless he was not as consistent an upholder of classical economy as was Ricardo or Malthus. Some of its principles he accepted fully and wholeheartedly; others he modified; still others he rejected entirely. His modifications and rejections are what made Mill a pioneer of social and economic policies distinctive of democratic liberalism, which repudiated classical economy by favoring government intervention in the relations between capital and labor.

What principles of classical economy did Mill at all times accept? These were freedom of enterprise and the maintenance of private property—principles that he never really modified and never really rejected. Free enterprise, so characteristic of modern capitalism, was to Mill the very touchstone of economic progress, without which mankind would be thrust back into the strait jackets of mercantilism and feudalism. And he regarded the security of private property as the one sure guarantee that economic progress would be maintained and strengthened. What

[30] Mill, *Representative Government*, 361–363.

he urged was the improvement of the system of private property so that everyone would share in its benefits.[31]

What principles of classical economy did Mill modify? One important principle that he modified, and modified very seriously, was the principle of *laissez faire,* the very keystone of "the obvious and simple system of natural liberty," to use the famous expression of Adam Smith. Mill came to the conclusion that there was a distinction between the nature of the forces which controlled the production of wealth and those which controlled its distribution, a distinction that he regarded as his most important contribution to economics. The production of wealth was determined, he held, by natural economic laws that operated inexorably, impersonally, and inevitably. But the distribution of wealth was a social matter, dependent on the human will; hence society had the power to arrange as it pleased the manner and form of distributing the wealth produced in a community.[32] Mill's view concerning the distribution of wealth directly contravened that of the master classical economist, Ricardo, according to whom economic laws rigidly determined the distribution of wealth among landlords, capitalists, and workers. In his last edition of the *Principles,* published in 1871, Mill' incorporated his changed views and advocated policies favorable to state intervention.

The economic situation in England in the seventies of the nineteenth century had much to do with Mill's renunciation of the Ricardian view of the distribution of wealth, so basic in classical economy. After an unparalleled industrial development, England exhibited gross inequalities of wealth, which brought many doubts to Mill as to the efficacy of economic laws to advance the principle so dear to him—"the Greatest Happiness for the Greatest Number." He was horrified when confronted with the hideous facts concerning the exploitation of the workers as revealed by the reports of the commissions of inquiry into the conditions in the factories (1833) and in the mines (1842). "Can political economy do nothing but only object to everything, and demonstrate that nothing can be done?[33] Mill asked plaintively. Trade was a

[31] Mill, *Principles of Political Economy,* with an introduction by W. J. Ashley, ed. (New York, 1909), 217, hereafter cited as Mill, *Principles.* See also Mill, *Autobiography,* 174–175.

[32] Mill, *Principles,* 199–201.

[33] *Ibid.,* 373.

"social act"; hence it was in the power of the government to prevent the antisocial practices of business. As his doubts increased concerning the validity of *laissez faire,* Mill's sympathetic nature recoiled from the bleak house that the classical economists had erected for the habitation of mankind. Slowly and tentatively he came to believe in the right and even in the duty of the government to intervene in the relations between capital and labor when the common good demanded it.[34]

It must be kept in mind, however, that Mill's change of attitude toward the working class came at a propitious time. That is why his new views were so influential in promoting the cause of social reform. The extension of the suffrage to the working class by the Reform Bill of 1867 was followed by the Forster Act of 1871, which established a national system of popular education. Mill clearly recognized that these reforms made the workers part of the public.[35] For the first time the nonpropertied masses began to feel that they, like the propertied classes, had a stake in the country. In fact, the workers had the greatest stake in the country, because their daily bread depended on its prosperity. Their interests as a class could be advanced through state intervention in economic matters. Irrefutable logic and the cohesive power of millions of poor would compel the state to assume a new role, that of mediator between the propertied and nonpropertied elements in the nation. *Laissez faire* was doomed when the control of the state passed from the hands of the middle class to those of the masses.

Mill threw a bombshell into the ranks of the classical economists by repudiating one of their cherished tenets—the wage-fund theory. At first he had strongly supported this theory and had denounced the efforts of trade-unions to raise wages as being both futile and pernicious. Now he declared that if an employer was compelled to pay higher wages to his workers, the increase came solely from his own pocket. Contrary to the wage-fund theory, the raising of wages of the organized workers through trade-union action would not be at the expense of the unorganized workers. Trade-unions, in the new view of Mill, were a rightful means of raising the standard of living of the

[34] *Ibid.,* 796, 977.

[35] *Ibid.,* 758. See also his "Chapters on Socialism," *Fortnightly Review,* XXXI (January–June, 1879), 218.

working class.[36] Mill urged the workers to organize, in order to protect their interests; unions and strikes he now considered "a valuable part of the existing machinery of society."[37]

During this period came Mill's final repudiation of *laissez faire*. Government intervention no longer appeared to him a useless and dangerous interference with the law of supply and demand and a violation of the principle of freedom of contract; it was, rather, a legitimate and necessary means of advancing the well-being of the people. Mill's changed views had the effect of lifting the curse pronounced on the working class by the classical economists, and the "door was thrown open for social reform, which was no small triumph."[38]

Mill, however, did not stop with social reform. Once he had broken away from his bondage to the "laws" of classical economy, he began to look forward "to a time, when society will no longer be divided into the idle and the industrious."[39] The economic system, which divided "society absolutely into two portions, the payers of wages and the receivers of them, is neither fit for nor capable of indefinite duration."[40] Mill realized, rather vaguely it is true, that political democracy was inadequate unless a new economic system was established in harmony with its egalitarian ideas. Political struggles, after the enfranchisement of the working class, he argued, would be between the propertied and nonpropertied classes, not, as previously, between landowners and factory owners. The workers were sure to question the rights of property; being no "longer enslaved or made dependent by force of law, the great majority are so by force of poverty." They were, therefore, debarred by the accident of birth from all the advantages that come from the possession of property.[41] As the workers became acutely conscious of their condition, they would resent being under the tutelage of their "betters," and would refuse to be governed or treated like children. Once they saw that their interests were opposed to those of their

[36] Mill, *Principles*, 991–993.
[37] *Ibid.*, 938.
[38] C. Gide and C. Rist, *Histoire des doctrines économiques* (Paris, 1926), 435.
[39] Mill, *Autobiography*, 162.
[40] Mill, *Principles*, 898.
[41] Mill, "Chapters on Socialism," *loc. cit.*, 222.

employers, the workers would not be content to remain permanently in the condition of wage earners.[42]

In view of this situation, Mill began to speculate on the possibilities of abolishing the capitalist system and became a convert to socialism. The "ideal of ultimate improvement" of both Mill and his wife went far beyond democracy, and would class them "decidedly under the designation of Socialists."[43] If a choice were to be made, he declared rather fervently, between socialism and all its uncertainties and capitalism with all its sufferings and injustices, all the difficulties of socialism "would be but as dust in the balance."[44] It is important to understand the nature of Mill's "socialism," on which much has been written that is misleading. In all his writings there is no reference to Marxism. Never at any time did he visualize a class struggle between *bourgeoisie* and proletariat, resulting in a revolutionary reconstitution of the social order. Not even in his most socialist mood did Mill believe that the workers were exploited by the capitalists. There is no anticapitalist note, in the Marxian sense, in all Mill's writings.

What, then, did Mill mean when he called himself a "socialist"? He had studied the works of the Utopian socialists, especially those of Saint-Simon and his disciples, whose criticisms of capitalism and of the competitive system started new trains of thought in his mind. Having come to the conclusion that the distribution of wealth was a matter of social arrangement, not of economic law, he was convinced that a cooperative society would accomplish a juster distribution of wealth than did the competitive society. During the Revolution of 1848 in France, he had followed with keen interest the socialist phase of the movement that had proclaimed the principle of the "right to work" and had set up what were called "national workshops." Socialism, in the opinion of Mill, had become irrevocably an outstanding movement in the political life of Europe.[45]

[42] Mill, *Principles*, 756–760.

[43] Mill, *Autobiography*, 162. Shortly before his death Mill had begun a book on socialism, but he did not live long enough to complete it. What he wrote on socialism appeared after his death in three articles, entitled "Chapters on Socialism," *loc. cit.*, 217–237, 373–382, and 513–530.

[44] Mill, *Principles*, 208.

[45] Mill, "Chapters on Socialism," *loc. cit.*, 220–222.

Mill asserted that cooperative associations of workers would retain all the good of capitalism without any of its evils. Gross inequalities of wealth would be abolished by these associations, formed "on terms of equality, collectively owning the capital with which they carry on operations and working under managers elected and removable by themselves."[46] In time the cooperative associations would be more successful in the production of wealth than individual capitalists; incentives to greater productivity would arise from the desire of greater profits by the members. The distribution of the profits would be made according to acknowledged principles of justice. Because of their greater productivity, their superior social aims, and the harmonious labor of the members, the cooperative associations would compete successfully with capitalistically organized enterprises and finally succeed in supplanting them. By this peaceful method, "without violence and spoliation," society would pass from a competitive to a cooperative basis.[47] According to Mill's new views, economics no longer condemned the mass of workers to eternal poverty, as had the "dismal science" of Ricardo and Malthus. It now held out hopes of a bright and happy future for all mankind.

From the Saint-Simonians Mill learned how the existing system of economic inequality could be put to a painless death: by severe limitations of the right of inheritance. Because of his tender regard for property rights, he made a rather tenuous distinction between the right of bequest and the privilege of inheritance: the former was part of the right of property, hence inviolable; whereas the latter was part of a social arrangement that could be changed in any way to advance the common good. No one, in Mill's opinion, should be permitted to lavish riches on some one individual who had done nothing to create them.[48] That a person, because of the accident of birth, should be certain of inheriting a large fortune was, he thought, very bad for society. He proposed that only the children of the deceased should have the privilege of being heirs, and they should inherit no more than was sufficient for them to be supported in a state of "comfortable inde-

46 Mill, *Principles*, 773.
47 *Ibid.*, 791.
48 *Ibid.*, 222.

pendence."[49] All above this amount left by the testator should go to the state, to be used for the common good.

One aspect of Mill's socialism had a revolutionary tinge: his attitude toward land as property. Mill vented all his "socialism" on the landlords, not on the capitalists. In his opinion the sacredness of property did not apply in the same degree to land, "the original inheritance of the whole species," as it did to other forms of property.[50] As a disciple of Ricardo, he regarded landed aristocrats as parasites on a capitalist economy, whose interests were always opposed to those of the consumers and the manufacturers.[51] "In no sound theory of private property," he declared, "was it ever contemplated that the proprietor of land should be merely a sinecurist quartered on it."[52] The landlords were a class "whom the natural course of things progressively enriches, consistently with complete passiveness on their own part." This increase in wealth, "an unearned appendage" to the income of the landowners, was not property in the rightful sense; hence it should be appropriated by the state for the common good. In other words, Mill favored the confiscation of the "unearned increment" in land values. However, Mill's sensitiveness to property rights, even to those not "sacred,". caused him to moderate his actions, if not his views. What he proposed was a special tax on land, which would gradually become heavier as the "unearned increment" of land values increased.[53] Mill's "modest proposal" implied the gradual socialization of land through the absorption by the state of all unearned increment.

The aristocratic land system of England, with its large estates, tenant farmers, and landless agricultural laborers, roused Mill's strongest opposition. A far better land system, in his opinion, was that in France, in which peasant proprietorship and equality of inheritance were the outstanding features. To reform the English land system,

[49] *Ibid.*, 228.

[50] *Ibid.*, 233*ff.*

[51] David Ricardo, "Principles of Political Economy," in *The Works of David Ricardo,* (J. R. McCulloch, ed., London, 1871), 202.

[52] Mill, *Principles,* 231.

[53] *Ibid.*, 817*ff.* Mill's views on the taxation of unearned increment in the value of land were applied by David Lloyd George in his famous budget of 1909.

Mill advocated the abolition of primogeniture and entail, the nationalization of idle land, and the establishment of a system of peasant proprietorship.[54] However, the landlords were not to be dispossessed without compensation. Parliament should "convert the whole body of landlords into fund-holders, or pensioners."[55] The final solution of the land problem, according to Mill, would be the socialization of land through cooperative societies that would exploit large agricultural areas.[56]

Mill's progress in the direction of democratic liberalism in its economic aspects was definite, though never very clear or very certain. Undoubtedly his sympathies were on the side of the impoverished masses, but his definite proposals were often tentative, halting, and even contradictory. In political parlance, Mill sat in the center, but looked toward the left. His view of government intervention "reflects a singular conflict of optimism and pessimism, of humanitarianism and expedience, of paternalism and self-reliance."[57] In reading Mill, one never gets the impression that he had definitely, once and for all, put classical economy behind him and was setting out on a new course of social reconstruction. Mill's new sympathies were not so deeply rooted as were his early ideas. Steeped from childhood in the principles of Bentham, Malthus, and Ricardo, he retained much of the substance and all of the forms of utilitarianism and classical economy. Always did Mill hesitate to repudiate the capitalist system, at which he leveled so many criticisms. Always did he hesitate to accept a socialist order, at which he cast so many wistful glances. Sometimes he oscillated between belief in the efficiency of competitive capitalism and faith in the ultimate triumph of the cooperative social order. As a consequence, contradictions appear in his writings, especially in the later ones: an economic "law" will suddenly arise to confound a humane ideal, or a socialist suggestion will blandly disconcert a "truth" of classical economy. This attitude of mind was extremely antipathetic to Karl Marx, who denounced Mill as a conspicuous example of

54 Mill, "Papers on Land Tenure," *Dissertations and Discussions*, V, 225–294. For a good discussion of Mill's views of the land problem, see Henri Sée, "Stuart Mill et la propriété foncière," *Revue internationale de sociologie*, XXXII (1924), 606–619.

55 Mill, *Principles*, 234.

56 *Ibid.*, 762–764.

57 *Planned Society* (F. MacKenzie, ed., New York, 1937), 139.

"shallow syncretism" because he tried to harmonize "capitalist political economy with the claims of the proletariat (claims that could no longer be ignored)."[58] Mill's hesitations and oscillations arose from a moralistic attitude toward social problems. Both in the definite reforms that he advocated and in his hazy vision of a cooperative commonwealth, he always stressed as the great desideratum the moral improvement of the individual rather than institutional reorganization. In this sense he was a moralist turned social reformer, whose moral ideals were touched with a social emotion and directed toward social ends.

This social moralism of Mill is best illustrated by his belief in the Malthusian "law of population," a belief that he consistently held all his life. Indeed, by relating the "law of population" to the "law of diminishing returns," he went so far as to give a gloomier emphasis to this theory than did Malthus himself. The disproportion between the increase in population and the yield from land, he argued, would be increased by the diminishing returns from greater investment in agriculture. Mill's criticism of large families among the poor took on a sharpness, even a harshness, that was foreign to his kindly, sympathetic nature. Poverty existed and would continue to exist, he asserted, primarily because men followed their brute instincts without due consideration for the future of their offspring.[59] Mill favored laws prohibiting individuals from marrying unless they offered reasonable guarantees that their children would have "the ordinary chances of a desirable existence." He enjoined upon the trade-unions to teach their members birth control, through moral restraint, because this was a better way of raising wages than by restricting the membership.[60] Only through the restriction of population could the conquest of nature by scientific discoveries become "the means of improving and elevating the universal lot."[61] Overpopulation was a problem, Mill argued, that has confronted society under capitalism and that would continue to confront it under socialism.[62] Even under the capitalist system, poverty

[58] Karl Marx, *Capital*, trans. from the German by E. and C. Paul (London, Everyman's Library, 1930), II, 868.

[59] Mill, *Principles*, 357 ff.

[60] *Ibid.*, 380.

[61] *Ibid.*, 751.

[62] Mill, "Chapters on Socialism," *loc. cit.*, 374.

could be abolished, provided universal education and birth control
were established.[63] One of the reasons why he favored the establishment
of peasant proprietorship in England was that, as in France, the owner
of a farm would then limit the size of his family in order to maintain
his economic status.

Malthusianism became almost an obsession with Mill, so frequently
and so insistently did he proclaim the limitation of offspring as a
sort of cure-all for the poverty of the toiling masses. One is tempted
to venture a psychoanalytic explanation of this obsession in Mill, in
whom wide sympathies and rational judgments were generally so
characteristic. As a child, he had been one of a large family, supported
with great difficulty by the stern, hard-driven James Mill. Young Mill
was required by his father to act as teacher to his younger brothers
and sisters, an arduous task for even so precocious a boy. The family
of his early recollection resembled a school, attended by poor children,
taught by an underpaid teacher, and kept by a stern taskmaster. It is
not surprising that, as a consequence of his childhood experiences,
Mill became a vehement Malthusian.

As a pioneer of democratic liberalism, Mill made more clear and
more certain than did any philosopher before him the vital importance
of intellectual freedom in promoting political and social progress.
He realized with piercing clarity and whole-souled conviction that,
given intellectual freedom, every reform could be achieved—in time.
Without it, nothing was possible except through the accidental and
spasmodic efforts of "benevolent despots," whose reforms might be
abolished by their malevolent successors. Of all Mill's writings, with
the possible exception of his *Autobiography, On Liberty* constitutes
his best claim to be considered a great writer. Even today *On Liberty*
is regarded as the complete and best expression of the faith of a
liberal in the progress of mankind through freedom of thought.
In no other book is the ideal of individual freedom as the great
objective of human striving so clearly stated, so coolly and logically argued, and so trenchantly advocated. All Mill's best qualities
of mind and heart, all that was best in the life of this fairest flower
of English liberalism, went into the writing of *On Liberty*. If ever
a book was a life, *On Liberty* was the life of John Stuart Mill.

[63] Mill, *Principles*, 209.

On Liberty appeared as a challenge to the wave of reaction that was sweeping Europe after the abortive Revolution of 1848. In Austria, in Prussia, in most of Italy, liberals were being hounded by the triumphant reactionaries. In France the prefascist Napoleon III was at the very height of his dictatorial power, and his heavy hand fell on all who were even suspected of being liberals. "Acre for acre, man for man, the political Europe of 1858 seemed not less hostile to the spirit that calls itself liberalism than seems the Europe of 1938."[64] To Mill the wave of reaction was not a "wave of the future" but a sudden and fearful storm, which had burst upon Europe and which would subside after its fury was spent. Every chapter, every line of *On Liberty* breathes a spirit of faith in the inevitable triumph of liberalism. Mill's faith was justified in his own day. When he died, in 1873, the map of liberalism in Europe showed extensive conquests. France was a democratic republic; Italy, a liberal monarchy; Germany and Austria-Hungary, semiliberal empires; Russia had abolished serfdom; and England had extended the franchise to the working class. These sweeping triumphs of the liberal cause convinced Mill, as it did his contemporaries, that the future of the world lay with liberalism.

The keynote of *On Liberty* is individual liberty, a keynote that is sounded in the introduction and is heard throughout the essay. The "sole end for which mankind are warranted, individually or collectively, in interfering with the liberty of action of any of their number is self-protection. That the only purpose for which power can be rightfully exercised over any member of a civilized community, against his will, is to prevent harm to others. His own good, either physical or moral, is not a sufficient warrant."[65] This was Mill's famous formula for the preservation of individual liberty. He went further than did the eighteenth-century libertarians, to whom individual liberty precluded the right of association; in a free society there were to be on the one hand, the state, and, on the other, a mass of "atomized" individuals. Mill, on the contrary, advocated the liberty of association, the right to combine for all legitimate purposes. He

[64] Robert C. Binkley, "Mill's 'Liberty' Today," *Foreign Affairs*, XVI (July, 1938), 563.

[65] Mill, *On Liberty*, in *Utilitarianism, Liberty and Representative Government* (London, Everyman's Library, 1914), 72–73.

advocated the repeal of the Combination Laws, enacted by Parliament to prevent the organization of trade-unions, because he believed in the right of laborers to combine to protect their interests.

In a democratic society the great problem, according to Mill, was how to erect a bulwark of principles of liberty against a tyranny that was little obvious, "the tyranny of the majority," and against a tyranny even less obvious, "the tyranny of the prevailing opinion and feeling," or the tendency of society to impose conventional ideas and practices upon those who refused to accept them. Social tyranny was likely to be more formidable than tyrannical laws, because it left the victim "fewer means of escape, penetrating much more deeply into the details of life, and enslaving the soul itself."[66] As an Englishman, Mill realized the danger of "the tyranny of the prevailing opinion and feeling" more keenly than did the liberals on the Continent. In England there was little to be feared from government interference, but much from conventional social opinion.[67] As a consequence, heretical opinions among the English, declared Mill, "never blaze out far and wide, but continue to smoulder in the narrow circles of thinking and studious persons among whom they originate, without ever lighting up the general affairs of mankind with either a true or a deceptive light."[68] The aristocratic cult of "good form" constituted an invisible coercive power to compel conformity to its own ideas and practices by socially ostracizing those who refused to accept them. The liberty of the individual could, in this way, be as effectively curtailed as by despotic laws and by tyrannical officials—perhaps even more efficiently, because to be "sent to Coventry" had more terrors for some than to be sent to jail.

It is important to note that Mill did not subscribe to the eighteenth-century doctrine that freedom of opinion was a natural right. To him, "opinion" implied views affecting the social order, not speculations concerning metaphysical abstractions; hence freedom of opinion was a "utility" for the practical purposes of life, in order to advance "the Greatest Happiness for the Greatest Number." Mill's entire concept of liberty was based on the idea that man is a rational being, interested in advancing his welfare, which could be best accomplished by ad-

[66] *Ibid.*, 68. See also 92*ff*.
[67] *Ibid.*, 71–72.
[68] *Ibid.*, 93.

vancing the public welfare. From the free competition of ideas in the market place would emerge "truth"—namely, the best method to accomplish this aim. Freedom of opinion was essential for maintaining this competition of ideas. Suppression of this freedom was an assumption of infallibility on the part of those in power and was "as noxious, or more noxious, when exerted in accordance with public opinion, than when in opposition to it."[69] Even wrong opinions had social value. They served to clarify and to vivify the right opinions; without them, the latter would degenerate into dead formulas; hence, wrong opinions gave a deeper understanding to those who held the right ones. "He who knows only his own side of the case, knows little of that."[70]

It was Mill's deep conviction that new ideas always came from minorities and from individual geniuses, especially from the latter, without whom "human life would become a stagnant pool."[71] Highly essential for the progress of the race, therefore, was the creation of an "atmosphere of freedom," wherein heretical minorities and gifted individuals would flourish. The dictum "that truth always triumphs over persecution," sagely observed Mill, "is one of those pleasant falsehoods which men repeat after one another . . . but which all experience refutes."[72] The greatest obstacle to progress in a democracy, according to Mill, was the tendency of the average man to accept conventional opinions as true, and prevailing practices as right. To overcome the coercive power of the prevailing social order, so powerful in England, Mill appealed to the enlightened members of the upper class—those "whose bread is already secured and who desire no favors from men in power, or from bodies of men, or from the public"—to become the leaders of unpopular causes. All that they had to fear was "to be ill-thought of and ill-spoken of, and this it ought not to require a very heroic mould to enable them to bear."[73]

Freedom of opinion was not only essential to social progress, it was also the only sure basis of stability in a democratic order. In the

[69] *Ibid.*, 79.
[70] *Ibid.*, 97.
[71] *Ibid.*, 122.
[72] *Ibid.*, 89.
[73] *Ibid.*, 92.

course of time, Mill reasoned, a body of universally accepted ideas would emerge from the conflict of opinions, which would grow larger as enlightenment spread. In this way, and only in this way, could a democratic order slowly establish a new type of stability. The more freedom there was to criticize the existing order, the greater would be the confidence in its essential rightness. In contrast to the petrified stability that was the outcome of the supression of opinion by a tyrannical government would be the dynamic stability of a free government, in which a prevailing system continued only until new knowledge and new conditions made a change desirable. The change would then be made smoothly and easily, because there would be a general agreement that it should be so made.

Mill's views were in harmony with the course of English history in his lifetime. The acceptance by the Tories of the political reforms inaugurated by the Reform Bill of 1832, the acceptance by the capitalists of the social reforms inaugurated by the Factory Acts, and the acceptance by the landowners of the economic reforms inaugurated by the repeal of the Corn Laws were so many illustrations of ideas and policies that were universally accepted after bitter conflicts of opinion. What Mill did was to universalize English experience during the nineteenth century. French experience during the same century was a tale of quite another sort.

Enlightened public opinion was all essential in the process of creating a body of universally accepted ideas. Mill, therefore, became an ardent advocate of popular education, which, he believed, would create an attitude of mind on the part of the masses favorable to progress. He did not have much confidence in the reasoning ability of the average man; but he did have great confidence in the desire of the average man to listen to reason, provided that the channels to truth were kept open: through appeal to facts, not to prejudices; through open discussion; and through freedom of assembly. It was only when these channels were kept open that the highly gifted individual, the genius, with a new vision of truth, could make an effective popular appeal, either to maintain existing laws against foolish or evil innovations or to adopt new laws to stabilize a progressive advance. No democracy, asserted Mill, "could rise above mediocrity, except in so far as the sovereign Many have let themselves be guided (which in their best times they always have done) by the counsels and influence of a more highly gifted and instructed One or Few."[74] Nothing else so clearly marked John Stuart Mill as a democratic liberal as his belief that the common man "can respond internally to wise and noble things," and would recognize wise leadership and support it faithfully. The bourgeois liberals of his day, Ricardo and James Mill among them, had no such faith in the common man, either in his good will or in his intelligence.

The right of every man to express his opinions had no stronger champion than Mill. But he was not a doctrinaire; hence he did not maintain that this right was valid at all times, in all places, and under all circumstances. Mill placed limitations, and very definite ones, on freedom of speech when it was used to incite to violence. "No one pretends," he declared, "that actions should be as free as opinions. On the contrary, even opinions lose their immunity when the circumstances in which they are expressed are such as to constitute their expression a positive instigation to some mischievous act. An opinion that corn-dealers are starvers of the poor, or that private property is robbery, ought to be unmolested when simply circulated through the press, but may justly incur punishment when delivered orally to an excited mob assembled before the house of a corn-dealer, or when handed about among the same mob in the form of a placard."[75] In other words, a man should not be permitted to shout "Hang the baker" during a bread riot, but he should be permitted to denounce capitalism at a public meeting. The aim of a popular agitation should not be to rouse the masses to revolutionary action but to convince those in power that the time was ripe for needed reforms. Hence the function of a popular press was "at once to raise the waves and to calm them."[76]

This distinction between opinion and incitement to violence, made by Mill, has become classic in discussions pertaining to freedom of speech. It was the distinction made by Justice Oliver Wendell Holmes of the Supreme Court of the United States in a famous opinion. The question of freedom of speech in every case, argued Justice Holmes,

[74] *Ibid.*, 124.

[75] *Ibid.*, 114.

[76] Quoted by F. A. von Hayek in his Introduction to John Stuart Mill, *The Spirit of the Age* (University of Chicago Press, 1942), xxxi–xxxii.

is "whether the words used are used in such circumstances and are of such a nature as to create a clear and present danger that they will bring about the substantive evils that Congress has a right to prevent. It is a question of proximity and degree."[77] A democratic order can function only when desirable changes are made peacefully as a consequence of free discussion.

By upholding freedom of opinion as a utility, not as a natural right, Mill made a distinct advance over the liberals of the eighteenth century. He realized more clearly than they that freedom of opinion was not the luxury of an esoteric group of intellectuals who wrote books but that it was a prime necessity in a progressive society, without which reforms would be fitful, hazardous, and uncertain. Mill's observation that changes, if made as a consequence of free discussion, became a stabilizing force, gave the weight of social necessity to his moral plea for the liberty of the individual. And for that very reason individual liberty became the battle cry of democratic liberalism, which sought to establish a new and more egalitarian social order.

In the main, the structure of the great argument in *On Liberty* still stands. In some respects it has become even stronger with the passing years. However, not all of Mill's fears or hopes contained in the treatise have been realized. Mill's great fear of the tyranny of the majority under democracy has proved to be groundless. As democracy spread from class to class and from the political to the economic sphere, liberty was more cherished and more sustained. The individual found greater, not less, freedom when the state became more pervasive by regulating social and economic matters. Although Mill renounced *laissez faire,* he never entirely succeeded in ridding himself of the eighteenth-century identification of government with tyranny. He did not fully realize that government under a democracy would be in a new relation to liberty—that of a friend and not that of an enemy, as was government under autocracy. Without the liberty of the individual, a democratic state could have no existence.

The generation that read *On Liberty* when it first appeared hailed it as a beacon light that both sought out the way to orderly progress and illumined it with a bright and steady glow. If as a consequence of the great advance of liberalism during the period 1870 to 1914

[77] Schenck v. United States of America, 249 U. S. 52 (1918).

Mill's pleas for individual liberty became so many platitudes, it was because he had helped to make them so. And what greater contribution can a social philosopher make to human progress than to be instrumental in making bold and unpopular ideas into platitudes that everyone accepts without argument!

Mill's importance in the history of the nineteenth century rests solely on his role as a pioneer of democratic liberalism. As an advocate of utilitarian philosophy and of classical economy he achieved a position of prominence by spreading the doctrines of Bentham, Ricardo, and Malthus. His views were received with great deference by the educated among his generation, to whom he appealed as the beloved and persuasive disciple of these unloved masters. But Mill would long since have passed into half-forgotten obscurity had he remained all his life a consistent upholder of the doctrines that had been implanted in him by his masters and that he advocated so persuasively. He became a more significant figure to the generations that followed his own, precisely because he questioned the validity of the doctrines that the bourgeois liberals of his day had accepted with the finality of natural laws. Unlike that other great Victorian liberal Macaulay, who never abandoned *laissez faire* and propertied suffrage, Mill had the social imagination to see that, if liberalism continued to be the expression of bourgeois ideals and the champion of capitalist interests, it would be overwhelmed by a storm of popular hatred that might spell revolution or reaction. Only by including the working class in its plans for human freedom could liberalism become a truly universal creed— one that would prove an inexhaustible source of inspiration to human progress. And the inclusion of the working class would inevitably lead to the recognition of the validity of socialism. Here again Mill, the devoted champion of individual liberty, was in a quandary. How could individual liberty exist in a collectivist state? According to Mill, the great problem of the future would be how to unite the greatest individual liberty of action with the common ownership of the means of production and the equal sharing by all in economic benefits. It would not be too much so say that Mill's was the most potent intellectual influence that prepared the way for the advent of democratic liberalism in England, with its wide extensions of the suffrage, with its establishment of popular education, with its emancipation of the trade-unions, and with its many-sided social reforms. Mill's influence was "far more effective in keeping men's minds open to the possibilities of social change than any socialist dogmatics. . . ." [78] When, in 1945, the British Labor party came into power, it set itself the task of solving the problem of uniting individual liberty with the socialist policy of nationalization of industry. Mill's benign spirit was invisibly present at the council table of the Labor party.

It is difficult in our day to recreate the intellectual climate of the age of Mill. That the cause of liberalism, despite setbacks, would inevitably triumph became an article of faith to Mill's generation. The only problem that confronted it was when and how liberal principles could be best advanced in lands that repudiated them. It never occurred to Mill, even in his most pessimistic moments, that any country that had once enjoyed liberty would repudiate it as an outworn ideal. The antiliberal elements that he knew were the reactionaries, such as the privileged noble and the intolerant priest, who rallied to the cause of the divine-right monarch in their endeavor to restore a vanished social and political order. Mill could not even imagine *revolutionary* antiliberal forces, like the totalitarian dictatorships of our time, when dictators stood "on the dead body of liberty" and proclaimed the advent of a new and a better social order.

Nothing is so painful as the rediscovery of the truth of a platitude. If anyone desires to undergo this experience, he can do no better than to read in *On Liberty* the well-known and oft-repeated pleas for individual liberty. The totalitarian opponents of liberty envisaged the subjugation of the individual in terms and in settings far beyond those of the reactionaries of former days. The world of the reactionaries was one in which the daily life and work of the individual was far removed from the authority of the state. What had chiefly concerned the absolute monarch was that his subjects pay taxes and obey his officials. Under a totalitarian dictatorship, all aspects of the individual's life—his work, his family, his movements, his opinions, his education, even his amusements—are forced to be in harmony with the ideas and ambitions of those in power. The totalitarian aim is nothing less than to coordinate the whole human being in a social order in which the individual would be an interchangeable part

[78] J. H. Clapham, *Economic History of Britain* (London, 1932), II, 482.

in a vast and complicated machine, operated by a dictatorial elite and responsible to no one, not even to God. As a consequence of mankind's experience with totalitarianism, Mill's pleas for individual liberty have become more compelling than when they were bold innovations and more persuasive than when they had been accepted platitudes.

Chapter 12. Alexis de Tocqueville
Pioneer of Democratic
Liberalism in France

The period in France from the Revolution of 1830 to the *coup d'état* of 1851 by Louis Napoleon is one of absorbing interest to students of modern society. The deadly conflict between the social classes that had raged in France since the French Revolution took new forms, aroused new emotions, and called into existence new forces of revolution and of repression. From the day of their triumph in 1830, the bourgeois liberals were assailed with doubts, hesitations, and fears. The bitter disappointment of the workers at being denied the benefits of the Revolution of 1830 awoke the passions of 1793. And the revival of the "Napoleonic legend" by Louis Napoleon inspired hopes of a new Eighteenth of Brumaire. During this absorbing time a thinker flourished whose writings constituted an extraordinary commentary on the great events of his day, and whose political vision was more far-reaching and more generous than that of his liberal contemporaries. That thinker was Alexis de Tocqueville.

The reign of Louis Philippe was not a propitious period for a social philosopher without a blueprint of a future society tucked away in his pocket. In this period of social ferment and bold speculation, the philosopher who had a system readily gained the ear of a public that was bitterly discontented with the existing order and was eagerly awaiting a new and better one. The situation was, therefore, not favorable to the appearance of a philosopher whose power lay primarily in analysis and whose hopes of a new and better order were often clouded with doubts, misgivings, and hesitations. Yet such a philosopher did appear, in the person of Alexis de Tocqueville, who, despite these handicaps, succeeded in attaining an eminent position in the

France of his day. Not having any system, De Tocqueville had no devout disciples, but he did have ardent admirers who regarded him as a luminous thinker with an unrivaled insight into the problems of democracy.

De Tocqueville was born in 1805, of an aristocratic family that had suffered during the French Revolution. When the Bourbons returned, his father became a strong supporter of the restored dynasty and was rewarded by being appointed to high governmental positions. Young De Tocqueville studied law, and at the age of twenty-two he was appointed to a judgeship in the lower courts. When the July Revolution established the Orleanist regime, De Tocqueville, being a supporter of the Bourbon cause, found himself *persona non grata* with the authorities. He asked and received leave to visit the United States for the purpose of studying the penal system in that country. Together with a friend, Gustave de Beaumont, he came to America in 1831, and stayed about a year. The young Frenchmen visited many of the states, journeying as far west as Michigan, then a frontier region.[1] They inspected prisons and studied methods of treating prisoners; the results of their observations were embodied in a report to their government.[2]

De Tocqueville's visit to America, like the visit of Montesquieu to England, was a voyage of intellectual discovery. It resulted in the publication of his book *De la démocratie en Amérique,* which, like Montesquieu's *Esprit des lois,* was a landmark in the history of political thought. What De Tocqueville saw in America gave him the thrill and excitement of discovery: the constitutional system, the popular passion for liberty, and the many opportunities for economic betterment. Moreover, his visit took place during the Jacksonian era, when a great wave of democratic sentiment swept the nation. The popular upheaval made a profound impression on De Tocqueville's sensitive, sympathetic nature. *Democracy in America* appeared in 1835 and created something of a literary sensation in France. Thirteen editions of the book were printed during the fifteen years following its publi-

[1] For an excellent study of the experiences in America of De Tocqueville and De Beaumont, see G. W. Pierson, *Tocqueville and Beaumont in America* (New York, 1938).

[2] Alexis de Tocqueville and Gustave de Beaumont, *Du système pénitentiaire aux États-Unis* (Paris, 1833).

cation, an unusual success at that time for a serious work on political science. It was translated into English in the same year that it was published in France. At the age of thirty De Tocqueville awoke to find himself famous. *Democracy in America* was compared with Montesquieu's *Spirit of Laws* as a profound and original contribution to political philosophy. "Since Montesquieu there has been nothing like it,"[3] was the opinion of Royer-Collard, an opinion that was echoed and reechoed.

The success of the book was due not to its merits alone, great as these were. It was due also to the fact that it appeared at a time when the democratic movement was on the upswing. The Revolution of 1830 in France and the Reform Bill of 1832 in England were followed by widespread agitations in both countries for manhood suffrage. Democracy was now a leading political issue, and naturally many were eager to learn about the great democratic experiment across the Atlantic. It would not be too much to say that De Tocqueville's book placed American democracy in the forefront of European opinion. For the first time the United States, as a nation and as a political experiment, became the subject of widespread discussion in almost every country in Western Europe. America had been rediscovered this time as the one successful democracy in the world.

In France a political philosopher was expected to take an active part in public life. Although De Tocqueville was temperamentally unfitted to be a politician, being shy, reserved, and a poor orator, nevertheless he felt called upon to enter politics. In 1839 he was elected to the Chamber, where he joined the constitutional opposition to the government of Louis Philippe. He remained in the Chamber until the February Revolution of 1848, which overthrew the July Monarchy. In 1849 he was elected to the Legislative Assembly of the Second Republic. For a few months he served in the cabinet as Minister of Foreign Affairs. The overthrow of the Second Republic, in 1851, by Louis Napoleon eliminated De Tocqueville from the political scene. He refused to accept the Second Empire and denounced the dictatorship of Napoleon III as a system of military terrorism that yoked France to the reactionary monarchs on the Continent. De Tocqueville

---

[3] Quoted in R. Pierre Marcel, *Essai politique sur Alexis de Tocqueville* (Paris, 1910), 88.

retired to private life and devoted the few years that remained to him to study and writing. He died in 1859, at the age of fifty-four.

De Tocqueville's life was comparatively short and he wrote few books, really only three. For all that, he has an important place in the intellectual history of Europe during the nineteenth century. It would not be correct to place him in the ranks of original and creative thinkers such as Montesquieu and Rousseau; his gifts were rather those of the keen observer and master analyst of the sociointellectual situation in his day. De Tocqueville had the style, the temperament, and the scholarship of a detached and discriminating analyst. In addition, he had a sympathetic social imagination, which gave to his analysis of a period, of a party, of a government the power of luminous suggestion of the historic forces and trends that were shaping civilization. In the opinion of Bryce, De Tocqueville was preeminent "for the acuteness of his observation, for the delicacy of his analysis, for the elegant precision of his reasonings, for the limpid purity of his style; above all, for his love of truth and the elevation of his character."[4] De Tocqueville's convictions were clear, strong, and steadfast, without being heightened by passion or narrowed by dogma. His style was elegant and cold, but not hard. In his analysis of political and social phenomena De Tocqueville exhibited a capacity for cool lucidity that gave an impression of "frozen logic." But this impression was dissipated by observations that revealed the author as a highly sensitive thinker, animated by generous sympathies and by an abiding love of mankind. As a writer De Tocqueville may be compared with an artist whose painting of a landscape gives the effect of softness, even of tenderness, by depicting the sun's rays breaking through a cold, gray atmosphere.

De Tocqueville called himself an "observer," which he was. Though not original in thought, he was original in method; his books bear the imprint of novel ways of dealing with a subject. *Democracy in America* was the first work that dealt with the impact of democratic principles on modern society, and the result of a firsthand study of the institutions of the country that embodied these principles. De Tocqueville did not limit himself to the study of American politics;

[4] James Bryce, *Studies in History and Jurisprudence* (New York, 1901), 320.

he made a full analysis of the cultural, social, and economic aspects of American life. His analysis of democratic practices and methods, blended with philosophic observation, made *Democracy in America* the outstanding work on America until the appearance of Bryce's *American Commonwealth,* more than a half century later.

De Tocqueville's *Recollections,* which appeared in 1850, is "among the abiding masterpieces in the literature of political memoirs."[5] In it may be found a luminous exposition of the social forces that clashed in the Revolution of 1848. The author appears as a spectator of historic scenes in which the contending parties are struggling for mastery over issues that had been projected on the screen of world history since the French Revolution. His observations on the first attempt to overthrow the social order by a socialist revolution, the "June Days" of 1848, read as though they had been written yesterday. No student of modern history can afford to neglect this little volume.

Equally remarkable is De Tocqueville's historic study *The Old Régime and the Revolution,* which appeared in 1856. It was the unobtrusive result of careful research, with little display of the apparatus of scholarship. According to De Tocqueville, the French Revolution was not a sudden break with the past but the last stage of a long process of transformation of the political and economic institutions of France. Centralization, peasant proprietorship, and the power of the *bourgeoisie* were forces that had been in train for centuries, but were accelerated and dramatized by the events of the French Revolution. The *Old Régime* was both a history and a philosophy of history. De Tocqueville's method in writing history was to arrange historical events in a pattern with a central theme, but pattern and theme varied with time, place, and circumstances. He felt a strong aversion to absolutist, dogmatic interpretations, "which represent all events of history as depending upon great first causes linked by the chain of fatality, and which, as it were, suppress men from the history of the human race. They seem narrow to my mind, under their pretense of broadness, and false beneath their air of mathematical exactness."[6]

[5] J. P. Mayer, *Alexis de Tocqueville,* trans. from the German by M. N. Bozman and C. Hahn (New York, 1940), 108.

[6] Alexis de Tocqueville, *Recollections,* trans. from the French by A. Teixeira de Mattos (New York, 1896), 80. Hereafter cited as *Recollections.*

Apart from his work as a historian and political philosopher, De Tocqueville has a unique position in the history of nineteenth-century liberalism. Like John Stuart Mill in England, he was in France the outstanding pioneer of democratic liberalism. But unlike Mill, De Tocqueville had a penchant for aristocracy because of his origin and early association. De Tocqueville did see the value of an aristocracy as the heir of past wisdom and as the bearer of political experience, which, he hoped, would be utilized by a wise democracy. Endowed with a social imagination, De Tocqueville clearly realized the limitations of bourgeois liberalism. As "a liberal of a new kind," he detested the principles and policies of the July Monarchy, as expounded and practiced by that preeminent bourgeois liberal Guizot. To De Tocqueville the rule of a capitalist oligarchy was the most revolting of all governments, since it was class despotism without class responsibility, a system offensive both to his aristocratic instincts and to his democratic sympathies. Moreover, bourgeois liberalism in France after 1830 exhibited a spirit of class selfishness and of crass materialism that was in conflict with the generous ideals of the nation. With much misgiving and with great hesitation, often in spite of his aristocratic inclinations, De Tocqueville was finally convinced that the solution of the problem would be to widen the outlook of liberalism by giving it a broader base. In other words, liberalism was to cease to be bourgeois and become democratic.

De Tocqueville had come to this conviction as a consequence of his study of history in general and of the French Revolution in particular. For centuries, he reasoned, the world had been witnessing a leveling process that was battering down the barriers of institutions, traditions, customs, and ideas that sheltered inequalities of all kinds—those of class, religion, race, sex, and nation. Behind this process was the drive of the supreme and persistent passion for equality throughout the ages, a passion that was "ardent, insatiable, incessant, invincible." It could best be satisfied by equality in freedom, but if that was impossible, then equality in slavery would be preferred by the people to inequality in a system dominated by aristocratic privilege. Men "will endure poverty, servitude, barbarism, but they will not endure aristocracy." At all times has this been true. And especially true was it, according to De Tocqueville, in his own day, when those who sought to resist the irresistible advance of equality would be swept aside or destroyed.[7]

The never-ending drive for equality, always present underneath all unequal social systems, appeared dramatically during the French Revolution. As the first *social* revolution of modern history, the French Revolution swiftly and ruthlessly destroyed a social system based on class privilege and established a new social system, in which equality was the all-pervading principle. As a Frenchman, De Tocqueville was profoundly influenced by the egalitarian aims of the French Revolution, though he revolted against the excesses of the Reign of Terror. During the Restoration the struggle between equality and privilege was resumed. In 1830 De Tocqueville witnessed a great popular uprising that defeated the efforts of the reactionaries to restore the Old Regime of privilege and inequality. During the reign of Louis Philippe a new upsurge of the passion for equality took place when the socialist movement fused political and economic ideas into a grand scheme for an egalitarian society. At one time equality between bourgeois and aristocrat had been the issue. Now, concluded De Tocqueville, the issue was equality between rich and poor.[8]

These events convinced De Tocqueville that the development of equality was a "providential fact" having all the chief characteristics of a divine decree, in that "it is universal, it is lasting, it constantly eludes all human interference and all events, as all men contribute to its progress."[9] Every step taken toward equality is immediately followed by an increased demand for greater equality. Politically the essence of equality was democracy. De Tocqueville "was one of the first to understand that democracy, with all its consequences and with all

[7] *Democracy in America,* The Henry Reeves text, as revised by Francis Bowen, now further corrected and edited by Phillips Bradley (New York, 1945), II, 97. Hereafter cited as *Democracy in America.*

[8] E. d'Eichthal, *Alexis de Tocqueville et la démocratie libérale* (Paris, 1897), 246–247. It is interesting to note that a new doctrine of inequality, that based on race, instead of descent or wealth, appeared in De Tocqueville's day. Arthur de Gobineau, in his pioneer book on racialism, *Essai sur l'inégalité des races humaines,* divided mankind into lower and higher races; hence inequality was inescapable in any social system. True to his principles, De Tocqueville severely condemned racialism as false and pernicious and as the primal source of all evil based on inequality, in that it furnished a justification for tyranny in every form. De Tocqueville predicted that the Germans would be most favorable to De Gobineau's doctrine of racial inequality. See *Correspondance entre Alexis de Tocqueville et Arthur de Gobineau* (Paris, 1908), 192, 291, 313.

[9] *Democracy in America,* I, 6.

its powers to transform everything for all time, was both inevitable and beneficent."[10] This attitude toward democracy was unusual in France during the first half of the nineteenth century. Representative liberals of the period, like Guizot and Thiers, dreaded popular rule even more than they dreaded the reactionary Bourbons, and with good reason. They regarded popular rule as a direct challenge to the control of the government by the *bourgeoisie,* and, because of the Jacobin heritage of French democracy, as a menace to established property interests. In De Tocqueville's long-range view, however, the political struggles and class divisions of his day were not danger signals of universal chaos, as they were to his contemporaries, but phases of the never-ending struggle to establish equality.

Would democracy, once established, constitute a danger to the freedom of the individual? Would not the unquestioned rule of the majority, the essential democratic principle, tend to flout the rights both of the individual and of minority groups? De Tocqueville was acutely sensitive to these dangers. "Liberty," he declared, "is my passion. This is the truth."[11] And it was. To De Tocqueville liberty had its own *charme*, apart from the benefits that it conferred, in the sheer pleasure of being free to think, to speak, and to act as one pleased. The despotism of the many could be as great an evil as the despotism of an absolute monarch—perhaps, even, a greater one. "For myself," he wrote, "when I feel the hand of power lie heavy on my brow, I care but little to know who oppresses me; and I am not the more disposed to pass beneath the yoke, because it is held out to me by the arms of a million men."[12] He was a hesitant optimist, fearing the tyranny that the majority might exercise, once it was recognized as the supreme and unlimited power in the state. A French aristocrat, not too far removed in time from the guillotine, De Tocqueville had no Jeffersonian faith in the people. The aims of democracy, he believed, were often capricious; its instruments, rude; and its laws, imperfect. Was the only alternative the rule of one man, a system of government that the conscience of mankind had definitely rejected, whether in the form of a divine-right monarch or of a military dictator? The problem that

[10] Henry Michel, *La Doctrine politique de la démocratie* (Paris, 1901), 19.

[11] Quoted in Antoine Redier, *Comme disait M. de Tocqueville* (Paris, 1925), 48.

[12] *Democracy in America*, II, 12.

confronted De Tocqueville was how to reconcile the rule of the majority "with respect for property, with deference for rights, with safety to freedom, with reverence to religion." In France democracy was identified with mob violence, confiscation, terrorism, and atheism, all of which he dreaded and hated. Intellectually De Tocqueville had an inclination toward democracy, but being an aristocrat by temperament, he despised and feared the mob. How could the "providential fact" of democracy be purged of its evil aspects, which had repelled so many Frenchmen?

America was the answer. De Tocqueville came to America not primarily to study American institutions but to study a democratic system of society and institutions of which America then offered the only outstanding example. "I confess that in America," he wrote, "I saw more than America; I sought there the image of democracy itself, with its inclinations, it character, its prejudices, and its passions, in order to learn what we have to fear or to hope from its progress."[13] His *idée-mère* in writing *Democracy in America* was, on the one hand, to moderate the extravagant hopes of those in Europe who regarded democracy as "a brilliant dream which could be easily realized." American democracy, as described in his pages, was not "a brilliant dream" realized, but a community that in some respects was backward and commonplace. On the other hand, he sought "to allay the terrors" of those to whom democracy was synonymous with "disorder, anarchy, spoliation, and murder," and "to bend their minds to the idea of an inevitable future" by showing democracy in America triumphant, moderate, and peaceful. The example of America was to be an inspiration to the democrats of Europe and, at the same time, an assurance to their opponents that democracy held no terrors for the future of mankind.[14]

The rich blend of the historian, the sociologist, and the philosopher— so distinctively De Tocqueville—was seen in the explanation that he gave for the success of America in solving the great riddle of modern government: the reconciliation of democracy with individual freedom. In part, America's success was due to fortunate circumstances: the ab-

[13] *Ibid.,* I, 14.

[14] De Tocqueville, "Correspondance," in *Oeuvres complètes* (Paris, 1864–1867), V, 425–427.

sence of historical obstacles and the English origin of most of the settlers in the Thirteen Colonies. The fact that America was a virgin continent, rich in natural resources, with land free for the asking, he observed, prevented the rise of bitter class conflicts like those which had proved so inimical to the progress of democracy in Europe. A society in which each individual would have something to keep and little to take from others was a society that made for social peace. Discontent could be drained off into the many channels of opportunity that America offered to acquire property, as a consequence of which there was an approach to economic equality consonant with the legal and political equality enjoyed by the citizens.[15] America was "virgin soil" in a social, as well as in a physical, sense. Here was a huge continent with marvelous and seemingly inexhaustible natural resources in food and raw materials in a "state of nature." Here was a social order in which there was opportunity for everyone to acquire the good things of life. Here was a political system that gave equal rights to all and special privileges to none. At last bountiful nature and a free society stood with doors wide open, through which the poor and oppressed of the old world could enter and create a new world based upon human equality. Unlike Europe, America had no such obstacle to equality as a landed aristocracy; no such obstacle to freedom as a military caste; and no such obstacle to religious toleration as a national church. To cap America's historic good fortune, most of its inhabitants had brought with them the traditions of liberty and self-government so characteristic of England.

Apart from fortunate circumstances, argued De Tocqueville, the success of democracy in America was due to the political wisdom of the astute and enlightened Founding Fathers. They created a constitutional system in which three major factors contributed powerfully to protect individual freedom: judicial power, federalism and local self-government, and decentralized administration. De Tocqueville analyzed with great care the independence of the judiciary and the judicial review, which, in his view, had for their object, not the foiling but the maturing of the popular will. Especially important was the power of the Supreme Court to interpret the constitution—a power that "forms one of the most powerful barriers that have ever been devised against the

[15] *Democracy in America*, I, 46*ff*., 288*ff*.

tyranny of political assemblies."[16] Just because the majority could not at all times exercise unlimited power in America, he observed, the minority felt assured of its rights. A mood of moderation was created under this system; majorities tended to be circumspect in their control of the government, lest what they did should be undone by the judiciary. The diffusion of political power between the federal, state, and local bodies and the decentralization of administration constituted "breakwaters" against despotic acts emanating from a highly centralized government, such as that in France. Moreover, local self-government constituted a training ground for citizenship in which the individual learned what his rights were and how best to defend them. The direct association between the citizens and the government was a guarantee of freedom in America.

Apart from governmental machinery, De Tocqueville saw in the right of political association a powerful means of maintaining freedom in a democracy. In his view this right was "almost as inalienable in its nature as the right of personal liberty. No legislator can attack it without impairing the foundations of society."[17] In no other aspect of his analysis of democracy was De Tocqueville so perspicacious as in his advocacy of the right of unlimited political association that flourished in America in the forms of parties, clubs, and conventions. As a result of his experiences in America, he came to regard the right of political association as a bulwark of political liberty. "In no country of the world," he wrote, "has the principle of association been more successfully used or applied to a greater multitude of objects than in America."[18] In a democracy the weakness of isolated individuals might encourage the majority to act tyrannically; but once the individuals combined into associations, they were "no longer isolated men, but a power seen from afar, whose actions serve for an example and whose language is listened to." [19] By showing their numerical strength, organized minorities diminished "the moral power of the majority," thereby deterring it from committing acts of tyranny.[20] Unlike the situation in

[16] *Ibid.*, 103.
[17] *Ibid.*, 196.
[18] *Ibid.*, 191.
[19] *Ibid.*, II, 109.
[20] *Ibid.*, I, 196.

America, the right of association was limited in France, where organizations of citizens were regarded with suspicion and fear, as conspiratorial groups that plotted to overthrow the government. Not so in America, where freedom to form political associations was regarded as a method of giving stability to the government by providing a safety valve to draw off popular discontent. As an illustration, he described a national convention meeting in Philadelphia in 1831, which adopted resolutions denouncing the tariff policy of the government. "Thus it is by the enjoyment of a dangerous freedom that the Americans learn the art of rendering the dangers of freedom less formidable."[21]

The question, however, remains: Why was De Tocqueville so much concerned about the tyranny of the majority? It was a recurrent theme in his writings, as it was in those of John Stuart Mill, his fellow pioneer of democratic liberalism.[22] The answer is the Reign of Terror. The confiscatory decrees, the summary executions, and the mob violence associated with the popularly elected National Convention caused even liberals like De Tocqueville and Mill to fear the tyranny of the majority. But the history of democratic government has proved their fears to have been groundless. One looks in vain for acts of oppression in England after the Reform Bills of 1867 and 1884 had made Parliament a democratic body, or in France after the establishment of the democratic Third French Republic. Quite the contrary. Scrupulous regard for the right of property, for individual liberty, and for the protection of minorities were outstanding features of democratic rule in England and in France. With the advent of totalitarianism in recent years, the great danger has been the tyranny of the organized minority, a danger all too real, which was not foreseen by the pioneers of democratic liberalism. Let it be noted that neither to De Tocqueville nor to Mill was democracy a radiant vision; rather was it a generous hope. They were pioneers, not prophets. Hence they were much alive to possible evils that might lie in their path. De Tocqueville, even more than Mill, feared these evils, and with good reason. Had not the radiant vision of popular sovereignty in the France of 1789 become the hideous nightmare of the Reign of Terror? It was to the credit of De Tocqueville that he set out for America, there to behold the true face of democ-

[21] *Ibid.*, II., 119.
[22] See *supra*, p. 265*ff*.

racy, which, he was convinced, was neither a vision nor a nightmare.

De Tocqueville was profoundly convinced that America was a land with a world mission, not a unique and isolated experiment that had no significance for the rest of the world. Only in America was the universal passion for equality freely expressed and freely applied. Democracy in America was the philosophic ideal of a freedom-loving people, not, as in Europe, the embittered creed of oppressed classes animated by hatred of those who ruled them. For this reason it was a bold and successful step in the march of history toward freedom and equality. America had created the pattern of the future of mankind. Sooner or later, De Tocqueville believed, the rest of the world would achieve a system of equality similar to that in America.

In the light of the present, *Democracy in America* reveals De Tocqueville as a thinker gifted with prophecy. In that far-away, scantily inhabited land, still in the frontier stage, he envisaged the future role of America as the world's champion of democracy. What a startling confirmation of the vision of this young Frenchman took place a century later! When the great threat to freedom arose during the First World War, the eyes of freedom-loving people throughout the world turned to America. The madly cheering crowds that greeted Woodrow Wilson in Europe were really cheering for America, which had come forward to make "the world safe for democracy." Again, when freedom faced its greatest crisis during the Second World War, America became the "arsenal of democracy," the powerful and determined champion of human freedom, the hope of mankind in the fearful struggle against the fascist dictatorships. Pearl Harbor touched off something more in America than resentment against a sneak attack by a treacherous foe.

Equally profound was De Tocqueville's observation that, in a war for survival, democracy would prove invincible. A despotic nation at war with a democracy, he observed, which "does not succeed in ruining the latter at the outset runs a great risk of being conquered by it." Inclined to be peaceful, a democracy was generally unprepared for war; consequently, it would meet early reverses when war broke out. However, if the war were of long duration, victory would go to the democracy, because the entire nation would be roused from its peaceful pursuits and "the same passions, that made them attach so much importance to the maintenance of peace will be turned to arms." A democratic people will "perform prodigious achievements when once they have taken the field." The enterprising and original minds of an entire nation, not merely those of a military caste, will come to the front, and great generals will appear, to lead the democratic armies.[23] The military prowess of America, France, and Britain during the First World War attested fully the validity of De Tocqueville's observations.

On his return from America De Tocqueville became absorbed in the political problems that agitated France. As already described in a previous chapter, two movements were in full swing and both had revolutionary implications. One was the movement for manhood suffrage, which aimed to overthrow the bourgeois monarchy of Louis Philippe and to establish a democratic republic. The other was a far more revolutionary movement, which aimed to destroy the property system and to usher in a cooperative socialist commonwealth. Property rights were being challenged by an influential body of opinion, led by the Saint-Simonians and by the revolutionary organizations of socialist workers. These attacks on property rights caused great uneasiness among the petty bourgeois, who, according to De Tocqueville, were more sensitive to attacks on property rights than were the rich. Being themselves "almost within the reach of poverty," the petty bourgeois dreaded nothing more than to be reduced to the level of the poor by a social revolution. Because of widespread ownership of property, America was better able to ward off social revolution than were the nations of Europe. Nowhere was "the love of property more active and more anxious than in the United States; nowhere does the majority display less inclination for those principles which threaten to alter, in whatever manner, the laws of property."[24]

Fear of social revolution would drive the small property owners to form a common front with the upper classes, the inevitable outcome of which would be a dictatorship to protect property rights. Parliamentary government and civil liberty would be swept away, and France would again be in the throes of reaction. De Tocqueville understood this situation very well. In his analysis of the property system, he revealed a keener insight into the problems confronting the democratic

[23] *Democracy in America*, II, 277–278.
[24] *Ibid.*, 253–256.

state than he did anywhere else. In a pregnant passage he described·
the position of property under modern conditions. "The French Revolution," he wrote, "which abolished all privileges and destroyed all
exclusive right has, however, allowed one to remain and that is the
right of property. However, property owners would delude themselves
if they entertained an idea that the right of property is a barrier that
can not be crossed because, up to the present, no part of this barrier
has been crossed. But our times are different from the past. When
the right of property was considered as the origin and the foundation
of many other rights it defended itself without difficulty; or more
correctly it was not attacked. Property rights formed the inner fortress
of society of which all the other rights were only outer defenses. Blows
could not reach it, hence property was not attacked. But today when
property rights, however sacred, are regarded as the last relics of a
ruined world, as isolated privileges in an egalitarian society, . . . they
have lost, for a time at least, the position that had made them impregnable. Relying on its own strength, property has to defend itself daily
against direct and incessant assaults of popular opinion."[25]

Though a strong upholder of the rights of property, De Tocqueville,
nevertheless, did see the contradiction involved between legal and political equality on the one hand and economic inequality on the other.
He was convinced that the people would not be content to be at the
same time "miserable and sovereign," and that the future would see
a social conflict far more serious than any in the past. "Can it be
believed," he asked, "that the democracy which has overthrown the
feudal system and vanquished kings will retreat before tradesmen and
capitalists?"[26] His view that democracy would sooner or later clash
with laissez-faire capitalism has been justified by all subsequent
history.[27]

Although he did not, like John Stuart Mill, live to become a socialist,
De Tocqueville realized even more keenly than did Mill the new

[25] De Tocqueville, "De la classe moyenne et du peuple," *Oeuvres complètes*, IX,
516–517.

[26] *Democracy in America*, I, 6.

[27] H. J. Laski, "Alexis de Tocqueville and Democracy," in *The Social and Political
Ideas of Some Representative Thinkers of the Victorian Age* (Hearnshaw, ed., London,
1933), 108.

dangers to freedom that came with the Industrial Revolution. It is nothing less than astonishing that he visualized the problems raised by modern industrialism as far back as the thirties of the nineteenth century, when it was in its infancy in both France and America—the only two countries that he studied. In cogent language he described the effect of the machine process on the worker and of the competitive system on the capitalist. As a consequence of the division of labor resulting from the use of machinery, he argued, the worker became demoralized by doing automatically the same thing all the time. The machine narrowed his interests and stifled his abilities; the less his natural ability, the greater his success as a tender of part of the machine. The capitalist, on the contrary, needed more and more ability, because competition, engendered by modern industry, drove incompetents to the wall. "This man resembles more and more the administrator of a vast empire, that man, a brute." The worker was assigned "a certain place in society, beyond which he cannot go; in the midst of universal movement it has rendered him stationary."[28] More remorseless than the feudal aristocracy in the past were the manufacturers, because, unlike the former, they had no responsibility to their dependents. The manufacturing aristocracy "first impoverishes and debases the men who serve it and then abandons them to be supported by the charity of the public."[29] Because it was not yet a caste and the personnel was constantly changing, the manufacturing aristocracy did not constitute so great a danger to freedom as did the feudal aristocracy. But he warned the friends of democracy to be on guard against a hereditary class of capitalists, which would surely come into existence, once industrialism succeeded in establishing "permanent inequality of conditions."

With prophetic insight, De Tocqueville realized that laissez-faire capitalism would result in bringing into existence a revolutionary movement to establish socialism. And the prospect of socialism terrified him. If it were unsuccessful, a socialist uprising would frighten the nation into reaction and military dictatorship. If it were successful, this "new formula for servitude" would mean the end of all freedom. No longer would the state be the means of realizing the freedom of every

[28] *Democracy in America*, II, 159.
[29] *Ibid.*, 161.

individual; it would become a monster that would reduce all men to lasting servitude by chaining them to dictatorial institutions. Under socialism, mankind would be dehumanized.[30]

To avoid either calamity De Tocqueville advocated political and social reform. He favored the establishment of manhood suffrage, which would give to the government a popular, hence a powerful, source of authority.[31] He also favored state intervention in the relations between capital and labor. Under the conditions of modern industry there was need of controlling and regulating the activities of capitalists because of their great economic power.[32] More than any other class did the industrial laborers, because of their dependence and misery, need "the special consideration of the legislator; for when the whole of society is in motion, it is difficult to keep any one class stationary."[33] Governments should make the welfare of the lower classes the chief object of their activity and not delude themselves into a state of security by creating "a kind of order in the midst of their wretchedness." In general governments should make every effort to abolish those inequalities that still remain and to assure the masses every comfort consistent with the rights of property.[34]

De Tocqueville was himself an example of the tragedy of French liberalism, which since the French Revolution has waged unceasing war on two fronts: against reaction on the right and against revolution on the left. His aristocratic temperament, which caused him to despise the bourgeois and to fear the mob, was in conflict with his intellectual conviction that democracy was both inevitable and desirable. In a sense, his *Democracy in America* was a providential solution of the problem raised by this conflict in France. Far away in the new world was a land with no Old Regime to restore, no mob of desperately poor to fear, no ambitious dictators to foil; hence democracy, which was inevitable in Europe in the course of history, had been providential from the very outset in America. What nature and a *tabula rasa* social order had

---

[30] De Tocqueville, "Discours prononcé à l'assemblée constituante," *Oeuvres complètes*, IX, 536–552.

[31] *Nouvelle correspondance entièrement inédite de Alexis de Tocqueville* (Paris, 1866), 239.

[32] *Democracy in America*, II, 309.

[33] *Ibid.*, 191.

[34] "De la classe moyenne et du peuple," *loc. cit.*, 519.

done for democracy in America, De Tocqueville hoped that a wise generosity on the part of the upper classes and a cautious restraint on the part of the lower classes would do for France. His experiences, however, during the Revolution of 1848, when he beheld the terrifying uprising of *le peuple* in the "June Days," filled him with great misgivings as to the capacity of the lower classes for ordered liberty. And the establishment of a Napoleonic dictatorship, with its ruthless suppressions, caused him to have grave doubts concerning the generosity of the upper classes. These experiences cast a melancholy shadow on the customary serenity of his thought. The shadow lengthened as he reflected that the Revolution of 1848 was but the continuation of the French Revolution, whose end now seemed to him "farther off and shrouded in greater darkness. Shall we ever . . . attain a more complete and more far-reaching social transformation than our fathers foresaw and desired, and than we ourselves are able to foresee; or are we not destined simply to end in a condition of intermittent anarchy, the well-known chronic and incurable complaint of old races? As for me, I am unable to say; I do not know when this long voyage will be ended; I am weary of seeing the shore in each successive mirage, and I often ask myself whether the *terra firma* we are seeking does really exist and whether we are doomed to rove upon the seas forever."[35]

Would, then, the American dream be realized in France? Was democracy really inevitable, as De Tocqueville had in his earlier days believed so hopefully and so confidently? The great reaction that swept over Europe after the Revolution of 1848 clouded his hopes and shook his confidence. He died in a state of wistful doubt.

[35] *Recollections*, 86–87.

Chapter 13. Heralds of Fascism:

I. Louis Napoleon Bonaparte Statesman

The failure of bourgeois liberalism in France was seen in the ease with which the July Monarchy was overthrown. Those chiefly responsible for the overturn were the "men of '48," socialist workers and *bourgeois éclairés* who were convinced that stability in France would come only when the government rested on the broad base of manhood suffrage and when government directed its efforts toward ameliorating the lot of "the most numerous and the most poor." Then and then only would the two Frances cease their struggling and divided France become united in a democratic republic.

However, the generous hopes of the "men of '48" were to be dashed to the ground. During the brief three years of the existence of the Second Republic, new revolutionary forces exploded, which threatened to destroy the social order that had survived Napoleon, the Restoration, and the July Monarchy. The easy success of the uprising in February, 1848, encouraged the socialists in their belief that the social order itself could just as easily be overturned. A political revolution that established a democratic republic was to be quickly followed by a social revolution to establish the cooperative commonwealth. Was not revolution the traditional method of progress in France? Once more the barricades went up in Paris. Both the reactionaries and the bourgeois liberals now faced the socialist threat of universal confiscation of property. They joined hands in defense of their interests, and the outcome was the tragic "June Days" of 1848. Into this situation came new forces, new personalities, new policies that can now be recognized as forming components in the pattern of fascism. The real significance of the Revolution of 1848 in France lay in its being a prologue to the dictatorship of Louis Napoleon—the strange interlude between the Second and the Third Republics.

The Revolution of 1848 was a European movement that began in Paris on February 22, with the uprising against Louis Philippe. It spread rapidly throughout Western Europe with more or less virulence. At first the success of the Revolution was startling: ancient thrones tottered; the absolute monarchs of Austria and Prussia were compelled to make humiliating concessions; and, in almost every country in Western Europe, constitutions were granted and parliaments were called into existence. In France, the July Monarchy made almost no defense against the onrush of its enemies, who came both from the left and from the right: democrats, republicans, socialists, Legitimists, clericals, and Bonapartists. Louis Philippe and Guizot hastily fled, driven into exile by the momentum of what was called *la révolution du mépris.* The magic word "Democracy" was spoken and that fortress of repression, the *Système Guizot,* quickly collapsed into a mass of ruins. "Such is the power of the word Democracy," declared Guizot, "that no government or party dares to raise its head, or believes its own existence possible, if it does not bear that word inscribed on its banner; and those who carry that banner aloft . . . believe themselves to be stronger than all the rest of the world."[1]

Social discontent played as great a part—perhaps even a greater one—in the Revolution of 1848 as did the political opposition to the corrupt and despotic rule of Louis Philippe. From 1846 to 1848 an economic depression had set in that had spread havoc in the industrial centers. Unemployment rose and wages fell, especially in the new cotton-manufacturing centers. Strikes and riots were almost daily occurrences and the government did nothing to remedy the desperate situation.[2] As usual in France, social discontent immediately flowed into revolutionary channels. Behind the barricades of the February uprising was the embattled proletariat, as eager to destroy capitalism as to overthrow the July Monarchy.

[1] François Guizot, *Democracy in France* (New York, 1849), 11.

[2] P. Louis, *Histoire de la classe ouvrière en France* (Paris, 1927), 57–68, 87; A. L. Dunham, "Industrial Life and Labor in France, 1815–1848," *Journal of Economic History,* III (1943), 138; and S. B. Clough, *France, A History of National Economics, 1789–1939* (New York, 1939), 158–160.

However, it was the idealistic *bourgeois éclairés* who became prominent in the uprising against Louis Philippe. A generation had come to
the fore that repudiated monarchical governments that depended for
support on wealthy minorities, aristocratic or bourgeois, and that favored
the establishment of a democratic republic as the best means of safe-
guarding the heritage of the French Revolution. There was no better
representative of the idealistic republicans than Alphonse de Lamartine
(1790-1869), who became head of the Provisional Government after the
abdication of Louis Philippe. The soul of the Romantic poet, which
had vibrated to the restless spirit of his age, now began to vibrate
to the political and social discontent of the Revolution. Lamartine
experienced "de façon inoubliable, le grand frisson libéral qui a secoué
son génération." [3] In his best known work on politics, *Sur la politique
rationelle,* Lamartine outlined policies and schemes of reform that
anticipated those of the Radical Socialists of the Third French Republic.
His great objective was to found what he called a *parti social,* which
would favor a democratic republic with full civil, religious, and political
liberty but with firm protection of property rights; and social reforms,
such as social insurance, popularization of credit through government
banks, and the recognition of trade-unions. Lamartine feared the
growing power of capitalism, with its unregulated competition and
ruthless exploitation of the laboring class. Manhood suffrage and social
reform, the twin virtues of democracy, would, according to Lamartine,
at last unite the two Frances and bring the long sought for stability
to the government of France. With his whole passionate nature, Lamartine opposed dictatorship of any kind, whether Bourbon, Bonapartist, or proletarian. Property, in his opinion, was the indispensable
basis of society; he, therefore, denounced socialism as a form of national
suicide. [4] On the morrow of the February Revolution, Lamartine
"appeared in the light of a saviour." As events progressed from idealistic declarations and proclamations to the bitter conflicts of parties
and of classes, Lamartine exhibited an incapacity to understand the
true situation and a weakness before the stern realities of class war
that caused him to be repudiated by all parties, left and right. He
was then quickly cast aside and relegated to political oblivion.

[3] P. Quentin-Bauchart, *Lamartine, homme politique* (Paris, 1903), 3–4.
[4] Lamartine, *Correspondance* (Paris, 1875), VI, 270.

Associated with Lamartine in the Provisional Government were representatives of the socialist workers. The leading socialist member was Louis Blanc, whose famous book *L'Organisation du travail* had a wide influence during the troubled year 1848. Blanc declared that the root of all economic evil was the competitive system, which ruined both worker and capitalist: the former through low wages and the latter through low profits. The only solution was the organization of cooperative societies financed by the government, the profits of which would go partly to the members, partly to finance social services, and partly to provide new capital. These cooperative societies would drive private enterprises out of business by successfully competing with them. In this peaceful way capitalism would disappear, to give place to a cooperative social order.

Owing to the influence of Blanc and the socialists, the Provisional Government proclaimed a new civil right—the "right to work," which later became the battle cry of the socialist movement throughout the world. The "right to work" was the socialist challenge to the capitalist order, as in the eighteenth century the doctrine of natural rights had been the liberal challenge to the feudal order. To put the new doctrine into effect, the Provisional Government established a commission, which issued decrees recognizing the trade-unions and establishing a ten-hour workday. It embarked on an ambitious scheme called "national workshops," which proved to be a caricature of Blanc's plan of cooperation. Men of all trades were given the "right to work," at forty cents a day, building fortifications around Paris.[5]

Even this caricature was important, as was shown by the desperate efforts of the socialists to maintain the "national workshops." Once granted, the principle of the "right to work" had the potential force of becoming a powerful weapon with which to batter down the citadel

[5] The doctrine of the "right to work" was inspired by the following article in the Constitution of the First French Republic (1793): "Public relief is a sacred debt. Society owes maintenance to unfortunate citizens either in procuring work for them or in providing the means of existence for those who are unable to labor." *The Constitutions and Other Select Documents Illustrative of the History of France, 1789–1907* (F. M. Anderson, ed., Minneapolis, 1908), 173.

For good accounts of the social reforms of the Second French Republic, see E. Levasseur, *Histoire des classes ouvrières et de l'industrie en France de 1789 à 1870* (Paris, 1903–1904), II, 337–454, and D. C. McKay, *The National Workshops* (Cambridge, 1933).

of property. At least, so it seemed to the affrighted property owners: aristocrats, bourgeois, and peasants. The conflict that now arose in France was not over class privileges but over the very existence of a class system in society, the abolition of which was demanded by the socialists as the most important step in the progress of mankind. De Tocqueville graphically described the new revolutionary attitude of the workers, now designated as the "proletariat." "How should the poor and humble, and yet powerful classes," he wrote, "not have dreamt of issuing from their poverty and inferiority by means of their power, especially in an epoch when our view into another world has become dimmer, and the miseries of this world become more visible and seem more intolerable? They had been working to this end for the last sixty years. The people had first endeavored to help itself by changing every political institution; but after each change, it found that its lot was in no way improved, or was only improving with a slowness quite incompatible with the eagerness of its desire. Inevitably, it must sooner or later discover that that which held it fixed in its position was not the constitution of the government but the unalterable laws that constitute society itself; and it was natural that it should be brought to ask itself if it had not both the power and the right to alter those laws, as it had altered all the rest. And to speak more especially of property, which is, as it were, the foundation of our social order— all the privileges which covered it and which, so to speak, concealed the privilege of property having been destroyed, and the latter remaining the principal obstacle to equality among men, and appearing to be the only sign of inequality—was it not necessary, I will not say that it should be abolished in its turn, but at least that the thought of abolishing it should occur to the minds of those who did not enjoy it?"[6]

Was economic equality to be attained through the abolition of property? The principle of the "right to work" and the social reforms adopted by the Provisional Government set the property nerve aquiver throughout France. The National Assembly, elected by manhood suffrage to draw up a constitution for the Second Republic, was democratic but not socialist. It clearly showed its antisocialist temper by

[6] Alexis de Tocqueville, *Recollections,* trans. from the French by A. T. de Mattos (New York, 1896), 99–100.

its opposition to the social experiments of the Provisional Government, especially to the "national workshops."

Hatred of the bourgeois, accumulated during the July Monarchy, now burst into fanatical fury among the Parisian workers. Leaders more radical than Blanc appeared, among them Louis Auguste Blanqui, who was as terrifying to the bourgeois of '48 as Marat had been to the aristocrats of '93. Even the tolerant, dispassionate De Tocqueville shrank in horror from Blanqui whom he described as a man who "had wan, emaciated cheeks, white lips, a sickly, wicked and repulsive expression, a dirty pallor, the appearance of a mouldy corpse; he wore no visible linen; an old black frock-coat tightly covered his lean, withered limbs; he seemed to have passed his life in a sewer, and to have just left it."[7]

When the National Assembly decreed the abolition of the "national workshops," fury rose high among the penniless unemployed workers. With the cry "Bread or Lead" they rose in insurrection under the red flag of socialism. The newly born democratic Republic was soon locked in deadly conflict with the newly born socialist revolution. A popular uprising against the Republic was strangely terrifying to the veterans of the February barricades. For the first time, France beheld the barricades dividing those who, so often in the past, had fought together on the same side against the upholders of the Old Regime. Now the same barricades divided the propertied of all classes from the nonpropertied. The bloody suppression of the uprising during the terrible "June Days" (June 23–26, 1848) impressed Karl Marx as "the most colossal event in the history of European civil wars."[8] The two Frances—bourgeois and proletarian—were divided by a chasm far deeper and wider than that which had divided royalists and republicans.

Fear of the Red Specter swept property-owning France. A socialist revolution would ruin the *bourgeoisie* even more completely than the French Revolution had ruined the aristocracy. Especially fearful were the peasant proprietors, who dreaded nothing so much as the confiscation of their lands by *les partageux*.[9] The elections to the Legislative

[7] *Ibid.*, 163.

[8] Karl Marx, "The Eighteenth of Brumaire of Louis Napoleon," *A Handbook of Marxism* (New York, 1935), 123.

[9] Albert Guérard, *Napoleon III* (Cambridge, Mass., 1943), 119*ff.*

Assembly, the unicameral parliament of the Second Republic, gave full expression to this fear on the part of all propertied classes. A large majority of the Assembly consisted of the Party of the Moral Order—monarchists who were determined to put an end to the democratic Republic. Promptly did the Assembly act to allay this fear. The electoral law of 1850, inspired by Adolphe Thiers, abolished manhood suffrage by depriving the "vile multitude" of the vote; over three million voters were erased from the electoral lists by this law.[10]

Voting or not, the workers continued to terrify bourgeois France. As in the period of the Restoration, fear of the masses caused many to see in religion the most effective means of combating the revolutionary spirit. A religious revival began among *les chrétiens de la peur,* the hitherto Voltairian bourgeois. The *bourgeoisie* had been liberal—even revolutionary—during the Restoration. After 1830, terrified by the rising discontent of the workers, it became conservative. After the "June Days" it became reactionary, clerical, and more than ever royalist. The Voltairian Thiers, no less than the Protestant Guizot and the Catholic Louis Veuillot, all were ready to use the church in defense of the established order. "Let us throw ourselves at the feet of the bishops. They alone can save us!" was now the cry of the fear-stricken propertied classes. Religion, according to Thiers, was "the indispensable rectifier of the ideas of the people." When one did not believe in God, observed Louis Veuillot, the militant clerical editor of *Univers,* it was necessary to be a proprietor in order to believe in property. The most trenchant and incisive statement on the utility of religion as a conservative force in society was made by Guizot: "You are surrounded by an immense and excited multitude; you complain that you want means to act upon it, to enlighten, direct, control, and tranquillize it; that you have little intercourse with these men, save through the tax-gatherer and the policeman; that they are given over, without defense, to the inflammatory declamations of charlatans and demagogues, and to the blind violence of their own passions. Dispersed among them, you have men whose express mission and constant occupation it is to guide their faith, to console their distresses, to show them their duties, to awaken and elevate their hopes, to exercise

[10] P. Muller, "M. Thiers," *La Révolution de 1848,* XII-XIII (September–October–November, 1917), 132–137.

over them that moral influence which you vainly seek elsewhere. And would you not second these men in their work, when they can second you so powerfully in yours, precisely in those obscure inclosures where you so rarely penetrate, and where the enemies of social order enter continually, and sap all their foundations?"[11]

Fear of the revolutionary proletariat led to a new education law, the *loi Falloux,* put through the Assembly in 1850 by Thiers. Under the Second Republic the new clericalism of the bourgeois gained a triumph that the old clericalism of the *émigré* aristocrats was unable to achieve under the Bourbon Restoration. This law gave to the church supreme power to supervise and to direct primary and secondary education in France, a power that was not broken until the passage of the Ferry Laws during the Third French Republic. This upsurge of clericalism among the Voltairian bourgeois followed the pattern of the reactionary philosophers De Maistre and De Bonald: beliefs and ideals concerning man's salvation in the next world were now put at the service of mundane class interests by those who feared for their possessions in this world.

Far more significant than the revival of clericalism was the revival of Bonapartism, in a new social setting with a political program, the significance of which has become clear only in our day. Into the new revolutionary situation created by socialism came the enigmatic figure of Louis Napoleon Bonaparte (1808-1873). The son of Louis Bonaparte, brother of Napoleon I, and his wife Hortense, the daughter of Empress Josephine by her first marriage, Louis Napoleon was thus related to Napoleon I by ties of blood and marriage. Driven from France after 1815, he became a wandering exile in various European lands. As the nearest relative of the great Emperor, Louis Napoleon came to be regarded as the embodiment of the "Napoleonic legend" and the hope of the Bonapartists in France. During the reign of Louis Philippe, Louis Napoleon returned to France and made two sensational attempts to overthrow the government. These attempts proved miserable failures and led to his imprisonment.

After the February Revolution in 1848 Louis Napoleon came prominently to the fore. His name, his romantic experiences, his appeals to the glorious memories of the First Empire made him a popular

[11] Guizot, *op. cit.,* 77-78.

figure. After the upheaval of the "June Days," Louis Napoleon appealed to many as the "savior of society," the strong "man on horseback" who would suppress the socialist terror as Napoleon I had suppressed the Jacobin terror. Nothing could be more ridiculous than the pose of Louis Napoleon as the embodiment of the "Napoleonic legend." The weak-chinned, short-legged, rouged "man on horseback" of 1848 was hardly even a caricature of the great Napoleon. The cynical French were not at all deceived by the romantic propaganda of the Bonapartist party. Louis Napoleon's appeal had a far more solid basis in that the propertied classes saw in him a powerful force able and willing to make use of a dictatorial government to save them from social revolution. He gained the solid support of all who feared a social revolution: property owners great and small, aristocrats, capitalists, peasant proprietors, shopkeepers, and professionals; Catholics, who dreaded a revival of attacks on the church by a socialist Reign of Terror; and people generally, who recoiled with horror at the prospect of class war. Barely a year after the February Revolution, the generous glow of democracy and republicanism gave way to a hardened resolve to establish a political system that would be neither democratic nor republican.

Wherein lay the appeal of Louis Napoleon as the "savior of society"? Nothing in his expressed views marked him as a conservative defender of vested interests and of class privileges. On the contrary, he had severely criticized capitalism and had asserted that his chief desire was to promote the welfare of the workers. Early in his career, Louis Napoleon had written three books, or rather pamphlets: *Idées libérales, Idées napoléoniennes,* and *De l'extinction du paupérisme,* in which he presented his views on the reconstruction of France. These writings breathed the atmosphere of Utopian socialism of the first half of the nineteenth century. Louis Napoleon's early associations were with the disciples of Charles Fourier and of Saint-Simon; he was an intimate of Louis Blanc; and he was sufficiently interested in Proudhon to have an extended discussion with him on social problems.

Louis Napoleon endorsed the socialist view that capitalism was a new feudalism imposed on mankind. "Property in land," he declared, "had its vassals and its serfs. The revolution enfranchised the land; but the new property—that of the manufacturers—growing daily, tended

. . . to have, like the first, its vassals and its serfs."[12] He denounced
the industrial system, which, he asserted, was responsible for starvation
amidst plenty. It was the disgrace of the nineteenth century that "a
tenth part of our population is in rags, and dying from starvation,
when there are millions of francs' worth of manufactured produce
which cannot find a sale, and millions of the productions of the earth
which cannot be consumed."[13] To create better conditions, Louis
Napoleon advocated the establishment of cooperative agricultural
colonies on unused land, to be financed by government loans. This
reform would absorb the unemployed and raise the standard of living
for millions. In this manner, he argued, prosperity would come to
the entire nation.

Louis Napoleon flatly and definitely repudiated the doctrine of
laissez faire. Government, he declared, was "the beneficent motive
power of all social organization." Its "basis is democratic, since all
the powers are derived from the people." However, the organization
of an efficient state should be according to hierarchical principles;
different grades were necessary to stimulate different capacities.[14]

Along with denunciation of capitalism and with concern for the
workers' welfare, an anti-Semitic note was sounded by the supporters
of Louis Napoleon, when he became a candidate for the presidency
of the Republic. Louis Napoleon, they asserted, was the true socialist,
who would destroy the "antisocial combination .of cosmopolitan
capitalists," such as the Jewish bankers, the Rothschilds, by abolishing
their financial privileges. A Bonapartist journal, *Organisation du travail,*
was established, "in the interest of democracy and of the proletariat,"
to exorcise the evil influence of Jewish finance in France. Another
Bonapartist journal, *Napoléon républicain,* held the Jews responsible
for the disasters suffered by France during the First Empire and for
the defeat of Napoleon I. "The infamous financiers of the period,
with the Jew Rothschild at their head," retarded the Emperor's campaign in Russia through their manipulations. That was the true cause

---

[12] Louis Napoleon Bonaparte, *Napoleonic Ideas,* trans. from the French by J. A. Dorr
(New York, 1859), 67.

[13] Louis Napoleon Bonaparte, *Extinction of Pauperism,* in *Political and Historical
Works* (London, 1852), II, 118.

[14] Louis Napoleon Bonaparte, *Napoleonic Ideas,* 17, 100.

of the Emperor's collapse. This interpretation of the fall of the First Empire has the familiar sound of the "stab in the back" by the Jews, popularized by Hitler to explain the downfall of the German Empire. Black lists appeared, bearing the names of bankers who, it was charged, became rich by robbing the people. Most of the names on the black lists were those of Jews and of foreigners, who were denounced as being responsible for all the evils in France.[15]

During the presidential campaign in 1848 the supporters of Louis Napoleon appealed to the workers to vote for him as the man who was both a democrat and a socialist. The success of Louis Napoleon's candidacy was so overwhelming that his appeal to the radical workers could not have been unheeded.[16] Not a few of them, discouraged by the suppression of the uprising in the "June Days," rallied to Louis Napoleon as a better choice than his bourgeois opponents. Socialism without terror was attractive to many radicals, who were convinced that Louis Napoleon would perform where the socialists had promised so hopefully and had failed so tragically in the fateful year 1848. There is no keener interpreter of the situation in France during the Revolution of 1848 than Proudhon. "Everywhere," he wrote, in 1848, "the socialist instinct and the deepest republicanism found themselves united by the name 'Napoleon,' who was and still is to the masses the Revolution incarnate."[17]

The struggle between the Assembly and the President, during the period 1848 to 1851, has been generally interpreted as that between a democratic Republic fighting for its life and an adventurer aiming to become a military dictator. Obviously that was not true; the Assembly, controlled by a royalist majority, had taken the first step to abolish the Republic by destroying its foundation—manhood suffrage. The real issue between the Assembly and the President was what method was to be used in order to allay the fears caused by the "June Days." The method offered by the Assembly was the old one, namely, a return

[15] For a study of the socialist and anti-Semitic appeals of the Bonapartists, see R. Pimienta, "La Propagande bonapartiste en 1848," *La Révolution de 1848*, V–VIII (May–June, 1910; July–August, 1910; and November–December, 1910).

[16] In round numbers, Louis Napoleon polled 5,500,000 votes, as against 1,500,000 for General Cavaignac, 370,000 for Ledru-Rollin, and 17,000 for Lamartine.

[17] Pierre Joseph Proudhon, "Mélanges," in *Oeuvres complètes* (Paris, 1866–1883), XIX, 232.

to monarchy buttressed by clericalism. This pattern of reaction had lost its appeal, except to the weak, discredited aristocracy and its clerical allies. What was needed was a new pattern of resistance to revolution. That was furnished by Louis Napoleon. His method to fight the revolutionary socialists, then as now called "communists," was by establishing a dictatorship, organized on a popular basis and committed to a program of social reform. "Now the reign of castes is over," declared Louis Napoleon, "multitudes are to be governed; they must therefore be organized that they may express their wishes, and be disciplined that they may be directed and enlightened for their own advantage."[18] This new type of dictatorial government would be able to defend property rights and to suppress revolutionaries with a vigor that neither the Bourbons nor Louis Philippe could exercise because they lacked the all-essential popular support. To conciliate the embittered workers and, at the same time, to quiet the fears of the propertied classes was the new political pattern presented by Louis Napoleon.

The overthrow of the Second Republic by the *coup d'état* of December 2, 1851, was the necessary and inevitable outcome of the election of Louis Napoleon to the presidency. And the proclamation of the Second Empire, which shortly followed the *coup d'état,* completed the strange, yet expected, turn of events in France. If the suppression of the Second Republic was the result of a conspiracy, it was an open conspiracy. No one was really surprised, as the *coup d'état* was ratified by a vote of 7,439,216 to 646,737. "The defeat of socialist democracy," observed Proudhon, "first in 1848 and 1849, and then in 1851 and 1852, is the very pivot of our present history. It is even now the principal reason for the existence of the Imperial government. In every political move that it makes the Second Empire never loses sight of this reason for its existence. . . . The danger of socialism brings to the support of the Empire the united forces of the conflicting groups now out of power: the Legitimists, the Orleanists, the moderate Republicans, and the Catholics."[19]

[18] Louis Napoleon Bonaparte, *Extinction of Pauperism,* 102.

[19] P. J. Proudhon, *De la capacité politique des classes ouvrières* (Paris, 1924), 234. This view was shared by De Tocqueville. See *Correspondence and Conversations of Alexis de Tocqueville with Nassau William Senior* (London, 1872), II, 7.

Like that of 1799, the *coup d'état* of 1851 was a revolutionary anti-dote to the revolutionary tradition in France. It was a desperate device born of the need to protect a social order established by one revolution from being overthrown by another. For this reason, the regime of Napoleon III was under the continuous necessity of proclaiming democratic ideals and of maintaining at least the appearance of democratic methods through plebiscites and elections. A naked autocracy, based on sheer despotism, could not have restrained for long the revolutionary forces in the nation.

The Second Empire was no more a restoration of the First Empire than the rule of the Bourbons, after 1815, was a restoration of the Old Regime. Despite the trappings and fittings of its Napoleonic prede-cessor, with which the Second Empire adorned itself, its advent marked the appearance of something new in political systems and in political ideologies. The real significance of the Second Empire is greater today than when it flourished. The methods that it employed, the policies that it pursued, and the ideas that it proclaimed anticipated in a vague, incomplete way what is now known as "fascism." Like fascism, it arose from similar conditions. During the reign of Louis Philippe the Industrial Revolution was fairly under way in France. In the transitional stage, from artisan manufacture to the factory system, economic dislocation resulted, which created widespread un-employment among the ruined craftsmen. The Industrial Revolution in France advanced rapidly enough to throw many out of work, but not rapidly enough to absorb them into the new industries. As a con-sequence, there was "an overwhelming mass of people without a career and a young generation without a future. . . . This was the chief reason for the constantly recurring agitations, the infinite source of public and private suffering."[20]

Two generations later there was a historic parallel to the overthrow of the Second French Republic. In Italy, after the First World War, a dangerous situation was created by the economic disorganization that followed the end of hostilities. There was widespread unemploy-ment and the government did little to alleviate the evil conditions under which millions were suffering. Deep resentment among the Italian workers led them to give a ready ear to those who preached

[20] Michel Chevalier, *Des intérêts matériels en France* (Paris, 1838), 15.

social revolution: socialists, syndicalists, and communists. The revolutionary temper of the embittered workers reached the boiling point in 1920, when they went on a general strike and seized the factories. Though the uprising quickly collapsed, there was great apprehension among the propertied classes, who feared that the seizure of the factories was but a rehearsal for a socialist revolution. And they consequently gave their powerful support to the movement, led by Mussolini, to establish a fascist dictatorship. France in 1848 strikingly resembled Italy in 1920. Fear that the "June Days" were but a rehearsal for a socialist revolution had impelled the propertied classes in France to rally behind Napoleon. Mussolini's March on Rome in 1922 paralleled Napoleon's *coup d'état* in 1851.

Like Mussolini, Napoleon puzzled and confused many of his contemporaries. Even the usually perspicacious and far-sighted De Tocqueville had no inkling of the real significance of Napoleon, of whom he held no high opinion. According to De Tocqueville, Napoleon's "intelligence was incoherent, confused, filled with great but ill-assorted thoughts, which he borrowed now from the examples of Napoleon, now from socialistic theories, sometimes from recollections of England, where he lived: very different, and often very contrary, sources." He was "naturally a dreamer and a visionary." And one could not be long in contact with him "without discovering a little vein of madness which was chiefly responsible for his success." [21] The powerful interests that, openly or secretly, rallied to Napoleon's support had no great opinion of his ability or confidence in the strength of his character. What they wanted him to do was to eliminate the socialists from the political scene with a strong hand and then to become their pliant tool in the government of France. Again to quote the observant De Tocqueville, the politicians expected to find in Napoleon "an instrument which they could handle as they pleased, and which it would always be lawful for them to break when they wished to. In this, they were greatly deceived." [22] Once in power, Napoleon swept aside the bourgeois politicians as ruthlessly as he suppressed the socialist revolutionists.

Nothing is easier than to find factual parallels in history. They

[21] De Tocqueville, *Recollections*, 286-287.
[22] *Ibid.*, 285.

are generally plausible, seldom convincing, and never instructive. To see the origins of great changes in history is a quite different—and more important—matter. As nature abhors a vacuum, history abhors changes without origins, whether immediate or remote. Fascism did not spring fully grown from the chin of Mussolini. It had historic origins, not so much in Italy itself as in France, which since the French Revolution has furnished many revolutionary patterns to Latin Europe.

The organization and policies of the Second Empire bore startling resemblances to the fascist dictatorships of our time. It was a dictatorship based on popular support, as expressed in plebiscites and in "elections." Napoleon realized what neither the Bourbons nor Louis Philippe had realized: that popular support was all essential in maintaining a government in postrevolutionary France. To obtain popular support he established a parliament, the *Corps législatif,* elected by manhood suffrage. The acid test of parliamentary government is the existence of an opposition that arises from free elections and that aims to assume power. No parliamentary opposition existed throughout the period of the Second Empire. The method of "official candidates," already established by the Bourbons and perfected into a system by the July Monarchy, concerned a small electorate, which was easily controlled. Under the Second Empire this system was applied thoroughly and efficiently to the huge electorate that came with manhood suffrage, punctiliously maintained by Napoleon. Official candidates were put in nomination in every district by a smoothly running political machine, organized by the government. For a time few, if any, opposition candidates appeared. Under the Second Empire there was a false majority in parliament, elected by manhood suffrage, as there had been false majorities in the parliaments of the Bourbon and Orleanist monarchies, which had been elected by small groups of property owners. As in the fascist dictatorships, the voters under the Second Empire went to the polls, not to elect representatives, but to endorse the list of candidates drawn up by the government; and parliament met not to pass laws but to ratify decrees presented by the government. In fact, though not in theory, elections were conducted on a one-party basis. It took a bold and courageous man to oppose the official candidate; an opposition candidate at the elections was sure to arouse the vindictive enmity of the government. Few dared to assume such a risk. In 1857 the government presented for reelection all the members of the outgoing parliament. This complete flouting of the democratic process created widespread resentment which found expression in the election of five opposition candidates. *Les cinq,* as the opponents of the government were known, constituted the beginning of a parliamentary opposition, which grew in numbers during the last decade of the Second Empire.

Public opinion in France, as expressed in the press, was traditionally antigovernment. Napoleon conceived the idea of having the entire press used as the mouthpiece of the government, an idea later applied in the fascist dictatorships. A highly organized censorship controlled, cajoled, directed, or terrorized the newspapers into becoming organs of the government. Opposition newspapers were suppressed and their editors jailed or exiled. Suppression of opposition newspapers was not a new thing in postrevolutionary France. What was new was the systematic use of the entire press to give the illusion that public opinion supported the government. Like manhood suffrage, the press was an integral part of the new type of dictatorship, which boasted of being the expression of the popular will.

What did the "socialist Emperor" do about labor? To allay the bourgeois terror of a class struggle between labor and capital, tradeunions were outlawed and strikes forbidden. In 1853 the government inaugurated a method of labor-capital cooperation through a system of industrial councils representing both sides. To these councils, *conseils des prud'hommes,* was given the task of regulating wages, hours, and conditions in the factories. Such bodies had existed before, but under the Second Empire they were used by the government to support its labor policies. Frequently men not even connected with the industry were appointed by the authorities as officials of the *conseils.*[23] As a system, the *conseils* suggested the Nazi Labor Front, in that they were intermediary groups between the workers and the government, under the political direction of the latter and used as a means of controlling the former. What the Emperor desired, writes a latter-day apologist of Napoleon, was "to create an army of workers of the same

[23] Albert Thomas, "Le Second Empire," in *Histoire socialiste* (Jean Jaurès, ed., Paris, 1907), X, 66-70.

type as that created by the National Socialists in Germany a century later."[24]

Another way of controlling the workers was through the *livret*.[25] In 1854 a law made more stringent the regulations of this industrial passport in order to enable the police to keep watch over the comings and goings of the workers. Since the "June Days" there was a great dread of the Paris worker, who was regarded as the uncompromising enemy of the social order, ever ready to overthrow it by mass insurrection. A secret report on the attitude of the working class, made by a government agent, asserted that the worker was a socialist as, before 1789, the bourgeois had been a *philosophe*. "The bourgeois sought to establish a system that they could use as a weapon against the dominance of the nobility and the clergy. The worker now favors a system which he can use to overthrow, if possible, all inequalities."[26] During the Second Empire the workers, cowed by repressive measures, were silent, industrious, and, to all appearances, submissive. Despite the great advance of industry during the regime of Napoleon, the condition of the mass of workers did not improve greatly. It was estimated that there were then in France about three million paupers and about six million who were often in a condition below the poverty line.[27]

What did Napoleon do to advance social reform, which had been the burden of his appeal to the workers? Very little. He did nothing at all to establish the agricultural colonies that he had advocated so fervently in his *De l'extinction du paupérisme*. Government subventions were given to associations having for their object old-age pensions and sickness insurance.[28] To diminish unemployment, the government instituted *les grands travaux,* public works of which the rebuilding of Paris was the most famous project. The social reforms of the Second Empire were meager performances, considering the

[24] H. N. Boon, *Rêve et réalité dans l'oeuvre économique et sociale de Napoléon III* (La Haye, 1936), 74.

[25] See *supra,* p. 160.

[26] Paul Bernard, *Le Mouvement ouvrier en France pendant les années 1852–1864* (Leyden, 1939), 256.

[27] Georges Weill, *Histoire du mouvement social en France, 1852–1924* (Paris, 1924), 29.

[28] For a description of the social reforms of the Second Empire, see Levasseur, *op. cit.,* II, 495–522.

generous promises that the Emperor had made when he was bidding for power.

The class that benefited most from the Second Empire was the *bourgeoisie*. Napoleon had learned from his early associates, the disciples of Saint-Simon, that a new historic era had come with the Industrial Revolution. Thenceforth, the capitalists, not the aristocrats, were to be the ruling class in society. The chief aim of the Saint-Simonians was the economic development of France. They were little interested in political rights and in popular government, and generally subordinated political to economic questions. If any intellectual group could be said to have been the mentors of the Second Empire, it was the Saint-Simonians. Closely associated with the government in its various economic enterprises were Michel Chevalier, the brothers Pereire, and Père Enfantin—all disciples of the famous Utopian socialist.

Napoleon did all in his power to encourage commerce and industry, which won for the government the powerful support of the new moneyed class. Anti-Semitism played no part in the Emperor's policies, despite its upflare during his campaign for the presidency; the Jewish bankers, the Rothschild family and the brothers Pereire, were very influential in government finance. The pace of industrialization in France after 1815 had been slow, hampered in part by aristocratic indifference, in part by socialist agitation. During the Second Empire, France was in a fever of business enterprise and machine production. Two new financial institutions, the *Crédit foncier* and the *Crédit mobilier,* financed the building of the great railway system of France, the rebuilding of Paris, and the organization of the French Line operating trans-Atlantic steamships. Railway mileage increased sixfold during the period of the Second Empire. Steel production was greatly increased by the expansion of the steel plant at Le Creusot. The horsepower of machines used in industry quintupled. France was beginning to catch up with England in the rapid development of modern industry.[29]

In his economic as well as in his political policies, reconciliation was the watchword of Napoleon III. He desired to reconcile capital with labor; authoritative government with manhood suffrage; and a rigid

[29] Clough, *op. cit.,* 163–200; A. Viallate, *L'activité économique en France* (Paris, 1937), 141–191; and J. B. Wolf, *France, 1815 to the Present* (New York, 1940), 280–297.

censorship with a free press. The prime motive of his reconciliation policy was to solve the as yet unsolved problem of the two Frances. Napoleon fully realized the vital importance of the problem, as well as the failure of the different political groups to solve it. The French Revolution, he declared, "had two distinct characteristics—one social, the other political. The social revolution has triumphed in spite of our reverses, while the political one has failed in spite of the victories of the people. That is the cause of all our discomfort now."[30] He came to the conclusion that all efforts to bring unity to France had failed because they had all been partisan in character: Legitimist, bourgeois liberal, or republican. Because he belonged to none of these parties, insisted Napoleon, he was best fitted to unite the two Frances. He would do so by a plan that incorporated the fundamental principle of each political element. From the Legitimists he would take the monarchical principle, by establishing a new dynasty. From the bourgeois liberals he would take the parliamentary principle, by establishing a representative body. From the republicans he would take the principle of popular sovereignty, by maintaining manhood suffrage. He would reassure the propertied classes by suppressing socialist revolts. To reassure the workers, "Saint-Simon on horseback," as Napoleon was called, would institute social reforms for the welfare of the masses. This uniting of the various conflicting elements would *terminer enfin la Révolution française,* and the two Frances at last would become one.[31]

There was to be a guarantee of this unity: authoritarian government. The dictatorial rule of Napoleon was carried out with great firmness. Thousands of recalcitrant republicans were exiled or imprisoned or were compelled to flee. The most famous of these new *émigrés* was Victor Hugo, whose denunciation of the Emperor and of his system was immortalized in his books *Napoléon-le-Petit* and *Histoire d'un crime.* All expressions of public opinion hostile to the Emperor, in the press, in popular assemblies, and in the schools, were ruthlessly suppressed. The famous historians Michelet and Quinet were ousted

[30] Louis Napoleon Bonaparte, *L'Idée Napoléonienne* in *Political and Historical Works* (London, 1852), II, 259.

[31] On this aspect of the politics of Napoleon III, see the penetrating analysis in the *Mémoires du Duc de Persigny* (Paris, 1896), 29–31.

from their academic chairs. The Legitimists and the Orleanists, less recalcitrant, were ignored. The church was cajoled into supporting the regime by the *loi Falloux* and by the encouragement given to the clergy. Napoleon was assiduous in showing deference to Catholic opinion by government support of Catholic societies, schools, and charities. Though the regime of the Second Empire was not "totalitarian" in the fascist sense, almost every institution in the land felt the hand of the government, which regulated, prescribed, punished, and suppressed opinions and activities that were hostile to Napoleon.

Did the Napoleonic dictatorship succeed in solving the persistent problem of uniting the two Frances? It certainly seemed so. All through the period of the Second Empire domestic peace reigned in France; no uprisings, no strikes of any consequence, and no serious parliamentary opposition disquieted the government. The nation appeared to be united behind the Emperor, who, toward the end of his reign, received an almost unanimous vote of confidence as a result of a plebiscite. But appearances belied the realities of the situation in France. On the morrow of the fall of the Empire there broke out the bloodiest uprising in the revolutionary history of France—the Paris Commune. Dictatorship had not been a solution.

In an extraordinary, penetrating pamphlet, *De l'esprit de conquête et de l'usurpation,* Benjamin Constant gave an analysis of the methods used by a dictator in ruling a nation. What he said referred to Napoleon I, but it applied even more forcefully to the methods used by Napoleon III. "The existence of public sentiment," he wrote, "being dangerous to dictatorship and the semblance of public sentiment being necessary to it, the dictatorship strikes the people with one hand to stifle any real sentiment; and it strikes them again with the other hand to compel them to act as if motivated by public sentiment." When a dictator "condemns innocence, he includes calumny so that his action will seem to be justified." When he decides on a policy, the dictator orders "a ridiculous investigation to serve as a prelude to what he had decided to do. This counterfeit liberty combines all the evils of anarchy and slavery. There is no end to a tyranny which seeks to drag forth tokens of consent. Peaceable men are persecuted for indifference, energetic men, for being dangerous." Dictatorship invents a falsified popular approval of the government; and the result is that fear "comes to ape all the appearances of courage, to congratulate itself on dishonor, and to give thanks for unhappiness." Dictatorship resorts to the practice of hiring corrupt journalists who parody freedom of the press. They "argue, as though trying to convince; they fly into a passion as though fighting an opposition; they fling insults as though there was any chance of replying." Under a despotic monarchy, the people are enslaved; but under a dictatorship, they are also degraded. A dictatorship "debases a people while oppressing them, and accustoms them to trample under foot what they once respected, to court what they once scorned, and even to scorn themselves."[32]

Nazi writers in Germany have evaluated the historic importance of Napoleon as a harbinger of fascism, despite the marked differences between the Second Empire and the Third Reich. A book, *Masse oder Volk,* written by Konstantin Frantz in 1852, was republished in 1933 with a significant preface by the Nazi Franz Kemper. "The rise to power of Louis Napoleon," wrote Kemper, "is the only historical parallel to the National Socialist revolution of our day."[33] According to Frantz, the Napoleonic state depended on mass support, without which it could not be maintained even by the powerful Imperial army. Only through social reform could the danger of socialism be eliminated.[34] In the view of another Nazi writer, Michael Freund, Napoleon was the only real revolutionist in 1848. "After the solemn republican respectability of 1848 it seemed that only with the Napoleonic experiment did a great revolutionary élan appear on the stage of history." The state created by Napoleon was antisocialist, but it was not the laissez-faire state of capitalism. The social ideals of the disciples of Saint-Simon were given by Napoleon, for the first time, a military and authoritarian aspect.[35] Still another Nazi, K. H. Bremer, diagnosed the situation of the Second Republic in the following manner. While the republicans of 1848 were trying to solve the constitutional question, he observed, Napoleon realized that the social question was the most important one. Parliamentarism, with its conflicting political parties and class struggles,

[32] Benjamin Constant, *De l'esprit de conquête et de l'usurpation* (Paris, 1814), 87–91.
[33] Franz Kemper, Introduction to Konstantin Frantz, *Masse oder Volk* (Potsdam, 1933).
[34] *Ibid.*, 76.
[35] Michael Freund, "Napoleon III. Eine Betrachtung zur Krise der Demokratie in Frankreich," *Deutsche Zeitschrift*, XLVIII (October, 1934–September, 1935), 181–183.

was incapable of solving the social question. Only a dictatorship with a social outlook, in the view of Napoleon, could solve it. His great aim was to establish a political system based upon the unity of all classes and of all interests in France. It was he, according to Bremer, who first created the new type of state in the form of authoritarian, plebiscitarian leadership.[36]

The prefascist pattern of Napoleon's dictatorship collapsed even before Sedan. What was called the "Liberal Empire," inaugurated in 1867, marked a definite trend toward liberalism. Elections became freer, and opposition parties appeared in parliament. The control of the press was relaxed. Public meetings were more freely permitted. Even more significant were the concessions made to the 'workers. Trade-unions were legalized, collective bargaining was recognized, and strikes were permitted.

What caused this transition from the fascist pattern of the dictatorship to the pattern of the "Liberal Empire"? Rising discontent among powerful elements in the nation forced Napoleon to make concessions to liberalism. The protectionists opposed his reciprocity treaty with England. The Catholics opposed his alliance with the Italian nationalists in the Austro-Sardinian war. The liberals loudly demanded a return to constitutional government and the restoration of "the necessary liberties." The disastrous failure of the Emperor's intervention in Mexico brought the discontented elements together in a common hostility to the Empire. Napoleon sought to ward off by timely concessions a revolutionary upheaval such as had overtaken his predecessor, Louis Philippe; hence, *l'Empire libéral*.

These explanations, while true enough, merely indicate the weakness of the Second Empire as a fascist experiment. Neither Hitler nor Mussolini made any concessions to liberalism throughout their dictatorships. *The weakness of the fascist pattern of Napoleon lay in that it did not include totalitarianism.* Napoleon never attempted "to coordinate" the political, economic, and social life of France into a uniform, unified, national system, run by a dictatorial machine. He would not have succeeded had he tried to do so. There were serious obstacles to totalitarianism in the France of his day. Despite fairly rapid industrial advance during the Second Empire, France continued to be

[36] K. H. Bremer, "Der sozialistiche Kaiser," *Die Tat*, XXX (June, 1938), 160–171.

primarily an agricultural nation. Land was cultivated by millions of peasant proprietors, passionately individualistic, who would quickly have resented any abrogation of their rights as independent cultivators. There did not then exist large combinations of basic industries, which easily lend themselves to government control and regulation. French industry generally was based on small competitive units that could not be "coordinated" even by the most despotic of dictatorships. Neither was there a large working class, organized in powerful trade-unions, that could be taken over and directed by a dictatorship. Totalitarianism requires, in addition, easy and rapid means of communication and transportation, such as radio, motion pictures, automobiles, and airplanes, which a dictatorship can use for propaganda purposes. It also requires a national school system in which the masses of the people can be indoctrinated with a common ideology. France of the mid-nineteenth century had none of these means of "coordination." Had Napoleon attempted to do what Hitler did so quickly and so successfully, the revolutionary tocsin would have been heard in every hamlet and in every quarter of France.

The social experiment of the dictatorship of Napoleon is the most significant aspect of the Second Empire. It has been obscured by the sensational foreign policies of the Emperor, which led to the Crimean, the Austro-Sardinian, and the Franco-Prussian wars, and finally to his dramatic downfall. In the light of fascism, it can now be discerned that a new political method of fighting social revolution had been devised, namely, to turn the revolutionary stream of working-class discontent into the new channel of a popular and socialized dictatorship. Napoleon's pioneer fascism failed, and its failure discredited the newly born legend of "Saint-Simon on horseback." It also discredited militarism, with which the experiment was so closely linked. The downfall of the Second Empire exploded the "Napoleonic legend" so violently that even Napoleon I was struck by the flying missiles. The great Napoleon, as well as Napoléon-le-petit, now appeared to the French as an "architect of ruin." Waterloo and Sedan became joined, in popular opinion, as the outstanding national disasters in the history of France.

Strangely enough, bourgeois liberalism also was discredited by the Second Empire. The social experiments of Napoleon, however tentative and halting, and the maintenance of manhood suffrage, however illusory and ineffective, yet kept alive a democratic sentiment in France. A restoration of bourgeois liberalism, with its neglect of the working class and with its capitalist rule, was as distasteful after 1870 as the restoration of the Bourbons had been after 1815. If it did nothing else, the Second Empire had accustomed the French people to think of government in its intimate relationship with their everyday problems. Was it possible to establish a new government on a truly democratic basis—one that would concern itself chiefly with the welfare of the masses? Such a government, of necessity, would be a republic, in order that it repudiate, at the same time, the bourgeois liberalism of the July Monarchy and the dictatorship of the Second Empire. It would have to make a powerful appeal for national unity, in order to face the grave problems that arose as a consequence of the defeat of France in the Franco-Prussian War. Would a democratic republic close the chasm that, for so long, had divided the two Frances? Out of these necessities was born the Third French Republic.

Chapter 14. Heralds of Fascism:

II. Pierre Joseph Proudhon

Revolutionist

The Second Empire was in truth a novel departure from traditional conservatism. It puzzled the reactionaries, confused the liberals, and confounded the socialists. What could be the significance of a dictatorial regime, professing democratic ideas and advocating radical social reforms? Did this preview of the great drama of twentieth-century fascism find intellectual expression? Nothing would be easier than to find fascist ideas in the writings of many famous authors. They can be found even in those of Plato. But to find a *pattern* of fascism with its attitude toward government and society and its solutions of political and social problems is quite another matter. It is the author's contention that the fascist pattern is to be found in a fairly clear and definite form in the writings of Pierre Joseph Proudhon and in those of Thomas Carlyle. For this reason the contributions of these famous writers will be reevaluated, with the purpose of exposing in them the intellectual origins of fascism.

An original thinker, like a prophet, is without honor not only in his own country but also in his own time. This is especially true when the original thinker is an inharmonious genius, at odds both with the orthodox upholders of the established order and with the heretics who repudiate it. Only rarely, very rarely, does such a genius arise, to confound the orthodox and to confuse the heterodox. He becomes the great misunderstood of his generation; and for this reason the true importance and real contribution of the inharmonious genius are not seen until future events reveal them. There is no better example in history of such a man than that of Rousseau, the great heretic of the eighteenth century, who was persecuted by the authorities and spurned by his fellow heretics the *philosophes*. Proudhon, like Rousseau, was an inharmonious genius. In his day Proudhon was persecuted by the government as a revolutionist and was denounced by his fellow revolutionists, the liberals and the socialists, who uneasily felt that, though he was with them, he was not of them. They were puzzled and disconcerted by "ce socialiste original, mal compris de ses contemporains, fantastique, plein d'idées souvent d'une perspicacité incroyable."[1]

Pierre Joseph Proudhon was born in 1809, in Besançon, France. His father was a humble artisan, a cooper by trade, who could do little to educate his son. Even as a child, Proudhon was obliged to help his family, which he did by working sometimes on a farm, sometimes in the local inn. An opportunity to get an education came to him when he was given a scholarship in the local college at Besançon. Despite his marked inclination for study, family needs compelled Proudhon to leave college before graduating. He learned the printer's trade, which for a time was his regular vocation. Proudhon's passionate interest, however, was study, and the interruption of his education by poverty incensed the ardent young student. "Poverty is no crime; it is something worse," was his resentful thought. He began to question the social order that put so many difficulties in the way of a poor boy seeking an education. Paris beckoned the ambitious young provincial as, in the eighteenth century, it had beckoned that other ambitious young provincial Diderot. At the age of thirty Proudhon went to Paris, where he began his career as a writer, supported in part by a small stipend granted to him by the college in Besançon. Poverty, however, drove him back to his native city, where he set himself up in the printing business. But the enterprise did not prosper, and he gave it up. In 1847 Proudhon returned to Paris, to resume his career as a writer, which he followed all the rest of his life.

Proudhon was almost entirely a self-educated man. He sought, by omnivorous reading, to acquire the necessary preparation for becoming a writer on social subjects. As in the case of many another self-educated man, Proudhon's reading was wide but unsystematic. It lacked the disciplined concentration and definite direction that characterizes scholarly study. Curiously enough, he drew his inspiration not from the

[1] Hendrik N. Boon, *Rêve et réalité dans l'oeuvre économique et sociale de Napoléon III* (La Haye, 1936), 54.

rich intellectual treasury of France but, as he said, from "the Bible first of all, then Adam Smith, and finally Hegel"[2]—an odd assortment of masters for anyone, especially for a French revolutionist.

In 1840 appeared Proudhon's first book, *Qu'est-ce que la propriété?* with its sensational answer, *La propriété, c'est le vol.* Both question and answer almost immediately gained for the author an audience in the France of his day, which was seething with revolutionary theories of all kinds. So deep was the discontent with the regime of Louis Philippe that anyone who attacked the social order from any angle or for any reason was sure to get a hearing. Proudhon's reputation as a social philosopher was assured by the appearance, in 1846, of his *Système des contradictions économiques, ou philosophie de la misère,* in which he sought to find a solution of the social problem other than that presented by the socialists or by the classical economists.

When the Revolution of 1848 broke out in February, Proudhon threw himself into the movement with great ardor. He became the editor of a radical journal, *Le Représentant du peuple,* in which he wrote articles that attracted considerable attention.[3] Proudhon became a popular figure in Paris and was elected to the National Assembly as a radical deputy. Because of his famous catchword, "property is theft," he was expected to be on the socialist left, along with Ledru-Rollin and Louis Blanc. Instead, he astonished his associates by voting against the famous resolution proclaiming the "right to work." He also voted against the adoption of the constitution establishing the democratic Second Republic, on the ground that he did not believe in constitutions.[4] His chief activity as a member of the Assembly was to introduce a bill to establish a system of free credit through a people's bank, which was to supersede the Bank of France. In the debate that followed, Proudhon proved no match for his opponent Adolphe Thiers, who ridiculed both the scheme and its author. The bill received only two votes, and Proudhon was howled down amid jeers and catcalls.

Proudhon was much more active as a journalist and pamphleteer than

[2] *Correspondance de P. J. Proudhon* (Paris, 1875), I, xxii; hereinafter cited as *Correspondance.*

[3] Arthur Desjardins, *P. J. Proudhon* (Paris, 1896), I, 120; Proudhon, *La Révolution sociale démontrée par le coup d'état du Deux Décembre* (Paris, 1936), 12.

[4] Desjardins, *op. cit.,* 1, 210; Edouard Droz, *P. J. Proudhon* (Paris, 1909), 163.

as a politician. He became notorious as a dissenter from the dissenters of his day: liberals, democrats, republicans, and socialists, especially the last. The socialists Louis Blanc, Ledru-Rollin, Leroux, and Considérant received the full measure of Proudhon's virulent invective. In 1849 he was arrested on the charge of writing violent articles against President Louis Napoleon, and was sentenced to prison for three years.[5] His prison cell provided Proudhon with an opportunity for leisure, of which he made good use by studying and writing. It was while he was in prison that Proudhon, at the age of forty, was married. His wife was a simple working woman to whom he was deeply attached all his life.

A number of books, as well as a wife, emerged from Proudhon's prison cell. A volume that appeared in 1852, *La Révolution sociale démontrée par le coup d'état du Deux Décembre,* created a sensation. In this volume Proudhon hailed the overthrow of the Second Republic as a great step of progress and extolled Louis Napoleon as the hope of revolutionary France. The book roused a storm of bewildered criticism, consternation, and bafflement among the democrats and socialists of the day. During the period of the Second Empire, Proudhon was actively engaged in writing. Book after book and pamphlet after pamphlet poured from his busy pen. He attracted the hostile attention of the government when, in 1858, he attacked the church in his book *De la justice dans la Révolution et dans l'église.* His arrest was ordered, but he fled to Brussels, where he lived for three years. In 1862 Proudhon returned to France, where he lived until his death in 1865.

Proudhon wrote voluminously and has been written about voluminously. His books, which had a wide audience, have greatly influenced the labor movement in France.[6] Not a little of Proudhon's influence came from the polemical character of his writings, which appealed to the mood and spirit of social criticism, traditional in France. He developed a manner of writing that was vehemently critical in tone, vivid in langauge, trenchant in style, and devastating in character.

[5] Proudhon, *Idée génerale de la révolution au XIXe siècle* (Paris, 1923), 5; Droz, *op. cit.,* 165.

[6] C. Bouglé, "La Résurrection de Proudhon," *Revue de Paris,* Sept. 15, 1910; W. Pickles, "Les Tendances proudhoniènnes dans la France d'après guerre," *Revue d'histoire économique et sociale,* XXIII (1936–1937).

Systems of thought, public policies, and famous reputations were demolished in a torrential verbal fury that left not a rack behind. Proudhon was profoundly convinced that he, and he alone of the many revolutionists of his day, was the complete and legitimate expression of the revolutionary movement in France.[7] In his own time and since, he has been regarded by many as the uncompromising champion of human liberty in every aspect and under all circumstances.

However, neither Proudhon's undoubted sincerity nor his great courage are of themselves sufficient to warrant accepting him on his own valuation as the complete revolutionist of his nation and of his age. The reader of Proudhon is frequently baffled by a curious and strange contradiction: lucidity in language and obscurity in thought. The language that he uses in analyzing social forces and political ideas is clear to the point of sharpness, and yet the reader fails to get a comprehensive idea of Proudhonian principles and remedies. The one outstanding exception is Proudhon's proposal for a bank of exchange to promote his favorite scheme of free credit, which is clearly outlined. Was, then, Proudhon merely a destructive critic of other men's ideas, with no ideas of his own? It would seem so were it not for sinister overtones that haunt his pages, of which the present-day reader soon becomes aware. Sometimes these overtones are heard faintly, sometimes with a loudness that is startling. It is these overtones that so puzzled his republican and socialist contemporaries and caused them to see in Proudhon a powerful destructive force, which launched missiles at the citadel of privilege, but from an angle and in a direction different from their own. As a consequence, they shied away from him as from a strange animal.

Proudhon was himself conscious that he was out of harmony with his age. "My body is in the midst of the people," he declared, "but my thought is elsewhere. Owing to the trend of my ideas I have almost nothing in common with those of my contemporaries."[8] Proudhon's attitude toward the Revolution of 1848, which saw a confluence of so many revolutionary streams, strikingly illustrated his enigmatic position of being both a product and an opponent of the revolutionary thought of his time. "And then the Revolution, the Republic, and

[7] *Correspondance*, VII, 36.
[8] *Ibid.*, II, 284.

socialism, one supporting the other," he declared, "came with a bound. I saw them; I felt them; and I fled before this democratic and social monster. . . . An inexpressible terror froze my soul, obliterating my very thoughts. I denounced the conservatives who ridiculed the fury of their opponents. I denounced still more the revolutionists whom I beheld pulling up the foundations of society with incredible fury. . . . No one understood me."[9]

Proudhon was not the intellectual leader of a revolutionary party, as was Louis Blanc; nor was he the founder of a school, as was Saint-Simon. Yet ardent disciples came to him, attracted more by the violence of his attacks on the social order than by the clarity of his social thought. They heard their master's word but did not see his vision, for he himself saw it but darkly. In truth, Proudhon was a revolutionist, not of his time, but of ours; hence he deserves a reevaluation in the light of the present.

Even an inharmonious genius does not arise in a vacuum. The France of Proudhon presented a situation wherein conflicting interests and ideas found the ready support of parties and classes struggling for mastery. As has already been indicated,[10] a new industrial France arose during the July Monarchy that shifted the struggle between the two Frances from that between aristocrat and capitalist to that between capitalist and worker. The complete control of the government by the wealthy *bourgeoisie,* commercial, industrial, and financial, roused opposition from two sources: the lower middle class and the industrial workers. The former, chiefly shopkeepers and artisans, regarded with increasing uneasiness the organization of joint-stock companies, which established large factories and consolidated transportation facilities. Big property was looming up as a threat to the existence of small property. The worker-owners, so numerous in France, felt the pressure of competition from the machine industries, which could easily and readily get capital from the banks to finance their expansion. Many worker-owners went to the wall or were reduced to the rank of laborers in the factories.[11] Even more bitterly opposed to the aristocracy of

[9] P. J. Proudhon, *Mélanges,* in *Oeuvres complètes,* 37 vols. (Paris, 1866–1883), XVIII, 6. Unless otherwise indicated, the citations from the works of Proudhon will be from this edition.

[10] See *supra,* p. 233.

[11] Pierre Quentin-Bauchart, *La Crise sociale de 1848* (Paris, 1920), 36*ff.*

money were the workers. Infuriated at being left voteless by the Revolution of 1830, and exasperated by the severe repression of trade-unions, they turned on the triumphant *bourgeoisie* as their hateful enemy. As has already been noted, the new revolutionary movement, known as "socialism," aimed to destroy the bourgeois ruling class in the only way that it could be destroyed as a class, namely, by abolishing property altogether. Strange as it may seem, property became a great issue as early as the thirties and forties of the nineteenth century and in a country, France, where property was more widely diffused than anywhere else in Europe.

There is an aspect of the social situation in France during the July Monarchy that is significant in the light of the present. The great mass of worker-owners, the petty bourgeois, were confronted by enemies on two fronts: consolidated capitalism, which would preserve property rights by driving them out of business through competition, and revolutionary socialism, which would establish economic equality by confiscating their property. The strong property sense of the petty bourgeois, nowhere else so strong as in France, led them to regard the capitalist with dislike as a competitor and with envy as a rich member of their class. But their dislike and envy were tempered by a keen regard for the security of property rights, which, in case of a crisis, would drive them to the side of the capitalist. Far different was the attitude of the petty bourgeois toward the worker. An overwhelming majority of the French workingmen were then employed in shops and in small factories; hence it was the small employer who was under constant pressure to make concessions to the workers' demands for better conditions. Behind demands for better wages and shorter hours the terrified bourgeois saw the specter of universal confiscation, proclaimed by the revolutionary proletariat. From this inharmonious historic background emerged the much misunderstood, fantastic Proudhon, "plein d'idées souvent d'une perspicacité incroyable."

How to preserve property rights and, at the same time, abolish capitalism? How to safeguard the small property owner against his economic enemies—big business and revolutionary socialism? These were the questions that agitated Proudhon. Sometimes his answers were plain, even blunt; at other times they seemed hazy and far afield; but at all times they were suffused by a strange kind of revolutionary fervor, which was both puzzling and exasperating.

La propriété, c'est le vol. Nothing could be clearer, sharper, and more definite in its repudiation of the established social order than this famous dictum of Proudhon. Property had been declared a natural right by the French Revolution, and every regime in France since 1789 had maintained it unswervingly. When Proudhon repudiated property so violently as to call it "theft," he was hailed, as he is regarded today, as an extreme revolutionist. Only by reading Proudhon carefully—and fully—is it possible to understand what he meant by "property" and why he regarded it as "theft." A false impression of Proudhon's views on this point, as well as on the other matters, is derived from such dicta.

According to Proudhon, property was in essence a privilege to obtain rent, profit, and interest without any labor whatsoever. It reaped without sowing, consumed without producing, and enjoyed without exertion. It was the "worst usurer as well as the worst master and worst debtor."[12] There could be no justification for property on any ground—natural right, law, or occupation—because, according to Proudhon, it creates and maintains social inequality, the prime source of all human woe. All efforts to abolish it had been in vain. The greatest of all changes in history, the French Revolution, did not abolish the rule of propertied classes; all that it did was to substitute the rule of bourgeois for that of aristocratic property owners. Therefore, the revolution must go on until property is abolished altogether. Then, and only then, will mankind enjoy equality.

But the "satanic" institution of property, in origin vicious and antisocial, could be made into a powerful instrument with which to establish a free and equal social order "by changing this angel of darkness into an angel of light."[13] How? By substituting *possession populaire* for *propriété aristocratique.* Under the property system, a man received an unearned income *sans main mettre,* because of his ownership of a wealth-producing estate or business. An unearned income, according to Proudhon, was the essence of privilege. Under a system of "possession" a man would earn his livelihood by actual labor on his farm or in

[12] Proudhon, *Théorie de la propriété* (Paris, 1866), 169.
[13] *Ibid.,* 208–210.

his shop; he would, therefore, be entitled to what he produced because it had been the product of his own labor.[14] To labor, then, should go the full product of its exertions. By establishing a widespread system of peasant proprietorship the French Revolution, in the view of Proudhon, had taken a great step toward the abolition of the system of property and toward the establishment of a system of "possession." Furthermore, by recognizing the *absolute right* of property and by abolishing the feudal notion of the trusteeship of property, the French Revolution had made property, *i.e.,* "possession," a great force for equality. "Possession" was the private ownership of the instruments of production without the unearned property income received by the functionless *rentier.* By abolishing the abuses that had grown up around property, the essentials of the system of property rights would be maintained more firmly, more clearly, and more strongly.[15]

It is plain that in his distinction between "property" and "possession" Proudhon aimed to justify property rights by universalizing property. It is also plain that he was strongly opposed to capitalism, with its factories, banks, stock exchanges, and great enterprises that demanded large investments of capital. Not even Marx was more bitter in his diatribes against capitalism than was Proudhon. He denounced capitalism as a *féodalité industrielle,* which brought chaos and disorder into the economic life of the world. By its perversion of the principle of the division of labor, capitalism made the worker more productive and more dependent at the same time. As a consequence, all the advantages under the new industrial system went to capital, not to labor.[16] Capitalism, asserted Proudhon, defended itself in the name of private property, the ideal of which it perverted and confiscated from a creation of freedom to a temptation to egosim and love of money. Furthermore, capitalism concentrated its great benefits in the hands of the privileged few. Through the doctrine of *laissez faire,* the capitalistic classical economists perverted the ideal of liberty by making it an end in itself, instead of a means of establishing a just economic system. Capitalism,

---

[14] *Ibid.,. 15ff.*

[15] The best analysis of Proudhon's view of property is to be found in A. Berthod, *P. J. Proudhon et la propriété* (Paris, 1910).

[16] *General Idea of the Revolution in the Nineteenth Century,* trans. from the French by J. B. Robinson (London, 1923), 48.

according to Proudhon, had some justification when it first appeared, because it had stimulated private enterprise. But its historical role was now over, as capitalists had become timid and conservative. The time was ripe for an economic revolution that would be in historical sequence to the religious, the philosophical, and the political revolutions of the past. This revolution would overthrow the system of property, with its injustices and its inequalities, and establish the egalitarian system of "possession."[17]

As Proudhon lived in France, the land of revolutionary traditions, and during the revolutionary period of 1848, it is important to understand clearly how he proposed to bring about what he considered the greatest of all revolutions in history. It cannot be asserted too emphatically that Proudhon was an uncompromising opponent of all popular uprisings to establish the new order of economic equality, which he had so much at heart. "I desire a peaceful revolution," he declared, "but I desire it at once and I desire it to be decisive and complete. I want to see the present system of oppression and of misery succeeded by a system based on general well-being and liberty. I want to see the present system of political control superseded by one based on the organization of economic forces. . . . Finally, in order to realize my hopes, I desire that the new order . . . should be a spontaneous, natural and necessary development from the old one."[18] Over and over again in the writings of Proudhon the term "revolution" is used to connote a peaceful, though rapid, establishment of a new social order. He strongly opposed the revolutionary activities of the socialists, whom he ridiculed and denounced in unmeasured terms. There was no greater crime, in the opinion of Proudhon, than to incite class war at any and at all times.[19] Violent language, habitual with Proudhon, was, in a sense, used by him as a substitute for violent action, to conceal the realities of his own program.

How was the peaceful revolution to take place whereby "the present system of oppression and of misery" would give way to a "system

[17] See C. Bouglé, *La Sociologie de Proudhon* (Paris, 1911).

[18] *Idée générale de la révolution au XIXᵉ siècle* (Paris, 1923), 240. In a letter to Marx, Proudhon repudiated violent methods as no longer necessary to accomplish social changes. See *Les Confessions d'un révolutionnaire* (Paris, 1929), 435.

[19] *Correspondance*, II, 200, 296; VI, 381.

based on general well-being and liberty?" Proudhon's answer was surprisingly definite. It was to be by means of a change in the financial system that would give free credit to anyone who asked for it. To grasp the significance of Proudhon's solution, it is essential to keep in mind that his anticapitalism was not the same as that of the socialists, Utopian or Marxian. The socialists directed their attacks on the capitalistic system of production; hence they sought to substitute socialization for private ownership—the Utopians, through cooperative societies, and the Marxians, through government ownership. To abolish competition would, Proudhon insisted, destroy the vital force that animated all society.[20] Not the system of production, but the system of exchange was the root evil of capitalism. And the capitalist mechanism of exchange was maintained by the financial organizations that functioned through the gold standard, the Bank of France, and the stock exchange.

Proudhon's anticapitalism took the unexpected form of hostility to finance. The term "capitalist" was to him synonymous with "financier," a man who performed no necessary function in economic life. He was a *rentier*, who lived without working by owning stocks and bonds, or a stock manipulator and banker, who juggled into his own pockets the wealth created by others. Finance was the quintessence of privileged, monopolistic capitalism, because it held the strategic position in the economic life of the people. In his book *Manuel du spéculateur à la bourse* Proudhon singled out the stock exchange as capitalism at its peak and at its worst. Of all monopolies, the most evil was that of finance, because it controlled the flow of the life blood of the entire economic system, namely, credit. The bank rate was established by the Bank of France, a legal monopoly created by the government. Money itself was a monopoly of the government or of a group of bankers designated by the government. And the value of money was fixed by the gold standard, which roused Proudhon to eloquent fury. "Gold is the talisman that congeals the force of life in society," he declared, "that restricts the circulation of goods, that destroys labor and credit, and that organizes all mankind into a system of mutual slavery."[21] It was the close and vital connection of finance with industry and with land that enabled the capitalist to exact profit and the landlord to exact rent.

20 *Système des contradictions économiques* (Paris, 1923), I, 249.
21 *Organisation du crédit*, in *Oeuvres complètes*, VI, 112.

The entire system of capitalist exploitation, established through this connection, would topple over through what Proudhon called a *révolution par le crédit*. Once the "leprosy of interest" was abolished and the "reign of gold" was over, the entire property system would collapse.

This revolution, the greatest in history, was to be accomplished by the establishment of free credit, *crédit gratuit*.[22] A "People's Bank" (*banque du peuple*) was to be established, to take the place of the Bank of France. Unlike the latter, the former was to have no capital, no stockholders, no gold reserve. It was neither to pay nor to charge interest, except a nominal charge to cover overhead. All business transactions in the nation were to be centralized in the People's Bank, which was to be a bank of exchange and a market for all the products of the nation. It was to issue notes based neither on specie nor on land but on goods or on actual business values. The producer or seller would consign his product to the bank and receive in return not money but exchange notes, the amount of which would be based on the value of the goods consigned, as determined by the amount of labor that produced them. The seller would use these notes to purchase whatever he needed. The goods would then be sold by the bank to buyers, who would give to the bank the same amount, in notes, as that paid to the sellers. No profit would result from either transaction. The chief function of the bank would be to universalize the bill of exchange by facilitating the exchange of goods between producers and consumers through exchange notes, instead of money.[23] Every commodity would become a medium of exchange, *i.e.*, "money." No risk would be run by the bank, as its notes would be based on real, not on speculative, values; and the amount issued would be regulated by the demands of business. By these methods the People's Bank would bring an end to the "reign of gold" under which mankind had suffered for so long.

The dominating virtue of this scheme, according to Proudhon, was free credit in the form of exchange notes, universally accepted. Credit

---

[22] References to this scheme are to be found in most of Proudhon's writings. The best exposition is contained in his *Organisation du crédit* and in his *Résumée de la question sociale*. See also *Proudhon's Solution of the Social Problem* (H. Cohen, ed., New York, 1927).

[23] *Organisation du Crédit*, 115.

was to be made accessible to all. Every producer would be able to get credit without paying interest charges, which would encourage many to engage in business enterprise. Artisans and small businessmen would not struggle under the burden of debt, once they could get free credit. Interest had a deterring effect on production, argued Proudhon, in that it was a premium paid to the financier before he would permit the use of his money for productive purposes. With free credit, a new economic order would arise, more free, more enterprising, more productive than capitalism. A profitless system of free enterprise, producing goods for use and not for profit, would result in low prices, thereby stimulating production. What better inducement could there be to secure an independent livelihood than by starting a business enterprise![24]

The new system of finance, according to Proudhon, would bring about revolutionary changes in the economic system and in the social order. The Proudhonian *révolution par le crédit* would result in the abolition of the property system established by capitalism and in the inauguration of the long-dreamed-of classless society. Capitalism would not be able to compete with a free-credit economy that functioned without profit and without interest. With capitalism would go the nonlaboring, nonfunctioning *rentier,* who amassed wealth through ownership, not through toil. Private enterprise would remain, and competition would continue to regulate market prices. What better protection could property have than an easy way to acquire it and no possible way of losing it? Exploitation of the laborers would be impossible under the free-credit system, as the door would be open to anyone to become a small worker-owner. This greatest of all revolutions in history would be effected, according to Proudhon, "without confiscation, without bankruptcy, without an agrarian law, without common ownership, without state intervention, and without the abolition of inheritance."[25]

The social order under free credit, according to Proudhon, would be the first classless society in history. It would arise not as a result of the

[24] Proudhon's ideas concerning money and credit, ridiculed in his day, have turned up in later times and in unexpected places. See Introdution in Silvio Gesell, *The National Economic Order* (San Antonio, Texas, 1934), and Dudley Dillard, "Keynes and Proudhon," *The Journal of Economic History*, May, 1942.

[25] Speech of Proudhon to the National Assembly, July 31, 1848, *Compte rendu des séances de l'Assemblée Nationale* (Paris, 1849), II, 772.

overthrow of the capitalists by a revolutionary proletariat but as a result of the elimination of the former through competition and of the rise of the latter into the middle class, which Proudhon called *la classe moyenne,* in contrast to the capitalists, which he called *la bourgeoisie.* The former, in his opinion, was the vital element in the nation—the element that "creates value, that produces, that exchanges, in a word that performs the functions of society, and truly represents the nation."[26]

Proudhon's deep concern for the interests of *la classe moyenne* led him to take a view of the class struggle that was different from that of the socialists. Unlike the latter, who regarded the class struggle as one between capitalists and workingmen, he saw it as one between *la bourgeoisie* and *la classe moyenne.* Bitter and unrestrained were Proudhon's invectives against the former, who, under the July Monarchy, had established "an ignoble feudalism, based on mercantile and industrial usury." Bourgeois hegemony had brought evils that were neither fewer nor less onerous than those of the old feudalism before 1789. The greatest danger to the nation lay in the triumph of *la féodalité industrielle,* aided by the privileges and concessions granted to it by the government. It would result in the mass expropriation of small property, in the concentration of capital, in the destruction of individuality, and in the elimination of freedom of enterprise for the benefit of a handful of insatiably greedy speculators.[27] The great bulwark against this danger was *la classe moyenne.* It was this class that was waging a war for its very existence on two fronts: against the competition of consolidated capitalism on one side, and against the demands of organized labor on the other side. Whatever movement, whatever ideology visualized the class struggle as that between capitalists and workingmen roused the strenuous opposition of Proudhon. The workingmen, he argued, were too poor, too ignorant, and too much inclined toward authoritarianism to lead a revolutionary movement. Moreover, the historic revolutionary class in France was the middle class, not the working class; it was the former that had overthrown the feudal aristocracy during the French Revolution and had created the class of

---

[26] *La Révolution sociale démontrée par le coup d'état du Deux Décembre* (Paris, 1936), 205.

[27] *Manuel du spéculateur à la bourse* (Paris, 1857), 451.

numerous small proprietors. Proudhon appealed to the *petite bour-geoisie* and to the workingmen to unite against *la féodalité industrielle,* on the ground that their common interests were fundamental, whereas their differences were superficial. The small employers were more likely to be sympathetic with their employees than were the impersonal administrators of large corporations, blind to human sentiment and to human needs.[28]

It is now clearly evident that the classless society of Proudhon's vision was entirely different from that of the socialists. Instead of the trium-phant proletariat of the socialists, it would be the triumphant middle class that would usher in the new order of economic equality. Proud-hon's ideal social unit was "the peasant family with its rigid customs and its individualistic outlook whose property, based on possession, had an absolute and sacred character."[29] His method of bringing the class-less society into existence was also strikingly different from that of the socialists of his time. It was the socialization of finance through the peaceful *révolution par le crédit,* in contrast to the socialist method of the socialization of the means of production and exchange by class war and the dictatorship of the proletariat. The proposal to renounce the principle of class war and to hold up the middle class as the hope of mankind roused all the furies in Marx, who had confidently con-demned this class to utter extinction, to be ground out of existence by the upper and nether millstones of capital and labor. Nothing appeared more preposterous to Marx than the notion that the revolution of the future would be in the interest of the middle class. He poured a stream of ridicule on Proudhon as a philosopher who "wished to soar as a man of science above the *bourgeoisie* and the proletarians; he is only the petty bourgeois, tossed about constantly between capital and labor between political economy and communism."[30]

All working-class movements of the day, such as trade-unionism, manhood suffrage, and socialism, encountered the uncompromising hostility of Proudhon. There was a menacing tone of bitterness in his

[28] *Manuel du spéculateur,* 466ff.; *Idée générale de la révolution,* 93–96.

[29] G. Pirou, "Proudhonisme et Marxisme," *La Revue du mois,* XX (1919), 238.

[30] Karl Marx, *The Poverty of Philosophy,* trans. from the German by Harry Quelch (London, 1900), 166.

vitriolic denunciation of these movements, not present in his attacks on capitalism. In his view, the aspirations of the workingmen were a diversion from the real issue in France and a perversion of his vision of a classless society. He denounced trade-unionism as a subversive movement directed against the public interest. Collective bargaining and the right to strike, argued Proudhon, would result in creating a labor monopoly. Competition, the only protection against monopoly and the only guarantee of economic freedom, would be destroyed by the trade-unions. The right to strike, asserted Proudhon, was a sinister power wielded by the workers that acted as a stimulus to their egoistic demand to rule the nation. It legalized class warfare, to which he was unalterably opposed. Moreover, he argued, trade-unionism brought no benefits to the workers. If, through collective bargaining, they won an increase in wages, up went the cost of living; and this left them in the same, or even in a worse, position. In the struggle between organized workers and their employers, the former were no match for the latter, who, having superior economic power, could break a strike by hiring strike breakers. Failing this, the employers had another resource, in that they could call upon the army to suppress a strike. Proudhon favored the reduction both of money wages and of prices, which, in the long run, would benefit both workers and employers. Low wages would lower the cost of production; and low prices would raise the volume of production, to satisfy the increased demand. The result would be more employment for the workers, whose real wages would suffer no diminution. He denounced the government for putting through the law of 1864 legalizing trade-unions; likewise did he denounce the opposition for not doing all in its power to prevent the passage of the law through parliament.[31] "The hostile attitude of Proudhon toward trade-unions during the years 1848-1849 . . . has done not a little to cause many to consider his doctrine as a fruitless, and even a retrograde attempt to preserve the independent craft industries, relics of medieval artisanry. . . . Proudhon always manifested his great preference for the middle class; artisans, small business men, and peasant proprietors, whom he considered the healthiest elements in the social body. . . . It is quite possible that in recommending his *révolution par*

[31] *De la capacité politique*, 372–400.

le crédit he hoped to furnish the middle class with a powerful means of defending itself" against capitalism.[32]

Proudhon's opposition to trade-unionism arose from his view of the class struggle as being that between the capitalists and middle class. What he persistently advocated was that the workers should unite with the middle class in the common war against the capitalists. The elimination of the latter from the economic life of France would result in the survival of that element in the nation which was closest to his heart, namely, the middle class. His scheme of free credit was expressly designed to ensure the economic health of this class and to guarantee its continued existence.[33] More, in the course of time it would eliminate the workers as a separate class by opening wide the opportunity for them to enter the middle class. In this manner class divisions in society would disappear altogether. The middle class would become the nation.

Even more violent than his attacks on trade-unionism were Proudhon's attacks on socialism and on socialists. By "socialism" he meant the Utopian socialism of Fourier and of Saint-Simon, and the radical social reforms advocated by Louis Blanc during the Second Republic. He ridiculed the Utopians for trying to transform *la rêverie religieuse* into *un avenir fantastique*.[34] Should they actually succeed in this attempt, the result would be a "pious and stupid uniformity." If the strong exploited the weak under the property system, the weak would exploit the strong under socialism.[35] Proudhon condemned socialism as a fantastic illusion, the value of which amounted to just nothing. All that the socialist movement would succeed in accomplishing would be to provoke a reaction far greater than any in the past. It would be suppressed by the power of the very state that it aimed to seize.[36]

Proudhon was equally hostile to the ambitious plans of social reform inaugurated by the Second Republic, such as the national workshops, the right to work, and the reduction of the hours of labor. He ridiculed these reforms as a *formation papyracée* that illustrated the incompetence

---

[32] A. Berthod, Introduction to *Idée générale de la révolution*, 36–37.

[33] See the keen observations of this aspect of Proudhon's ideas by Friedrich Engels in *Karl Marx, Friedrich Engels, Briefwechsel* (Berlin, 1929), 239–243.

[34] *Système des contradictions économiques*, in *Oeuvres complètes*, IV, 103.

[35] *What is Property?* trans. from the French by B. R. Tucker (Princeton, N. J., 1876), 259–261.

[36] *Les Confessions d'un révolutionnaire*, 325.

of revolutionary governments. In Proudhon's opinion, Louis Blanc, the leading protagonist of these reforms, was an absurd person, whose ideas and formulas poisoned the minds of the workers. Blanc, like all the contemporaries of Proudhon, was puzzled by the antilabor views of this bitter enemy of capitalism. Proudhon, Blanc declared, was "completely outside the movement of his century," and he would be admired by the reactionaries for initiating the attack on the socialists.[37]

Even more bitter and uncompromising than his opposition to socialism was Proudhon's opposition to democracy. His great power of invective almost exhausted itself in the denunciation of democracy, its ideals, its methods, and its organization. He unleashed a furious, almost obscene, assault on what he contemptuously called the "political poverties," namely, popular sovereignty, natural rights, constitutions, parliaments, manhood suffrage, and majority rule. In practice, according to Proudhon, democracy was "disguised aristocracy," because government was controlled by a few men, called "representatives," generally nonworkers, elected by the workers. It was the most unstable of governments, continually oscillating between the absurd and the impossible. Its consequences were "the strangling of the public conscience, the suicide of popular sovereignty, and the apostasy of the Revolution."[38] Manhood suffrage created the worst of all governments because it was "the idea of the state infinitely extended."[39] To be ruled by a popularly elected assembly was far worse than to be ruled by a dictator; the latter was responsible, but not so the former.[40] He, Proudhon, would under no circumstances devote any of his labor, of his time, or of his substance to defend such *enfantillage* as democratic government.[41] Rousseau, the father of the doctrine of popular sovereignty and the fountainhead of democracy, became a target for Proudhon's bitter attacks. There never lived another man, he declared, who so completely united as did Rousseau "pride of spirit, the lowest desires, and aridness of soul."[42] The social contract was a "pact of hatred," a

[37] Louis Blanc, *Questions d'aujourd'hui* (Paris, 1880), III, 162-163.
[38] Desjardins, *op. cit.*, II, 214*ff.*
[39] *Les Confessions d'un révolutionnaire*, 185.
[40] *Ibid.*, 221.
[41] *Idée générale de la révolution*, 214.
[42] *Ibid.*, 194.

"covenant of class war" against the disinherited proletariat in the interest of the propertied classes.[43] He poured withering scorn on Rousseau's disciples, the Jacobins, who, he asserted, were just like their enemies, the royalists, because, like the latter, they desired to use the state to dominate the people. Robespierre, the Jacobin chief, was an "empty-headed viperous denunciator," and a "cowardly rhetorician."[44] As a theory, popular sovereignty was just plain nonsense; and its application to government in the form of manhood suffrage was "worn out childishness"—at worst, counterrevolution. Manhood suffrage was political atheism in the worst sense of the word, as if a general idea could be created by adding whatever number of opinions. The complete absurdity of this doctrine was evident, in that the vote of an Arago or a Lamartine counted no more than that of a beggar.[45] Proudhon's contempt and hatred of democracy overflowed all decent bounds, and he descended to a degree of disgusting vilification reached only by the fascists of our day. "All this democracy disgusts me," he wrote. "It wishes to be scratched where vermin causes itching, but it does not at all wish to be combed or to be deloused. What would I not give to sail into this mob with my clenched fists!"[46]

An opponent of democracy, Proudhon also opposed its Siamese twin, liberal nationalism. He saw nothing bad in the partition of Poland and nothing good in the Polish national movement of his day. Poland, he declared, had been "at all times the most corrupt of aristocracies and most disorderly of states." He condemned the efforts of his fellow countrymen on behalf of the Polish patriots as useless and hopeless.[47] Proudhon was likewise opposed to the unification of Italy, which, he said, was advocated by those who wanted to use a united Italy against France, *la patrie, patrie française, patrie de la liberté.* He advised the Italian patriots "to preach resignation to their followers and to get out, as quickly as possible, of the misleading road into which they had strayed."[48]

[43] *Ibid.*, 191.

[44] *Ibid*, 233.

[45] For Proudhon's views on democracy, see P. Bourgeau, *P. J. Proudhon et la critique de la démocratie* (Strasbourg, 1933), 41–42.

[46] *Correspondance,* XI, 197.

[47] *Ibid.*, 23; L. Abensour, "P. J. Proudhon et la Pologne," *La Grande revue,* CIII (1920).

[48] *Correspondance,* XII, 54; *La Fédération et l'unité en Italie* (Paris, 1862), 8.

Proudhon's opposition to democracy arose from his contempt for the common man. The great mass of people, in his opinion, consisted of puffed-up bourgeois, miserable peasants, and stupid proletarians. He loved to embroider this theme with many verbal designs. The bourgeois were "greedy, cowardly, as much without generosity as without principles," and they stole through speculation because they hated to work for a living. The peasant never felt the "beat of national honor in his heart. He believes that tyranny is good provided it keeps down the city folks. Instinctively he hates science, philosophy, art, and industry . . . and is ever ready to respond to the appeals of the clericals to fight against liberty." All that the worker desired was better wages, fewer hours of work, low cost of living, and high taxes for the rich. He had no vision of a new and better social order. "Corrupt, envious, and slanderous the worker mistakes hatred of employers for patriotism. He gets his greatest pleasure in witnessing the massacre of those who champion his cause." His contempt for his fellow worker, his hatred for his employer, his love of pomp and show "always drive him to the side of authority."[49]

All true progress, according to Proudhon, was accomplished, not directly by the masses, but by *des esprits d'élite* who, openly or secretly, drove them in the right direction.[50] The masses were predisposed to autocratic rule, not to self-government. They needed a ruler as they needed a God. "For me," Proudhon declared, "it is an economic truism that the class which is the most numerous and the most poor is by that very fact the most envious, the most immoral, and the most cowardly."[51] Humanity does not consist of the mass of brutalized "bipeds" but of the small group of elite, which had always been the ferment in history. He questioned whether humanity ever consisted of more than ten thousand persons.[52]

Proudhon's diatribes against democracy arose from his repudiation of what he called "political" government, whether absolute monarchy, constitutional monarchy, or democratic republic. Authority and subordination, so destructive of human individuality and personal freedom,

---

[49] *Correspondance*, V, 138–139; *Manuel du spéculateur à la bourse*, in *Oeuvres complètes*, XI, 404.

[50] *Correspondance*, V, 57–58.

[51] *Ibid.*, IV, 267.

[52] *Ibid.*, 154–155.

were the fundamental principles of every state, "the unpaid prostitute of knaves, monks, and old soldiers."[53] The state, under whatever form, was a conservative force; it could not, therefore, ameliorate social conditions just because it was the state. If anything, democracy was worse than other forms of government because, depending on political methods, it never came to grips with economic problems. The great illusion of the Jacobins of 1789, as of the socialists of 1848, according to Proudhon, was their conviction that political equality could solve the problem of economic inequality. All true revolutionists must abandon forever *la constitution politique* and become the protagonists of *la constitution sociale*.[54] The great problems since the French Revolution —an "unfinished" revolution—have been economic, not political. The most important of them concerned the abolition of property rights; this greatest of all reforms could come only with the abolition of the state. Proudhon went so far as openly to avow himself an anarchist and to praise anarchy as the condition of a mature society.[55]

What was "economic" government, which, according to Proudhon, was to supplant the "political" government that he condemned so loudly, so persistently, and so profusely? He devoted a volume, *Du Principe fédératif,* to the explanation of the scheme; and references to it are to be found scattered throughout Proudhon's writings. Nevertheless, it is difficult, very difficult, to get a clear idea of the scheme of economic government that Proudhon called "mutualism." Generalizations, keen and brilliant, there are plenty, but nowhere a ground plan. Under mutualism there would be organized, in each industry, voluntary autonomous associations of producers for specified and limited purposes. These associations were to function with the object of exchanging, not producing, commodities. Production was to be individual, not collective. Proudhon was an anticollectivist; hence, he was opposed to the all-absorbing "association" advocated by the Utopian socialists. Each "mutualist" association would specialize in a product; and the exchange of products would be made through the agency of the People's Bank, the exchange notes of which would be honored by all members of every association. Under capitalism, argued Proudhon, producers and

[53] *Idée générale de la révolution,* 344.
[54] *Ibid.,* 126–127, 143; *Confessions d'un révolutionnaire,* 217.
[55] *Mélanges* in *Oeuvres complètes,* XIX, 9; *Idée générale de la révolution,* 199.

consumers were brought together through the intermediary of monopolistic banks that charged high rates of interest; but under mutualism, they would be brought together more easily and more freely by the system of free credit, established by the People's Bank. All existing economic organizations, whether those of capital or of labor, were to be dissolved in favor of the mutualistic associations. Relations between individuals and associations would be based on voluntary contracts, not on coercive laws.[56] Competition between the voluntary, autonomous, economic associations under mutualism would function in a healthy manner; whereas, under capitalism, competition between individuals was destructive and chaotic. In these ways, mutualism would prove superior to the individualism of the capitalists and to the collectivism of the socialists.

There was to be a political aspect to mutualism, namely, federalism. The various associations would form a hierarchy of federations, at the top of which would be two national federations, one of producers and another of consumers. Supreme authority would be vested in a council chosen by the various associations, with power to regulate their common affairs, such as transportation, credit, insurance, defense, security, etc. The federations of economic associations would displace all existing political organizations, whether local or national. Instead of the centralized, sovereign state, exercising coercive power over the people, France would become a "cluster of sovereignties," one guaranteeing the other. The sterile "citizen" would give way to the creative "producer," and the economic despotism exercised by the *féodalité financière et industrielle* would give way to the free, autonomous *fédération agricole-industrielle*.

Economic mutualism with its political counterpart of federalism would inaugurate what Proudhon called the *troisième monde*. This would be the first truly classless society in history—a society that was destined to succeed capitalism as the latter had succeeded feudalism. *Le troisième monde* would arise from the soil of capitalism without class conflicts, through a *révolution par le crédit*. Although arising from capitalism, it will have none of the capitalistic evils, like the "lily, which repudiates the onion from which it stems."[57] For an

---

[56] *Idée générale de la révolution*, 301–302.
[57] *La Guerre et la paix* (Paris, 1927), 191.

understanding of the significance of the type of decentralization advocated by Proudhon, it must be related to the situation in France during the reign of Louis Philippe. Who were now the masters of the centralized governmental machine, constructed by the French Revolution and Napoleon? The great capitalists, who manipulated it in the interests of the owners of "property," so bitterly hated by Proudhon. How, then, could the control of the government be shifted to the "possessors," namely, the great mass of petty bourgeois? By a system of decentralization that was economic, not geographic. That was the "anarchy" of Proudhon in his schemes of mutualism and federalism. The new order would maintain private enterprise, freedom of contract, competition, and private property. Unlike capitalism, it would not tolerate financial and industrial overlordships, with the attendant economic inequalities, class conflicts, and political tyrannies. All classes would fuse into one, *la classe moyenne,* and the great dream of a society of equals would at last be realized.

The unique aspect of Proudhon's blurred blueprint of *le troisième monde* was his outlawing of government from the social order. It caught the attention of those revolutionists in France who, in the four short years from 1848 to 1852, had seen rapid and violent changes of government. When the Second Empire gave evidence of its ability to maintain itself against all opposition, whether royalist, republican, or socialist, certain elements among the revolutionists became convinced that stable government was synonymous with despotism. On the sudden collapse of the seemingly all-powerful Empire at Sedan, these revolutionists saw their opportunity of destroying despotism forever by abolishing government altogether. The voice of Proudhon rang loudly in the ears of the revolutionists of the Paris Commune, who aimed to destroy the central government of France and to establish in its place a federation of autonomous communes.[58]

However, nothing would have astounded and infuriated Proudhon more than being hailed as the inspirer of a bloody uprising by the revolutionary proletariat. This contemner of all government, this "anarchist" hailed the dictatorial Second Empire as the long-promised,

[58] Concerning the influence of Proudhon's ideas on the Paris Commune see Bourgin, *Proudhon,* 81*ff.;* D. W. Brogan, *Proudhon* (London, 1934), 85; and E. S. Mason, *The Paris Commune* (New York, 1930) 42*ff.,* 190, 211, 250, 302.

passionately hoped for, historical event that would usher in *le troisième monde*. After the *coup d'état* of December 2, Proudhon addressed Louis Napoleon in the following manner: "You are the revolution of the nineteenth century; you can not be anything else. Apart from this, Deux Décembre would be only an historic accident without principle and without significance."[59] The true object of Deux Décembre, according to Proudhon, was to inaugurate the social revolution that had proved too great a task for every government in France since the First Empire. There was only one possible program for Louis Napoleon to follow, and that was a revolutionary one.[60] In the light of his great mission, the suppression of the socialists during the "June Days" and the overthrow of the Second Republic were not reactionary acts. On the contrary, they prepared the way for the advent of the true revolution of which Louis Napoleon was the leader.[61] "Let him proclaim frankly and loudly that the reason for Deux Décembre was social revolution."[62]

Proudhon offered to collaborate with Louis Napoleon and to guide him in the new revolutionary course "for the glory of the country, for the well-being of the masses, and for the progress of mankind."[63] He counseled the republicans and the socialists to rally to the banner of Louis Napoleon, the champion of the masses, despite the fact that he was regarded by the reactionaries as an agent of counterrevolution.[64] By supporting Louis Napoleon, republicans and socialists would become the leaders and moderators of the true revolution demanded by the proletariat, who desired not political slogans but economic renovation.[65]

Forcefully and repeatedly Proudhon drove home the idea that a social revolution could be accomplished only through the dictatorship of one man. Because of party divisions, the revolution, so necessary to France, could not come from the deliberations of a popular assembly but from the dictatorship of one man, supported by the people.[66] The Revolution of 1848, Proudhon asserted, exposed the incompetence of

[59] *La Révolution sociale*, 108.
[60] *Correspondance*, IV, 281.
[61] *La Révolution sociale*, 177.
[62] *Ibid.*, 269.
[63] *Correspondance*, V, 154.
[64] *La Révolution sociale*, 284*ff.*
[65] *Idée générale de la révolution*, 121.
[66] *La Révolution sociale*, 215.

the babblers and visionaries, and its suppression by the *coup d'état* cleared the way for the efficient, practical revolution of Louis Napoleon. He, not the socialist, was the true revolutionist. Did he not question all institutions: property, interest, income, privilege, constitution, dynasty, church, army, school? Not by theories but by acts did Louis Napoleon show how fragile was the social structure and how weak were the principles that supported it.[67] The "anarchist" Proudhon, who so hated political government that he voted against the adoption of the democratic constitution of the Second Republic, now welcomed the constitution of the Second Empire, which established the dictatorship of Louis Napoleon.

Like every other French thinker during the nineteenth century, Proudhon was keenly aware of the problem of the two Frances, between which yawned the chasm of the French Revolution. His solution of the problem was the establishment of one party, based on *la classe moyenne.* He poured scorn, wrathful, withering, and inexhaustible, on the many political parties during the Second Republic. Was this the product of the united, centralized France of which everyone was so proud? Napoleon had sought to unite France by means of the poetry of war, but Louis Napoleon would improve on this by using the "prose of economics." How? Proudhon's answer had a sinister significance. It was possible and desirable, he argued, that one party should swallow all the other parties. This party must represent the interests of *la classe moyenne* and those of the proletariat, fused into one national interest. Deux Décembre alone could do it, because it represented social revolution. To Louis Napoleon had now come the opportunity to take this great step, which would unite the two Frances.[68]

Who were the powerful and intractable enemies of Louis Napoleon? Not the republicans or socialists, who had been eliminated from the political scene. They were, according to Proudhon, the capitalists and the Catholics, who would exert every effort to ruin his great mission as *mandataire de la révolution.* What the capitalists desired of Louis Napoleon was to use him as their tool: first, to suppress the socialists, and second, to advance their class interests.[69] Especially must he be-

[67] *Ibid.,* 219.
[68] *Ibid.,* 268–269.
[69] *Ibid.,* 177.

ware of the international financiers, who would ruin him as they had ruined Napoleon I. It was the stock exchange, asserted Proudhon, that had triumphed at Waterloo; the financiers had stabbed the great Emperor in the back by encouraging his enemies. The quotations on the stock exchange had followed the great captain in his marches and countermarches, "in order to condemn him in case of victory, and to overwhelm him in the case of defeat."[70]

The Catholics, likewise, were the deadly enemies of Louis Napoleon. To them he represented "revolutionary impiety," because he espoused the emancipation of the proletariat, the equality of classes, free labor, and free thought. "Let Deux Décembre organize and proclaim anti-Christianity as its life principle, which means antitheology, anticapitalism, antifeudalism. *Tel est son mandat, telle est sa force.*"[71] Its great mission was to emancipate the masses, to transform befuddled believers into rational beings, to create a superior race, and finally to revolutionize, first Europe, and then all the world.[72]

Outside France the greatest enemy of the revolutionary dictatorship of Louis Napoleon was England, the very heart of capitalism and the representative of *la féodalité capitaliste* in the modern world. Economic weapons would prove effective in conquering England, the same weapons that she herself had used in conquering other lands. By establishing her economy on a free-credit basis, France would have an economic system superior to that of capitalist England. She would then be able to drive the latter from the markets of the world by the force of competition. Her world trade ruined, England would go the way of Carthage.[73]

Proudhon was doomed to suffer great disappointment in his ardent hopes of Deux Décembre. In an interview with Louis Napoleon in 1848, he had proposed to the latter his scheme for free credit to inaugurate peacefully the great social revolution. After Louis Napoleon became Emperor, Proudhon insistently urged him to adopt his scheme, in order to fulfill the great revolutionary promise of Deux Décembre. But the Emperor paid no heed whatever to Proudhon's exaltation of

[70] *Manuel du spéculateur à la bourse*, 27–28.
[71] *La Révolution sociale*, 191.
[72] *Ibid.*, 192.
[73] *Ibid.*, 278–279.

him as the greatest revolutionist of all times, or to his scheme of
révolution par le crédit. Chagrined at his failure to convert Louis
Napoleon, Proudhon became very hostile to the Second Empire. Had
the Emperor betrayed the social revolution? Had he, instead, supported
the industrial revolution of the capitalists and the bankers? Proudhon's
passionate resentment of what he considered a betrayal of the greatest
mission in history led him to conclude bitterly, yet correctly, that the
Second Empire was a bourgeois government with a romantic
Napoleonic façade.[74] The great advance of industry and finance that
was taking place with the active encouragement of the government
was, in Proudhon's view, a retrograde movement to exploit the French
people. What was the government doing for the masses and for his
favorite class, *la classe moyenne?* Nothing, he replied. As the Second
Empire became more liberal in its political and more capitalistic in
its economic policies, Proudhon became more bitter in his hostility to
Louis Napoleon. "After handing over our souls to the Jesuits," he
complained, "the Emperor hands over our patrimony to the Jews."[75]
Public opinion under the Second Empire, Proudhon asserted, was
dominated by Jews, Saint-Simonians, liberals, Jesuits, and bohemians.
Especially influential were the Jews, "who dominated the press and
controlled the government."[76]

More than once was the note of anti-Semitism sounded by Proudhon.
During the supreme hour of European liberalism, the Revolution
of 1848, he had denounced the Jews as the bulwark of *la féodalité
capitaliste,* hence the enemies of the people at all times. "The Jews,
again the Jews, always the Jews!" he exclaimed. "Under the Republic,
as under Louis Philippe, and as under Louis XIV we have always
been at the mercy of the Jews."[77] Proudhon identified capitalists
with bankers, and the latter with Jews, and he regarded all three as
an unholy trinity indissolubly united in exploiting *la classe moyenne*
and in defending reaction in France. "One group of counterrevolution-
ists," he declared, "consists of the moneyed elements, industrialists,
merchants, and bankers, who are responsible for all the tyrannies per-

[74] *Ibid.,* 82; *Correspondance,* V, 55.
[75] *Correspondance,* V, 242.
[76] *Ibid.,* XI, 354; XII, 65.
[77] *Mélanges* in *Oeuvres complètes,* XIX, 31.

petrated by reaction. These elements recognize the Jews as their leaders."[78] Do you believe, he asks, in putting up tariff barriers to protect
home industry? If you do, you have the same ideas concerning trade
and currency as do Fould and Rothschild. "Then you are not at all
an apostle of human brotherhood; you are a Jew."[79] Proudhon had
the tendency, inevitable in the anti-Semite, to see in the Jews the
prime source of the nation's misfortunes, and to associate them with
persons and groups that he hated. Whenever he drew up a catalogue
of anathemas he nearly always included the Jews. He denounced
Jews along with "Saint-Simonians, pimps, brutal drunkards, and
contemptible pedants."[80]

Anti-Semitism, always and everywhere the acid test of racialism,
with its division of mankind into creative and sterile races, led Proudhon to regard the Negro as the lowest in the racial hierarchy. During
the American Civil War he favored the South, which, he insisted,
was not entirely wrong in maintaining slavery. The Negroes,
according to Proudhon, were an inferior race, an example of the
existence of inequality among the races of mankind. Not those who
desired to emancipate them were the true friends of the Negroes
but those "who wish to keep them in servitude, yea to exploit them,
but nevertheless to assure them of a livelihood, to raise their standard
gradually through labor, and to increase their numbers through
marriage."[81]

What astounded Proudhon's contemporaries even more than his
support of the dictatorship of Louis Napoleon or his anti-Semitic
outbursts or his defense of Negro slavery was his glorification of
war. Hatred of war and longing for universal peace has been an
almost universal characteristic of all modern revolutionary thinkers—
the *philosophes* in the eighteenth, the democrats in the nineteenth,
and the socialists in the twentieth century. The contradictions between
the revolutionist Proudhon and the revolutionary thought of his
day became even more puzzling, even more strange, when Proudhon
appeared as a glorifier of war for its own sake. His book *La Guerre*

[78] *Résumé de la question sociale*, 36.
[79] *Mélanges*, in *Oeuvres complètes*, XIX, 19.
[80] *Correspondance*, XII, 55.
[81] *La Guerre et la paix*, 179.

et la paix, which appeared in 1861, was a hymn to war, intoned in a more passionate key than anything produced by the fascists of our time. "This book," remarks Henri Moysset, editor of the volume, "arises from the very well-spring of Proudhonism; ordered and fully completed by the pressure of events, it is truly the product of the intellectual soil and moral climate in which the spirit of Proudhon grew and matured."[82]

"Hail to war!" exclaimed Proudhon. "It is only through war that man was able to rise from the lowest depths to his present dignity and worth. Over the body of a fallen foe he had the first vision of glory and immortality. . . . Death is the crowning of life, and how can an intelligent, free, moral creature like man end his life more nobly than on the battlefield?"[83] War, in its very nature, was divine, being the revelation of religion, of justice, and of the ideal in human relations. Man was "above all else a warrior animal. . . . It is through war that his sublime nature becomes manifest. It is war alone that makes heroes and demigods."[84]

In the view of Proudhon, war was inherent in the very nature of man and was itself the prime source of human progress. From force arose the entire system of rights, political, social, and economic; therefore war would last as long as man existed and as long as moral and social values prevailed in human society.[85] Universal and perpetual peace would mean the end of all progress. What would become of literature, of poetry, and of art if what was inconceivable actually happened, namely, the abolition of war? What would become of justice, of freedom? Of the independent, free, autonomous nations? Everything would degenerate in a world at peace, and life would become a *siesta éternelle.* As war was the beneficent, though terrible, cause of human progress, its very origin was divine. The conscience that produced religion and justice also produced war. The fervor and enthusiasm that inspired lawgivers and prophets also inspired the warrior heroes.[86] War was the only possible method of establishing

[82] *Ibid.,* Introduction, lvi.
[83] *Ibid.,* 31.
[84] *Mélanges,* in *Oeuvres complètes,* XIX, 65.
[85] *La Guerre et la paix,* 55 ff.
[86] *Ibid.,* 31, 72.

justice on earth. As every nation sincerely believed that its cause was just, war was the only way of settling disputes between nations. And the victor always represented the justice of mankind. The profoundest sentiment felt by the masses of mankind was that there were "mysterious bonds" that united might and right. Because of this sentiment a nation, no matter how low she fell, would never perish as long as she kept burning in her heart "the just and regenerating flame of the right to make war."[87]

After several hundred lyrical, almost hysterical, pages in praise of force as the supreme manifestation of spiritual power, Proudhon comes to the paradoxical conclusion that war is the original sin of organized mankind. Its primal cause is poverty, and only when poverty is abolished will war disappear. "Considered as the judgment of force," he writes, "war is sublime! It is the mean between justice, of which it is a manifestation, and religion, from which arises its poetry and enthusiasm. But considered in relation to its primal cause, poverty, war is soiled with every iniquity." Its evil practices belie its sublime inspiration. To reform the institution of war only just indemnities should be levied, pillage and marauding should be prohibited, and conquered territory should be annexed without violence.[88]

Almost always has the militarist been hostile to the emancipation of women. Not being warriors themselves, women could be the wives and mothers of warriors. Hence to relegate women to domestic duties was the best way of ensuring a strong, virile nation. Moreover, woman's subordination to man and her inferior status in government and in society was the militarist pattern of command and obedience applied to the very foundation of the social order, namely, the family. In Proudhon's day George Sand, in France, and John Stuart Mill, in England, sounded the beginnings of the movement to emancipate women by granting them equal rights with men. Women's rights encountered the furious opposition of Proudhon. "I regard as baneful and stupid," he declared, "all our dreams of emancipating woman. I deny her every political right and every initiative. For woman liberty and well-being lie solely in marriage, in motherhood, in domestic duties, in the fidelity of her spouse, in chastity, and in seclu-

[87] *Ibid.*, 86, 91.
[88] *Ibid.*, 441; see also 426–437.

sion."[89] The emancipation of women, in the opinion of Proudhon, would sap the foundation of the family, the sanctity of which always roused his deepest emotions. He opposed inheritance taxes, because such levies weakened the family by transferring its property to the state.

Proudhon's attitude toward religion is likewise mystifying. Though bitterly anti-Catholic, he was not at all a materialistic atheist, as befitted a "father" of anarchy. On the contrary, Proudhon was fundamentally a religious man. His three-volume work *De la justice dans la révolution et dans l'église* is a diffuse discussion of abstract ideas concerning justice, truth, morals, in which religious overtones are distinctly heard.[90] In Proudhon's writings on religion, as in those on politics and economics, can be seen the spirits of anarchy and authority in juxtaposition to each other, each unaware of the other's presence.

What can be the explanation of this astonishing phenomenon of the "complete revolutionist's" being, at the same time, the complete militarist, the defender of slavery, the passionate hater of democracy and of socialism, and the bitter opponent of working-class movements and of the emancipation of women? The search for intellectual paternity sometimes leads to strange and disconcerting discoveries. Both by his disciples and by his detractors Proudhon has been exalted as the father of anarchosyndicalism. To assert that both groups are mistaken involves a drastic reevaluation of the ideas of this enigmatic thinker and of his significance in modern history.

According to authoritative syndicalist writers, notably Hubert Lagardelle, Proudhon was the inspirer of the anarchosyndicalist movement, which came prominently to the fore in France during the two decades before the First World War.[91] Proudhon's repudiation of both capitalism and socialism, his flouting of political government, and his scheme of free, autonomous economic groups became the fundamental theories of anarchosyndicalism. A resolution adopted by the great federation of French trade-unions, the *Confédération Générale du Travail,* was permeated with this Proudhonian doctrine. It de-

[89] *Correspondance,* IV, 377.

[90] See the interesting article by H. de Lubac, "Proudhon, religieux," *Cahiers du monde nouveau,* I (1945), and *Proudhon et le Christianisme* (Paris, 1945).

[91] Pirou, *Proudhonisme et syndicalisme révolutionnaire* (Paris, 1910), 5.

manded the establishment of a new social order "based not on authority but on exchange, not on domination but on reciprocity, not on sovereignty but on freedom of contract."[92]

It is true that Proudhon's vague ideas concerning the future "mutualist" society influenced the equally vague ideas of the syndicalists concerning the future organization of society. Concretely and definitely, however, syndicalism was a revolutionary labor movement that depended on trade-unions, general strikes, and class violence to bring about a social revolution. Proudhon was certainly not a champion of organized labor. Concretely and definitely he opposed trade-unions, strikes, and violent class conflicts.

There still persists the legend of the "anarchist" Proudhon. He did, it is true, repudiate the state and all political government whatsoever, which gave him the specious reputation of being the "father" of anarchy. In discussing the social and political issues of his day, Proudhon did not at all apply his anarchist views. They seemed to form no part of his vigorous attacks on the ideas of his opponents, whether on the left or on the right. His hatred of socialism, which Proudhon regarded as the worst of all social poisons, drove him to advocate anarchy as its very opposite. What he really saw in anarchy was not a solution of social problems but an antidote to socialism. It is important to note that the historically important contribution of Proudhon to social thought was not his repudiation of the state but his new version of the class struggle in Western Europe. As the champion of the cause of the middle class, in opposition both to capitalists and to workingmen, Proudhon's anarchism evaporates with furious abruptness. His advocacy of personal dictatorship and his laudation of militarism can hardly be equaled in the reactionary writings of his or of our day.

It is equally surprising that the royalists in France have claimed Proudhon as one of the "masters of counterrevolution." What especially attracted them to Proudhon was his vitriolic denunciation of Jacobinism and of socialism. In the office of the royalist journal, *Action française,* there hung on the wall a picture of the "complete revolutionist."[93] In his book *Les Maîtres de la contre-Révolution* the royalist writer, Louis Dimier, declared that Proudhon had a comprehensive

[92] See *Proudhon et notre temps* (C. Bouglé, ed.), 3.
[93] Bouglé, *La sociologie de Proudhon*, Introduction, viii.

philosophy of counterrevolution only in outline; in parts only was it fully completed.[94] Though Proudhon gave to himself and to his contemporaries the impression of being a revolutionist, in reality, asserted Dimier, his ideas had the essence of conservatism. Therefore, the "revolution" of Proudhon could be more correctly described as "reaction," especially in those of his writings that were most striking and most penetrating.[95] The well-known anti-Semite Edouard Drumont hailed Proudhon as one who had clear understanding, in his day, of the nature of masonic and cosmopolitan—*i.e.,* Jewish—conspiracies. By his sense of what was politically useful to France and "by his instinctive horror of cosmopolitanism, he was the first of the nationalists."[96] The Nestor of French royalism, Charles Maurras, praised Proudhon for his pitiless exposure of democracy and democrats and of liberalism and liberals. As a nationalist, he asserted, Proudhon wrote in the spirit of the ancient monarchy, which had done so much to advance the interest of France.[97]

However, Proudhon was not a reactionary, despite the claims of the royalists. Nothing in his writings or in his life indicates that he desired to reestablish the Old Regime in France or that he had any sympathy with the reactionary ideas of De Maistre and De Bonald. The royalists, like the syndicalists, mistook their man. Before the First World War, anyone in France who opposed democratic ideas, parliamentary government, trade-unions, or socialism was considered a counterrevolutionist. That may have been true of others, but not of Proudhon.

It was indeed an inharmonious age that produced Proudhon. The period in French history, 1830 to 1852, saw the revival of an old hope, that of fulfilling the democratic promise of the French Revolution, and the appearance of a new hope, that of creating a socialist commonwealth. Ideological conflicts had a great importance in France because of the tendency of radical ideas, in that land, to jump from the pages of a book into the melee of a barricade. Proudhon was a product of this revolutionary period, in that he was one of those who voiced

[94] Louis Dimier, *Les Maîtres de la contre-Révolution* (Paris, 1917), 282.
[95] *Ibid.,* 239, 241–251.
[96] "Le Centenaire de Proudhon," *La Grande revue,* LIII (1909), 140.
[97] Charles Maurras, *Dictionnaire politique et critique* (Paris, 1933), IV, 220*ff.*

its discontents. In this sense he was a minor revolutionary figure, much less important than his fellow revolutionists Louis Blanc, Blanqui, and Lamartine. Far more significant, however, was the fact that Proudhon was a prophet of future discontents, which gives him a greater position in history than that of his revolutionary contemporaries. The true significance of his writings can be seen only in the light of the political and social movement of our day known as "fascism." It would be a great error to regard fascism as a counterrevolutionary movement directed against the communists, as was that of the reactionaries against the liberals during the first half of the nineteenth century. Fascism is something unique in modern history, in that it is a *revolutionary* movement of the middle class directed, on the one hand, against the great banks and big business and, on the other hand, against the revolutionary demands of the working class. It repudiates democracy as a political system in which the bankers, capitalists, and socialists find free scope for their activities, and it favors a dictatorship that will eliminate these elements from the life of the nation. Fascism proclaims a body of doctrines that are not entirely new; there are no "revelations" in history. With what ideas in Europe's past could they be related? With what great thinkers could they be associated?

It is the thesis of the author that the great French polemicist, Proudhon, was a harbinger of fascist ideas. Otherwise, his views would be as bewildering to us as they were to his contemporaries. To them his writings had a revolutionary trend, but in an unfamiliar direction, and a violence of language that yet clothed an anxious conservatism. They baffled reactionaries, liberals, and socialists alike. Proudhon was a revolutionist, in that he repudiated established political and economic institutions and in that he proclaimed a new social order inspired by a new ideology. Yet his bent of mind was conservative. His intense devotion to the institution of the family, his never-failing championship of the interests of the middle class, and his advocacy of the inheritance of property reveal his essentially conservative outlook. At bottom therefore Proudhon was a conformist. But there was nothing in the France of his day to which he could conform, neither to the traditions of the aristocratic past, nor to the ideas of the bourgeois present, nor to the hopes of the socialist future. The mental configuration of Proudhon, with its strange contrasts,

produced an attitude toward social and political problems that is under-
standable only in the light of present discontents. His attacks on the
capitalist system were similar in manner, in direction, and in objective
to those made familiar today by fascist writings. He it was who first
sounded the fascist note of a *revolutionary* repudiation of democracy
and of socialism. These were the overtones of fascism, frequently heard
in Proudhon's writings.

Proudhon was the intellectual spokesman of the French middle
class, so numerous and yet so timorous. Like the fascists of our time,
and unlike the Marxists of any time, he realized that there was a
powerful class interest apart from capitalists and workingmen and
hostile to both. With the upswing of modern industry and with
the growth of socialism, the middle classes were in constant fear of
losing their little farms, their little shops, their little savings, either
through confiscation by the revolutionary proletariat or through competition of powerful capitalists who would grind them into poverty
or out of existence. Fear, especially, of socialist confiscation continued
in France all during the nineteenth century, and even later, down
to the Second World War. The taunt that Marx threw at Proudhon—
that he was a champion of the petty bourgeois, interested in the survival of this class—was true. But the contemptuous tone that Marx
used showed that he had no understanding of the power and revolutionary possibilities of the middle class. This error of Marx became
an article of faith to his disciples. The contemptuous disregard of
the middle class by the Marxist Social Democrats and Communists,
during the period between the two world wars, was to have fatal
consequences in the triumph of fascism, the revolutionary creed of
the middle class.

In stressing banking and Jewish bankers for his line of attack
against the established order, Proudhon betrayed an almost unerring
sign of fascist anticapitalism. That banking was predatory—not productive—capitalism, and that it characterized the economic activity
of the Jews were the emphatic appeals of the Nazis to the impoverished middle class in their crusade to abolish "interest slavery." "In
singling out predatory capital national socialism treads in the footsteps of Proudhon, who, in his *Idée générale de la révolution au
19e siècle* demanded the liquidation of the Banque de France and

its transformation into an institution of public utility."[98] In Proudhon's day, his scheme of free credit was regarded by revolutionists as a tiny and sickly mouse that had emerged from the enormous mountain of his devastating attacks on the capitalist system. In the light of fascism, it was an important and significant weapon with which to attack capitalism in the interest of the middle class.

Proudhon's hostility to labor, whether organized industrially in trade-unions or politically in socialist parties, had a fascist edge. The vehemence of his denunciation of working-class movements arose from his bitter hostility to labor *as a separate class interest.* During the middle of the nineteenth century most French workers were employed in small shops; hence class consciousness on their part was less a challenge to the capitalists than to *la classe moyenne,* whose interests Proudhon had so much at heart. He was indeed concerned with the welfare of the workers, but only when they were willing to merge their interests with those of the middle class in the war against capitalism.

It was again Proudhon who proclaimed the novel idea that a dictatorship, to be successful under modern conditions, must have a popular basis and a revolutionary social program. This conception of dictatorship became distinctively fascist. Proudhon's was the only revolutionary voice that hailed the dictatorship of Louis Napoleon as a continuation of the French Revolution in the economic sphere. It caught the attention of many anxious minds in France who were seeking a stable, united France without resorting to Legitimist reaction, bourgeois class rule, or socialist terrorism. The new class conflict, that between bourgeois and workingmen, which culminated in the "June Days" of 1848, created a social crisis in France similar to that in Italy and in Germany after the First World War. The emergence of a "savior of society" in the person of Louis Napoleon may be compared to the emergence of Mussolini and Hitler, who also claimed to have saved society from the revolutionary onslaught of the communists. The significance of Proudhon, in the crisis of 1848, was his self-

98 Franz Neumann, *Behemoth* (New York, 1942), 320. The most prominent exponent of economic anti-Semitism was the Nazi economist Werner Sombart. See his books *The Jews and Modern Capitalism,* trans. from the German by M. Epstein (London, 1913), and *A New Social Philosophy* (Princeton, N. J., 1937).

appointed role of intellectual cicerone to Louis Napoleon, a role difficult to play a century before it could be appreciated. That explains why he was rejected both by those whom he sought to guide and by those who had regarded him as a fellow revolutionist.

There is no hint of the totalitarian corporative state in Proudhon's writings. The economic condition of France, in his day, was such that a totalitarian state of the fascist type was inconceivable, even by the bold social imagination of Proudhon. There existed no large working class, no concentrated industries that could be organized into state-controlled "corporations." What was conceivable was a dictatorship based on a mass of small property owners who desired a strong state to protect them against their class enemies and to make their interests those of the nation. That is why Proudhon, the spokesman of this class, supported the *coup d'état* of Louis Napoleon. That is why he proclaimed the latter to be the chosen of history and implored him to carry out his mission as a social revolutionist. That is why he supported dictatorial government against *toute la gente candidate*.

Fascist writers both in Germany and in France have not been slow to recognize Proudhon as the intellectual forerunner of fascism. One of these writers, Willibald Schulze, hailed him as the *Wegweiser* of the Third Reich, because he repudiated democracy, capitalism, and socialism. Of all the social philosophers of former times, he asserted, Proudhon was nearest to National Socialism, in that he upheld the principle of private enterprise and was, at the same time, opposed to profit and to interest.[99]

Proudhon, asserted another Nazi writer, Karl Heinz Bremer, saw the necessity of popularizing a social idea that was antiliberal, in order to give a social significance to the Second Empire. What Louis Napoleon needed was an ideology that expressed the relationship of the workers to the Second Empire, which only Proudhon could supply. But the Emperor rejected him, because he desired the rapid success of his regime. Instead, he catered to the banking interests and to the Jews, as a consequence of which Louis Napoleon failed to solve the social problem within the framework of national and *völkisch* ideas.[100]

[99] Willibald Schulze, "War Proudhon Anarchist?" *Deutschlands Erneuerung*, XXIII (1939).

[100] Karl Heinz Bremer, "Der sozialistiche Kaiser," *Die Tat*, XXX (1938), 160*ff*.

A significant article contrasting Marx and Proudhon appeared in a Paris fascist journal devoted to French collaboration with Nazi Germany. "Marx, the revolutionary disciple of Hegel," it declared, "placed a violent contradiction at the basis of society, a contradiction which could be dissolved only by violence. Proudhon, being infinitely more comformable to the spirit of France, was well aware of individual values. He, therefore, found a way to resolve the economic contradictions of society. According to Marx, it is the individual; but, according to Proudhon, it is wealth that is the evil. Proudhon welcomed into his 'people,' the middle class, who are the brains of the body social, a class that Marx would have stood up against a wall to be shot down."[101]

In the powerful polemicist of the mid-nineteenth century, it is now possible to discern a herald of the great world evil of fascism. An irritating enigma to his own generation, his teachings misunderstood as anarchy by his disciples, Proudhon is destined to have a new and more prominent place in intellectual history. This will come with the reevaluation of the nineteenth century as the prelude to the world revolution that is now called the Second World War.

[101] *Les Nouveaux temps* (Paris, May 2–3, 1943).

Chapter 15. Heralds of Fascism:

III. Thomas Carlyle

Prophet

England escaped serious disturbance during the Revolution of 1848. Neither the democratic demand for manhood suffrage nor the socialist menace of social revolution threatened, as in France, the rule of the propertied classes. All this despite the fact that only in England was there a fairly large working class concentrated in factory towns and organized in trade-unions, that could offer a serious challenge to bourgeois rule. This potential rather than actual threat to the established order did find intellectual expression in the prefascist pattern of the philosophy of Thomas Carlyle.

Every master must, in time, undergo reevaluation, and a reevaluation of a social philosopher can be made only in the light of the present. His writings, on reexamination, may reveal what was little understood by his contemporaries or even by the master himself. This is particularly true of the great Victorian Carlyle, whose writings acquire a new and startling significance when viewed in the light of the great events of our day. Admired, even revered, by his contemporaries, as a preacher of righteousness, Carlyle now emerges as a prophet with a sinister message for our generation. His views on social and political problems, divested of their moral appeal, imply an attitude of mind characteristic of fascism of our time.

Thomas Carlyle was born in 1795, in a village in Dumfries, Scotland. His father was a workman, a stonemason, in humble circumstances. The atmosphere in the Carlyle home was typical of many Scottish folk, whether poor or rich: it was deeply and sternly Calvinist and Presbyterian. Unlike the situation in the England of the time, there were opportunities in Scotland for a poor boy to get a college

education. Carlyle was sent to Edinburgh University, where he
studied for a time. For a brief period he devoted himself to
teaching in a private school and, in his spare time, to studying for
the Presbyterian ministry. But neither the calling of a teacher nor
that of a minister appealed to him very much. He felt an irrepressible
urge to write, to express the thoughts that came tumbling into his
mind; and he decided, come what may, to embark on the uncertain
career of a writer.

Another decisive event in Carlyle's life occurred when he fell in
love with Jane Welsh, a young woman well connected socially, well
educated, and gifted intellectually. Her influence gave the necessary
spark to his literary talent. His first books, published during 1824 and
1825, dealt with German literature, then a novelty in educated England. His translation of Goethe's *Wilhelm Meister* and his *Life of
Friedrich Schiller,* published during these years, attracted some attention, chiefly because they dealt with an unexplored literary land.

Carlyle then embarked on his next life venture, marriage. He and
Jane Welsh were married in 1826. Their married life—a long and,
on the whole, an unhappy one—lasted until the death of Mrs. Carlyle
in 1866. Much has been written and much more whispered about
the unhappy marital life of the Carlyles. She was brilliant, caustic,
and fond of society. He was a prophet, a dyspeptic, and, at times, a
morose recluse. If, according to Voltaire, one cannot argue with a
prophet, it is even more difficult to live with one, especially for a
vivacious, clever woman to do so.

As did so many other talented natives of Scotland, the Carlyles,
in 1834, moved to London to seek fame and fortune. For a number
of years Carlyle struggled hard to make a living by writing and lectur-
ing. His *Sartor Resartus* first appeared serially in *Fraser's Magazine*
during 1833 and 1834. Its grotesque theme of a philosophy of clothes
and its picturesque style—part Biblical, part satirical—did not, at first,
attract favorable attention. With the publication of *The French Revolution, a History,* in 1837, and *Oliver Cromwell's Letters and Speeches,*
in 1845, Carlyle's success as a writer was assured, and he became a
literary lion. Carlyle reached the very pinnacle of literary success
and was almost universally hailed throughout the English-speaking
world as a great social philosopher, who, in addition, was a literary

man of genius. His home in Chelsea, London, became a place of pilgrimage for people from all parts of the world who came to seek light on the social and moral problems of the day. Rarely had a famous writer maintained an attitude toward life and toward life's problems with such consistency and such integrity as did Carlyle. From the time that *Sartor Resartus* appeared until his death, in 1881, Carlyle's philosophy, style, and manner of life were all of one piece. Although everything around him was changing, he changed not at all.

Of all the famous Britons of Victorian England, Carlyle may be said to have been the only one who was not, in any sense of the word, a liberal. He was not an aristocratic liberal, as was the Tory Sir Walter Scott; neither was he a bourgeois liberal like Macaulay; nor a democratic liberal like John Stuart Mill; nor a socialist liberal like Robert Owen. Carlyle was a lone figure on the intellectual landscape of the England of his day. Despite this fact, he was the most widely read and most greatly admired social philosopher of his time. He was regarded by his contemporaries as an inspired prophet who had awakened the nation to its greatest and most pressing responsibilities and who had given a moral imperative to the need of solving the grave social problems that confronted Victorian England. Carlyle was a prophet not without honor in his own land and in his own day.

Carlyle, like Proudhon, was an inharmonious genius, out of sympathy with the spirit of his age and of his nation. For all that, he cannot be understood and his popularity cannot be correctly estimated unless he is considered in relation to the historic background from which he emerged. That historic background was England between the Reform Bill of 1832 and that of 1867. This period witnessed the industrial rise of England as the "workshop of the world." As previously described, capitalism was given free rein and succeeded in establishing political, social, and economic conditions favorable to the new class in power, the capitalists. Bitter opposition to the new order spread among the industrial working class, more numerous and better organized than any other working class in Europe. It was the England of Carlyle that first felt the impact of the social problem as it affected labor. After the Reform Bill of 1832 the workers were in a rebellious mood against the triumphant middle class, which had used them to oust the aristocrats from the seats of power that they now filled. Voteless and propertyless, the workers often resorted to violent methods to express their discontent.[1] The Manchester riots in 1819 so frightened the propertied classes that the government, in direct violation of the traditional civil liberties, passed the Six Acts restricting freedom of assembly and of the press. But working-class discontent was not dampened by repressive measures. Despite restrictive laws against unions, trade-unionism spread rapidly; and strikes, often attended by violence, frequently took place. "No week passes," wrote Friedrich Engels, "scarcely a day, indeed, in which there is not a strike in some direction."[2] The advent of Chartism resulted in coordinating working-class discontent into a mighty movement to establish an egalitarian order in England.

Was England to undergo a social revolution? This was the question that continually haunted Carlyle. It was this fear that turned his attention to the study of the French Revolution. Carlyle's famous work, *The French Revolution, a History,* is less a history than a moral tract; less a study of conditions in France than a foreboding of universal chaos. Carlyle was firmly convinced that all that had been accomplished by the French Revolution was the violent overturn of an old, bad system in a welter of chaos and anarchy. "Sans-culottism" was the evil spirit, set loose by the French Revolution, that generated the disintegrating, anarchic social conflicts that were devastating Europe.

Fear of social revolution dominated Carlyle's views on government and society. He was a frightened philosopher, who saw in every manifestation of popular discontent a portent of social disintegration. What groups could effectively check sans-culottism, which was threatening to bring on universal chaos? Not the landed aristocracy, the traditional defenders of the established order. Carlyle belabored the aristocrats unmercifully as a degenerate class, "near dead in somnolent delusions," who were idle consumers of rents and who wasted their time and energy in partridge shooting. Not the masters of industrial England, the newly rich capitalists. No socialist poured such withering scorn on what he called the "millocracy" as did Carlyle. He denounced the capitalists as a profit-mad class, interested only in making money, "spellbound amid money-bags and ledgers," who were insensitive to the

---

1 See *supra,* pp. 202*ff.*

2 Friedrich Engels, *Condition of the Working-class in England in 1844* (London, 1926), 224.

sufferings of the workers and indifferent to the welfare of the nation.[3] Carlyle looked to another source for the salvation of England and gave hints of the coming of a new force that alone would be capable of curbing sans-culottism.

What kind of Engand did Carlyle visualize? Being a prophet, he had no blueprint of a future society. Being a moralist, he emphasized spiritual, not social, values. Nevertheless, he did have a vision of an ideal social order in which England would find security, well-being, and stability. Security would be achieved by the state's assuming responsibility for every man's being employed; well-being, by everyone's getting a fair day's wage for a fair day's work; and stability, by establishing a hierarchical social order in which the most worthy would be on top and the least worthy on the bottom. This new order could be organized by a dictatorial government in which "heroes" ruled because of their natural capacity for leadership.

It is quite evident that Carlyle's vision of the future in England centered in his overmastering belief in the doctrine of inequality among men. Carlyle's view of human nature was such that he believed that, at all times, the masses have desired to be ruled by the masterful few. He termed this a "beneficent instinct" of mankind. Inequality was, therefore, of natural—even divine—origin; hence, all ideals of human equality proclaimed by the French Revolution were, according to Carlyle, baseless, and all efforts to realize them, futile. Whatever was fruitful and creative in human life arose from inequality, the only sound basis of a just political and social order. However, his conception of inequality diverged sharply from the aristocratic view of a hierarchy of social castes with mutual obligations, with privileges at the top and discriminations at the bottom. Carlyle was no uncompromising, recalcitrant Tory who desired to restore England's old regime, the order prior to 1832. He had as little use for aristocratic Tory England as he had for liberal parliamentary England. His vision of a new social order was based on the elite principle, according to which the masterful few ruled the people, organized into a hierarchy, not of classes but of disciplined economic groups that functioned in a military fashion of command and obedience. Society, organized on the principle of inequal-

[3] *Past and Present*, 153, 154, and 273. The citations from Carlyle's writings are from the centenary edition of *The Works of Thomas Carlyle*, 30 vols. (London, 1898–1901).

ity, would be patterned on the universe itself, which was "a Monarchy and a Hierarchy."[4] Inequality was transformed by Carlyle from an aristocratic idea of privilege into a moral imperative that was both universal and eternal.

Inequality achieved its most striking manifestation in history according to Carlyle, by the appearance of great men, superior individuals whom he called "heroes." Great men were the prime movers of all great historical events; hence the biographies of great men constituted the history of mankind. Heroes arose from no special group or privileged class, but spontaneously from any group or class, and were self-chosen because of their inborn capacity for leadership. It is well to note that Carlyle did not admire great men as highly gifted, farseeing, devoted individuals who led the people in the struggles for freedom and for a more abundant life. His hero was a sort of god, leading a life apart from the people, whom he ruled as master. He came in a mysterious way, to destroy old values and to create the new forms of art, the new systems of government, the new religious beliefs that marked the advance of civilization. When a hero appeared, asserted Carlyle, the masses instinctively recognized his superiority and said to him: "We do not quite understand thee; we perceive thee to be nobler and wiser and bigger than we, and will loyally follow thee."[5] As his power was due neither to hereditary privilege nor to free election, the hero had a God-given right to rule the people, nearly all of whom were weak, irrational, docile, "mostly fools." Whatever he said and whatever he did, the hero was always right because he alone saw the real and true causes of events. Wise, brave, virtuous, and strong, the hero demanded and received unflinching obedience. He could rule only arbitrarily and would rule only justly. Democracy, according to Carlyle, could never produce heroes. The best that the people, being fools, could do was to choose knaves to rule over them.

The great event in the life of a nation was the appearance of the hero—a Cromwell in England and a Frederick the Great in Germany. When he appears, commanded Carlyle, "raise *him* to the supreme place, and loyally reverence him: You have a perfect government for that country; no ballot-box, parliamentary eloquence, voting, constitu-

4 "Present Time," *Latter-day Pamphlets,* No. I, 21.
5 "New Downing Street," *Latter-day Pamphlets,* No. IV, 142.

tion-building, or any other machinery whatsoever can improve it a whit."[6] But how is the hero to be found? Carlyle prescribed no definite method, because he was convinced that the instinct of obedience among the masses would cause them to recognize and to submit to their divinely appointed ruler when he appeared. What if they did not recognize him and therefore refused to obey him? Then the hero was justified in using force to compel obedience.[7] In this case, force was not brutal violence but a spiritual power exercised to establish the rule of those divinely ordained.

Passionately convinced of the doctrine of inequality, Carlyle fought a lifelong, truceless war against democracy and representative government. No opponent of democracy before him or in his own time, not even De Maistre or Proudhon, attacked democratic ideals with such devastating fury, with such poetic eloquence, with such saturnine humor, and with such acrimonious determination. Parliamentary government had, in Carlyle's day, been accepted by all classes in England, even by those who were still voteless. What the unenfranchised lower classes demanded was not the abolition of Parliament but the right to elect its members in order to make that body the fulcrum of democracy in England. Carlyle ridiculed Parliament, reformed or unreformed, as the "National Palaver," which "by its very nature can not do work but can do talk only."[8] Much less could it be the means of making necessary reforms in the social order. "Penny-newspaper parliaments cannot legislate on anything."[9] They would always consist of talkers, who, being inefficient, neglected important matters in order to keep themselves in office. Never would parliaments produce "Herculean men," able to diffuse "a light of Heavenly order in the nation." How could a parliament be otherwise than the collective entity of folly? Was it not chosen by fools? If, out of ten men, nine are recognizable as fools, "how, in the name of wonder, will you ever get a ballot-box to grind out a wisdom from the votes of these ten men?"[10]

Pending the arrival of the all-wise, all-powerful hero, how should

[6] *On Heroes, Hero-worship and the Heroic in History*, 197.
[7] *Past and Present*, 218–219.
[8] "Parliaments," *Latter-day Pamphlets*, No. VI, 225.
[9] "Shooting Niagara," *Critical and Miscellaneous Essays*, V, 46.
[10] "Parliaments," 238.

England be governed? Carlyle suggested the formation of a "Sovereign Body of Rulers and Administrators," an "Acting Apparatus," composed of a half dozen or a dozen men appointed by the crown, without regard to rank or party, who should rule the nation.[11] Unless such a reform were made, he declared, anarchy would spread over the land "with ever-accelerated pace."[12] What about Parliament? Should it be abolished? "No," replied Carlyle, not in England, where that institution "is like second nature" and hence indispensable. But Parliament should be transformed, so that it would represent the instincts, not the opinions, of the people. Carlyle had the fascist idea of the role of the masses, whose instincts were "wise and human" and "well deserve attending to," but whose opinions were "of little wisdom" in government. Although Parliament was a "Condensed Folly," it would be useful for the rulers to know its "pitch," so that they could judge what might "safely be attempted with said Folly." In this manner the rulers of the nation would plumb the instincts of the masses, in order to find out what measures the latter would "assent to willingly, what unwillingly, what they will resist with remonstrances, what with armed rebellion." Just as a prudent rider consulted his horse's desires as to food, so should the rulers consult the instincts of the people as to government.[13]

These views of Carlyle concerning the uses of a parliament strikingly resemble those of the fascists. To fascism the common man is not an end in himself, with opinions of his own, but an irrational creature whose powers, like those of an animal, are to be used by his master as a means to promote good ends. Universal suffrage and elections are maintained by the fascists, not for the purpose of establishing a government, but as a means of giving popular approval to the rule of the elite.

Carlyle's hostility to democratic government was rooted in his contempt for the common man. No writer, except Nietzsche, has expressed such withering contempt of the common man and such fervent exaltation of the elite as did Carlyle. In his view the masses of mankind had no power of reflection and followed a leader like a flock of sheep. And, like sheep, they were gregarious, stupid, and cowardly. Left to

[11] "Downing Street," *Latter-day Pamphlets*, No. III, 93.
[12] "Parliaments," 248.
[13] *Ibid.*, 239–244.

themselves, the "multitudinous *canaille*" would become a menace to
civilization by creating anarchy and chaos through revolution. England
and America received the full measure of Carlyle's castigation, as the
lands where representative government was established and where
democratic ideals received popular acclaim. England, Carlyle declared,
contained twenty-seven million inhabitants, "mostly fools."[14] America,
where the exaltation of the common man had become a national cult,
roused Carlyle to furious derision. "What great human soul," he
exclaimed, "what great thought, what great noble thing that one could
worship, or loyally admire, has yet been produced there? None. . . .
They have begotten, with a rapidity beyond recorded example, Eighteen
Millions of the greatest *bores* ever seen in this world before."[15]

When the movement to expand the suffrage began in the fifties of
the nineteenth century, it encountered the vituperative hostility of
Carlyle. He was opposed to any extension of the suffrage beyond that
established by the Reform Bill of 1832. Democracy would give even
more power to Parliament, which, in Carlyle's opinion, already had
too much. And, far worse, democracy would establish the political
equality of the common man with the elite. He ridiculed the theory
of natural rights—the only "right" that an ignorant man had was to
be guided, peacefully or forcibly, by those wiser than he. There was
only one natural law, and that was the law which said that the stronger
in mind and body should rule mankind. It was the everlasting privilege
of the masses, being fools, to be governed by an aristocracy of talent,
naturally wise and virtuous. The masses, "full of beer and nonsense . . .
can not but be wrong."[16] According to Carlyle, democracy, in its very
nature, was a "self-cancelling business," which, in the long run, would
give "a net result of zero."[17] It would bring about the consummation
of all evil in government, because it made the vote of Judas Iscariot
equal to that of Christ.[18] Under a system of manhood suffrage, the
worthy candidate would have a poor chance of election as against a
quack. That a majority of the Members of Parliament should rule was

14 *Ibid.*, 225.
15 "Present Time," 21.
16 "Parliaments," 242.
17 "Chartism," *Critical and Miscellaneous Essays,* IV, 158.
18 "Nigger Question," *Critical and Miscellaneous Essays,* IV, 363.

bad enough; but that this majority should be chosen by manhood suffrage was, according to Carlyle, a direct violation of his fundamental doctrine of inequality. Minorities, not majorities, were always right. "Witness Cromwell and his Puritans, a minority at all times, by a count of heads; yet the authors or saviors, as it ultimately proved, of whatsoever is divinest in the things we can still reckon ours in England." The few have dominated the many because "in a dim, instinctive, but most genuine manner, they were doing the commandment of Heaven."[19]

Carlyle's opposition to manhood suffrage arose from his flat denial of the dignity and worth of every man, irrespective of his talents or station. Could anyone seriously claim, he asked, that "Quashee Nigger" was equal to Socrates?[20] Democracy, according to Carlyle, was a form of anarchic rebellion among the masses, blindly groping for leadership. "Bellowings, inarticulate cries as of a dumb creature in rage and pain; to the ear of wisdom they are inarticulate prayers: 'Guide me, govern me! I am mad and miserable, and can not guide myself.'"[21] Happy was he who had found a master!

When Parliament, under the leadership of Disraeli, passed the Reform Bill of 1867, which extended the suffrage to the working class, Carlyle fell into an uncontrolled rage. "Shooting Niagara," he called the reform, the evil work of the "superlative Hebrew Conjuror," who led the great of England "by the nose, like mesmerized somnambulant cattle."[22] He prophesied disaster to England as a consequence of the reform. It would result in "new supplies of blockheadism, gullibility, bribeability, amenity to beer and balderdash."[23] The Reform Bill had been the outcome of agitation organized by the trade-unions, which planned to use Parliament to advance the interests of the working class. Carlyle realized this full well, and it enraged him still more. He declared that working-class suffrage would encourage the trade-union, "with assassin pistol in its hand," to demand an eight-hour workday and a daily wage of eight shillings.[24] Such a demand seemed

19 "Parliaments," 246–247.
20 "Shooting Niagara," 4.
21 "Chartism," 157.
22 "Shooting Niagara," 11.
23 *Ibid.*, 9.
24 *Ibid.*, 31.

to that prophet of righteousness something so monstrous as to presage the end of all things.

Now that the working class was enfranchised, the onrushing tide of democracy, Carlyle was convinced, threatened to engulf all civilization. How to stem this tide? Pending the arrival of a hero or while preparing for the coming of one something must be done. So he made a suggestion that revealed his essentially fascist mentality. He recommended the formation of a "noble Few" who would constitute an "Aristocracy of Nature," consisting of the elite among the capitalists and the elite among the aristocrats—"brothers born; called and impelled to cooperate and go together." These aristocrats should cease to be idle partridge shooters and consecrate themselves to "a noble and valiantly cosmic life." And these capitalists should cease to be a "millocracy," devoted to profit seeking, and become "Captains of Industry," consecrating their talents to the common welfare. The capitalist was "almost an aristocrat by class." He could do no better "than unite with this naturally noble kind of aristocrat by title" in the struggle against the rabble and their spokesmen. United, they will "take command of the innumerable Foolish."[25] By what method would the "noble Few" of aristocrats and capitalists conquer the "innumerable Foolish"? It is startling to read in the pages of Carlyle an outline of the fascist technique for destroying democracy by violent methods on the part of an organized minority. The forces of "Anti-Anarchy," he declared, should prepare to deal with "Anarchy, however million-headed," to whom no victory was possible. "Patience, silence, diligence, ye chosen of the World! Slowly or fast, in the course of time, you will grow to a minority that can actually step forth (sword not yet drawn, but sword ready to be drawn), and say: 'Here are we, Sirs; we also are now minded to *vote* —to all lengths, as you may perceive.' "[26] What would avail "the noisiest anarchic Parliaments" against such a challenge!

With the overthrow of democratic parliaments a new social order would be ushered in by the "noble Few." It was to be hierarchical in character—organized, however, along *military,* not economic, lines. It is important to note that Carlyle was not at all class conscious; he was not the intellectual spokesman of the propertied classes in their

25 "Present Time," 34; "Shooting Niagara," 30–31.
26 "Shooting Niagara," 44.

struggle with labor. What he feared in the rising discontent of the working class was the destruction of organized society and the consequent relapse of civilization into barbarism, not the overthrow of the capitalist system and the establishment of a socialist commonwealth. Society, not the capitalist system, was to be saved by the "noble Few," and in the interest of civilization, not in that of the "millocracy."

Another startlingly fascist note is heard in Carlyle's plan for the militarization of labor. Carlyle had a penchant for militarism; his favorite heroes were the militarists Frederick the Great and Oliver Cromwell. In his *Life of Frederick the Great* he lingers over his hero's many battles, of which he gives long descriptions filled with passionate details. Military discipline, therefore, came readily to his mind as the best method of curing the disorders of democracy and of promoting the national interest efficiently and energetically. According to Carlyle's scheme, which is hazy, yet darkly suggestive, a universal "system of Drill" should be introduced for all men between sixteen and sixty, having both military and civil objectives. Regimentation was to begin with the paupers, who were to be put to work in labor battalions; then it was to be applied to all classes, up to the highest ranks of society. The factory workers, seeing the blessedness of regimentation, would then say to their employers: "Masters, you must regiment us a little; make our interests with you permanent a little, instead of temporary and nomadic." The "Captains of Industry," with their armies of laborers, would then cooperate with the state, with its armies of soldiers. Their fields would meet and coalesce, "and there will be no unregimented worker, or such only as are fit to remain unregimented, any more." [27] Previously, the capitalists had lacked the military iron and divine light necessary to create a "noble just Industrialism and Government by the Wisest." [28] In the new regimented order, corporal punishment would be inflicted on those refractory workers who violated the rules that held them to their jobs. Employers were to be ready and willing to shoot down their workers, should the need arise.

The social order envisioned by Carlyle is plainly fascist in its militaristic and totalitarian patterns. The supremacy of the civil authorities

[27] *Ibid.,* 42; "New Downing Street," 166; "Inaugural Address," *Critical and Miscellaneous Essays,* IV, 476–477.

[28] *Past and Present,* 271.

over the military has been a distinctively liberal principle of government ever since it was adopted in England by the Mutiny Act of 1689. Even under a militaristic regime, such as that in the German Empire, there had existed a separation between the civil and the military powers in the state. It remained for the fascists, in both Fascist Italy and Nazi Germany, to fuse both powers into one—and that one, military. This was the true meaning of the totalitarian state. All labor, all industry, was regimented, in order that the nation should "Believe! Obey! Work! Fight!" under the rule of the self-chosen elite. Carlyle's plan of regimenting labor had no military objectives. For all that, it does suggest the totalitarian state with all its implications. Logically and inevitably, the plan involved the suppression of freedom of speech and of assembly, to which Carlyle was not at all averse. His comment on Mill's classic exposition of intellectual freedom, *On Liberty,* was that it was "the greatest nonsense I ever read."[29] True liberty, he asserted, consists in a man's "finding out, or being forced to find out, the right path, and to walk thereon. To learn, or to be taught, what work he actually was able for; and then by permission, persuasion, and even compulsion, to set about doing of the same!" That was liberty and the maximum of well-being.[30]

Carlyle's anticipation of totalitarianism is, indeed, surprising. In part, it may be explained by the historic situation in which he found himself. The England of Carlyle was unique in the world of that period, in that it was an industrialized state with large factories and a numerous working class. A philosopher like Carlyle, with a social imagination and dictatorial beliefs, could envisage a system of society in which economic life would be regulated, controlled, and coordinated by a dictatorial state. However, Carlyle had only a glimpse, not a full view, of totalitarianism, which required for its application a far greater concentration of industry than that which existed in Victorian England.

There was another aspect in which England was unique: she was the mistress of a world-wide empire. She had acquired vast domains, not only peacefully through settlement but through many colonial wars with Spain, Holland, and France. In the British Empire were

[29] Quoted in D. A. Wilson, *Carlyle to Threescore-and-ten* (London, 1929), 557.
[30] *Past and Present,* 212.

many peoples in all stages of civilization, ruled by the English. To Carlyle the victorious career of the English and their overlordship in the Empire marked them as a superior race and nation. He applied his master-principle of inequality, not only to individuals, but also to races and to nations, especially to the former. Racial doctrines were not fully developed in Carlyle's day, but he anticipated them in fitful gleams that betrayed the passionate racial consciousness of the fascist. According to Carlyle, there existed an elite among the races of mankind who imposed its rule on the lesser breeds as part of the natural order that determined their place in history. In modern times, the racial elite were the Teutons, represented chiefly by the English and the Germans, who, alone among the races of mankind, had an inborn capacity to rule. They alone could produce heroes. The "silent" English, racially rooted in Teutonism, were superior to the "jabbering" French. In his eyes, the Teutonic races are virtuous, Protestant, and inspired by a moral intuition above reason. The Latin races are "corrupt, worldly, selfish and addicted to barren logic."[31] The English, in Carlyle's view, whether they were found in Arkansas, India, London, or Lancaster,[32] were an "indomitable rock-made race of men," who proved their superiority by ruling the inferior races in the Empire. It is to be expected, of course, that Carlyle would have no admiration for the Irish. "The Irish National Character," he declared, "is degraded, disordered; till this recover itself, nothing is yet recovered. Immethodic, headlong, violent, mendacious: what can you make of the wretched Irishman?"[33]

Carlyle was a strong upholder of imperialism. Although he wrote little about the subject, what he did write left no doubt that he regarded the English as a chosen people, whose mission was to open the uninhabited lands of the world.[34] He denounced the antiimperialists of his day, notably the Manchester school, because they believed that the colonies did not pay. Must, then, the Empire "be dismembered to bring the ledger straight?" he scornfully asked. He favored peopling the colonies through state-directed emigration to the thinly populated

31 Crane Brinton, "Thomas Carlyle," *Encyclopedia of the Social Sciences*, III, 229.
32 "Chartism," 175.
33 *Ibid.*, 137.
34 *Ibid.*, 171.

regions of the Empire. The colonies were to be governed by the English, with no concessions of self-government to the inhabitants.[35]

In the racial ladder, those on the lowest rung, according to Carlyle, were the Negroes. Human inequality as applied to them was dramatized by slavery—an institution that legally, socially, and morally denied human equality by making one human being the property of another. The movement to emancipate the Negroes from slavery had no more uncompromising opponent than Carlyle. He denounced the abolition of slavery in the British Empire, which had taken place in 1833. And he was bitterly opposed to the American abolitionists, whom he stigmatized as "rabid Nigger-Philanthropists." Carlyle's contempt for the Negro was unbounded—a contempt that he showed by using the vulgar expression, "Nigger." Fervently Carlyle insisted that God had ordained slavery for the Negro.[36] In the hierarchy of humanity, the "wisest Man" was at the top and the Negro was at the bottom.[37] Whom God had made a slave "no parliament of men nor power that exists on Earth can render free," because he was chained by fetters that parliaments could not break. To proclaim emancipation was, therefore, a "Devil's Gospel," harmful alike to the enslaved and to the free. Nations were noble and happy in so far as they settled rightly who was slave and who was free.[38] Carlyle saw even in slavery an antidote to *laissez faire.* Happy was he who had found a master! By contrast with the "nomadism" of *laissez faire,* slavery exhibited permanency and security.[39] Slavery argued Carlyle, was a "contract of long continuance," especially suited to the racially inferior Negro. He favored the South during the American Civil War. In his view, it was a conflict in which the racially superior Anglo-Saxons were killing each other in a "Nigger-Agony" to decide which was the best way to hire servants. Another illustration of Carlyle's hostility to the Negro was in the famous case of Governor Eyre. In 1865, a Negro riot broke out in Jamaica, in which a number of whites were killed. The British governor, Edward John Eyre, took savage reprisal by military action, in which four hundred

[35] "New Downing Street," *passim;* C. A. Bodelson, *Studies in Mid-Victorian Imperialism* (London, 1924), 22–32.
[36] "Shooting Niagara," 5; "The Nigger Question," 371.
[37] "The Nigger Question," 361.
[38] "Parliaments," 249–250.
[39] "The Nigger Question," 367.

and fifty Negroes were killed and six hundred severely beaten. There was a great outcry in England on the part of liberals at the conduct of Governor Eyre, and he was recalled in disgrace. Carlyle, almost alone among the British intellectuals, came to the defense of Eyre, whom he hailed as one of his heroes.

What was Carlyle's attitude toward the Jews—always the acid test of racial intolerance? He rarely mentioned the Jews, but whenever he did so it was always in vindictively derogatory terms. "Harpy Jews" was a typical Carlylean expression of hostility. He justified the savage persecution of the Jews during the Middle Ages.[40] Like the Nazis of our day, Carlyle was convinced that the Jews were uncreative exploiters, incapable of any heroism.[41] Whenever Carlyle saw a Jewish head appear on the literary or the political horizon, he promptly smote it. Heinrich Heine had attracted favorable attention in England, which roused the ire of Carlyle. He denounced Heine as a "slimy and greasy Jew," and a "filthy foetid sausage of spoiled victuals." He virulently berated all those who admired him.[42] Carlyle cordially detested Disraeli, the only man of whom, as he said, he had "never spoken except with contempt." There were legitimate reasons why some of Disraeli's contemporaries disliked him, but Carlyle's dislike arose from a racial aversion to the statesman, whom he ridiculed as "a cursed old Jew not worth his weight in bacon." His anti-Semitism extended even to religion. Carlyle once planned to write a book with the object of liberating the spirit of religion from worn-out theological traditions that he stigmatized as "Hebrew Old Clothes," a reference to Jews as dealers in second-hand clothing.[43]

Although he was a Scot of the Scots, Carlyle's mind had migrated to Germany, where it found a congenial home. Repudiating the liberal heritage of his own nation, he instinctively saw in the Germans

[40] *Past and Present*, 59, 92, and 181.

[41] Theodor Deimel, *Carlyle und der National-sozialismus* (Würzburg, 1936), 128–129.

[42] David A. Wilson and David W. MacArthur, *Carlyle in Old Age* (London, 1934), 218; see also Sol Liptzin, "Heinrich Heine, 'Blackguard' and 'Apostate': a Study of the Earliest English Attitude towards Him," *Publications of the Modern Langauge Association of America* (1943), LVIII, 179.

[43] For examples of Carlyle's anti-Semitism, see E. R. Bentley, *A Century of Hero-worship* (Philadelphia, 1944), 35; "Thomas Carlyle," *Dictionary of National Biography*, III, 1030 and 1033; Wilson and MacArthur, *op. cit.*, 358–359.

the only people in Western Europe who had little or no liberal heritage; whose ideals of government were dictatorial, not parliamentary; and among whom force was a popular ideal and racialism a widespread belief. It was the "magnetism of German thought which helped him to polarize very definitely the instincts of his nature."[44] Carlyle helped greatly to popularize German literature in England, where it had been little known prior to his time.[45] Of his German masters, he greatly admired Goethe, Schiller, Fichte, and Novalis—especially, the first. The passionate adoration of the Olympian Goethe, whose supreme interest lay in the culture of the individual, by the stormy Scottish prophet calling modern society to judgment was, indeed, rather strange. It may be explained by the extreme contrast in their natures. Not only distance in space and in time, but also distance in temperament lends enchantment.

As a devotee of the cult of Teutonism, Carlyle did much to spread admiration for the Germans among the English. "The German race, not the Gaelic," he wrote, "are now to be protagonist in that immense world drama; and from them I expect better issues."[46] He had come to regard the Teutonic race "as a measuring rod with which to judge other races."[47] Germany, according to Carlyle, was the greatest force for good in the modern world; and within Germany, it was Prussia; and within Prussia, the Prussian army. During the Franco-Prussian War, Carlyle favored Prussia. He praised Bismarck as "a magnanimous, noble and deep-seeing man."[48] The annexation of Alsace-Lorraine by Germany received Carlyle's full endorsement, on the ground that it would benefit the whole world—even France herself.

[44] E. Legouis and L. Cazamian, *History of English Literature*, trans. from the French by H. D. Irvine (New York, 1939), 1160.

[45] C. E. Vaughan, "Carlyle and his German Masters," *Essays and Studies* by members of the English Association (Oxford, 1910); C. F. Harrold, *Carlyle and German Thought* (Yale University Press, New Haven, 1934).

[46] *Critical and Miscellaneous Essays*, V, 57.

[47] W. Vollrath, *Th. Carlyle und H. St. Chamberlain, zwei Freunde Deutschlands* (Munich, 1935), 53. On the relation of Carlyle to Nazi Germany, see, in addition to the book of Vollrath: Deimal, *op. cit.;* Olga Hess, *Carlyles Stellung zum Germanentum* (Freiberg, 1926); H. J. C. Grierson, *Carlyle and Hitler* (Cambridge, 1933); Ernest Seillière, *Un précurseur du national-socialisme* (Paris, 1939); and J. E. Baker, "Carlyle Rules the Reich," *Saturday Review of Literature*, X (1933), 291.

[48] Quoted in N. Young, *Carlyle, His Rise and Fall* (London, 1927), 312.

"That noble, patient, deep, pious and solid Germany," he wrote, "should be at length welded into a Nation, and become Queen of the Continent, instead of vaporing, vainglorious, gesticulating, quarrelsome, restless and oversensitive France, seems to me the hopefulest public fact that has occurred in my time."[49] Such hearty support by so influential a writer could not go unrewarded. Ostensibly for his *Life of Frederick the Great,* but really for his support of Prussia, Carlyle received the Order of Merit from the Prussian government.

Reading Carlyle today is a difficult task. The great mass of words, rolling like a continuous stream of lava from a verbal volcano in a constant state of eruption, soon tires even the most persistent reader. Time has dulled the glow of the lava and stilled the rumble of the volcano. The reader becomes confused by a jumble of words, often without any clear design; or he becomes irritated by rhetorical ejaculations and splenetic denunciations that crowd on almost every page. In truth, Carlyle's intellectual acumen was not very great; and his verbosity often—too often—outran his real intelligence. "The bareness, the scantiness, to which Carlyle's political thought is easily reducible is at first pause astonishing."[50]

As a social philosopher, Carlyle cannot be compared with his great contemporaries, the liberal John Stuart Mill and the socialist Karl Marx. Carlyle's knowledge of economics was most meager and his understanding of the political and social trends in Victorian England was superficial. "As far as I could judge, I never met a man with a mind so ill adapted for scientific research," said Charles Darwin of Carlyle.[51] He had no real grasp of the economic forces set loose by the Industrial Revolution. Carlyle's denunciations of laissez-faire capitalism were apocalyptic diatribes, not social criticisms of the new economic order.

Neither can Carlyle be considered a great historian. He was too much the prophet and too little the scholar to make permanent contributions to the study of history. His famous *French Revolution,* once so popular and so much admired, is now seldom even referred to by historians of the movement. Carlyle knew little of conditions in France under the

[49] *Critical and Miscellaneous Essays,* V, 59.

[50] Crane Brinton, *English Political Thought in the Nineteenth Century* (London, 1933), 165.

[51] *Life and Letters of Charles Darwin* (Francis Darwin, ed., New York, 1896), I, 64.

Old Regime. Neither did he have a thorough knowledge of the Revolution itself as it affected the fate of France and that of Europe. His interpretation of the French Revolution was that it was a punishment visited by an angry God upon the rulers of France because they had strayed from the "eternal verities." It proclaimed no new principles, produced no heroic figures, and created nothing that was good and substantial. The famous work is "less a history than a series of tableaux."[52] About the only value that it now possesses consists in Carlyle's extraordinarily vivid sketches of the leading revolutionists and in the "flame pictures" of the sensational incidents. In his *Life of Frederick the Great,* on which he spent many years, Carlyle failed to appreciate the historic role of that knave of genius. In the eight volumes of the work there is almost nothing about the social and economic situation in Prussia, almost nothing of the classes and their relation to one another, almost nothing on the system of laws and of the methods of administration. It is filled with detailed descriptions of battles, of delineations of personalities, of denunciations of German historians of the Frederician period, and of adulation of Frederick. Carlyle did regard the Prussian king as a "questionable" hero; yet he continually idealized him as a great creative force with a sense of the realities of history. He gave hearty and enthusiastic approval of Frederick's aggressions, tyrannies, treacheries, and duplicities. The partition of Poland was "Heaven's Justice." As a history, the work is disfigured by distortions, partisanship, biased judgments, and significant omissions. Carlyle's favorite hero in history was Cromwell. In his *Letters and Speeches of Oliver Cromwell* he did succeed in giving Cromwell a new and better place in history. Although Carlyle's work was chiefly that of an editor, his "Introduction" and his comments present the Puritan Revolution almost exclusively as a religious movement. He exalted Cromwell as a soldier and statesman who heard the voice of God and faithfully executed His commands. Carlyle had as little understanding of the historic importance of the Puritan Revolution as he had of the French Revolution.

[52] G. P. Gooch, *History and Historians in the Nineteenth Century* (London, 1935), 326. For a more favorable view of Carlyle as a historian, see Louise M. Young, *Thomas Carlyle and the Art of History* (London, 1939), and C. F. Harrold, "Carlyle's General Method in *The French Revolution,*" *Publications of the Modern Language Association of America,* XLIII (1928), 1150–1170.

Wherein, then, lies Carlyle's importance in the intellectual history of modern Europe? As in the case of Proudhon, it lies in the fact that he was one of the influential writers in the nineteenth century who continued the intellectual tradition that led to fascism. Carlyle's pre-fascist ideas, unlike those of Proudhon, were not disturbing overtones that disconcerted and baffled his readers. On the contrary, they were proclaimed in thunderous tones and repeated often and insistently in nearly all his books. It is now plain that Carlyle's political and social views were those that are today recognized as being distinctively fascist. He anticipated the fascists in his social demands, in his views on the form and function of the state, on the organization of economic life, and on the right and duty of the racially superior Teutons to rule the world.[53] His "hero" is none other than the Nazi "Fuehrer," dressed in moral garments tailored for him by the Puritan Carlyle. His hatreds, no less than his loves, proclaim him the prophet of fascism. The weight of his attack was directed against liberalism, its ideals, its methods, and its policies, upon which he poured mordant ridicule while savagely tearing it to pieces.

What is misleading in Carlyle is that his views are saturated with a *moral* purpose and are proclaimed in an apocalyptic manner. That is in sharp contrast with the cynical brutality and cold ferocity of the fascist. But Carlyle's moral appeal obscured his real message. He was the product of a national tradition—Scottish Puritanism—that he could not renounce; and he flourished in Victorian England, which would listen only to those who spoke in moral terms, whatever the message. As a consequence, he became the victim of a confusion that was typical of so many prophets—a confusion between right and might. So greatly did Carlyle admire force, and yet so deep were his moral roots, that right and might became synonymous to him. The intensity of his conviction that "right made might brought him perilously near saying that might made right"—a dictum that Carlyle expressly disavowed.[54] His exaltation of power as a moral force in the universe was so great that the effect of his teaching was to clothe dictatorial rule with the mantle of divinity. He, more than any other modern philosopher, always excepting Nietzsche, beheld in the egoism of the dictator the

[53] Deimel, *op. cit.*, 12.
[54] Emery E. Neff, *Carlyle and Mill* (New York, 1926), 280.

supreme manifestation of heroic virtues and in the exercise of force the supreme manifestation of efficient organization.

The problem remains how to explain Carlyle's enormous popularity. It cannot be that his contemporaries accepted his message. They certainly did not. His prophecy of a new dispensation for England, when heroes—not a "palavering" parliament—should rule the nation, fell on deaf ears. England listened eagerly to her flaming prophet but heeded him not at all. Once started on her liberal path by the Reform Bill of 1832, England continued to follow it doggedly, faithfully, and unswervingly. Carlyle's popularity may be ascribed, in the first place, to the magic of style, which, in his case, was the most individualistic in English literature. His prose gleamed and darkened with strange lights and. mystic shadows. A Niagara of words—colorful, irritating, stimulating, startling, and threatening—overwhelmed the reader and put him in a state of dazed exaltation. "The sudden relaxations and irruptions, the broken rhythms of this style, its discordant harmony, its profound congruence with the vehemence, the bitterness, the irony and the humor of the thought it conveys, make it a unique instrument, the work of a unique temperament, an instrument which adds an unforgettable note to the choir of English prose."[55] In Carlyle's case, style was not only the man, it was the message.

Carlyle was a prophet and, like all prophets, a sensationalist. He excelled in combining the glory and the truth of his message with dire threats to those who flouted it and in making glowing promises of the new dispensation with pronouncements of the impending doom of the existing order. His capitalized rhetoric, his half-finished sentences, his grim and mordant characterizations made Carlyle's writing almost audible to his readers. His moral fervor, always at white heat, made all criticism seem like questioning the moral law itself. Not one of Carlyle's famous contemporaries ever entered into a debate with him. Brought up on the King James Bible, clinging to his Puritan heritage, the prosaic mid-Victorian reader of Carlyle was verbalized into a Biblical trance and felt himself to be, for a time at least, a crusader for social righteousness. Few others could create for his contemporaries so well the mood of moral exaltation in relation to social problems.

[55] L. Cazamian, *Carlyle*, trans. from the French by E. K. Brown (New York, 1932), 286.

Carlyle was also adept in the art of generating an atmosphere of intellectual terrorism. The rising tide of popular discontent after 1832 led to Chartism, which, though essentially constitutional in aim, caught the revolutionary fever of 1848. The threat of a violent overthrow of the social order flung bourgeois England into a state of panic. Was there to be a new eruption of sans-culottism? Carlyle was quick to ring the tocsin violently. He denounced the uprisings in Europe in the Revolution of 1848 as disastrous and humiliating events in European history. "Everywhere immeasurable Democracy rose Monstrous, loud, blatant, inarticulate as the voice of Chaos."[56] Nothing worse, according to Carlyle, had happened since the barbarian invasions. His *Chartism, Past and Present,* and *Latter-day Pamphlets* exaggerated the dangers of a social revolution in England; at the same time, their message was that Parliament was unequal to the task of solving the "condition of England question" in order to avoid revolution. Many were attracted to Carlyle because he expressed in language that was startling, yet reassuring, their fear of a social upheaval. His "eternal verities" gave assurance to his readers that inequality in society was part of the divine order of things, hence indestructible. What was necessary was to make inequality a moral ideal and to strengthen those forces in society that upheld it.

However, the most important and the more legitimate aspect of Carlyle's influence lay elsewhere. It might be said, though with some exaggeration, that Carlyle, in contrast with nearly all of his famous contemporaries, did have a social sense. He it was who saw most clearly and expressed most vividly the evils imposed on the English workers by laissez-faire capitalism. The doctrine of *laissez faire* had become an article of faith in Victorian England, largely because it blended the English ideal of individual freedom with the selfish interests of the capitalist class that was now in power. What evoked a great response to Carlyle's message, and still does, were his eloquent attacks on *laissez faire* and on its supporters, especially the classical economists. These attacks were more vehement, more direct, than were those even of the socialist Robert Owen. The freedom of the individual, so much lauded by the classical economists, was, as Carlyle said, the freedom to die of starvation. Unregulated competition set man against man, which

[56] "Present Time," 186.

created anarchy and chaos in the life of the nation. It reduced human relations to a "cash-nexus," which resulted in a defilement of man's finer instincts and a dampening of his noblest aspirations. The "general downbreak of Laissez faire in these days,—may we not regard it as a voice from the dumb bosom of nature, saying to us: 'Behold! Supply-and-demand is not the one Law of Nature; Cash-payment is not the sole nexus of man with man,—how far from it!' "[57]

Laissez faire, according to Carlyle, was not only evil in itself; it was the primal source of all evils in the body social. As a principle it was "false, heretical, and damnable, if ever aught was." [58] It created insecurity among the workers by giving them the status of "Servant-ship on the nomadic principle." Carlyle saw full well the sinister implication of freedom of contract when applied to the helpless wage earner confronting the capitalist. And he denounced freedom of contract as a device to starve the laborer, " 'My starving workers'? answers the rich mill owner: 'Did I not hire them fairly in the market? Did I not pay them to the last sixpence, the sum covenanted for? What have I to do with them more?' "[59] By adhering to the teachings of the classical economists, it became possible, as it was said, "to freeze one's heart and yet live at peace with one's conscience." Acting on the principle of *laissez faire,* observed Carlyle, society became an economic jungle, in which each sought to devour the other; and the outcome was the survival of the most brutal, the most cunning, and the most unscrupulous. He denounced the new class of capitalists as "Gamblers swollen *big.* Paltry Adventurers for most part; worthy of no worship; . . ."[60]

Carlyle also saw the contradictions of laissez-faire capitalism, which created immense concentrated wealth on one side and immense concentrated poverty on the other side. England had become the workshop of the world, producing superabundant commodities; but vast numbers of her people were starving amid plenty, because they did not earn enough to benefit from this wealth production. Millions were struggling in the lowest depths, engaged in a lifelong battle with famine. "In the midst of plethoric plenty the people perish; with gold walls and

[57] *Past and Present,* 180.

[58] *Critical and Miscellaneous Essays,* IV, 131.

[59] *Past and Present,* 147.

[60] "Hudson's Statue," *Latter-day Pamphlets,* No. VII, 262.

full barns, no man feels himself safe or satisfied."[61] *Laissez faire* had failed doubly; it had failed to give opportunities to work, and it had failed to give a fair day's wage for a fair day's work. And Carlyle placed the blame for this evil state of affairs squarely where it belonged, on the state that had failed to coordinate and regulate the new industrial order so that the masses might have security and a fair living standard. *Laissez faire* was "an *abdication* on the part of the governors."[62] English liberty, "shuddering to interfere with the right of capital," brought unemployment, poverty, and unsanitary conditions into home and factory. If this was the result of liberty, Carlyle declared, then he would "lay it on the shelf a little."[63]

To many of his contemporaries Carlyle was an antidote to the metallic rationalism of the utilitarians and to the cool identification by the classical economists of universal economic laws with capitalist class interests. His revulsion from both had an Old Testament flavor, which greatly appealed to those Victorians who had begun to question the economic ruthlessness set loose by modern industrialism. Carlyle was acclaimed as the leader in the revolt that set in against the rule of "economic man." He was unquestionably one of the powerful influences that brought about the fall of *laissez faire* in the new England that appeared after 1870.

It is, indeed, true that Carlyle had a social sense, but it was the perverted social sense of the fascists of our day. His diatribes against *laissez faire* were not inspired by compassion for the poor and disinherited. He had no social vision of a happy humanity freed from want and living in security and abundance—the social vision of the socialists in France and of the Chartists in England. Fundamentally, Carlyle was not at all a humanitarian—which is clearly seen in his attitude toward Negro slavery. It is also seen in his attitude toward prison reform, which became prominent in his day. He denounced the humanitarian attitude of the criminal-law reformers, and he strongly opposed their reform measures.[64] The evils that Carlyle visualized in England were inefficiency and planlessness, which led to disorganiza-

---

[61] *Past and Present*, 6.
[62] "Chartism," 156.
[63] "Present Time," 30.
[64] "Model Prisons," *Latter-day Pamphlets*, No. 2.

tion in society and bred revolutionary discontent among the workers, who suffered most from these evils. Like the fascists, Carlyle believed that these evils could be cured by state control of economic life, which would result in making the workers more productive and more contented at the same time. A worker having security, receiving good wages, and living in a comfortable home would work harder for his employer, fight better for the state, and serve loyally the "noble Few" who ruled him.

Carlyle was convinced that the "condition of England question" could be solved neither by the "partridge-shooting" aristocracy nor by the profit-seeking "millocracy." Least of all would it be solved by the "multitudinous *canaille*," bent on revolutionary destruction. Like the fascists, he believed that social problems could be solved only by a ruling elite, who would give to the masses what they really wanted, namely, economic security, not democratic equality. Democracy, Carlyle insisted, could not abolish the evils produced by capitalism, because democracy was "the consummation of No-government and Laissez-faire."[65] Carlyle's specific proposals for the solution of the "condition of England question" were surprisingly moderate, even in his day. These were (1) government regulation of working hours and working conditions, (2) factory and housing reform, (3) government-directed emigration of workers to the colonies, and (4) compulsory education.[66] What a small mouse emerged from that enormous mountain that rumbled so ominously!

Carlyle had no followers, no disciples in Britain, excepting John Ruskin and James Fitzjames Stephen—not even friends and associates to carry forth his message, as had his contemporaries Robert Owen, Charles Kingsley, and John Stuart Mill. He was without British progeny, as he was without British ancestors. He was not part of the main stream of English thought, which had its fountainhead in John Locke and has flowed steadily and evenly to this day. For this reason, there was no more lonely man in Britain than the most popular of all British philosophers. Neither in his day nor since have the British people as a whole or any significant section of them favored the overthrow of

[65] "Chartism," 159.

[66] *Ibid.*, 197–203; *Past and Present*, 265–267.

parliamentary government in favor of dictatorship. Instead, the powers of Parliament were increased and its base was broadened by the extension of suffrage to all men and women. Today the popularly elected House of Commons exercises supreme and unchallenged power in the government of Britain. The complete unity of the British people behind their government when confronted by Nazi Germany during the Second World War was dramatic proof that Carlyle had been a false prophet in his own land.

It would not be true to say that Carlyle's writings exerted any direct influence on those who brought about the triumph of fascism in the twentieth century. Once the fascist movement got under way, however, it sought to find respectability in the writings of the great thinkers of the past. Then it was that Carlyle was discovered by the fascists, who were delighted to find their ideas proclaimed in eloquent words by the great Victorian. Carlyle's writings were translated and widely circulated in Fascist Italy. A prominent Fascist writer, G. Liciardelli, wrote a book on Mussolini and Carlyle, the thesis of which was that Carlyle was the prophet of a new social order and that the historic mission of Mussolini was to establish it on solid foundations. Among the precursors of fascism, "none had expressed as clearly as did Carlyle the principles and ideas that were later adopted by the leaders of fascism." Liciardelli especially praised Carlyle's views on the regimentation of labor, as foretelling the coming of a society in which workers and employers would be united, not by the "cash-nexus," but by a system in which the worker would render obedience, "wise, noble, and loyal," in return for the noble leadership of the employer. In the opinion of Liciardelli, Mussolini incorporated Carlyle's views on labor into his famous "Charter of Labor."[67]

Carlyle's popularity was even greater in Nazi Germany. Three hundred thousand copies of a book of selections from his works, translated into German, were sold during the period 1926 to 1932. His *Heroes and Hero-worship* was widely read in Nazi schools.[68] Far

[67] For the above quotations and for a discussion of Carlyle's influence on fascism, see the excellent study by A. C. Taylor, *Carlyle et la pensée latine* (Paris, 1937), 364–366 and 378–382.

[68] Emery E. Neff, *Carlyle* (New York, 1932), 268–269.

more than to the Italians did Carlyle appeal to the Germans. Had he not singled out the Teutons as the master race and Germany as the "Queen of the Continent"? Had he not expressed fascist principles in language that flamed across the century? It is no wonder that the Nazis recognized in Carlyle a kindred spirit whose ideas had anticipated their own.

Chapter 16: The Historic Importance
of Bourgeois Liberalism

Bourgeois liberalism was not a passing episode or a strange interlude, but a vital link in "the chain of being" in modern civilization. Hence only a historical appraisal can reveal what was temporary and what was permanent in its ideas and policies. What is the historic importance of bourgeois liberalism? What was the heritage that it gave to democracy? It is an historic truth that in both the political and social spheres the bourgeois liberals aimed to advance chiefly the interests of the middle class. Yet in the process of doing so, they unwittingly and inevitably created political machinery that served wider interests; inaugurated policies that benefited the nation as a whole; and proclaimed a political and social philosophy which, in the end, was to be turned against the very class whose interests they championed. Bourgeois liberalism has the unique distinction of having created a way of life and thought that outlived the historic circumstances that had brought it forth. In it was the promise of a larger liberty and of a greater equality than that envisioned by its champions in England and France during the 1830's.

The creation of the liberal state constitutes the outstanding achievement of bourgeois liberalism. A tremendous innovation in the theory and practice of government took place when, almost for the first time in history, the state became the protector of the freedom of the individual and the most efficient instrument of social progress. This new role of the state was clearly envisaged by that most bourgeois of bourgeois liberals Jeremy Bentham. Previously the state had been the chief bulwark of caste privilege and the most efficient instrument of the suppression of individual freedom. Fear of the state as their enemy was almost universal among the disinherited of mankind. The law was always against them: to keep them in ignorance, in servitude, and in poverty. With the advent of liberalism, even in its restricted, bourgeois form, the state appeared in the guise of a friend of the common man and acted—even though haltingly—to improve his lot and to protect him against oppression. Before that the state had acted in the interest of the economically strong; now it acted in the interest of the economically weak. Despite the fact that the bourgeois liberals used the state to promote the interests chiefly of the middle class, the very nature of the liberal state made such a policy self-defeating in the long run. Even in their heyday of power, the class policies of the bourgeois liberals were not entirely successful. This is made clear by the comprehensive factory laws passed by Parliament, where the champions of these laws, notably Shaftesbury, were supported by humanitarians, irrespective of party or of class. Such drastic reforms in the interest of the workers would have been well-nigh impossible prior to 1832. Parliament then was not fashioned to become the instrument of such reforms.

It was the liberal state that succeeded in reconciling government with liberty. Previously, government had been the enemy, and its opponents, the friends of human liberty. Before the advent of bourgeois liberalism, every movement for liberty was a movement against the government as an organized system of repression manipulated by those in power to protect their special interests. Almost the first act of a newly established liberal state was the proclamation of a Bill of Rights or a Declaration of the Rights of Man, guaranteeing the civil liberty of all citizens, including those who opposed the government. At last there was effected a great reconciliation—that between government and liberty.

Later in the nineteenth century, when the social question came to the fore, the liberal state again assumed a new role. It was that of mediator between the contending classes. The liberal state did not aim to liberate one class at the expense of another, as had been done during the French Revolution. That was *social* revolution, which all liberals of whatever school have repudiated. The aim of the liberal state was to modify and, in time, even to abolish the class structure of society through continuous social reform, modest at first but increasing in scope and in intensity. In order to accomplish this aim without too much friction, liberals developed the method of compromise, according to which the propertied classes were given protection against confiscation, and the nonpropertied classes, protection against poverty. The functioning of the liberal state in all its political and social phases can now be clearly seen in the extensive reforms put through by the British Labor party.

Equally revolutionary was the new basis of authority adopted by the liberal state, in that it was based on numbers, not on supernatural sanction, or on a hereditary elite, or on military power. Supreme authority lay in a representative assembly; an election gave power, and an election took it away. The road to power lay clear and open to any group that had the backing of a majority of the electorate. As a consequence, revolution gave way to reform as a method of progress, and repression gave way to popular support as a means of maintaining stability. There was now a new "legitimacy" for government, not the old legitimacy of divine right but the new one of majority rule. It was this new legitimacy that made possible both progress and stability.

But the great shortcoming of bourgeois liberalism was that it greatly narrowed the basis of representation by its insistence on a propertied suffrage. In truth, the equality preached by the bourgeois liberals was in essence the equality of property owners—landlords, industrialists, merchants, and financiers. That is why they so strongly opposed aristocratic privileges, which gave the landlords a position of supremacy over all the property owners. And that is why they opposed manhood suffrage, which sought to establish political equality between the propertied and nonpropertied classes. It was widely believed among bourgeois liberals that the "lower orders" lacked sufficient rationality to weigh public questions; hence they should not be entrusted with the suffrage. Parliamentary government demanded that the electors be "comfortable" in worldly goods. And, in the opinion of the bourgeois liberals, the masses were unlikely to attain, in the near future, the degree of "comfort" necessary to fit them to become electors.[1] Hence they supported a political system, based on numbers, which kept the greatest number out of political life. So intense was the belief of the bourgeois liberals in property that they became afflicted by a kind of social myopia. They failed to see a new governing class in

[1] Walter Bagehot's political views were typical of those English liberals of his time. See Bryon Dexter, "Bagehot and the Fresh Eye," *Foreign Affairs,* XXIV (October, 1945).

the industrial capitalists and a new exploited class in the industrial workers. On the very morrow of the triumph of bourgeois liberalism in England and France, a sharp challenge was heard from the property-less masses. "The antagonism which formerly arose between the *bourgeoisie* and the aristocracy now begins to assert itself by degrees between the proletariate and the *bourgeoisie*. Beneath the veil of universal Liberalism, the *bourgeoisie* disguised a privilege similar to that once flaunted by the aristocracy. . . ."[2]

Class rule in the liberal state, however, soon became difficult—before long, impossible. It was a patent violation of its very reason for existence and a repudiation of the principles that had animated its creators. In their struggle for power against the aristocrats, the *bourgeoisie* had need of a universal appeal, to give moral validity to their claims and to win popular approval of their policies. Hence they espoused the principles of liberty and equality, and asserted that their policies would advance the greatest happiness of the greatest number. As a consequence, the system created by bourgeois liberalism contained an inner contradiction: the broad libertarian framework could not be manipulated by a narrow class interest. To resolve this contradiction, bourgeois liberalism developed a power, previously unknown in history, the power of political elasticity, which began to accommodate itself, fairly early and fairly easily, to the new forces in society that developed with the rise of the working class. The transition from bourgeois to democratic liberalism was considered inevitable by those farsighted liberal thinkers John Stuart Mill and Alexis de Tocqueville. By about 1870 manhood suffrage had virtually become an accomplished fact in England and France.

Another problem confronted the bourgeois liberals. How could freedom of the individual be justified in the face of widespread poverty and misery? Would the masses for long be content to remain "sovereign and miserable"? Because of their "atomic" view of society, the bourgeois liberals did not see that the individual apart from the society in which he was integrated was "a mere abstraction, a logical ghost, a metaphysical specter, a mere negation." In truth, the individual was a "bundle of relations" whose every activity and whose every thought was condi-

[2] G. de Ruggiero, *The History of European Liberalism*, trans. from the Italian by R. G. Collingwood (Oxford University Press, 1927), 48.

tioned by the social order in which he lived, moved, and had his being. He could not "paddle his own canoe" in an industrial system based on highly concentrated capital investments. In such a system, the problem of the relation of the individual to society was primarily a social problem; hence every method to give strength and bring happiness to the individual must, of necessity, be undertaken through social reform. And only through state intervention could social reform be made permanent and effective.

The bourgeois liberals failed to see the necessity for state intervention, largely because of their dogmatic insistence that government and economics were separate spheres of human activity and that only by keeping them separate could freedom be assured in the former and prosperity, in the latter. They had little understanding of the economic limitations on human freedom that they defended so ardently. The bourgeois liberals did not realize that the full enjoyment of civil rights and even of manhood suffrage depended on the possession of property or of unusual ability. By separating economics from politics, they ignored the political relevance of economic power. Their stout adherence to the doctrine of *laissez faire* was founded primarily upon this error, the consequence of which became only too clear, even in their own day. Ugly social facts continually negated beautiful economic theories. The great poverty that accompanied the vast accumulations of wealth was a direct contradiction of the almost unshakable belief of the bourgeois liberals that, once capital was free to invest and labor free to work, the entire community would be happy and prosperous. As between the individual worker and the individual employer, freedom of contract was based on a fictitious equality between the economically weak and the economically strong. It did not work and could not work, as was shown in the bitter industrial strife that was continually taking place. When a strike occurred, the government promptly emerged from the cold neutrality of the "political" world to intervene on the side of the employer. The good reason given for this intervention was to protect property rights; the real reason was to protect the property owner. The only protection that the worker had in his struggle for better conditions was the trade-union. Here, too, the government intervened, not however to protect the worker but to render him defenceless by outlawing unions. In mitigation of the lack of social vision on the part of the bourgeois liberals, it may be said that the economic problem in the early stage of the Industrial Revolution was to increase production and to decrease its cost. Long hours and low wages then seemed the easiest and quickest way of solving this problem.

For all their limitations, the economic ideas of the bourgeois liberals were the historic concomitants of the new economy of the industrial age, with its mass production and expanding markets. *Laissez faire* was originally designed as a weapon against the beneficiaries of mercantilism and feudalism, not against the legitimate demands of the workers. Only later did it become so. It must be kept in mind that the central aim of the classical economists—increased production and widespread consumption—has been accepted as a permanent contribution to modern economy. What the proponents of *laissez faire* did not realize is that it would result in new inequalities, in some ways more onerous than the old ones.

However, the principle of equality, once applied in the juridical and political fields, was bound to be applied before long in the social and economic fields. The very success of bourgeois liberalism was to prove its undoing through the repudiation of its chief doctrine *laissez faire*. Despite its class predilections, bourgeois liberalism did have a concept of public interest, a concept virtually unknown in the period of aristocratic rule. While it is true that by the "public" the bourgeois liberals meant the propertied elements, especially the middle class, yet the concept was a generous and an all-inclusive one. In order to create the "public," bourgeois liberalism swept away the caste-bound social order by abolishing slavery, serfdom, monopolistic guilds and corporations, and aristocratic privileges. Once the role of the state was admitted in adjusting social and economic relations, the limits set by bourgeois liberalism could not be maintained. The pace of reform was accelerated with the advent of democracy, when public interest became the prime mover in the great social and socialist reforms enacted in England and France during the nineteenth and twentieth centuries.

Yet so deep was the impact of bourgeois influence on the liberal movement between 1815 and 1870, that liberalism became synonymous with bourgeois class interest, with laissez-faire policies, and with a capitalist economy. Today liberalism has become identified with working-class interests, with state intervention, and even with an emerging socialist economy. Nevertheless, the bourgeois "taint" still haunts liberalism. There are still many who do not or cannot see the great transformation that liberalism has undergone since 1870. It is, indeed, a peculiar illustration of "cultural lag" when opposition to a system outlasts the system itself.

Bourgeois liberalism has long ago ceased to be a factor of importance in England and France. Its shortcomings have been derided by reformers, socialist and nonsocialist. Its contributions have been accepted —and forgotten. Those who still cherish its central doctrine of *laissez faire* are regarded as relics of a past that has receded even more in opinion than in time. Yet bourgeois liberalism did perform a historic function the greatness of which merits recognition. It was the fascist threat to parliamentary government and civil liberty, a heritage from bourgeois liberalism, that solidified the English people in the critical year 1940. And it was this same heritage that, in France, inspired the Resistance movement which led to the creation of the Fourth Republic. In the new pattern of life and thought that is now emerging, in which socialized democracy is in the foreground, bourgeois liberalism is clearly seen as the background. The prime object of this book has been to emphasize the great and lasting values that bourgeois liberalism gave to democracy and to "its way of life."

Bibliography

Bibliography

CHAPTERS 1 TO 3

GENERAL: On the general subject of modern liberalism innumerable volumes have been written. Few, however, treat the subject specifically as a system of thought and of policy; and still fewer are of great value at the present time. The following list will be found valuable to a student of modern liberalism. It includes Guido de Ruggiero, *History of European Liberalism,* trans. from the Italian by R. G. Collingwood (London, 1927); Benedetto Croce, *History of Europe in the Nineteenth Century,* trans. from the Italian by H. Furst (New York, 1933); L. T. Hobhouse, *Liberalism* (London, 1911); Emile Faguet, *Le Libéralisme* (Paris, 1912) L. von Mises, *Liberalismus* (Jena, 1927); Harold J. Laski, *Rise of European Liberalism* (New York, 1936); John Dewey, *Liberalism and Social Action* (New York, 1935); G. H. Mead, *Movements of Thought in the Nineteenth* Century (University of Chicago Press, 1936); and W. A. Orton, *The Liberal Tradition* (Yale University Press, 1945). Chapters dealing with liberal ideas and practices are to be found in F. J. C. Hearnshaw, ed., *The Social and Political Ideas of Some Representative Thinkers of the Age of Reaction and Reconstruction* (London, 1932) and *The Social and Political Ideas of some Representative Thinkers of the Victorian Age* (London, 1933); B. F. Lippincott, *Victorian Critics of Democracy* (University of Minnesota Press, 1938); A. N. Holcombe, *The Foundations of the Modern Commonwealth* (New York, 1923); and C. J. Friedrich, *Constitutional Government and Politics* (New York, 1937).

ENGLAND: The standard general histories of England during the first half of the nineteenth century are Élie Halévy, *A History of the English People,* trans. from the French by E. I. Watkin and D. A. Barker, 3 vols. (New York, 1924-1934); and *The Age of Peel and Cobden,* trans. from the French by E. I. Watkin (London, 1947). On the economic and social aspects: J. H. Clapham, *An Economic History of Modern Britain,* 3 vols. (Cambridge University Press, 1930-1932); S. Maccoby, *English Radicalism,* 2 vols. (London, 1935-1938); G.D.H. Cole, *A Short History* of the British Working Class Movement, 1789–1925, 3 vols. (London, 1925–1927). Sidney and Beatrice Webb, *Industrial Democracy* (London, 1920); and K. Polanyi, *The Great Transformation* (New York, 1944). On the theoretical aspects: A. V. Dicey, *Lectures on the Relation between Law and Public Opinion in England* (London, 1914); Crane Brinton, *English Political Thought in the Nineteenth Century* (London, 1933); and R. H. Murray, *Studies in the English Social and Political Thinkers of the Nineteenth Century,* 2 vols. (Cambridge, 1927).

FRANCE: The best general histories of France during the period 1815 to 1870 are in the series edited by E. Lavisse, *Histoire de France contemporaine,* vol. IV, S. Charléty, *La Restauration, 1815–1830* (Paris, 1921); vol. V, by the same author, *La Monarchie de Juillet* (Paris, 1921); vol. VI, Charles Seignobos, *La Révolution de 1848—Le Second Empire* (Paris, 1921); vol. VII, by the same author, *Le Déclin de l'Empire et l'établissement de la 3ᵉ République, 1859–1875* (Paris, 1921). Other notable general histories of France are Georges Weill, *La France sous la monarchie constitutionelle* (Paris, 1912) and *Histoire du parti républicain en France, 1814–1880* (Paris, 1928); P. Thureau-Dangin, *Le Parti libéral sous la Restauration* (Paris, 1876); Frederick B. Artz, *France under the Bourbon Restoration* (Harvard University Press, 1931); J. B. Wolf, *France, 1815 to the Present* (New York, 1940); and P. Bastid, *Doctrines et institutions politiques de la Seconde République* (Paris, 1945). On the economic and social aspects: E. Levasseur, *Histoire des classes ouvrières et de l'industrie en France de 1789 à 1870,* 2 vols. (Paris 1903–1904); Henri Sée, *La Vie économique de la France sous la monarchie censitaire, 1815–1848* (Paris, 1927) and *Histoire économique de la France: Les temps modernes (1789–1914)* (Paris, 1942); Shepherd B. Clough, *France, A History of National Economics, 1789–1939* (New York, 1939); A. Viallate, *L'Activité économique en France de la fin du XVIIIᵉ siècle à nos jours* (Paris, 1937); Georges Weill, *Histoire du mouvement social, 1852–1924* (Paris, 1924); P. Louis, *Histoire de la classe ouvrière en France depuis la Révolution* (Paris, 1927); and E. Dolléans, *Histoire du mouvement ouvrière,* 2 vols. (Paris, 1936–1939). On the theoretical aspects: Émile Faguet, *Politiques et moralistes du dix-neuvième siècle,* 3 vols. (Paris, 1891–1899); H. Michel, *L'Idée de l'état* (Paris, 1895); R. Soltau, *French Political Thought in the Nineteenth Century* (Yale University Press, 1931); George Boas, *French Philosophers of the Romantic Period* (Johns Hopkins Press, 1925).

CHAPTERS 4 TO 7 AND 9

UTILITARIANISM: John Bowring, ed., *The Works of Jeremy Bentham*, 11 vols. (Edinburgh, 1843); Leslie Stephen, *The English Utilitarians,* 3 vols. (London, 1900); A. V. Dicey, *Lectures on the Relation between Law and Public Opinion in England* (London, 1914); E. Albee, *A History of English Utilitarianism* (London, 1902); W. L. Davidson, *Political Thought in England; the Utilitarians from Bentham to J. S. Mill* (London, 1915); C. M. Atkinson, *Jeremy Bentham* (London, 1905); H. G. Lundin, *The Influence of Jeremy Bentham on English Economic Development* (Iowa City, 1923); C. Phillipson, *Three Criminal Law Reformers: Beccaria, Bentham, Romilly* (London, 1903); W. Seagle, *Men of Law* (New York, 1947); C. W. Everett, *The Education of Jeremy Bentham* (Columbia University Press, 1931); C. W. Everett, ed., *Bentham's Comments on the Commentaries* (Oxford, 1928); E. L. Kayser, *The Grand Social Enterprise; A Study of Jeremy Bentham in His Relation to Liberal Nationalism* (New York, 1932); Jeremy Bentham, *The Theory of Legislation* (C. K. Ogden, ed., New York, 1931) and *A Fragment on Government* (F. C. Montague, ed., Oxford, 1931); and John Stuart Mill, "Utilitarianism," in *Utilitarianism, Liberty and Representative Government* (London, Everyman's Library, 1914), and "Bentham," *Dissertations and Discussions* (New York, 1874), I, 355–417.

CLASSICAL ECONOMY: Charles Gide and Charles Rist, *History of Economic Doctrines from the Time of the Physiocrats to the Present Day,* trans. from the French by R. Richards (Boston, 1915); L. H. Haney, *History of Economic Thought* (New York, 1920); E. Whittaker, *A History of Economic Ideas* (New York, 1940); J. Bonar, *Philosophy and Political Economy* (London, 1909); David Ricardo, *Works* (J. R. McCulloch, ed., London, 1888) and *Principles of Political Economy and Taxation* (E. C. K. Gonner, ed., London, 1891); J. H. Hollander, *David Ricardo* (Baltimore, 1910); C. C. North, *The Sociological Implications of Ricardo's Economics* (Chicago, 1915); F. H. Knight, "The Ricardian Theory of Production and Distribution," *Canadian Journal of Economic and Political Science,* I (1935); Thomas R. Malthus, *An Essay on the Principle of Population* (London, 1890) and *Principles of Political Economy* (London, 1936); C. R. Drysdale, *Life and Writings of Thomas R. Malthus* (London, 1892); J. Bonar, *Malthus and His Work* (London, 1924); G. T. Griffith, *Population Problems of the Age of Malthus* (Cambridge University Press, 1926); and S. Leon Levy, *Nassau W. Senior: The Prophet of Capitalism* (Boston, 1944).

PHILOSOPHIC RADICALISM: Élie Halévy, *The Growth of Philosophic Radicalism,* trans. from the French by Mary Morris (London, 1928); James Mill, *Essays* (London, n.d.); Alexander Bain, *James Mill* (London, 1882); Graham Wallas, *Life of Francis Place* (London, 1919); C. B. R. Kent, *The English Radicals* (London, 1899); and A. S. Pringle-Pattison, *The Philosophical Radicals* (London, 1907).

CHARTISM: J. L. and Barbara Hammond, *The Age of the Chartists* (London, 1930); E. Dolléans, *Le Chartisme,* 2 vols. (Paris, 1912); M. Hovell, *The Chartist Movement* (London, 1918); J. West, *A History of the Chartist Movement* (New York, 1920); F. F. Rosenblatt, *The Chartist Movement in its Social and Economic Aspects* (New York, 1916); and P. W. Slosson, *The Decline of the Chartist Movement* (New York, 1917).

CHAPTERS 8 AND 10

BOURGEOIS LIBERALS: Books dealing with the "Doctrinaires": C. H. Pouthas, *Guizot pendant la Restauration* (Paris, 1923); A. de Barante, *La Vie politique de M. Royer-Collard,* 2 vols. (Paris, 1861); E. Spuller, *Royer-Collard* (Paris, 1895); Robert de Nesmes-Desmarets, *Les Doctrines politiques de Royer-Collard* (Paris, 1908); and Gabriel Rémond, *Royer-Collard* (Paris, 1933).

CONSTANT: The writings and speeches of Constant are to be found in *Cours de politique constitutionnelle,* 2 vols. (Paris, 1872); *Discours à la chambre des députés,* 2 vols. (Paris, 1827–1828); and *De l'esprit de conquête et de l'usurpation* (Paris, 1918). Critical studies dealing with the work of Constant are G. de Lauris, *Benjamin Constant et les idées libérales* (Paris, 1904); C. Bouglé, "La philosophie de Benjamin Constant," *Revue de Paris* (March, 1914); E. W. Schermerhorn, *Benjamin Constant* (Boston, 1924); J. de La Lombardière, *Les Idées politiques de Benjamin Constant* (Paris, 1928); J. Hiestand, *Benjamin Constant et la doctrine parlementaire* (Geneva, 1928); L. Dumont-Wilden, *La Vie de Benjamin Constant* (Paris, 1930); P. L. Léon, *Benjamin Constant* (Paris, 1930); and F. Wagner, *Der liberale Benjamin Constant* (Munich, 1932).

GUIZOT: The chief works of Guizot are *Mémoires pour servir à l'histoire de mon temps,* 8 vols. (Paris, 1858–1867); *Histoire parlementaire de France,* 5 vols. (Paris, 1863–1864); *Histoire des origines du gouvernement représentatif,* 2 vols. (Paris, 1874); History of Civilization, trans.

from the French by W. Hazlitt, 2 vols. (New York, 1899); and *De la démocratie en France* (Paris, 1849). The chief works on Guizot are Charles H. Pouthas, *Guizot pendant la Restauration, 1814–1830* (Paris, 1923), and *Le jeunesse de Guizot, 1787–1814* (Paris, 1936); M. A. Bardoux, *Guizot* (Paris, 1894); and E. P. Brush, *Guizot in the Early Years of the Orleanist Monarchy* (Urbana, Ill., 1929).

THE REACTIONARIES: General works dealing with the reactionary philosophers are Harold J. Laski, *Authority in the Modern State* (New Haven, 1919); L. Dimier, *Les Maîtres de la contre-Révolution* (Paris, 1917); Charlotte T. Muret, *French Royalist Doctrines since the Revolution* (New York, 1933); and A. Roche, *Les Idées traditionalistes en France de Rivarol à Charles Maurras* (Urbana, Ill., 1937).

DE MAISTRE: The most important works of De Maistre are *Considération sur la France* (Paris, 1936), *Essai sur le principe générateur des constitutions politiques* (Lyon, 1924), *Du pape* (Paris, 1903), and *Les Soirées de Saint-Petersbourg* (Paris, 1924). The leading works on De Maistre are G. Cogordan, *Vie de Joseph de Maistre* (Paris, 1894); C. Latreille, *Joseph de Maistre et la papauté* (Paris, 1906); G. Goyau, *La Pensée religieuse de Joseph de Maistre* (Paris, 1921); P. R. Rohden, *Joseph de Maistre als politischer Theoretiker* (München, 1929); and F. Bayle, *Les Idées politiques de Joseph de Maistre* (Paris, 1945).

DE BONALD: The collected works of De Bonald are *Oeuvres complètes* by J. P. Migne, 3 vols. (J. P. Migne, ed., Paris, 1859). The leading works on De Bonald are R. Mauduit, *Les Conceptions politiques et sociales de Bonald* (Paris, 1913); H. Moulinié, *De Bonald* (Paris, 1915); R. A. Nisbet, "De Bonald and the Concept of the Social Group," *Journal of the History of Ideas* (June, 1944); and A. Koyré, "Louis de Bonald," *Journal of the History of Ideas,* VIII (January, 1946).

CHATEAUBRIAND: The collected works of Chateaubriand are *Oeuvres complètes de Chateaubriand,* 12 vols. (Paris, 1859–1861). Works dealing with the ideas of Chateaubriand are H. P. Spring, *Chateaubriand at the Crossways* (New York, 1924); H. Sée, "Les Idées et les tendances politiques de Chateaubriand," *Revue d'histoire littéraire de la France,* XXXII (1925); V. Giraud, *Le Christianisme de Chateaubriand,* 2 vols. (Paris, 1925–1928); P. André-Vincent, *Les Idées politiques de Chateaubriand* (Montpellier, 1936); and E. Sevrin, "L'Évolution politique de Chateaubriand sous la Restauration," *Revue des études historique,* CV (October, 1938).

CHAPTER 11

JOHN STUART MILL: The chief works of John Stuart Mill are *Utilitarianism, On Liberty, Representative Government* (London, Everyman's Library, 1914); *Socialism* (W. P. D. Bliss, ed., New York, 1890); *Principles of Political Economy,* with an Introduction by W. J. Ashley, ed. (New York, 1909); *Dissertations and Discussions,* 4 vols. (New York, 1874); *Letters of John Stuart Mill* (H. S. R. Elliott, ed., 2 vols., London, 1910); *A System of Logic* (New York, 1900); *The Subjection of Women* (New York, 1911); *Three Essays on Religion* (London, 1874); *On Social Freedom,* with an Introduction by Dorothy Fosdick (New York, 1941); and *The Spirit of the Age,* with an Introductory Essay by Frederick A. von Hayek (University of Chicago Press, 1942). Books and articles dealing with the life and work of Mill are Alexander Bain, *John Stuart Mill* (London, 1882); Leslie Stephen, *The English Utilitarians* (New York, 1902), III; Emery E. Neff, *Carlyle and Mill* (New York, 1926); Henri Sée, "Stuart Mill et la propriété foncière," *Revue internationale de sociologie,* XXXII (1924), 606–619; H. Gehrig, "John Stuart Mill als Sozialpolitiker," *Jahrbuch fur Nationalökonomie und Statistik,* 3d Ser., XLVII (1914), 176–201; and George Morlan, *America's Heritage from John Stuart Mill* (Columbia University Press, 1936).

CHAPTER 12

ALEXIS DE TOCQUEVILLE: The original writings of De Tocqueville are *Oeuvres complètes,* 9 vols. (Paris, 1864–1867); *Correspondence and Conversations of Alexis de Tocqueville with Nassau William Senior,* 2 vols. (M. C. M. Simpson, ed., London, 1872); *Correspondance entre Alexis de Tocqueville et Arthur de Gobineau, 1843–1859* (Paris, 1909); *Souvenirs* (Paris, 1944); *Recollections,* trans. from the French by A. Teixeira de Mattos (New York, 1896); *The Old Regime and the Revolution,* trans. from the French by J. Bonner (New York, 1856); and *Democracy in America,* the Henry Reeves text as revised by Francis Bowen, now further corrected and edited by Phillips Bradley, 2 vols. (New York, 1945). Books and articles on De Tocqueville are John Stuart Mill, "M. de Tocqueville on Democracy in America," *Dissertations and Discussions,* II (New York, 1874); E. d'Eichthal, *Alexis de Tocqueville et la démocratie libérale* (Paris, 1897); James Bryce, *Studies in History and Jurisprudence* (London, 1901); R. P. Marcel, *Essai politique sur Alexis de Tocqueville* (Paris, 1910); L. Schemann, *Alexis de Tocqueville* (Stuttgart, 1911); A. Redier, *Comme disait Monsieur de Tocqueville* (Paris, 1925); G. W. Pierson, *Tocqueville and Beaumont in America* (New York, 1938); J. P. Mayer, *Alexis de Tocqueville,* trans. from the German by M. M. Bozman and C. Hahn (New York, 1940); M. Leroy, "Alexis de Tocqueville," *Politica* I (August, 1935); F. Roz, "Cent ans après—Alexis de Tocqueville et *La Démocratie en Amérique," Revue des deux mondes,* XXVIII (1935); A. Salomon, "Tocqueville, Moralist and Sociologist," *Social Research,* II (1935), and 'Tocqueville's Philosophy of Freedom," *The Review of Politics,* I (October, 1939); S. J. Copans, "Tocqueville's Later Years," *Romanic Review,* XXXVI (April, 1945); and J. Wach, "The Role of Religion in the Social Philosophy of Alexis de Tocqueville," *Journal of the History of Ideas,* VIII (January, 1946).

CHAPTER 13

LOUIS NAPOLEON BONAPARTE: For a complete bibliography dealing with Napoleon III, see R. Schnerb, "Napoleon III and the Second Empire," *Journal of Modern History,* VIII (1936), 338–355. The most important works dealing with the ideas of Napoleon and with the history of the Second Empire are Napoleon III, *Oeuvres,* 4 vols. (Paris, 1854–1856); Louis Napoleon Bonaparte, *Political and Historical Works,* trans. from the French, 2 vols. (London, 1852); Pierre de La Gorce, *Histoire de le Second Empire,* 7 vols. (Paris, 1894–1905); Albert Thomas, *Le Second Empire,* vol. X of Jean Jaurès, *Histoire socialiste* (Paris, 1907); F. A. Simpson, *The Rise of Louis Napoleon* (London, 1925), and *Louis Napoleon and the Recovery of France* (London, 1923). An excellent book on world conditions dealing with the period 1848 to 1860, especially with its economic aspects, is C. H. Pouthas, *Démocraties et capitalisme (1848–1860)* (Paris, 1941). Unusually good historical novels dealing with Napoleon III are those by Alfred Neumann: *Another Caesar,* trans. from the German by E. and C. Paul (New York, 1935), and *Man of December,* trans. from the German by E. and C. Paul (London, 1937). In recent years books have appeared that aimed to rehabilitate Napoleon III as a social reformer. H. N. Boon, *Rêve et réalité dans l'oeuvre économique et social de Napoléon III* (La Haye, 1936) praises the Emperor as a far-sighted progressive statesman and blames his ministers for the collapse of the Second Empire. Albert Guérard, *Napoleon III* (Harvard University Press, 1943), contends that the Emperor was deeply devoted to the cause of the masses, was a leader of "unfailing gentleness" and "profound generosity, and was a better democrat than Gambetta and a better socialist than Marx."

CHAPTER 14

PIERRE JOSEPH PROUDHON: The latest edition of Proudhon's complete works is *Oeuvres complètes de P. J. Proudhon,* 14 vols. (C. Bouglé and Henri Moysset, eds., Paris, 1923–1938). An older edition is P. J. Proudhon, *Oeuvres complètes,* 37 vols. (Paris, 1866–1883). A collection of miscellaneous notes, "Carnets de Proudhon," was published in *La Grande revue,* L–LI. Proudhon's correspondence, which is as interesting as it is voluminous, is to be found in *Correspondance de P. J. Proudhon,* 14 vols. (Paris, 1875), and in *Lettres au Citoyen Rolland* (Paris, 1946). The biographies of Proudhon are K. Diehl, *P. J. Proudhon, Seine Lehre und sein Leben,* 3 vols. (Jena, 1888–1896); A. Desjardins, *Proudhon,* 2 vols. (Paris, 1896); and E. Droz, *P. J. Proudhon* (Paris, 1909). Books dealing with the various ideas of Proudhon are Herbert Bourgin, *Proudhon* (Paris, 1901); Gaetan Pirou, *Proudhonisme et syndicalisme révolutionnaire* (Paris, 1910); Aimé Berthod, *P. J. Proudhon et la propriété* (Paris, 1910); C. Bouglé, *La Sociologie de Proudhon* (Paris, 1911); C. Bouglé, ed., *Proudhon et notre temps* (Paris, 1920) and *Proudhon* (Paris, 1930); Alfred G. Boulen, *Les Idées solidaristes de Proudhon* (Paris, 1912); Laurent Labrusse, *Conception proudhoniènne du crédit gratuit* (Paris, 1919); Shi Yung Lu, *The Political Theories of P. J. Proudhon* (New York, 1922); Nicholas Bourgeois, *Proudhon, le fédéralisme et la paix* (Paris, 1926); Henry Cohen, ed., *Proudhon's Solution of the Social Problem* (New York, 1927); Jeanne Duprat, *Proudhon, sociologue et moraliste* (Paris, 1929); Pierre Bourgeau, *P. J. Proudhon et la critique de la démocratie* (Strasbourg, 1933); Denis W. Brogan, *Proudhon* (London, 1934); Jacques Chabrier, *L'Idée de la révolution d'après Proudhon* (Paris, 1935). Chapters and articles on Proudhon are to be found in Émile Faguet, *Politicians and Moralists of the Nineteenth Century,* trans. by Dorothy Galton (London, 1928); Max Nettlau, *Der Anarchismus von Proudhon zu Kropotkin* (Berlin, 1927); Georges Gurvitch, *L'Idée du droit social* (Paris, 1932); Silvio Gesell, *The Natural Economic Order* (San Antonio, Tex., 1934); Louis Dimier, *Les Maitres de la contre-Révolution* (Paris, 1917); Dorothy W. Douglas, "P. J. Proudhon: A Prophet of 1848," *American Journal of Sociology,* XXXIV-XXXV (1929); Dudley Dillard,

"Keynes and Proudhon," *Journal of Economic History,* II (May, 1942); M. Amoudruz, *Proudhon et l'Europe* (Paris, 1946) and H. de Lubac, *Proudhon et le Christianisme* (Paris, 1945).

CHAPTER 15

THOMAS CARLYLE: The centenary edition of *The Works of Thomas Carlyle* (London, 1898–1901) consists of thirty volumes. The best known biographies of Carlyle are J. A. Froude, *Carlyle: A History of the First Forty Years of His Life* (New York, 1890) and *Carlyle: A History of His Life in London* (New York, 1884); and D. A. Wilson, *Carlyle,* 6 vols. (London, 1923–1934). Books dealing with various aspects of Carlyle's moral and social philosophy are Leslie Stephen, *Hours in a Library* (New York, 1899), IV; J. MacCunn, *Six Radical Thinkers* (London, 1907); C. E. Vaughan, "Carlyle and His German Masters," *Essays and Studies,* by members of the English Association (Oxford, 1910); C. Cestre, "La Doctrine sociale de Carlyle," *Revue du mois,* XVI (1913), 553–580; G. P. Gooch, *History and Historians in the Nineteenth Century* (London, 1935); Else Kemper, "Carlyle als Imperialist," *Zeitschrift für Politik,* XI (1918), 115–166; F. W. Roe, *Social Philosophy of Carlyle and Ruskin* (New York, 1921); N. Young, *Carlyle, His Rise and Fall* (London, 1927); B. H. Lehmann, *Carlyle's Theory of the Hero* (Durham, N. C., 1928); Olga Hess, *Carlyle's Stellung zum Germanentum* (Freiberg, 1926); O. H. Burdett, *The Two Carlyles* (London, 1930); L. Cazamian, *Carlyle,* trans. from the French by E. K. Brown (New York, 1932); Emery E. Neff, *Carlyle* (New York, 1932) and *Carlyle and Mill* (New York, 1926); H. J. C. Grierson, *Carlyle and Hitler* (Cambridge, 1933); C. F. Harrold, *Carlyle and German Thought* (New Haven, 1934); W. Vollrath, *Th. Carlyle und H. St. Chamberlain, zwei Freunde Deutschlands* (Munich, 1935); Theodor Deimel, *Carlyle und der National-sozialismus* (Würzburg, 1936); A. C. Taylor, *Carlyle et la pensée latine* (Paris, 1937); B. E. Lippincott, *Victorian Critics of Democracy* (Minneapolis, 1938); V. Basch, *Carlyle, l'homme et l'oeuvre* (Paris, 1938); Ernest Seillière, *Un précurseur du national-socialisme: l'actualité de Carlyle* (Paris, 1939); Louise M. Young, *Thomas Carlyle and the Art of History* (London, 1939); A. Ballmer, *Carlyles Stellung zu Theorie und Praxis des modernen Kapitalismus* (Basel, 1940); Hill Shine, *Carlyle and the Saint-Simonians* (Baltimore, 1941); E. R. Bentley, *A Century of Hero-worship* (Philadelphia, 1944).

Index

Index

A

America, and Bentham, 125
  and Carlyle, 378
  and De Tocqueville, 291, 302
  liberalism in, 8, 18–19
Anarchism of Proudhon, 352, 363
Anglican church, and Disraeli, 205
  and Philosophic Radicals, 127–128
  position of, 128–129
  and propertied classes, 218–219
Anticlericalism, in France, 42, 172–173
  and liberalism, 6–7
Antiimperialism in England, 196–199
Anti-Semitism, of Carlyle, 385
  of Proudhon, 358–359, 366
  under Second French Empire, 325
  under Second French Republic, 317–318
Aristocracy, Carlyle on, 373
  position of, in England, 64, 67, 75, 111–112
  in France, 141–142, 159, 223–224
Association, right of, 11–12, 300–301

B

Ballot, secret, 125, 269–270
Bank, People's, as planned by Proudhon, 334, 342–343
Bastiat, Frédéric, 235
Bentham, Jeremy, disciples of, 46–47
  early career of, 44–45
  against English constitution, 46
  opinions of, 49, 119–121, 123, 133–134, 197, 209
  criticism of, by Carlyle and Marx, 58
  personality of, 47–48
Benthamism (see Utilitarianism)
Blackstone, William, criticism of, by Bentham, 46

Blackstone, William, on English constitution, 27-28
Blanc, Louis, opposition of, to July Monarchy, 243
  to *laissez faire*, 237
  Proudhon against, 349
  and Revolution of 1848, 311
Blanqui, Louis Auguste, 242, 313
Bolingbroke, Lord, 25
Bonald, Vicomte de, 166–167
Bourgeois, petty, defense of, by Proudhon, 345, 348
  position of, in France, 337–338
Bourgeoisie, importance of, 66–67, 229–232
  influence of, in England, 121–123
  and liberalism, 3
  opposition to, by workers and aristocrats, 73–74
  origin of, 61–65
  position of, in France, under July Monarchy, 223–224
  under Old Regime, 33
  under Restoration, 140–141, 143, 144
  triumph of, with Reform Bill of 1832, 183, 201
Burke, Edmund, 29

C

Cairnes, John Elliott, 71
Candidates, official, under July Monarchy, 249
  under Restoration, 174-175
  under Second French Empire, 322
Capitalism, against aristocratic rule, 30
  in France, 242–243, 337
  Mill, J. S., on, 278
  and progress, 109
  Proudhon on, 340

Capitalists, and aristocracy, 65, 74, 216–218, 224
  Carlyle on, 373
  classical economists for, 74
  De Tocqueville on, 295, 305
  importance of, 62–64, 109–110
  origin of, 61–62, 73
  and reform, 135
  (*See also* Bourgeoisie)
Carlyle, Thomas, admiration of, for Germany, 385–387
  character and views of, 373–376
  early life of, 370–372
  for fascistic methods, 380–382
  fascists for, 395
  for imperialism and racialism, 383–384
  literary style of, 390
  against manhood suffrage, 378–379
  prefascist views of, 389–390
  for rule by elite, 377
  shortcomings of, 387–388
Catholic church, as bulwark against revolution, 314–316
  during French Revolution, 41
  under Restoration, 170–171
  under Second French Empire, 327
Censorship, in England, 131
  in France, 177–178, 323
Charte, 140–141, 147, 149–150
Chartism, 202–203, 215
Chateaubriand, Vicomte de, 167–169
Class struggle, capitalists in, against landlords, in England, 74–76, 185
  in France, 145, 156
  against workers, in England, 215
  in France, 345–346
Clericalism, in France, 163–172
  support of, by *bourgeoisie*, 168, 315
Cobbett, William, 129
Cobden, Richard, 101, 102, 195
Combination Laws, 101–103
Conservative party, 204
Constant, Benjamin, character and views of, 150–151
  on dictatorship, 327–328
  political ideas of, 154–156, 176
Constitution, English, Bentham on, 46
  Blackstone on, 27-28

Corn laws, 78, 135, 192–196
Credit, free, Proudhon on, 343–344

D

Democracy, Carlyle on, 375, 377–378
  De Tocqueville on, 296–297, 302–303
  fear of, in England, 121
    in France, 153, 297
    unjustified, 265, 301
  Guizot on, 245–246
  Macaulay against, 203
  Mill, J. S., on, 264–266, 268
  Philosophic Radicals against, 122–124
  and property, 304
  Proudhon on, 349–350
Diminishing returns, law of, 79, 88
Disraeli, Benjamin, 23, 204–205
Doctrinaires, 148–149
Dominion system in British Empire, 199
Dumont, Etienne, 46–47

E

East India Company, 200
Economists, classical, for capitalism, 81
  dismal views of, 78–80
  importance of, 68–69
  influence of, in England, 106
    in France, 235
  on nature, 106–107
  against workers, 84–85, 94, 96, 98
Education, popular, in England, 273
  in France, 252, 315
  and liberalism, 20
  utilitarians for, 53, 91, 266
Emigrés, French, 140, 142
Equality, and economic conditions, 67–68
  and French Revolution, 36–37, 40
  and liberalism, 8–9
  utilitarians on, 55

F

Fascism, and Carlyle, 380–381
  prelude to, in Second French Empire, 320–324, 329
  and Proudhon, 365–369

Federalism of Proudhon, 353
Feminism, and Mill, J. S., 264–265
  and Proudhon, 361–362
Finance, power of, in France, 233–234, 325
Frances, the two, 146–147, 163, 173, 180
    under July Monarchy, 222, 239, 243, 248, 254
    Proudhon on, 356
    under Second Empire, 326–327
    under Second Republic, 308–313

G

Germans, Carlyle on, 385–387
Gladstone, William E., 7, 186–187, 218
Greatest happiness principle (*see* Utilitarianism)
Guizot, François, for bourgeois rule, 251
  career of, 224–225
  education law of, 252
  for inequality, 245
  for monarchy, 251
  and parliament, 248
  personality and opinions of, 225–228
  political views of, 157–158, 176
  for religion, 314–315

H

Helvétius, Claude, 257
Heroes, government by, 375, 376
Human nature, utilitarian view of, 50, 52–53

I

Imperialism, Carlyle for, 383–384
  liberals against, 198–199
  utilitarians against, 197–198
Individualism, 9–10, 210–211
Industry, progress of, in England, 196
  in France, 143, 233, 324
Inequality, the new, 82, 99
  De Tocqueville on, 305
  justification of, by Carlyle, 374
    by classical economists, 84
    by Guizot, 232, 245
    by Malthus, 99

Inheritance, right of, 276–277
Intellectual freedom and liberalism, 10–11

J

Joint-stock company, 61
July Monarchy, 222–224, 237–238
June Days of 1848, 168, 307, 313, 321, 367

L

Labor as commodity, 75, 81, 92
Laissez faire, and capitalism, 211–212
  De Tocqueville on, 305
  in England, 206–209
  in France, 235, 236
  and labor, 103–105
  Mill, J. S., on, 272–274
  opposition to, by Carlyle, 391–393
    by Disraeli, 205
    by Louis Napoleon, 317
    by Proudhon, 340
  support of, by Guizot, 236
  system of, 206–209
  and the state, 15–18
  and workers, 212
Lamartine, Alphonse de, 310
Laski, Harold J., 6
Laws, economic, and capitalism, 72, 81
  and distribution of wealth, 69–70
  and labor, 85, 93
Le Chapelier, loi, 40, 160
Lefebvre, Georges, 37
Liberalism, bourgeois, contributions of, 397–399
  De Tocqueville on, 295
  in England, 114, 182–183, 219–220
  in France, 148, 151, 161, 163, 221–222, 251
  Louis Napoleon on, 317
  shortcomings of, 399–402
  and *bourgeoisie,* 3
  and education, 20
  English, 27, 33
  and equality, 8–9
  French, 33–34
  and human nature, 3–5

Liberalism, and individualism, 9–10
  and intellectual freedom, 10–11
  and nationalism, 12
  and progress, 12–13
  and reason, 5–6
  and religion, 6–7
  and revolution, 2–3
  and rights of minorities, 11–12
  and the state, 13–15, 18, 209, 397–399
Liberals, English, 186
  French, 150
Liberties, civil, 8, 251–252
Liberty, intellectual, in England, 23
  and liberalism, 10–11
  Mill, J. S., on, 280–286
Locke, John, 22
Lords, House of, 125–127, 183, 269
Louis Napoleon, career of, 315–316, 318–
  319, 326–327
  and Napoleonic legend, 243
  Nazis for, 328–329
  personality and views of, 316–318
  Proudhon for, 355

M

Macaulay, Lord, 136, 208
McCulloch, J. R., 96
Machine, and labor, 107
  nature and influence of, 60
Maistre, Joseph de, 164–166
Malthus, Thomas Robert, career of, 85–86
  influence of, 91
  Mill, J. S., for, 279–280
  principle of population of, 87–90, 93–94
  refutation of, 91–92
  on wages, 93–95, 98, 104–105
Manchester school, 213
Marx, Karl, 214, 242–243, 278–279, 313,
  346
Maurras, Charles, 168–169, 364
Middle class (*see Bourgeoisie*)
Militarism, Carlyle for, 380–382
  Proudhon for, 360–361
Mill, James, against imperialism, 197–198
  on labor, 92
  for middle class, 66, 116
  personality and career of, 47, 114–115
  plan of, for reforming the Lords, 127

Mill, James, for popular education, 53
  relations of, with Mill, J. S., 257
  on suffrage, 122–123
Mill, John Stuart, and capitalism, 66, 271
  career of, 257–262
  conversion of, to socialism, 275
  on government, 263–264
  on imperialism, 198
  importance of, 260, 262, 287–288
  against landed aristocracy, 67, 76, 277–
    278
  for liberty, 280–286
  for limitation of inheritance, 276–277
  for Malthusianism, 98, 279–280
  on middle class, 124
  for nationalism, 270–271
  for popular education, 266
  on progress, 95
  for state intervention, 104
  on suffrage, 123, 264, 265
  on trade-unions, 102, 273
  on utilitarianism, 52, 263
  on wages, 273
  on woman, 261
  and workers, 274–275
Monarchy and Philosophic Radicals, 125–
  126
Mutualism, 352–353

N

Napoleon III (*see* Louis Napoleon)
Napoleonic legend, 243, 315
National workshops, 311, 313
Nationalism, and liberalism, 12
  Mill, J. S., for, 270–271
  Proudhon against, 350
Natural rights, Bentham on, 49
  and French Revolution, 35

O

Opposition, lack of, in France, 175–176,
  247, 250
  and liberal state, 17
  origin of, in England, 24–26
Owen, Robert, 105, 129

P

Parliament, Carlyle against, 376-377
  English, control of, by aristocracy, 28-30,
    113
    reform of, 31
    and Revolution of 1688, 22
    (*See also* Reform Bill of 1832)
  French, under July Monarchy, 247
    under Restoration, 173
    under Second Empire, 322
Parties, political, English, 28-29, 186-187
  French, 173-174, 246-247
Pays légal, 246, 249
People's Bank as planned by Proudhon,
  334, 342-343
Philosophes and revolution, 32-33, 35-36
Philosophic Radicals, influence of, 134-135
  organization of, 116-117
  for parliamentary reform, 117-118
  political activity of, 119, 130-131, 187
  political views of, 120-124
  (*See also* Mill, James)
Place, Francis, 48, 102
Plural voting, 267-268
Poor Law, English, 189-192
Population, principle of (*see* Malthus,
  Thomas Robert)
Poverty, attitudes toward, 107-108
  Malthus on, 110
  and surplus economy, 83-84
Press, Paris, 177, 248, 252
Progress, and capitalism, 109
  and liberalism, 12-13
  Proudhon on, 351, 360
  and subsistence, 94
  and utilitarianism, 52
Property, rights of, and capitalism, 64-65
  De Tocqueville on, 304
  in France, 40-41, 140, 158, 161-162,
    241, 303, 304, 312, 338
  and French Revolution, 34-35, 41
  Proudhon on, 339-340
  support of, by Mill, J. S., 271
    by Philosophic Radicals, 133-134
    by utilitarians, 55
Proprietors, peasant, in France, 34, 40, 144-
  145

Proudhon, Pierre Joseph, for anarchism, 352
  as anti-Semite, 358-359
  career of, 333-335
  on classless society, 345-346
  against democracy, 349-350
  for dictatorship, 355, 358
  against finance, 341-342
  as herald of fascism, 365-369
  as militarist, 360-361
  for mutualism and federalism, 352-353
  against nationalism, 350
  for Negro slavery, 359
  personality and opinions of, 335-337
  on religion, 362
  against rights of property, 339-340
  against rights of women, 361-362
  against socialism and social reform, 348-
    349
  against trade-unions, 347

R

Racialism, Carlyle for, 382-383
  De Tocqueville against, 296*n*.
  (*See also* Anti-Semitism)
Radicalism (*see* Philosophic Radicals)
Reform, factory, in England, 213-214
  in France, 253
  utilitarians for, 210
  prison, Bentham for, 45-46
    Carlyle against, 393
  social, De Tocqueville for, 306
    Disraeli for, 205
    in France, 311, 324
    Louis Napoleon for, 316-318
Reform Bill of 1832, 136-137, 182-183
Reforms, Tory, 132
Reign of Terror (*see* Revolution, French)
Religion, and clericals, 164-169
  and education in France, 252
  freedom of, in England, 23
    in France, 23
  Guizot on, 314-315
  and liberalism, 6-7
  and Philosophic Radicals, 128
  Proudhon on, 362
Rent, law of, 74-76

Representation, proportional, Mill, J. S., for, 268–269
Republicanism, Bentham for, 125
in France, 246–247
Résistance, La, 250
Responsibility, ministerial, in England, 184
in France, 175, 223
Revolution, English, of 1688, 22–24
French, 34–38, 139
of 1830, 180–181
of 1848, 308–310
Ricardo, David, for capitalism, 69–70
career of, 68
importance of, 68–69
and labor, 92
"law of rent," 74–76
for propertied suffrage, 123
Right to work, principle of, 275, 311
Rights of Man, Declaration of (*see* Liberties, civil)
Roebuck, John Arthur, 119, 135, 185
Royer-Collard, Pierre Paul, career and influence of, 149–150
political views of, 152–154, 175–176, 241
religious views of, 172
and Revolution of 1830, 221

S

Sacrilege Law, 171
Saint-Simon, Henri de, 62–63
Say, Jean Baptiste, 235
Secret societies in France, 247–248
Shaftesbury, Lord, 213-214
Sismondi, Charles de, 235–236
Slavery, Negro, abolition of, 197, 199–200
Carlyle for, 384–385
Proudhon for, 359
Smith, Adam, 72, 78, 85, 209
Snyder, Carl, 69
Socialism, Blanc, Louis, for, 311
in France, 239–241, 325
Mill, J. S., for, 275–276
Proudhon against, 348
(*See also* June Days of 1848; Marx, Karl)

Societies, secret, in France, 247–248
Speenhamland system, 89, 189, 190
Spencer, Herbert, 105
State, liberal, 209, 397–399
stationary, 77, 79
Stephen, Leslie, 43
Subsistence theory of wages, 75, 77, 92–94
Suffrage, manhood, Carlyle against, 378–379
De Tocqueville for, 255, 306
in England, 202–203
in France, establishment of, 38, 312, 322
issue of, 153–156, 243–244, 255, 314
Proudhon against, 349–350
propertied, in England, 39, 137
in France, 39, 140–141, 222–223
woman, Mill, J. S., for, 265
Syndicalism, 362
Système Guizot, 249–251, 253–254

T

Tamworth Manifesto, 185
Tennyson, Lord, 219
Thiers, Adolphe, 246
Tocqueville, Alexis de, on America, 298–302
on *bourgeoisie,* 237, 238, 250–251, 295
career of, 291–293
character and opinions of, 294
on class struggle, 156–157
contributions of, 295
and democracy, 255, 295–297, 306
on Louis Napoleon, 321
on property rights, 312
Tories, in England, 25, 214
Totalitarianism, and Carlyle, 382
and liberty, 288–289
and Proudhon, 368
Trade-unions, in England, 100–102, 195, 196
in France, 40, 160, 240, 329
Mill, J. S., for, 273–274
Proudhon against, 347

U

Utilitarianism, and capitalism, 71–72
  Carlyle against, 58
  contributions of, 58–59
  Marx against, 58
  as middle-class philosophy, 56–57
  popularity of, 44, 57–58, 187, 188
  principles of, 50–52, 54–55
    (*See also* Bentham)

V

Victorian Compromise, 133, 186, 215

W

Wages, fund theory, 95–98, 273
  versus profits, 77
  subsistence theory of, 75, 77, 92–94
Walpole, Sir Robert, 26–27
Whigs, 25, 132
Working class, condition of, in England,
    82, 129, 201
  in France, 159, 234, 309, 323–324
  discontent of, in England, 108–109, 201–
    203, 373
    in France, 160, 232–233, 244–245,
    305